T0211627

Communications in Computer and Information Science 1472

More information about this series at http://www.springer.com/series/7899

Fernando De La Prieta · Alia El Bolock ·
Dalila Durães · João Carneiro · Fernando Lopes ·
Vicente Julian (Eds.)

Highlights in Practical Applications of Agents, Multi-Agent Systems, and Social Good

The PAAMS Collection

International Workshops of PAAMS 2021
Salamanca, Spain, October 6–9, 2021
Proceedings

Springer

Editors
Fernando De La Prieta ⓘ
University of Salamanca
Salamanca, Spain

Dalila Durães ⓘ
University of Minho
Braga, Portugal

Fernando Lopes ⓘ
National Laboratory of Energy and Geology
Lisbon, Portugal

Alia El Bolock
German University in Cairo
New Cairo City, Egypt

João Carneiro ⓘ
Polytechnic Institute of Porto, ISEP
Porto, Portugal

Vicente Julian ⓘ
Polytechnic University of Valencia
Valencia, Spain

ISSN 1865-0929   ISSN 1865-0937 (electronic)
Communications in Computer and Information Science
ISBN 978-3-030-85709-7   ISBN 978-3-030-85710-3 (eBook)
https://doi.org/10.1007/978-3-030-85710-3

This Springer imprint is published by the registered company Springer Nature Switzerland AG
The registered company address is: Gewerbestrasse 11, 6330 Cham, Switzerland

Preface

The PAAMS Workshops complemented the regular program with new or emerging trends of particular interest connected to multi-agent systems. PAAMS, the International Conference on Practical Applications of Agents and Multi-Agent Systems, is an evolution of the International Workshop on Practical Applications of Agents and Multi-Agent Systems. PAAMS is an international yearly tribune for presenting, discussing, and disseminating the latest developments and the most important outcomes related to real-world applications. It provides a unique opportunity to bring multi-disciplinary experts, academics, and practitioners together to exchange their experience in the development of agents and multi-agent systems.

This volume presents the papers that were accepted in the workshops during the 2021 edition of PAAMS: Workshop on Character Computing (C2), Workshop on Deep Learning Applications (DeLA), Workshop on Decision Support, Recommendation, and Persuasion in Artificial Intelligence (DeRePAI), Workshop on Multi-agent-based Applications for Modern Energy Markets, Smart Grids, and Future Power Systems (MASGES), and Workshop on Smart Cities and Intelligent Agents (SCIA). Each paper submitted to PAAMS went through a stringent peer review by three members of the international Program Committee of each track. From the 42 submissions received, 26 were selected for presentation at the workshops.

We would like to thank all the contributing authors, the members of the Program Committees, the sponsors (IBM, AEPIA, APPIA, and AIR Institute) and the Organizing Committee for their hard and highly valuable work. We thank the Regional Government of Castilla y León and FEDER for funding the project "XAI: Sistemas inteligentes auto-explicativos creados con modelos de mezcla de expertos" (Id. SA082P20).

Thanks for your help – PAAMS 2021 would not exist without your contribution.

July 2021

Fernando De la Prieta
Alia El Bolock
Dalila Durães
João Carneiro
Fernando Lopes
Vicente Julián

Organization

General Co-chairs

Frank Dignum — Umeå University, Sweden
Juan Manuel Corchado — University of Salamanca and AIR Institute, Spain
Fernando De la Prieta — University of Salamanca, Spain

Workshop Chair

Fernando De la Prieta — University of Salamanca, Spain

Advisory Board

Bo An — Nanyang Technological University, Singapore
Paul Davidsson — Malmö University, Sweden
Keith Decker — University of Delaware, USA
Yves Demazeau — Centre National de la Recherche Scientifique, France
Tom Holvoet — KU Leuven, Belgium
Toru Ishida — Kyoto University, Japan
Takayuki Ito — Nagoya Institute of Technology, Japan
Eric Matson — Purdue University, USA
Jörg P. Müller — Clausthal Technical University, Germany
Michal Pěchouček — Technical University in Prague, Czech Republic
Franco Zambonelli — University of Modena and Reggio Emilia, Italy

Organizing Committee

Juan M. Corchado Rodríguez — University of Salamanca and AIR Institute, Spain
Fernando De la Prieta — University of Salamanca, Spain
Sara Rodríguez González — University of Salamanca, Spain
Javier Prieto Tejedor — University of Salamanca and AIR Institute, Spain
Pablo Chamoso Santos — University of Salamanca, Spain
Belén Pérez Lancho — University of Salamanca, Spain
Ana Belén Gil González — University of Salamanca, Spain
Ana De Luis Reboredo — University of Salamanca, Spain
Angélica González Arrieta — University of Salamanca, Spain
Emilio S. Corchado Rodríguez — University of Salamanca, Spain
Angel Luis Sánchez Lázaro — University of Salamanca, Spain
Alfonso González Briones — University of Salamanca, Spain
Yeray Mezquita Martín — University of Salamanca, Spain

Javier J. Martín Limorti	University of Salamanca, Spain
Alberto Rivas Camacho	University of Salamanca, Spain
Elena Hernández Nieves	University of Salamanca, Spain
Beatriz Bellido	University of Salamanca, Spain
María Alonso	University of Salamanca, Spain
Diego Valdeolmillos	AIR Institute, Spain
Sergio Marquez	AIR Institute, Spain
Marta Plaza Hernández	University of Salamanca, Spain
Guillermo Hernández González	University of Salamanca, Spain
Ricardo S. Alonso Rincón	AIR Institute, Spain
Javier Parra	University of Salamanca, Spain

Contents

Workshop on Decision Support, Recommendation, and Persuasion in Artificial Intelligence (DeRePAI)

Workshop on Multi-Agent-Based Applications for Modern Energy Markets, Smart Grids, and Future Power Systems (MASGES)

Workshop on Smart Cities and Intelligent Agents (SCIA)

Workshop on Character Computing (C2)

Workshop on Character Computing (C2)

The fourth consecutive Workshop on Character Computing presented the emerging field and the opportunities and challenges it poses. Character computing is any computing that incorporates the human character within its context (for more details see https://www.springer.com/gp/book/9783030159535 and https://en.wikipedia.org/wiki/Character_computing). The character includes stable traits (e.g., personality) and variable affective, cognitive, and motivational states as well as history, morals, beliefs, skills, appearance, and socio-cultural embeddings, to name a few. As the next step towards further putting humans at the center of technology, novel interdisciplinary approaches such as character computing are developing. The extension and fusion between the different computing approaches, e.g. affective and personality computing, within character computing is based on well-controlled empirical and theoretical knowledge from psychology. This is done by including the whole human character as a central part of any artificial interaction.

Character computing has three main modules that can be investigated and leveraged separately or together: 1) character sensing and profiling, 2) character-aware adaptive systems, and 3) artificial characters.

The aim of the workshop is to inspire research into the foundations and applications of character computing by investigating novel approaches by both computer scientists and psychologists. C2 addresses applications, opportunities, and challenges of sensing, predicting, adapting to, affecting, or simulating human behavior and character.

This workshop seeks to promote character computing as a design material for the creation of novel user experiences and applications by leveraging the evolving character of the user.

The main goal of this workshop is to:

- Provide a forum for computer science, technology, and psychology professionals to come together and network for possible future collaboration.
- Share experience obtained and lessons learned from past projects to understand the current state of the art of research conducted related to character computing.
- Identify challenges and opportunities the researchers faces to set up a current R&D agenda and community in this field.

C2 aims to bring together researchers and industry practitioners from both computational and psychology communities to share knowledge and resources, discuss new ideas, and build foundations of possible future collaborations. The main aim is to further the research into character computing by discussing potential ideas, challenges, and sharing expertise among the participants. The workshop was held in a hybrid format like the conference, allowing registrants the choice to participate virtually or in-person in Salamanca, Spain.

Organization

Organizing Committee

Alia El Bolock	German University in Cairo, Egypt, and Ulm University, Germany
Cornelia Herbert	Ulm University, Germany
Slim Abdennadher	German University in Cairo, Egypt

Program Committee

Friedhelm Schwenker	Ulm University, Germany
Patrick Weis	Ulm University, Germany
Walid El Hefny	German University in Cairo, Egypt
Jailan Salah	German University in Cairo, Egypt

Anxiety Detection During COVID-19 Using the Character Computing Ontology

Nada Elaraby[1(✉)], Alia El Bolock[1,2(✉)], Cornelia Herbert[2(✉)], and Slim Abdennadher[1(✉)]

[1] German University in Cairo, Cairo, Egypt
{nada.elaraby,alia.elbolock,slim.abdennadher}@guc.edu.eg
[2] Ulm University, Ulm, Germany
cornelia.herbert@uni-ulm.de

Abstract. The lifestyle changes resulting from the COVID-19 pandemic increased the risk of suffering from anxiety and depression. We need the cooperation between psychologists and computer scientists to provide technology solutions to help mitigate negative mental well-being early on. CCOnto is an integrated ontology that models the interactions between behavior and character states and traits in specific situations following the framework of the inter-disciplinary domain of Character Computing. CCOnto is parts of an going research cooperation between computer scientists and psychologists for creating character-based interactive applications. The knowledge represented in the ontology is modular separating core knowledge from rules. In previous work, the rules were extracted from the literature. In this paper, we present an approach for generating rules from existing datasets. The main contribution of this paper is the generation of if/then rules from a dataset collected during the first lockdown. The rules are added to CCOnto in form of SWRL rules and used as a backend for an anxiety detection application.

Keywords: Character computing · Anxiety · Ontology · Psychology · Human-based computing

1 Introduction

Acute stress, anxiety, and depressive symptoms have been prevalent among college students during the COVID-19 pandemic [24]. Stressful times are not the only stimulant for stress, anxiety, and depression. Studies show that there is an established relationship between personality traits and depression, as well as between personality traits and anxiety [8]. The demand for technology solutions during the pandemic is higher than ever before. Personality traits, a person's emotional state, and the pressing situation can contribute to someone facing anxiety or depression. This calls for seamless integration between psychologists and computer scientists for developing technology solutions that help people understand and change their behavior as proposed by Character Computing [6]. Character Computing is an interdisciplinary field spanning between psychology

© Springer Nature Switzerland AG 2021
F. De La Prieta et al. (Eds.): PAAMS Workshops 2021, CCIS 1472, pp. 5–16, 2021.
https://doi.org/10.1007/978-3-030-85710-3_1

and computer science which advocates that affect and personality alone are not enough to capture the essence of a person, and their behavior [1,6,19]. Character Computing is based on a holistic, psychologically driven model of human behavior in the context of the Character–Behavior–Situation triad (CBS). Human behavior is modeled and predicted based on relationships between a situation and character state and trait markers [11], e.g., personality, affect, socio-economic embedding, culture, cognitive state, and well-being. The CBS triad is modeled using an ontology-based approach and presented in [12,13]. CCOnto models human character and its interaction with behavior and situation to provide domain experts with an intelligent interface for modeling, testing, and unifying rule-based hypotheses on the interaction between the three. The knowledge included in the ontology is mainly based on psychological evidence. The ontology is used in an application for evaluating sleep and healthy eating habits during the novel COVID-19 pandemic based on user-input data (named CCleep) [12]. CCleep is a Java-based web application where the user is prompted to answer a couple of questions about the type of food he/she eats, the kind of activities he/she performs, the emotion he/she experiences within the two hours before going to bed. Accordingly, the application infers the user's personality and sleep quality. The inference is done by the ontology reasoner based on a set of rules from literature and domain experts. CCOnto was also used for monitoring psychological and educational factors during COVID-19 in [14]. This paper presents another usage domain for CCOnto for mental well-being and another approach for obtaining behavior correlations rules from datasets. We illustrate that on part of a dataset that has been collected during the first lockdown and published in [20]. The dataset results from a self-assessment questionnaire measuring personality traits, the current emotional state of a person using a discrete scale (valence, arousal), the anxiety state, and whether he/she undergoes depression. The followed approach for generating the rules consists of (a) clustering the features of the dataset into two clusters (low/high), (b) converting numeric values into categorical ones, (c) identifying the features that highly correlate with state anxiety and depression, and (d) generating rules from a transformed dataset in the form of if/then statements where state anxiety and depression are the main consequents using association rules. The generated rules are further integrated into CCOnto in the form of rules in the Semantic Web Rules Language (SWRL). An anxiety detection application based on this version of CCOnto was created to infer whether the user is anxious/depressed. The remainder of this paper is organized as follows. Section 2 gives an overview of the CCOnto and CCleep application. In Sect. 3, we present the process of collecting data and describing the dataset. The mining of association rules in the datasets is discussed in Sect. 4 and the anxiety detection application is discussed in Sect. 5. The conclusion is presented in Sect. 6.

2   CCOnto: Character Computing Ontology

Character Computing is an interdisciplinary field spanning psychology and computer science. It is based on the holistic psychologically-driven model of the interaction between human character and behavior in a specific situation (CBS Triad). CCOnto[1] [12,13] is the first integrated ontology modeling the CBS triad. The CBS triad is a model representing the interaction between the three factors. At any given time, any two of the triad edges can be used to explain the third. By knowing the person's character(e.g., personality traits, emotional states,..etc.) in a specific situation, we can deduce how he/she might behave. The process of developing CCOnto was based on the METHONTOLOGY methodology[15]. CCOnto(as a whole with its three sublevels) is based on integrating related concepts from other ontologies that fit our scope. EmOCA [5], Emotions Ontology (EM) [18], HeLiS [27], Human Disease Ontology (HDO) [26] and the APA Psychology Terms [3] ontology are example of ontologies integrated with CCOnto. since the domain is too big, the ontology is modularized into three smaller ontologies which are: (a) CCOnto-Core ontology (b) CCOnto-Domain ontologies (c) CCOnto-App ontology. The generic core concepts of the CBS are represented in the CCOnto-Core ontology. Each core concept included is represented by psychological model:- (a) personality through the Five-Factor Model (FFM) [9] (b) emotion is represented through multiple model as the Two-Factor Theory [30], affective processes [18], continuous (valence and arousal) [28] and discrete emotions (Eckman's six basic emotions) [10]. Rules for the interactions in a specific domain(extended T-Box + SWRL Rules) are included in CCOnto-Domain ontologies. The CCOnto-Domain ontologies extend CCOnto-Core ontology. CCOnto-PhW[2] is one of the forms of CCOnto-Domain ontology, where it represents one of the six well-being dimensions, namely, physical well-being [21]. CCOnto-App ontologies extend CCOnto-Domain with application-specific information to enable utilizing the ontology (extended T-Box + SWRL + A-Box). CCleep[3] is an instance of CCOnto-App. CCleep relies on CCOnto to reason about sleep quality and its relation to personality, emotions, and other physical well-being factors based on a set of rules from literature and domain experts. This paper will discuss another form of obtaining rules and use it to make inferences about anxiety/depression. The application collects self-report behavior data (e.g. Food, physical activity, general behaviors) for the two hours before sleep and infers sleep quality and personality traits. The user is prompted to select from ontology-populated choices about certain activities performed two hours before sleeping. This includes (1) age, gender, (2) consumed foods and stimulants (e.g., alcohol and caffeine), (3) performed physical activities, (4) bodily feelings and emotions, (5) entertainment activities (e.g., TV, reading, video games), and (6) sleep-related activities (e.g., daytime napping, bed quality,.. etc.). An example of the CCleep application is illustrated in Fig. 1.

---

[1] https://github.com/CharacterComputingResearch/CCOnto/blob/main/CCOnto.owl.

[2] https://github.com/CharacterComputingResearch/CCOnto/blob/main/CCOnto-Full-PhW-Sleep.owl.

[3] https://charactercomputingsleep.herokuapp.com/introServlet.

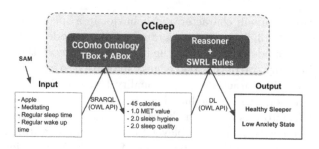

Fig. 1. Running example of CCleep Application[12]

3   Dataset Description

The dataset presented in [20] consists of multi-modal self-report data from 221 participants (50% female) during the first lockdown of COVID-19 (May 2020). The dataset is already published and is only used here as a proof of concept application for generating ontology rules from existing datasets. The main focus of the questionnaire was to analyze which characteristics(personality traits, emotion...etc.) highly affect a person's mental state (whether suffering from anxiety and depression) during a stressful time like the lockdown. The used sub-set of the self-assessment test measures personality traits, the current emotional state of a person using a discrete scale (valence, arousal), the anxiety state of a person, and whether he/she undergoes depression. By computing the relationship between features (e.g., personality traits, valence, arousal, dominance, state anxiety, trait anxiety, alexithymia, and depression). The self-assessment test includes different dimensions of a person's character. Tests included in the process are: (a) Big Five Inventory (BFI-10) [29], (b) self-assessment manikins (SAM) [17], (c) State-Trait Anxiety Inventory (STAI) [32], (d)Toronto Alexithymia Scale (TAS) [4], (e)Patient Health Questionnaire (PHQ-2) [25], and (f) general demographics. The BFI [29] (big five inventory) is the best accepted and most commonly used model of personality in academic psychology. The Big Five personality traits are extraversion, agreeableness, openness, conscientiousness, and neuroticism. In this process, we used the abbreviated version, which contains 10-items. BFI test was originally a 44-items questionnaire. We used SAM [17] to measure the three-dimensional scales of emotions: arousal, valence, and dominance. Arousal can range from inactive (e.g., uninterested, bored) to active (e.g., alert, excited), whereas valence ranges from unpleasant (e.g., sad, stressed) to pleasant (e.g., happy, pleased). Dominance ranges from a helpless and weak feeling (without control) to an empowered feeling (in control of everything). The TAS is a 20-item instrument that is one of the most commonly used measures of alexithymia [4]. Alexithymia refers to people who have trouble identifying and describing emotions and tend to minimize emotional experience and focus attention externally.

It has three subscales for measuring: (a) difficulty describing feelings (DDF), (b) difficulty identifying feelings (DIF), and (c) externally oriented thinking (EOT). The State-trait anxiety inventory (STAI) [32] is used to measure via self-report the presence and severity of current symptoms of anxiety and a generalized propensity to be anxious. It includes a scale for state anxiety (S-Anxiety) evaluating the current state of anxiety and another for trait anxiety (T-Anxiety) evaluating relatively stable aspects of anxiety proneness. The Patient Health Questionnaire-2 (PHQ-2) [25] is a 2-item depression screener. It inquires about the frequency of depressed mood and anhedonia over the past two weeks. The test also includes some general questions, e.g., age and gender. The main purpose of collecting these features is to identify which characteristics stimulate anxiety, depression, and the current situation(lockdown). The correlation matrix of the collected data after cleaning, transforming data presented in Fig. 2) shows that:

- State anxiety is highly negatively correlated with valence ($p = -0.66$), positively correlated with neuroticism ($p = 0.57$), and positively correlated with PHQ (moderately with $p = 0.47$)
- For trait anxiety, there is a slightly positive correlation with conscientiousness and extraversion and a negative correlation with neuroticism.
- For PHQ values, there is a moderate negative correlation with valence ($p = -0.48$), state anxiety ($p = 0.47$), and neuroticism ($p = 0.37$) and a positive correlation with the "Difficulty Describing Feelings" scale of TAS ($p = 0.48$).

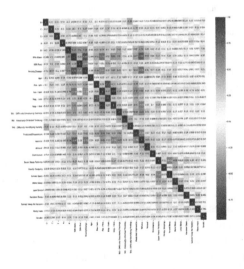

Fig. 2. Correlation Matrix between Features (personality traits, valence,arousal, TAS, S-Anxiety, Trait-Anxiety...etc.)

4   Implementation

CCOnto is the first integrated ontology representing human character and its interaction with behavior and situation to provide domain experts with an intelligent interface for modeling, testing, and unifying rule-based hypotheses on the interaction between the three. CCOnto is part of a joint project to develop an inter-disciplinary and inter-cultural Character Computing platform created by and for computer scientists and psychologists. Rules included in the ontology were based on some psychological theories. In this paper, we introduce a new method where rules are generated from datasets. We only used part of the dataset that is related to anxiety/depression. The approach shown in Fig. 3 includes the following steps: (a) clustering data of a single feature (for example, neuroticism into low/high), (b) converting numeric values into categorical ones, (c) identifying features that highly affect state anxiety, trait anxiety, and depression, (d) generating rules from categorical data with consequent of state anxiety, trait anxiety and depression using association rules, (e) adding rules in the form of SWRL to CCOnto, and (f) creating java application to infer whether a person is anxious/depressed using CCOnto.

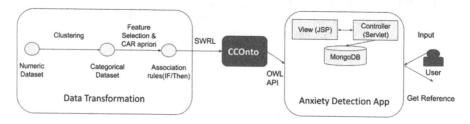

Fig. 3. Overview of the rule generation process through data transformation and the anxiety detection application.

4.1   Categorical Data and Feature Selection

The generation of rules in the form of if/then statements requires the data to be categorical to use in the current version of CCOnto. To convert numeric data into categorical ones, we used K-means clustering to group data values for each feature into two categories (for neuroticism features, it is grouped into low neuroticism and high neuroticism). K-means clustering [22] is an unsupervised learning algorithm used to solve clustering problems in machine learning or data science. The algorithm starts with the first group of randomly selected centroids, which are used as the beginning points for every cluster. It then performs iterative (repetitive) calculations to optimize the positions of the centroids. Figure 5a and Fig. 5b show the range of low and high values for each big five personality trait (conscientiousness, neuroticism). The range of state and trait anxiety scores is presented in Fig. 5c. Figure 4 presents the included categorical data.

	Openness	Conscientiousness	Extraversion	Agreeableness	Neuroticism	S-Anxiety	T-Anxiety
0	LowOpenness	LowConscientiousness	LowExtraversion	HighAgreeableness	LowNeuroticism	LowS-Anxiety	HighT-Anxiety
1	LowOpenness	LowConscientiousness	LowExtraversion	HighAgreeableness	HighNeuroticism	LowS-Anxiety	LowT-Anxiety

Fig. 4. Conversion of numeric data to categorical ones

In feature Selection, we aim to identify the features that highly correlate with anxiety/depression. We used the chi-squared test for feature selection. The main focus was on testing the following hypotheses for all features of the dataset:

- **H0:** Feature x does not contribute to anxiety/depression.
- **H1:** Feature x contributes to anxiety/depression.

Chi-squared [16] is used to measure the degree of association between two categorical variables. For state anxiety, the ten best features that highly associate with it are illustrated in Fig. 6b. For trait anxiety, the ten best features that highly associate with it are presented in Fig. 5d. For depression, the 10 best features that highly associate with it are illustrated in Fig. 6a. For each of these features, we will choose the top 3 or 4 features. For example, depression correlates with valence, difficulty describing feelings(TAS), and neuroticism. We used the best features that correlate with anxiety/depression as the antecedents to generate the rules. After the categorical conversion of data and identifying features that highly correlate with anxiety/depression, the next step is to create rules.

4.2 Generating Rules

The generation of psychological rules in the form of if/then statements are produced using association rule mining. Association rule mining is one of the most important and well-researched techniques of data mining [2]. It aims to extract interesting correlations, frequent patterns, associations, or causal structures among sets of items in transaction databases. These rules should satisfy the predefined minimum support, and confidence [23]. An association rule is an implication expression of the form $A \rightarrow C$, where A and C are disjoint itemsets [33]. Metrics used for evaluating association rules and setting selection thresholds are support, confidence, and lift. The confidence of a rule $A \rightarrow C$ is the probability of seeing the consequent in a transaction given that it also contains the antecedent [2].

$$confidence(A \rightarrow C) = \frac{support(A \rightarrow C)}{support(A)}, range : [0, 1]. \tag{1}$$

The support metric is defined for itemsets, not association rules [2]. Support is used to measure the abundance or frequency of an item set in a database.

$$support(A \rightarrow C) = support(A \cup C), range : [0, 1]. \tag{2}$$

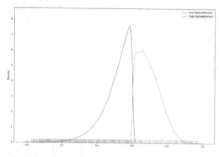

(a) Grouping of normalized values of Conscientiousness scores obtained from BFI

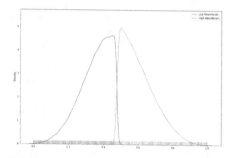

(b) Grouping of normalized values of Neuroticism scores obtained from BFI

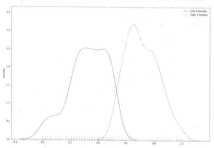

(c) Range of State Anxiety scores obtained from STAI

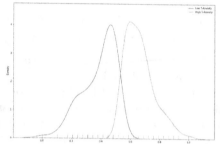

(d) Categorization of Trait Anxiety scores from STAI

Fig. 5. Ranges of BFI and STAI test scores

```
              Specs        Score
21           valence    29.340661
 9           NegIfeel    17.259539
10            TAS-DDF    16.346930
 4        Neuroticism    15.558599
22          Dominance     5.953109
11            TAS-EOT     4.304163
 1  Conscientiousness     3.779931
18         RandomSleep     3.577752
 8            NegIam      3.414511
23            Arousal     3.074909
```

```
                       Specs        Score
21                    valence    46.608358
 9                    NegIfeel    35.379789
 4                 Neuroticism    21.163909
10                     TAS-DDF     9.720121
22                   Dominance     7.982064
13           SameSleepPatterns     5.945949
23                     Arousal     5.281457
15                 TurnedSleep     4.812324
 8                      NegIam     4.712703
 1           Conscientiousness     3.335086
```

(a) 10 best features that associate with depression

(b) 10 best features that associate with state anxiety

Fig. 6. The 10 best features associated with depression and state anxiety

The lift metric is commonly used to measure how much more often the antecedent and consequent of a rule $A \rightarrow C$ occur together than we would expect if they were statistically independent. If A and C are independent, the lift score will be precisely one [7].

$$lift(A \rightarrow C) = \frac{confidence(A \rightarrow C)}{support(C)}, range : [0, \infty] \qquad (3)$$

The Apriori algorithm [34] is one of the algorithms used for generating association rules. The Apriori principle allows us to prune all the supersets of an itemset that does not satisfy the minimum threshold condition for support.

The algorithm consists of generating all frequent itemsets and all confident association rules from them. A frequent itemset is an itemset that has transaction support above minimum support *minsup*. A confident association rule is a rule with confidence above minimum confidence *minconf*.

The class association rules (CAR) apriori algorithm [31] is used to satisfy only rules with some fixed target items on the right-hand side and also meets minimum support and minimum confidence. We are interested in rules that have consequent state anxiety, trait anxiety, or depression with minimum support of 0.15 and confidence of 0.6. Rules generated from CAR apriori algorithm that has state anxiety as a consequent is represented in Fig. 7a. The generated rules include the features that already have a high correlation with state anxiety. The generated rules that have depression as a consequent are represented in Fig. 7b. The generated rules include the features that already have a moderate correlation with depression. This indicates needing further pruning or the inclusion of additional features for depression prediction. For example, the resulting rules for state anxiety include that people who have a negative valence, i.e., experiencing negative emotions and have high neuroticism tend to suffer from high state anxiety.

	LHS	RHS	Support	Confidence
0	['NEGIFEEL@HIGH', 'HighNeuroticism']	HighS-Anxiety	0.312	0.870
1	['valence@NegativeValence', 'NEGIFEEL@HIGH', '..	HighS-Anxiety	0.181	0.975
2	['DDF@high', 'HighNeuroticism']	HighS-Anxiety	0.271	0.833
3	['DDF@high', 'NEGIFEEL@HIGH', 'HighNeuroticism']	HighS-Anxiety	0.172	0.868
4	['DDF@low', 'NEGIFEEL@LOW']	LowS-Anxiety	0.199	0.750

(a) Rules generated with consequent of state anxiety

	LHS	RHS	Support	Confidence
0	['LowNeuroticism', 'valence@PositiveValence']	PHQ@minimaldepressed	0.199	0.705
1	['valence@NegativeValence', 'HighNeuroticism']	PHQ@depressed	0.258	0.825
2	['DDF@high']	PHQ@depressed	0.376	0.723
3	['NEGIFEEL@NORMAL']	PHQ@minimaldepressed	0.156	0.857
4	['DDF@high', 'valence@NegativeValence', 'HighN...	PHQ@depressed	0.156	0.886

(b) Rules generated with consequent of depression

Fig. 7. Rules generated with consequent of state anxiety and depression

5   Anxiety Detection Application

The Anxiety Detection App[4] is used to reason about anxiety and depression during the current pandemic and its relation to personality, emotions, and other factors. It is Java-based web application using OWLAPI [5] on top of MongoDB database, as shown in Fig. 3. The application collects daily self-report data (e.g., personality traits, emotions, etc.) and infers anxiety level(low, high) and depression level(low/high). The application is written in Java using "Eclipse IDE for Java EE Developers", Java Web Application is used to create dynamic websites,

---

[4] https://anxiety-collection-app.herokuapp.com/login.

[5] http://owlapi.sourceforge.net/.

and it also provides support for web applications through Servlets and JSPs. Java Servlet and JSPs are server-side technologies to extend the capability of web servers by providing support for dynamic response and data persistence. Java enables the deployment of applications in a Tomcat Web application server. The app measures the emotional state of the user daily. The daily test includes (a) answering "who I am" in five different responses, (b) answering "how I feel" in five different responses, and (c) the current emotion (e.g., happy, sad), following [20]. At any time, the user can proceed to the weekly report to see the inference of anxiety/depression. In this step, for verification purposes, the user has to take PHQ-2 and S-Anxiety tests. The application records stable markers of the user's character(e.g., personality traits), then through the daily report, the user records his/her emotional state and inputs five responses for "who I am", and "how I feel". Then, the application inserts the rules obtained from the dataset into the ontology in the form of SWRL rules. It then collects data from users daily for a week. The application then calculates the scores of the included questionnaires and performs sentiment analysis of the free-text responses using the Java library[6]. A DLQuery containing the processed, collected data is sent to the CCOnto ontology to get the anxiety/depression inference from the reasoner. Finally, the results are saved in the database and displayed to the user.

6   Conclusion

CCOnto is an integrated conceptualization of Character Computing, modeling the interactions between character and behavior in a specific situation. The ontology is modularized into three smaller ontologies separating levels of domain knowledge and two modules separating core knowledge from flexible rule-based knowledge. The anxiety detection application is an instance of CCOnto extended with the knowledge needed for representing mental well-being and developing an anxiety detection application. The application infers the anxiety/depression level from his/her personality traits, emotional states, and behavior attributes. The CCOnto inference rules used in the application are generated from a previously collected dataset through:

- Converting each numeric feature to categorical ones.
- Identifying the features that highly correlate with anxiety and depression.
- Using CAR association rule mining to generate rules that have state anxiety and depression as consequent.

The rules are added to the ontology in the form of SWRL rules. The application was tested on daily input records of users over a week. The application uses the ontology and generated rules to infer the anxiety/depression level according to the collected data.

---

[6] https://stanfordnlp.github.io/CoreNLP/.

References

1. Abaalkhail, R., Guthier, B., Alharthi, R., El Saddik, A.: Survey on ontologies for affective states and their influences. Seman. Web **9**(4), 441–458 (2018)
2. Agrawal, R., Imieliński, T., Swami, A.: Mining association rules between sets of items in large databases. In: Proceedings of the 1993 ACM SIGMOD International Conference on Management of Data, pp. 207–216 (1993)
3. Walker, A., Garcia, A.: I.G.: psychology ontology. In: BioPortal (2014). https://bioportal.bioontology.org/ontologies/APAONTO
4. Bagby, R.M., Parker, J.D., Taylor, G.J.: The twenty-item toronto alexithymia scale–i. Item selection and cross-validation of the factor structure. J. Psychosom. Res. **38**(1), 23–32 (1994)
5. Berthelon, F., Sander, P.: Emotion ontology for context awareness. In: 2013 IEEE 4th International Conference on Cognitive Infocommunications (CogInfoCom), pp. 59–64. IEEE (2013)
6. Bolock, A., Abdelrahman, Y., Abdennadher, S.: Character Computing. Human-Computer Interaction Series, Springer International Publishing, heidelberg (2020). https://books.google.com.eg/books?id=VZXHDwAAQBAJ
7. Brin, S., Motwani, R., Ullman, J.D., Tsur, S.: Dynamic itemset counting and implication rules for market basket data. In: Proceedings of the 1997 ACM SIGMOD International Conference on Management of Data, pp. 255–264 (1997)
8. Bunevicius, A., Katkute, A., Bunevicius, R.: Symptoms of anxiety and depression in medical students and in humanities students: relationship with big-five personality dimensions and vulnerability to stress. Int. J. Soc. Psychiatry **54**(6), 494–501 (2008)
9. Costa, P.T., Jr., McCrae, R.R.: The Revised NEO Personality Inventory (NEO-PI-R). Sage Publications Inc., Thousand Oaks (2008)
10. Ekman, P., Cordaro, D.: What is meant by calling emotions basic. Emot. Rev. **3**(4), 364–370 (2011)
11. El Bolock, A.: What is character computing? In: El Bolock, A., Abdelrahman, Y., Abdennadher, S. (eds.) Character Computing. HIS, pp. 1–16. Springer, Cham (2020). https://doi.org/10.1007/978-3-030-15954-2_1
12. El Bolock, A., Elaraby, N., Herbert, C., Abdennadher, S.: Cconto: the character computing ontology. In: RCIS, pp. 313–329 (2021)
13. El Bolock, A., Herbert, C., Abdennadher, S.: CCOnto: towards an ontology-based model for character computing. In: Dalpiaz, F., Zdravkovic, J., Loucopoulos, P. (eds.) RCIS 2020. LNBIP, vol. 385, pp. 529–535. Springer, Cham (2020). https://doi.org/10.1007/978-3-030-50316-1_34
14. Elbolock, A., Abdennadher, S., Herbert, C.: An ontology-based framework for psychological monitoring in education during the covid 19 pandemic. Front. Psychol. **12**, 2879 (2021)
15. Fernández-López, M., Gómez-Pérez, A., Juristo, N.: Methontology: from ontological art towards ontological engineering (1997)
16. Freeman, J.V., Julious, S.A.: Scope. The analysis of categorical data. **16**(1), 18–21 (2007)
17. Grimm, M., Kroschel, K.: Evaluation of natural emotions using self assessment manikins. In: IEEE Workshop on Automatic Speech Recognition and Understanding, 2005, pp. 381–385. IEEE (2005)

18. Hastings, J., Ceusters, W., Smith, B., Mulligan, K.: The emotion ontology: enabling interdisciplinary research in the affective sciences. In: Beigl, M., Christiansen, H., Roth-Berghofer, T.R., Kofod-Petersen, A., Coventry, K.R., Schmidtke, H.R. (eds.) CONTEXT 2011. LNCS (LNAI), vol. 6967, pp. 119–123. Springer, Heidelberg (2011). https://doi.org/10.1007/978-3-642-24279-3_14

19. Herbert, C., El Bolock, A., Abdennadher, S.: A psychologically driven, user-centered approach to character modeling. In: El Bolock, A., Abdelrahman, Y., Abdennadher, S. (eds.) Character Computing. HIS, pp. 39–51. Springer, Cham (2020). https://doi.org/10.1007/978-3-030-15954-2_3

20. Herbert, C., El Bolock, A., Abdennadher, S.: How do you feel during the covid-19 pandemic? A survey using psychological and linguistic self-report measures, and machine learning to investigate mental health, subjective experience, personality, and behaviour during the covid-19 pandemic among university students. BMC Psychol. **9**(1), 1–23 (2021)

21. Hettler, B.: Six dimensions of wellness model (1976)

22. Kanungo, T., Mount, D.M., Netanyahu, N.S., Piatko, C.D., Silverman, R., Wu, A.Y.: An efficient k-means clustering algorithm: analysis and implementation. IEEE Trans. Pattern Anal. Mach. Intell. **24**(7), 881–892 (2002)

23. Kotsiantis, S., Kanellopoulos, D.: Association rules mining: a recent overview. GESTS Int. Trans. Comput. Sci. Eng. **32**(1), 71–82 (2006)

24. Li, Y., et al.: Mental health among college students during the Covid-19 pandemic in China: a 2-wave longitudinal survey. J. Affect. Disord. **281**, 597–604 (2021)

25. Löwe, B., Kroenke, K., Gräfe, K.: Detecting and monitoring depression with a two-item questionnaire (PHQ-2). J. Psychosom. Res. **58**(2), 163–171 (2005)

26. Lynn M. Schriml, E.M.: The disease ontology: fostering interoperability between biological and clinical human disease-related data

27. Dragoni, M., Bailoni, T., Maimone, R., Eccher, C.: HeLiS: an ontology for supporting healthy lifestyles. In: Vrandečić, D., et al. (eds.) ISWC 2018. LNCS, vol. 11137, pp. 53–69. Springer, Cham (2018). https://doi.org/10.1007/978-3-030-00668-6_4

28. Olson, D., Russell, C.S., Sprenkle, D.H.: Circumplex model: systemic assessment and treatment of families. Routledge (2014)

29. Rammstedt, B., John, O.P.: Measuring personality in one minute or less: a 10-item short version of the big five inventory in English and German. J. Res. Pers. **41**(1), 203–212 (2007)

30. Schachter, S., Singer, J.: Cognitive, social, and physiological determinants of emotional state. Psychol. Rev. **69**(5), 379 (1962)

31. Slimani, T.: Class association rules mining based rough set method. arXiv preprint arXiv:1509.05437 (2015)

32. Spielberger, C.D.: State-trait anxiety inventory for adults (1983)

33. Tan, P.N., Steinbach, M., Kumar, V.: Introduction to Data Mining. Pearson Education, India (2016)

34. Yabing, J.: Research of an improved apriori algorithm in data mining association rules. Int. J. Comput. Commun. Eng. **2**(1), 25 (2013)

XReC: Towards a Generic Module-Based Framework for Explainable Recommendation Based on Character

Fatma Elazab[1]([✉]), Alia El Bolock[1,2], Cornelia Herbert[2],
and Slim Abdennadher[1]

[1] German University in Cairo, Cairo, Egypt
{fatma.hossam,alia.elbolock,slim.abdennadher}@guc.edu.eg
[2] Ulm University, Ulm, Germany
cornelia.herbert@uni-ulm.de

Abstract. The ongoing improvements of technology worldwide helped humans and businesses in different aspects by enhancing human-computer interactions. Especially after the outbreak of the COVID-19, people head to the virtual world by shopping online instead of going to the actual store, watching movies on platforms like "Netflix" instead of going to cinemas, or companies are applying different methods to continue their internal operations online. So most companies now invest much effort to enhance their online platforms to cope with the occurring situation. One way of enhancing the online system, especially in E-commerce, E-learning, and entertainment platforms, is by building robust recommendation algorithms. Recommender systems play a massive role in improving the online experience by suggesting to the user relevant items. However, treating all users the same by applying recommendation strategies that do not include the user her-/himself as the center of the algorithm may lead to an unpleasant user experience as each user has a different personality, taste, and different needs. Thus, in this paper, a structured review of the efforts invested in creating personalized recommendation systems is studied to explore the personal factors included in previous trials. Accordingly, we propose XReC, a generic framework for building character-based recommender systems based on Character Computing principles, including all the aspects that influence human behavior. As a result of integrating multiple human aspects, the system's complexity will arise. A personalized explanation accompanying each recommendation is provided to improve our framework's transparency, trustworthiness, persuasiveness, effectiveness, and user satisfaction.

Keywords: Character computing · Recommender systems · Explainability

1 Introduction

Recommendation systems play a crucial role in E-commerce and multimedia platforms as they help users make decisions by suggesting relevant content. Especially

F. De La Prieta et al. (Eds.): PAAMS Workshops 2021, CCIS 1472, pp. 17–27, 2021.
https://doi.org/10.1007/978-3-030-85710-3_2

nowadays because of the COVID-19 outbreak [1], people were forced to stay home which affects businesses, local shops, and also the customers that need to fulfill their demands. As a result, both parties headed to the virtual world to survive. Companies invest much effort to enhance their online services to meet the users' satisfaction, and on the other side, users search for effective services that replace the lack of in-person communication. This is when the need for robust explainable recommendation systems arises. However, recommender systems should not treat all users the same by applying recommendation algorithms that do not include the user her-/himself as the center of implementation. It may lead to an unpleasant user experience as each user has a different personality, taste, and different needs. Thus personalization is required. Studies such as [2, 18, 25] show that incorporating the user personality into the recommendation techniques outperform the state of the art algorithms by improving the accuracy and quality of recommendations. Additionally, Affective Computing considers the user's emotional state [16]. In Character Computing, all aspects that influence the character are considered, such as the personality traits, the affective state, the behavior, and situation [29–31]. Accordingly, character-based recommender systems will surpass systems that consider one aspect of the human character such that the personality traits only, emotional state, or demographic data. According to [17], user-centric models are much more effective to suggest accurate items. Recommendation systems can be applied in different domains such as entertainment platforms, E-commerce, and E-learning. In this paper, a structured review of the efforts invested in creating personalized recommendation systems in different domains is studied to explore the personal factors included in previous trials. Accordingly, we propose a generic module-based framework for building character-based recommender systems based on Character Computing principles, including all aspects that influence human behavior. As a result of integrating multiple human aspects, the system's complexity will arise. Here comes the need for an explanation accompanying each recommendation. Explanations models are responsible for answering the question of **Why** a particular item is recommended by explaining the reason to the user, which will improve the transparency, trustworthiness, persuasiveness, effectiveness, and user satisfaction of our framework [38]. Additionally, an implementation approach of our framework is presented.

The rest of this paper is organized as follows. The related work and background information is given in Sect. 2. In Sect. 3, the generic framework for character-based explainable recommendation is proposed. Section 4 discusses an implementation approach of our framework. Finally, the conclusion and future work are presented in Sect. 5.

2   Background

2.1   Related Work

In this section, a systematic review of the state-of-the-art recommender systems is presented, along with the current attempts to create personalized recommender systems and explainable recommendations.

Recommendation Systems Techniques. Recommendation systems can be classified according to the recommendation algorithm used, such as content-based recommendation, collaborative filtering(CF) recommendation, hybrid approach, demographic-based and knowledge-based recommendation [5,6]. In content-based recommendation, the recommendation is based on item features. It recommends items that are similar to previously liked items by the user [7,8]. The recommendation in collaborative filtering is based on the choices of other individuals who share similar interests; customers giving an identical rating to any product are considered as customers of similar interests [9]. It is based on the idea that people with the same evaluation of items in the past are most likely to agree again in the future. A hybrid technique could be used to achieve a more powerful recommendation. It combines two or more recommendation techniques such as content-based and collaborative filtering because it helps to avoid some of the recommendations challenges. The demographic-based recommendation is based on the assumption that users with similar demographic data share the same taste(rate items similarly). Some of the demographic data can be the gender, age, and location of the user [10]. Finally, for complex domains such as real estate or automobile where a low number of available ratings exists, a knowledge-based recommendation technique is used where the user is needed to set its requirements explicitly [15].

Challenges of Recommender Systems. Recommender systems can face multiple challenges that affect the quality of recommendations. One of the challenges recommender systems face is the cold start problem which happens when a new user enters the systems or a new item is added so the system does not have enough ratings, history, or information to suggest items. Trust is also a challenge for recommender systems. It happens when there is a lack of trust between the user and the system as a result of missing explanations [5,13,14].

Personalized Recommender Systems in Different Domains. Recommendation systems can be applied to different domains. According to [5], the main application areas of recommendation systems are entertainment, e-commerce, and e-learning. Entertainment includes music and movies platforms in which recommendation algorithms suggest relevant items such as a movie, a song, or a playlist to the user. In [20], they personalized the recommendation by including the users' current mood extracted from social media content such as posts or comments. They classified the users' mood into *happy, sad, calm, and angry* and by classifying the songs to moods as well based on the lyrics and songs' audio, they were able to recommend relevant songs that enhance the users' mood. The user's current mood is also used in [21]. They designed a framework that classifies the songs according to the mood and asks users about their listening preferences when they are in a specific mood to suggest songs that match their moods. The personality traits are used as well in [22] to identify the relation between users' personality and their behavior, and needs, and different ways to infer users' personality social media. In [26], the influence of personal values on music taste is studied to introduce a value-based personalized music recommendation algorithm. Additionally, the personality traits were examined to identify their role in movie recommender systems by incorporating the different dimensions of personality to a collaborative filtering technique to achieve more personalized recommendation [2]. Also, It has been proved that incorporating the user personality into an existing recommendation technique such as collaborative filtering could enhance the recommendation as it addresses the cold start problem [24]. E-Commerce includes online shopping platforms, health, and tourism. In [28], they proposed a framework for a personalized itinerary recommendation that maximizes user satisfaction. E-learning platforms provide learning materials, online courses, and certificates to users. Thus, recommender systems aim to aid users in finding relevant and interesting materials among the huge resources. In [12], they designed a personalized recommender system for e-Learning by considering the users' background knowledge, interests, and their capacity of storage.

Explainable Recommendation. Explainable recommendations are important as it increases the trustworthiness, effectiveness, persuasiveness, and user satisfaction of the system. [38] provides an extensive review of explainable recommendation techniques and models in different domains. Mainly, explainable recommendations can be classified into two dimensions: *the display style of explanations based on the information source* and *the model responsible for generating the explanations.* The type of information source and style can be divided into two parts. Firstly, explanations that usually related with certain types of recommendation algorithm such explanations based on relevant users or items(*Collaborative filtering*), feature-based explanation(*content-based*), and opinion-based explanation. Secondly, how the explanations are displayed. The explanations can be in the form of textual sentences, visual explanations, and social explanations. Some explainable recommendation models can be divided into models that generate explanations based on the recommendation algorithms or the recommendation results themselves. Explainability can be applied to different recommendation applications such as entertainment, E-commerce, and E-learning, as discussed before. According to [38], the knowledge-enhanced explainable recommendation needs to be investigated as most of the explainable recommendation research is based on unstructured data; however, if extensive knowledge about the domain of recommendation is known, this will result in high fidelity scores. Additionally, context-aware explanations need further examination since personalized recommendation could be context-aware; thus, the explanation should be context-aware as well.

The existing work done into achieving personalized explainable recommender systems considers one aspect of the user. It can be the user's personality or affective state. Thus our goal is to incorporate all the dimensions that build the human character, such as the personality traits, affective state, behavior, and situations towards achieving a character computing model-based generic framework for explainable recommendations.

2.2 Character Computing

Focusing on the interaction between the human and technology is known as Human-Computer-Interaction (HCI). HCI aims to design usable systems, provide effective user and computer interaction, and enhance the user experience. Personality Computing and Affective Computing are considered sub-fields of the HCI domain. Personality Computing focuses on putting the user personality at the center of the design. The user personality could be measured using multiple psychological models of personality; one of them is the Five-Factor Model (FFM) [35]. On the other hand, Affective Computing adapts the system based on the emotional state of the user instead of the user's personality traits [16]. On the other side, the Character Computing field suggests considering the whole character instead of considering the personality or affect individually [29]. The human character consists of general stable factors that include personality traits, demographic data, socio-culture embeddings, and current factors such as the affect, mood, behavior, and situation [30,31]. The principles of Character Computing are used in [32] to build a character-based chatbot that has multiple n-dimensional traits based on the human character components where the user can choose between to create their preferred character. In [33], the authors aimed to develop a character-based meta recommender system for movies that is adaptive in the way it recommends. Therefore, the field of Character Computing is promising as it integrates different aspects of the human character instead of considering only one aspect, which will improve the quality of recommendations.

3 Framework for Character-Based Explainable Recommendation

We propose a generic module-based framework for character-based explainable recommendations. The idea of separate modules will allow us to customize each module according to the domain and purpose of the recommender system without affecting the rest of the system. We aim to integrate all the dimensions of the human character into the design to improve the recommendation quality.

Our framework consists of different modules that interact with each other to reach our goal. As shown in Fig. 1, the main modules are as follows: the character module, the database module, and the XReC module that includes the recommender module and the explainability module.

The character module is solely based on the Character Computing principles that suggest integrating the character as a whole into the design and implementation instead of taking only one part of the human character, such as considering the current mood only or the user's demographic data. The character is a complex model; it consists of general stable factors that include the personality traits, demographic data, socio-culture embeddings, and current factors such as the affect, mood, and situation [29]. Thus, the character module in our framework consists of four different sub-modules. The sub-modules are personality traits, demographic data, affect, and the situation, which represents

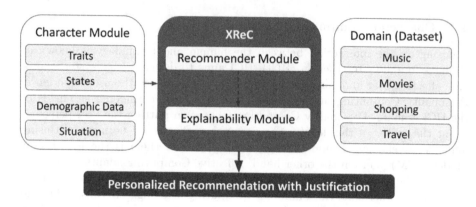

Fig. 1. Generic approach for character-based explainable recommendations

the state. The personality module is the module in which the user personality traits are collected. Personality traits are the main component of a human character. There are multiple psychological models of personality; however, the most commonly used trait model is the Five-Factor Model(FFM), also known as the Big-Five(BF) and OCEAN. The five personality traits measured are openness to experience (O), conscientiousness (C), extraversion (E), agreeableness (A), and neuroticism (N) [34]. Openness to experience measures how open the person is to experiences and new ideas. Conscientiousness measures how organized, persistent, and goal-oriented a person is. Extraversion measures how energetic and outgoing the person is. Agreeableness measures how cooperative and considerate the person is. Neuroticism measures the sensitivity of a person to negativity and stress.

For the demographic data sub-module, data such as gender, age, and location are collected. It has been proved that integrating user's demographic data in recommender systems will enhance the quality of recommendation [10].

Part of Character Computing principles is including the affective state of the user. The user's affective state comprises the current emotion, which is a temporary state as it varies quickly based on external factors. On the other hand, there exist the mood, which is a more general affective state as it lasts longer and could not get influenced by external factors easily [29]. Multiple affect models can be used to measure the user's affect, such as The Positive and Negative Affect Schedule (PANAS-X) model that includes two mood scales; one can measure the positive affect and the other for measuring the negative affect. PANAS-X also supports different temporal instructions; it can measure short transitory emotions, and long-lasting moods [36,37].

Each user goes through many situations that affect their current emotion and, accordingly, their behavior. Thus, the user's current situation should be gathered as well to complete all aspects of the character module. The recommendation domain is specified by including datasets. Possible recommendation domains are, for example, movies, music, shopping items, or travel destinations. If the domain is movies, the dataset could contain *the movie name, main actors, year of release, genre, and duration,* as the MovieLens dataset [23] used in [33]. If the domain of choice is music, music attributes and features should be added to the dataset such as *valence, energy, liveness, beats per minute(BPM), and much more.* This will allow us to customize our framework on different domains by simply changing the dataset without affecting the other modules. Finally, the XReC module. It is divided into the recommender module and the explainability module. The recommender module is responsible for the personalized recommendation. The inputs to the recommender module are taken from the character module and the dataset module since we aim to integrate the Character Computing principles into the design to achieve character-based recommendations. So user's personality traits, demographic data, current emotion, and situation, along with the chosen domain features, are fed to the recommender algorithm that is in charge of suggesting relevant items to the users. Recommendation algorithms can be based on state-of-the-art approaches such as content-based, collaborative filtering, hybrid approach, knowledge-based, or demographic-based, as discussed in the previous section. The explainability module is responsible for answering the question of why a particular item is recommended by explaining the reason to the user [38]. The need for an explainable module in our suggested framework is essential as our system consists of multiple dimensions that influence the recommendation; thus, the system became more complex.

4   Explainable Recommender Application

In this section, we outline how to implement an explainable recommender applications using our proposed framework. The proposed framework consists of multiple modules as shown in Fig. 1. Thus the application needs to go through different phases; each phase corresponds to one module to reach our goal of providing the user personalized explainable recommendation as shown in Fig. 2.

To implement the first module, which the "Character Module", users' characters must be collected. The Five-Factor Model(FFM) is used as it has been proved that it is a valid and reliable way to measure the five personality traits along with the demographic data(age, gender, location, occupation), current affect using emotion tests such as the PANAS-X and finally the current situation.

The domain we chose to implement our application is the music domain because of the shortness of duration for songs which makes users able to listen to the recommended song/playlist in a small amount of time; thus, the user will be more engaged in the testing process, accordingly will give fast and reliable feedback. The dataset is built from a combination of different datasets collected from "www.spotify.com".

The following features exist for each song: the year it was released, the artist, beats per minutes(BPM) which is the tempo of the song, energy which measures how energetic the song is, valence which measures how cheerful the song is, the danceability which measures how easy is to dance to that song, loudness which measures how loud is the song, liveness that detects if the track was

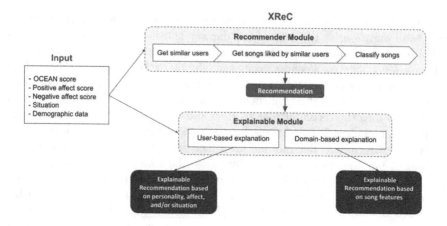

Fig. 2. XReC

performed live or not, acousticness which measures how acoustic a song and finally the duration of the song. The most important two features for our system are "valence" and "energy". Because we can classify songs to happy songs or sad songs based on the valence value, valence value ranges from 0 to 1; the lower the value, the sadder the song, and higher value means happier song. In addition to valence, energy value measures how fast and energetic the song is. It ranges from 0 to 1 as well, the lower the value the slower the song, and the higher the value the faster the song.

We propose an enhanced version of the collaborative filtering approach that instead of finding similar user groups in terms of their ratings, it finds similar user groups based on the whole character model; thus, multiple dimensions are included in finding the similarity between users, which results in more accurate similar user groups. When a new user enters the system, its personality traits, demographic data, current situation, and emotion are used to find the most similar user groups according to those factors. Afterward, items chosen by the matching user groups will be classified based on its attributes. For example, songs will be classified based on the valence and energy values as discussed before. To overcome the cold start problem that the collaborative filtering approach could cause, we can collect initial data for populating our database in advance.

The output from the recommender algorithm is further used to be explainable before it is displayed to the user. The explanations will be based on two parts; the first part is generated based on the recommendation algorithm itself. Since the suggested recommendation approach is collaborative filtering, we can benefit from its nature of classifying users into similar user groups(user-based collaborative filtering) by taking into consideration multiple dimensions like the personality traits, demographic data, emotion and situation to generate explanations such as "users with a personality and a situation similar to yours when they are in this mood loved this item". The second part is that the explanation generated from the first part can be combined with a knowledge-based explanation of the recommended domain as suggested in [32]. For example, in a music domain, we can explain the features of the recommended song; if the recommended song has high valence, it means that it is a happy song, so one way of explanations could be "we recommend you this song as it is a happy song that will lift your mood". In this way, the transparency, trustworthiness, persuasiveness, effectiveness, and user satisfaction of the framework are improved as each user will now get as an output a personalized explanation accompanying each personalized recommendation.

5 Conclusion and Future Work

Recommendation systems play a significant role in E-Commerce and entertainment platforms as they help users make decisions by suggesting relevant items. However, recommender systems should not treat all users the same. The user should be the center of any recommendation algorithm to improve the quality and effectiveness of the recommendation. After reviewing the current personalized recommender systems, we propose XReC, a generic module-based framework for explainable recommendation based on the Character Computing principles by incorporating all aspects and dimensions that influence the human character into designing and implementing the recommendation and explanation algorithms. A proposed application is presented that is based on the four main modules of our framework.

In the future, we can apply our framework for different domains to be evaluated. We can expand our recommender module by adding additional recommendation algorithms and applying different explanation styles such as visual and audible explanations instead of textual sentences. We can further investigate the effect of each character trait individually and collectively on the output and notice the differences.

References

1. Bhatti, A., Akram, H., Basit, H.M., Khan, A.U., Raza, S.M., Naqvi, M.B.: E-commerce trends during COVID-19 pandemic. Int. J. Future Gener. Commun. Netw. **13**(2), 1449–1452 (2020)
2. Nalmpantis, O., Tjortjis, C.: The 50/50 recommender: a method incorporating personality into movie recommender systems. In: Boracchi, G., Iliadis, L., Jayne, C., Likas, A. (eds.) EANN 2017. CCIS, vol. 744, pp. 498–507. Springer, Cham (2017). https://doi.org/10.1007/978-3-319-65172-9_42
3. Vinciarelli, A., Mohammadi, G.: A survey of personality computing. IEEE Trans. Affect. Comput. **5**(3), 273–291 (2014). https://doi.org/10.1109/TAFFC.2014.2330816
4. Konstan, J.A., Riedl, J., Borchers, A., Herlocker, J.L.: Recommender systems: a grouplens perspective. In: Recommender Systems: Papers from the 1998 Workshop (AAAI Technical Report WS-98-08), pp. 60–64. AAAI Press, Palo Alto (1998)

5. Santosh Kumar, V.: Survey on personalized web recommender system. Int. J. Inf. Eng. Electron. Bus. (IJIEEB) **10**(4), 33–40 (2018)

6. Kumar, P., Thakur, R.S.: Recommendation system techniques and related issues: a survey. Int. J. Inf. Technol. **10**(4), 495–501 (2018). https://doi.org/10.1007/s41870-018-0138-8

7. Van Meteren, R., Van Someren, M.: Using content-based filtering for recommendation. In: Proceedings of the Machine Learning in the New Information Age: MLnet/ECML2000 Workshop, vol. 30, pp. 47–56 (2000)

8. Pazzani, M.J., Billsus, D.: Content-based recommendation systems. In: Brusilovsky, P., Kobsa, A., Nejdl, W. (eds.) The Adaptive Web. LNCS, vol. 4321, pp. 325–341. Springer, Heidelberg (2007). https://doi.org/10.1007/978-3-540-72079-9_10

9. Breese, J.S., Heckerman, D., Kadie, C.: Empirical analysis of predictive algorithms for collaborative filtering. arXiv preprint arXiv:1301.7363 (2013)

10. Said, A., Plumbaum, T., De Luca, E.W., Albayrak, S.: A comparison of how demographic data affects recommendation. User Model. Adapt. Personalization (UMAP) 7 (2011)

11. Yan, L.: Personalized recommendation method for e-commerce platform based on data mining technology. In: 2017 International Conference on Smart Grid and Electrical Automation (ICSGEA), pp. 514–517 (2017). https://doi.org/10.1109/ICSGEA.2017.62

12. Benhamdi, S., Babouri, A., Chiky, R.: Personalized recommender system for e-Learning environment. Educ. Inf. Technol. **22**(4), 1455–1477 (2016). https://doi.org/10.1007/s10639-016-9504-y

13. Jariha, P., Jain, S.K.: A state-of-the-art recommender systems: an overview on concepts, methodology and challenges (2018)

14. Khusro, S., Ali, Z., Ullah, I.: Recommender systems: issues, challenges, and research opportunities. In: The Adaptive Web. LNEE, pp. 1179–1189. Springer, Singapore (2016). https://doi.org/10.1007/978-981-10-0557-2_112

15. Aggarwal, C.C.: Knowledge-based recommender systems. In: Recommender Systems. LNEE, pp. 167–197. Springer, Cham (2016). https://doi.org/10.1007/978-3-319-29659-3_5

16. Tao, J., Tan, T.: Affective computing: a review. In: Tao, J., Tan, T., Picard, R.W. (eds.) ACII 2005. LNCS, vol. 3784, pp. 981–995. Springer, Heidelberg (2005). https://doi.org/10.1007/11573548_125

17. Paul, D., Kundu, S.: A survey of music recommendation systems with a proposed music recommendation system. In: Mandal, J.K., Bhattacharya, D. (eds.) Emerging Technology in Modelling and Graphics. AISC, vol. 937, pp. 279–285. Springer, Singapore (2020). https://doi.org/10.1007/978-981-13-7403-6_26

18. Song, Y., Dixon, S., Pearce, M.: A survey of music recommendation systems and future perspectives (2012)

19. Lin, K., Xu, Z., Liu, J., Wu, Q., Y., Chen, Q.: Personalized music recommendation algorithm based on tag information (2016). https://doi.org/10.1109/ICSESS.2016.7883055

20. Wishwanath, C.H.P.D., Weerasinghe, S.N., Illandara, K.H., Kadigamuwa, A.S.T.M.R.D.S., Ahangama, S.: A personalized and context aware music recommendation system. In: Meiselwitz, G. (ed.) HCII 2020. LNCS, vol. 12195, pp. 616–627. Springer, Cham (2020). https://doi.org/10.1007/978-3-030-49576-3_45

21. Al-Maliki, M.: Music recommender according to the user current mood. In: Arai, K., Bhatia, R., Kapoor, S. (eds.) FTC 2018. AISC, vol. 880, pp. 828–834. Springer, Cham (2019). https://doi.org/10.1007/978-3-030-02686-8_61

22. Ferwerda, B., Schedl, M.: Personality-based user modeling for music recommender systems. In: Berendt, B., Bringmann, B., Fromont, É., Garriga, G., Miettinen, P., Tatti, N., Tresp, V. (eds.) ECML PKDD 2016. LNCS (LNAI), vol. 9853, pp. 254–257. Springer, Cham (2016). https://doi.org/10.1007/978-3-319-46131-1_29

23. Harper, F.M., Konstan, J.A.: The movielens datasets: history and context. ACM Trans. Interact. Intell. Syst. (TIIS) **5**(4), 1–19 (2015)

24. Hu, R., Pu, P.: Enhancing collaborative filtering systems with personality information. In: Proceedings of the Fifth ACM Conference on Recommender Systems, pp. 197–204 (2011)

25. Tkalcic, M., Chen, L.: Personality and recommender systems. In: Ricci, F., Rokach, L., Shapira, B. (eds.) Recommender Systems Handbook. LNCS (LNAI), pp. 715–739. Springer, Boston, MA (2015). https://doi.org/10.1007/978-1-4899-7637-6_21

26. Manolios, S., Hanjalic, A., Liem, C.: The influence of personal values on music taste: towards value-based music recommendations, pp. 501–505 (2019). https://doi.org/10.1145/3298689.3347021

27. Balakrishnan, V., Arabi, H.: HyPeRM: a hybrid personality-aware recommender for movie. Malays. J. Comput. Sci. **31**, 48–62 (2018). https://doi.org/10.22452/mjcs.vol31no1.4

28. Chen, L., Zhang, L., Cao, S., Wu, Z., Cao, J.: Personalized itinerary recommendation: deep and collaborative learning with textual information. Expert Syst. Appl. **144**, 113070 (2019). https://doi.org/10.1016/j.eswa.2019.113070

29. El Bolock, A.: What is character computing? In: El Bolock, A., Abdelrahman, Y., Abdennadher, S. (eds.) Character Computing. HIS, pp. 1–16. Springer, Cham (2020). https://doi.org/10.1007/978-3-030-15954-2_1

30. El Bolock, A., Salah, J., Abdelrahman, Y., Herbert, C., Abdennadher, S.: Character computing: computer science meets psychology. In: Proceedings of the 17th International Conference on Mobile and Ubiquitous Multimedia, pp. 557–562 (2018)

31. Bolock, A.E., Salah, J., Abdennadher, S., Abdelrahman, Y.: Character computing: challenges and opportunities. In: Proceedings of the 16th International Conference on Mobile and Ubiquitous Multimedia, pp. 555–559 (2017)

32. El Hefny, W., El Bolock, A., Herbert, C., Abdennadher, S.: Towards a generic framework for character-based chatbots. In: De La Prieta, F., et al. (eds.) PAAMS 2020. CCIS, vol. 1233, pp. 95–107. Springer, Cham (2020). https://doi.org/10.1007/978-3-030-51999-5_8

33. Bolock, A.E., Kady, A.E., Herbert, C., Abdennadher, S.: Towards a character-based meta recommender for movies. In: Alfred, R., Lim, Y., Haviluddin, H., On, C.K. (eds.) Computational Science and Technology. LNEE, vol. 603, pp. 627–638. Springer, Singapore (2020). https://doi.org/10.1007/978-981-15-0058-9_60

34. Allport, G.W., Odbert, H.S.: Trait-names: a psycho-lexical study. Psychol. Monogr. **47**(1), i (1936)

35. Goldberg, L.R.: The development of markers for the big-five factor structure. Psychol. Assess. **4**(1), 26 (1992)

36. Watson, D., Clark, L.A.: The PANAS-X: manual for the positive and negative affect schedule-expanded form (1999)

37. Boyle, G.J., Helmes, E., Matthews, G., Izard, C.E.: Measures of affect dimensions. In: Measures of Personality and Social Psychological Constructs, pp. 190–224. Academic Press, Cambridge (2015)

38. Zhang, Y., Chen, X.: Explainable recommendation: a survey and new perspectives. arXiv preprint arXiv:1804.11192 (2018)

How to Deal with Incongruence? The Role of Social Perception and Bodily Facial Feedback in Emotion Recognition in Human Agent Interaction – Evidence from Psychology as Potential and Challenge for Multimodal User-Centered Approaches

Cornelia Herbert[(⊠)]

Department of Applied Emotion and Motivation Psychology,
Institute of Psychology and Education, Ulm University, 89081 Ulm, Germany
`cornelia.herbert@uni-ulm.de`

Abstract. Human computer applications are available in every domain of human live. Even human-human interaction has been augmented or replaced by agent-based communication systems. The aim of these systems is to decode the user's emotions, thoughts and experience from the user's overt behavior, e.g., his/her text messages, voice, gestures or his/her expressive facial behavior. However, understanding the interactions between the information conveyed by the different modalities (text, voice, face) is also relevant, especially also when information between modalities is incongruent, (e.g., the user expressing a smile while judging a positive text message (congruent) or a negative text message (incongruent)). In this paper, evidence from psychology and results from an experimental study on social perception will be presented to demonstrate how the user's affective judgments of the very same input - here words describing the user's own or other people's feelings - can change depending on whether the user's facial expressions are congruent or incongruent with the verbal input. Furthermore, inter-individual differences and their possible influence on emotion processing are explored. The results demonstrate the relevance of incongruence in computer and agent-based human interaction. The research question, the experimental design as well as the results of this study provide new impetus, theoretical and empirical proof for user-centered computational approaches that aim at modeling the "true" emotion of the users.

Keywords: Agent-based human interaction · Psychology · Multimodal · Emotion recognition · Social perception · Experimental manipulation · Character computing · User-centered

1 Introduction

Human computer applications have found their way into almost every aspect of human live. Especially, in recent years, there has been a tremendous boost in options for tracking human behavior by means of computer systems and algorithms in principally any

F. De La Prieta et al. (Eds.): PAAMS Workshops 2021, CCIS 1472, pp. 28–39, 2021.
https://doi.org/10.1007/978-3-030-85710-3_3

situation, be it in private or public life. This has motivated scientists, companies, stakeholders and societies to replace or augment human-human interaction by agent-based communication systems, such as, for example, expressive personal assistants, embodied conversational agents (ECAs) or virtual Chatbots to name but a few systems. The underlying computational models of these systems have become quite intelligent in an attempt to recognize the human user's feelings, sentiments, intentions, motivations and emotions, and respond to it [1]. Many agent systems integrate artificial intelligence (AI) and machine learning to allow automated interaction with human users in real time.

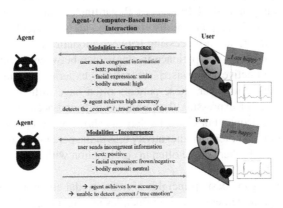

Fig. 1. Agent interaction with a human user. Upper panel: agent dealing with congruent information conveyed by the user; lower panel: agent dealing with incongruent information conveyed by the user.

Because human interaction is multimodal and heavily depending on social perception and emotions, many agent-based systems aim to decode, detect and recognize the user's emotions, his or her current mood state from his/her overt behavior including text messages, gesture, the voice or the expressive bodily or facial behavior of the user [2–4]. Despite vast progress in the field of decoding the user's emotions from different modalities (voice, text, etc. …), human-centered agent-based systems also need to account for the interactions between the different modalities (text, voice, face). Consider a virtual agent-based system (e.g., Chabot) for recognizing the user's emotions from his/her smartphone text messages. The Chatbot's task is to try to "understand" the user's emotions and reply emotionally and empathetically back to him/her (see Fig. 1). Maybe the system can also monitor the user's heart rate, voice or facial expressions to make emotion detection and emotion recognition more versatile. As illustrated in Fig. 1, the system will have a high accuracy in decoding the "correct or true" emotion, if information from all input channels or modalities (e.g., text, voice, face, heart rate) is congruent (Fig. 1, upper panel). However, accuracy will most likely drop, if information from the multimodal input channels is incongruent (Fig. 1, lower panel). In the latter case, reduction to only one modality or input channel (e.g., text or expressive behavior only) could even lead to false decoding results.

Thus, from a psychological point of view, truly interactive and human-centered computer systems should be emotionally intelligent and smart enough to reason and understand how information from different modalities (e.g., text, voice, face, …) inter-acts and contributes to the user's self-report to accurately sense the user's experience. Understanding modality interactions is imperative for developing truly human-aware agent-systems that decode, simulate and imitate humans based on data produced by real humans. Importantly, as illustrated in the examples in Fig. 1, these systems need to learn to deal with inconsistencies or incongruence in the data sent by the user and interpret it correctly. Knowing how to computationally model congruent and incongruent informa-tion is especially relevant for certain agent-based applications in the field of Psychology, such as the development of negative behavior intervention, mental health prevention and in research on inter-individual differences. Regarding certain mental disorders (e.g., depression, anxiety) or developmental disorders (e.g., autism), these are characterized by discrepancies in information processing between modalities. In other words, these patients show and maybe also experience incongruence between the information per-ceived and how it is affectively appraised, subjectively experienced and expressed e.g., verbally or physically. Moreover, these patients often have difficulties in accurately describing, identifying or expressing their own feelings and accurately responding to the emotions of other people. For example, they are showing a preference to neutralize or suppress their emotion or tend to a negativity bias in the perception and affective eval-uation of the Self and of other people often in combination with blunted or exaggerated facial expression to these [5, 6].

Therefore, knowing the basic principles of multi-modal emotion processing and of social perception and implementing these principles into agent-based systems will con-stitute key challenges for an agent technology that aims to best serve its human users. In this paper evidence from psychology and results from an experimental study on social perception and the role of bodily emotional feedback in emotion perception will be pre-sented and discussed to demonstrate how human appraisal and affective evaluation of the very same input - here words describing the user's own or other people's feelings -can change depending on whether facial expressions are congruent or incongruent with the verbal input during affective evaluation. Furthermore, inter-individual differences in emotion processing as assessed by standardized psychological questionnaires assessing depressive symptoms as well as trait and state anxiety as well as their possible influ-ence on emotion processing are explored. Finally, the implication of the results of this experimentally controlled study will be discussed as a potential and challenge for human-centered approaches in agent-based communication and possible recommendations will be given how information about multimodal incongruence effects can be integrated in user-centered approaches using psychology-driven character computing as an example [7–9].

2 Methods

2.1 Participants, Study Design and Methods

The study was conducted at Ulm University, Germany. The study and data collection were hosted by the Department of Applied Emotion and Motivation Psychology. N = 45 volunteers (all university students) (n = 36 women, n = 9 men) with a mean age of 18 – 32 years took part in the study. All participants were fully debriefed about the purpose of the study and gave written informed consent prior to participation. After arrival at the psychological laboratory, the volunteers were randomly assigned to three experimental conditions/groups. Depending on the experimental groups, the facial emotion expression of the participant was either inhibited (Group A: Emotion suppression, n = 14; n = 11 women) or facilitated (Group B: Emotion facilitation; n = 17; n = 14 women) by asking participants to hold a wooden stick either with their lips (Group A) or between the front teethes (Group B), see Fig. 2 for an overview. As shown in Fig. 2, holding the stick with the lips inhibits a smile and consequently any positive emotion expression by the lower part of the face including mouth, lips, cheeks controlled by the face muscles including the *m. zygomaticus* for smiling. In contrast, holding the stick between teeth elicits positive emotion expression by stimulating the facial muscles responsible for smiling. In Group C (control group, n = 13; n = 11 women), facial expressions were not inhibited nor facilitated. Instead, participants received a gummy drop, so called "Myobands" (ProLog GmbH; [10]), which they had to keep in their mouth. The drops avoid under- or over-expressive facial expressions but still allow facial mimicry, i.e., spontaneous emotion expression and facial imitations of the emotions perceived. Experimental manipulations of this kind have been used in previous studies as an implicit experimental procedure to inhibit positive facial expression (smile) or induce positive emotion expression in a controlled laboratory environment. The manipulation is aimed at testing effects of facial inhibition and of congruent vs. incongruent facial feedback on social and emotion perception [11–13].

Fig. 2. Left: Group A (Emotion suppression, i.e., "inhibition of a smile"; right: Group B (Emotion facilitation, i.e., "smile").

The participants of the three groups received detailed instructions of how to keep the wooden stick or the drop (Group C) with their lips, mouth or tongue. Next, all participants were asked to perform the same experimental task, the so called His-Mine-Paradigm developed by the author in [14] and existing in different experimental variants [e.g., 15, 16, 17]. In the HisMine Paradigm, participants are presented emotionally positive and negative nouns or neutral nouns. The nouns are matched in terms of linguistic features (e.g., word length, word frequency) and in terms of emotional features including the big two emotional dimensions of valence and arousal [18]. The nouns are presented together with possessive pronouns of the first person (self) or third person (other person) or an article (control condition, no person reference). All stimuli were presented in German language to native speakers of German. The participants were instructed that the words presented on the screen describe their own emotions, feelings, attitudes or neutral objects, or the emotions, feelings or objects of a third person (e.g., possible interaction partner) or do make no specific person reference to a particular person including oneself. The pronoun-noun or article-noun pairs were presented randomly on the computer screen

and therefore could not be anticipated by the participants, see Fig. 3 for an illustration
of the paradigm.

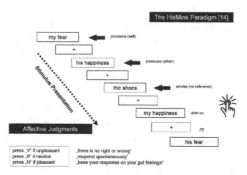

Fig. 3. The HisMine Paradigm [14] for measuring the user's affective judgments of self- and other-
related emotional and neutral concepts in an emotional evaluation task with self- and other-related
words and words without person reference (controls).

The participant's task was to read each word pair attentively and evaluate the feelings
the word pair elicits. They were instructed to not think too much about the meaning of
the word and respond spontaneously by following their gut feelings. They were told
to decide as spontaneously as possible. The stimuli were presented in trials and trials
were separated by an intertrial interval (ITI) in which a fixation cross was shown (see
Fig. 3 for an illustration). The words (including ITI) were presented for 4000 ms on
the computer screen. The participants were asked to indicate their valence judgments
- positive/pleasant, negative/unpleasant or neutral - by pressing a key on the keyboard
and indicate their preferred evaluation (positive/pleasant: key N; negative/unpleasant:
key V; neutral: key B). Reaction time and accuracy (number of valence congruent key
presses) were recorded and statistically analyzed. The experiment was programmed with
Presentation® software (Neurobehavioral Systems, Inc.). Statistics were performed with
Statistica (TIBCO® Data Science). Before and after the experiment (duration: 20 min),
participants were asked to fill in standardized psychological questionnaires asking for
mood (positive and negative affect, PANAS [19], state and trait anxiety (STAI, [20]),
and current depressive symptoms (last two weeks, BDI-2, [21]).

3 Results

Result patterns (accuracy and reaction times as dependent variables) were analyzed
for each experimental group separately by within-subject repeated measures designs
(ANOVA) with "emotion" (negative/unpleasant, positive/pleasant or neutral) and "reference" (self, other, no person reference) as within-subject factors. P-values are reported
adjusted (Greenhouse Geisser corrections) in case sphericity assumptions were not met
(F-statistic and degrees of freedom are reported uncorrected). No between-group factor
was included in the ANOVA designs to avoid biases due to unequal and small sample
sizes (n = 17 vs. n = 14 vs. n = 13 per group). In summary, the following hypotheses

were tested. First, the hypothesis (**H1a**) was tested that participants respond differently to emotional and neutral words giving emotional content priority in processing over neutral content, as predicted by emotion theories and converging previous empirical evidence [18]. Therefore, affective evaluations of positive and negative words were expected to differ from affective evaluations of neutral words (significant effect of the factor "emotion"). Second, because humans are social perceivers, it was expected that this emotion effect is modulated by the self- vs. other-reference of the words (**H1b**: interaction effect of the factors "emotion" x "reference"). The interaction of "emotion" x "reference" was expected for accuracy and reaction time measures and to be most pronounced in group C, i.e., the control group who performed the task without facial expression manipulation. Previous findings suggest that healthy participants differ in their affective evaluation of self and other, showing faster evaluation of content related to their own (positive) emotions compared to content describing other people's emotions [22], an effect known as self-positivity bias in social perception [23]. Third, the influence of congruency vs. incongruency and inhibition of information between modalities was tested (**H2**). If feedback from the body (here: facial emotion expression) influences affective judgments and in particular the process of relating one's affective judgments about self and others to one's gut feelings, it was expected that experimental manipulation of facial expressions will impact emotion processing and particularly its modulation by self- other-reference. Therefore, it was expected that Group A and Group B will show different response patterns than Group C, although performing the same affective judgment task as group C. To determine the individual effects of the three experimental conditions/groups, the results of the ANOVA designs (accuracy and reaction times as dependent variables) of each of the three experimental groups were further analyzed by means of planned comparisons including parametric (t-tests) where appropriate. In total, from all possible comparisons across stimulus categories, only a few planned comparisons were made to test H1a, H1b and H2. The planned comparison tests compared per dependent variable, affective judgments of emotional and neutral words within the reference category of "self" or "other" or "article/no person reference". In addition, the comparisons included comparisons within the same emotion category (positive/pleasant or negative/unpleasant or neutral) across the reference categories (self vs. other vs. no person reference). The advantage of the strategy of planned comparisons is that multiple testing can be avoided and only comparisons that can be meaningfully interpreted with respect to the hypotheses are selected and tested. Finally, exploratory analyses were performed to investigate (**H3**) how inter-individual differences in affect, self-reported depressive symptoms, trait or state anxiety impact affective judgments when facial feedback is blocked (Group A), facilitated (Group B) or not manipulated (Group C). H3 was explored by correlation analysis (Pearson) between the self-report data and reaction time and accuracy measures. Correlations were performed separately for each experimental group. Results were considered significant for comparisons of $p < .05$ (alpha $= 95\%$).

H1a and H1b: As predicted, the control group (Group C) showed a significant "emotion" effect and a significant "emotion" x "reference" effect in accuracy ("emotion": $F(2,24) = 23.14, p < .002$; "reference": $F(2,24) = 1.05, p = .36$; "emotion x reference": $F(4,48) = 3.2, p < .02$) and in reaction times ("emotion": $F(2,24) = 4.71, p < .02$; "reference": $F(2,24) = 8.26, p < .02$; "emotion" x "reference": $F(4,48) = 3.19, p <$

.05). As illustrated in Fig. 4, participants of Group C had a significantly higher accuracy for negative as compared to neutral words for all words irrespective of whether these described negative emotions of the own person or a third person or no particular person (p < .05). For positive emotions, accuracy was significantly higher for judgments of own emotions, particularly of positive ones (e.g., "my happiness") compared to emotion of others (e.g., "his happiness"), p < .05. This supports previous findings that healthy subjects find it more difficult to evaluate a positive word as positive when it describes the emotion of another person compared to when it refers to one's own emotion or when the word describes the same emotion without a person reference (e.g., "the happiness"). Moreover, participants of Group C were least accurate for self-related neutral words, i.e., on average only half of the words were judged as neutral when they were self-related, p < .05, and accuracy dropped below 50%. This difference was also reflected in differences in reaction times. Participants were fasted in accessing their feelings in their judgment for positive words that were referenced to themselves (p < .05), and took significantly longer in their decision for neutral words, specifically when neutral words were related to another person or had no person reference (e.g., "his shoes", "the shoes"), all p < .05. Again, this supports previous findings of social perception, namely that healthy subjects show positive self-evaluations [22, 23].

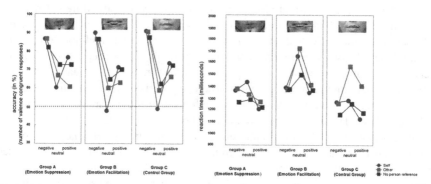

Fig. 4. Results. Accuracy (left) and reaction times (right). The results are described in detail in the text.

H2: As predicted and as illustrated in Fig. 4, facial emotion suppression and facial emotion facilitation, here the inhibition of a smile (Group A) or its induction (Group B) had a significant impact on the participants' response patterns. Group B, who held the stick between their teeth showed a significant "emotion" effect and a significant "emotion" x "reference" interaction in the accuracy data ("emotion": F(2,32) = 15.2, p < .001; "reference": F(2,32) = 1.68, p = .2; "emotion" x "reference": F(4,64) = 4.24, p < .02). However, producing a smile reduced the speed of the judgments for self- and other-reference: the interaction effect between "emotion" x "reference" was not significant in Group B ("emotion": F(2,32) = 11.44, p < .001; "reference": F(2,32) = 2.16, p = .13; "emotion" x "reference": F(4,64) = 2.04, p = .13). As shown in Fig. 4, Group A, in whom positive facial emotion expression was blocked during affective judgments, showed no significant "emotion" effect nor a significant interacting of "emotion" x "reference" in reaction times indicating that blocking facial feedback reduces the influence of emotion and of social perception on affective judgments by decreasing the speed of discriminating between emotional and neutral content and between self vs. other ("emotion": $F(2,26) = 2.87$, $p = .1$; "reference": $F(2,26) = 2.05$, $p = .14$; "emotion" x "reference": $F(4,52) = 1.71$, $p = .18$). Interestingly, blocking one's smile seemed to improve accuracy for self-related neutral content (accuracy increased above 50%), as was indicated by significant interaction of "emotion" x "reference", $F(4,52) = 3.57$, $p = .03$, in this group, see Fig. 4, accuracy, left column.

H3: Correlations between self-report measures, accuracy and reaction time measures revealed no significant effects in Group C. However, in Group B, trait as well as state anxiety were significantly positively correlated with the speed of affective judgments for self- and other-related negative words and negatively correlated with accuracy for positive self- and other-related words (Pearson correlations; all $p < .05$, two-tailed). Similarly, depressive symptoms were negatively correlated with accuracy for other-referenced positive words and this was also observed when smiling was inhibited in Group A (all $p < .05$). In addition, in Group A, who inhibited a smile, positive affect was negatively correlated with accuracy for negative self-related words and positively correlated with reaction times for positive self-related words (all $p < .05$). The results suggest that in healthy subjects, inter-individual differences in emotion perception including positive affect and negative emotion experience in terms of anxiety proneness (state and trait) and depressive symptoms can significantly interact with affective judgments, specifically in conditions in which incongruence between affective and bodily signals occurs.

4 Discussion

Humans send text messages, share private experiences in internet forums, and like or dislike others for their comments, thereby quite intuitively transferring their thoughts, emotions and feelings via the internet from a sender to a receiver, be it human or a digital agent. Regardless of the sensory modality (e.g., visual, auditory) in which the information is presented and communicated (e.g., text, audio, video, ...), in humans it is rapidly decoded, the content is implicitly appraised for the relevance for the perceiver and affectively evaluated by the perceiver on the basis of his/her gut feelings and this often without direct cognitive control or reflection. Spontaneous human information processing is a dynamic and highly complex social and emotional process. There is a cascade of processes triggered and information or signals from different modalities are being integrated while humans are perceiving information and evaluating it for their social and emotional relevance. Notably, the perception of self and of other people including affective evaluation of own emotions and feelings play a critical role in human interactions. Psychological research has shown that reading single words carrying positive or negative emotional connotations are rapidly and preferentially processed, eliciting changes in brain networks responsible for emotion perception and preparation of action (fight-flight), for an overview see [24]. Moreover, it has been shown that the content of the same words re-enacts bodily emotional and motivational systems (e.g., facial muscle expression, startle reflex) differently depending on whether their content is related to the user's own feelings or describing other people's feelings, for an overview see [24].

There seems no doubt that humans can emotionally feel what they read and intuitively and affectively differentiate between self and others by embodying or bodily suppressing their feelings. Especially, there is ample evidence that with regards to bodily signals, specifically facial expression of emotions significantly shape the perception of self and of other people by influencing how people affectively evaluate information about self and others [27, 28]. For instance, inhibiting facial expression leads to a significant decrease in understanding the emotions of others - be it during reading, during watching videos or pictures of other people or while interacting in real time with others.

This feedback from facial expressions could be so strong that it might significantly impact the user's decisions, for instance whether he or she likes or dislikes other users in an internet forum for their comments. Not being aware of the fact that social processing and emotion processing are multimodal processes in which information from one modality interacts with the information conveyed by other modalities can lead to wrong predictions in automated emotion recognition tools if these focus on only one modality or do not have theoretical or empirical knowledge of how to weigh and combine cross-modal congruent and incongruent information. For that reason, user-centered agent-based systems need to be able to deal with incongruence a) between information processing modalities or b) in information between sender and receiver. An example of an incongruence in a) is, that e.g., what is said by the user is incongruent with how it is expressed by the user. For example, the user sends a positive text message but displays a negative facial expression. An example for incongruence in b) is that the message of a sender is incongruent with the emotion/mood of the receiver or with the context in which the perceiver or receiver decodes the message. This sender-receiver incongruence also holds true for messages sent by the virtual agent itself [25]. For instance, if a virtual agent is sending incongruous emotional information to the human receiver of the message (visual: smile, auditory: sad voice). Incongruence effects on the agent's side can have a number of negative side effects on the user's behavior and feelings. It can lead to significantly fewer trust of the user in the agent, a decrease in the user's self-disclosure motivation and in turn produce inconsistent emotional expression on the user's side, thereby significantly impairing human-agent interaction qualitatively and quantitatively. Whether a) or b), emotion psychology as well as concomitant research including the results of the current study impressively demonstrate that information from that information from different modalities as well as incongruence of information between the modalities matter and should not be ignored in human-computer interaction. Therefore, focusing on only one decoding signal of the user might lead to inconsistent results because incongruent effects become unnoticed if not tracked across modalities. As a consequence, the user's true or correct emotional experience cannot be accurately detected. One can think of many instances in virtual agent-based human communication in which detecting an accurate reaction from the user does not reflect the true emotional state of the user. This is the case, when a person wishes to disguise his/her emotion or hide feelings by faking a smile or by mimicking a poker face while posting his/her text message. In other instances, the user may implicitly suppress his/her emotion without even being explicitly aware of it when posing a different emotion inconsistent with the message sent. Similarly, when in a depressed or negative mood or when suffering from depression or anxiety, emotion processing often becomes difficult including describing, identifying and expressing emotions. Computationally modeling such discrepancies in perception, feeling and action in the user becomes most relevant for agent-systems that aim at supporting e-mental health interventions. Regardless which use-case one might imagine, the importance of multimodal processing and how to integrate information that signals incongruence between modalities as meaningful information into computational models of user-centered agent systems is of central relevance, especially in light of novel developments such as multimodal sentiment analysis or "the emotive Internet".

Nevertheless, so far, incongruence effects still remain a challenge and an issue of investigation in human-computer interaction [4, 25]. As pointed out in [25], "much work remains to be done before sophisticated multimodal interaction becomes a common place, indispensable part of computing", cited from [25]. The present study was aimed to experimentally demonstrate the impact and power of incongruence in emotion processing in the laboratory by experimentally manipulation the participants' facial expressions by holding a wooden pen with lips or teeth or letting participants freely express themselves. Furthermore, despite small sample sizes, the present study also showed that inter-individual differences in emotion processing can and should not ignored as they mutually interact with the strength of such incongruence effects.

5   Conclusion and Future Outlook

Much effort and scientific work has been invested in the field of multimodal human computer interaction and human-robotics to provide computational solutions for data fusion, data interfacing, data classification or multimodal sensor engineering to allow for multimodal tracking of the user's behavior from principal any device and make virtual agents (including robotic behavior) as communicative interaction and communication partners more humanoid and thus "real" for the human user. While there is agreement that enriching agent-based human interaction by multiple modalities can increase the accuracy of the computational system in its attempt of detection, prediction and simulation of human behavior, multimodality is still a complicated tasks when it comes to dealing with ambiguity or incongruence in the data while mapping for instance the user's emotional states. Here, the challenge is not to treat these inconsistencies as error or noise in data preprocessing but as meaningful information. Up to know, the problem of incongruence is receiving more and more attention by researchers in the field. First solutions for theory-driven and data-driven hybrid approaches have also been already proposed [26]. Character Computing [7–9] constitutes one of these ambitious approaches that takes the human user in the center of its investigation and that attempts to go beyond simple emotion tracking. The novelty of Character Computing is its joint approach from Computer Scientists and Psychologists. Crucially, its framework as well as its underlying computational architecture and models are psychologically-driven and based on psychological reasoning including both a theory-driven and a data-driven approach. As outlined in [7–9], Character Computing tries closing the gap between the knowledge gained from psychological research and its application by computer scientists. It is a multimethod, multimodal approach that based on well-controlled psychological experiments already has proven successful in combining multimodal input with automated signal decoding routines. For instance to give one example, in [9], a study is discussed in which participants watched simple character trait and character state words to elicit positive or negative attitudes - amongst others about one's body appearance (in terms of size and shape) - while participants' responses were tracked by sensors recording the participants' eye blink data and heart rate to measure their implicit bodily arousal and approach or withdrawal behavior towards these words and thereby detect potential risk for body dissatisfaction and eating disorder. Next, the special prediction tested in the psychological studies as the one in [9] as well as the one presented in the present study can be directly integrated into an information ontology in order to represent the knowledge gained from the interactions between modalities.

To conclude, this paper asked how to deal with incongruence in agent-based human interaction and demonstrated its relevance by investigating how processes related to social perception and bodily facial feedback influence the user's affective judgments of emotional and neutral concepts. The research question, the experimental design as well as the results of this study provide an important theoretical framework and empirical proof for user-centered research aimed at solving incongruence detection in uni- and multimodal agent-based systems for the sake of modeling the "true" emotion of its users and for improving the user's trust in keeping up communication with virtual agents as empathetic and equal conversation partners.

References

1. Jennings, N.R.: Agent-oriented software engineering. In: Garijo, F.J., Boman, M. (eds.) Multi-Agent System Engineering. LNCS, vol. 1647, pp. 1–7. Springer, Heidelberg (1999). https://doi.org/10.1007/3-540-48437-X_1
2. Ivanović, M., et al.: Emotional agents-state of the art and applications. Comput. Sci. Inf. Syst. 12(4), 1121–1148 (2015)
3. Jaimes, A., Sebe, N.: Multimodal human–computer interaction: a survey. Comput. Vis. Image Underst. 108(1–2), 116–134 (2007)
4. Turk, M.: Multimodal interaction: a review. Pattern Recogn. Lett. 36, 189–195 (2014)
5. Suslow, T., Junghanns, K., Arolt, V.: Detection of facial expressions of emotions in depression. Percept. Mot. Skills 92(3), 857–868 (2001)
6. Paulus, M.P., Angela, J.Y.: Emotion and decision-making: affect-driven belief systems in anxiety and depression. Trends Cogn. Sci. 16(9), 476–483 (2012)
7. El Bolock, A., Abdennadher, S., Herbert, C.: Applications of character computing from psychology to computer science. In: El Bolock, A., Abdelrahman, Y., Abdennadher, S. (eds.) Character Computing, pp. 53–71. Springer, Cham (2020). https://doi.org/10.1007/978-3-030-15954-2_4
8. Herbert, C.: An experimental-psychological approach for the development of character computing. In: El Bolock, A., Abdelrahman, Y., Abdennadher, S. (eds.) character computing, pp. 17–38. Springer, Cham (2020). https://doi.org/10.1007/978-3-030-15954-2_2
9. Herbert, C., El Bolock, A., Abdennadher, S.: A psychologically driven, user-centered approach to character modeling. In: El Bolock, A., Abdelrahman, Y., Abdennadher, S. (eds.) Character Computing, pp. 39–51. Springer, Cham (2020). https://doi.org/10.1007/978-3-030-15954-2_3
10. Garliner, D.: Myofunktionelle Therapie in der Praxis - Gestörtes Schluckverhalten, gestörte Gesichtsmuskulatur und die Folgen - Diagnose, Planung und Durchführung der Behandlung. Thieme, Stuttgart (1989)

11. Wingenbach, T.S., Brosnan, M., Pfaltz, M.C., Plichta, M.M., Ashwin, C.: Incongruence between observers' and observed facial muscle activation reduces recognition of emotional facial expressions from video stimuli. Front. Psychol. **9**, 864 (2018)

12. Strack, F., Martin, L.L., Stepper, S.: Inhibiting and facilitating conditions of the human smile: a nonobtrusive test of the facial feedback hypothesis. J. Pers. Soc. Psychol. **54**(5), 768–777 (1988)

13. Effron, D.A., Niedenthal, P.M., Gil, S., Droit-Volet, S.: Embodied temporal perception of emotion. Emotion **6**(1), 1 (2006)

14. Herbert, C.: Emotions on our mind: cognitive appraisal and its contribution to verbal emotion processing and emotion regulation (2015). https://gepris.dfg.de/gepris/projekt/184218848

15. Herbert, C., Herbert, B.M., Ethofer, T., Pauli, P.: His or mine? The time course of self–other discrimination in emotion processing. Soc. Neurosci. **6**(3), 277–288 (2011)

16. Herbert, C., Pauli, P., Herbert, B.M.: Self-reference modulates the processing of emotional stimuli in the absence of explicit self-referential appraisal instructions. Soc. Cogn. Affect. Neurosci. **6**(5), 653–661 (2010)

17. Herbert, C., Sfärlea, A., Blumenthal, T.: Your emotion or mine: labeling feelings alters emotional face perception-an ERP study on automatic and intentional affect labeling. Front. Hum. Neurosci. **7**, 378 (2013)

18. Lang, P.J., Bradley, M.M., Cuthbert, B.N.: Motivated attention: affect, activation, and action. In: Lang, P.J., Simons, R.F., Balaban, M. (eds.) Attention and Orienting: Sensory and Motivational Processes, pp. 97–135. Psychology Press (1997)

19. Watson, D., Clark, L.A., Tellegen, A.: Development and validation of brief measures of positive and negative affect: the PANAS scales. J. Pers. Soc. Psychol. **54**(6), 1063 (1988)

20. Laux, L., Spielbeger, C.D.: Das State-Trait-Angstinventar: (STAI). Theoretische Grundlagen und Handanweisung (Beltz-Test). Beltz-Testgesellschaft, Weinheim (1981)

21. Beck, A.T., Steer, R.A., Hautzinger, M.: Beck-Depressions-Inventar: (BDI): Testhandbuch. Huber (1994)

22. Weis, P.P., Herbert, C.: Bodily reactions to emotional words referring to own versus other people's emotions. Front. Psychol. **8**, 1277 (2017)

23. Mezulis, A.H., Abramson, L.Y., Hyde, J.S., Hankin, B.L.: Is there a universal positivity bias in attributions? A meta-analytic review of individual, developmental, and cultural differences in the self-serving attributional bias. Psychol. Bull. **130**(5), 711 (2014)

24. Herbert, C., Ethofer, T., Fallgatter, A.J., Walla, P., Northoff, G.: The Janus face of language: where are the emotions in words and where are the words in emotions? Front. Psychol. **9**, 65 (2018)

25. Tsiourti, C., Weiss, A., Wac, K., Vincze, M.: Multimodal integration of emotional signals from voice, body, and context: effects of (in) congruence on emotion recognition and attitudes towards robots. Int. J. Soc. Robot. **11**(4), 555–573 (2019). https://doi.org/10.1007/s12369-019-00524-z

26. Mortillaro, M., Meuleman, B., Scherer, K.R.: Advocating a componential appraisal model to guide emotion recognition. Int. J. Synth. Emot. (IJSE) **3**(1), 18–32 (2012)

27. Niedenthal, P. M., Halberstadt, J. B., Margolin, J., Innes-Ker, Å. H.: Emotional state and the detection of change in facial expression of emotion. European J. Soc. Psychol. **30**(2), 211–222 (2000)

28. Weis, P. P., Herbert, C.: Bodily reactions to emotional words referring to own versus other people's emotions. Fron. Psychol. **8**, 1277 (2017)

Contributions of Character Computing to AI Based Adaptive Learning Environments – A Discussion

Dirk Reichardt[✉]

DHBW Stuttgart, Stuttgart, Germany
dirk.reichardt@dhbw-stuttgart.com

Abstract. During the covid-19 pandemic, the use of elearning and online learning increased significantly. Learning management systems provide a large data basis which can be exploited for personalized learning using AI based approaches of XAI and active learning. Integrating concepts of character computing enables a more robust adaptation to the learner's needs. The paper discusses future application scenarios of XAI, virtual learning companions and social learning.

Keywords: Character computing · AI · XAI · Active learning · Learning management system · Learning theory · Education · Personalization

1 Introduction

Within the last year, the pandemic situation led to a disruptive change in education. In unprecedented speed, schools and universities switched to a new form of education which did not necessarily require the presence of students and lecturers. The methods and even the technologies used where not new, though. Learning Management Systems existed before, but since march 2020, for example 50,000 new sites with the LMS moodle were launched. An increase of more than 30%. Google Trends also shows an enormous increase in the interest in learning management systems. The share of elearning and blended learning will most likely remain much higher than it was before 2020 and we will have a new "normal" situation in education.

In the last decade machine learning gained more and more application fields and interest. Applying AI techniques in learning environments also becomes more interesting with a larger acceptance and use learning platforms. In education, personalized learning is a widely discussed concept and is supposed to offer great opportunities. Nevertheless, it requires a lot of effort and resources of the education system. In the emerging new situation of widely used software supported online learning environments, there are good chances of an implementation of personalized learning in our education system.

Motivation is known as one of the key factors of learning and educational success. In an education system which has certain predefined learning objectives, the main key to success is the elicitation of motivation which is in line with these objectives. How can that be achieved best? If you know the learner, his or her history and background, the

F. De La Prieta et al. (Eds.): PAAMS Workshops 2021, CCIS 1472, pp. 40–47, 2021.
https://doi.org/10.1007/978-3-030-85710-3_4

beliefs, skills and preferences, the personality and even the affective and motivational state, it's much easier to set anchors and use this knowledge in order to motivate a person. Character computing addresses exactly this field and is a promising approach to individualized learning [1, 2].

This paper intends to set the basis for a scientific discussion on the role of AI based adaptive learning in future learning environments and especially the contributions of character computing in this field. It brings together basic learning and education theories, current developments in technological learning support and AI methods. Eventually, four future application scenarios are discussed.

2   Education, Learning and Personalized Learning

In order to set a scientific basis, this chapter will give a brief insight in learning theories and personalized learning.

2.1   Behaviorism, Cognitivism and Constructivism

Learning and learning processes can be seen from many different perspectives. Therefore, a number of theories on learning has been published and discussed. Three main theories have been established and today we can also associate them to separate learning contexts and situations:

- Behaviorism
- Cognitivism
- and Constructivism.

In behaviorist theories, learning is based on reinforcement where the subject of research are responses to stimuli. This is still a learning approach which seems to fit well in foundational learning with clear criteria and instructions. Cognitivist theories try to analyze the cognitive processes leading to a shown behavior. This is in contrast to behaviorism where this part is considered a black box and intends to build up a model of knowledge and knowledge processes, memory and representations. In constructivist theories, learning is a self-regulating process which is supposed to build up and dynamically modify its own model and constructing new meanings. In advanced learning scenarios, cognitivist and constructivist theories are considered as best fitting. These scenarios are open learning situations rather than pre-structured acquisition along fixed criteria. Learning in these scenarios takes place by discovery and exploration and provide an integral importance of learning from mistakes. Teaching approaches are more complex and more open than in foundational learning. The main role of a teacher is to provide scenarios which cause a cognitive conflict with the learner's existing model in order to make the learner develop it further. A crucial aspect of constructivism is the situation and social context a in which knowledge is built and used. So learning is always situated and is formed by social interaction [3].

2.2 Learning Types, Categories and Instructional Events

In the mid of the last century, the educational psychologist Robert Gagné developed a scheme of learning types which is often used and referenced. In a hierarchical order, eight categories of learning are introduced as: signal learning, stimulus-response learning, chaining, verbal association, discrimination learning, concept learning, rule learning and problem solving. Moreover, Gagné defined five categories of learning outcomes: intellectual skills, verbal information, cognitive strategies, motor skills and attitudes. He introduces a scheme of nine instructional events which serve as a guideline for designing instruction in an educational environment:

- gaining attention of the learner
- informing the learner of the objective of the learning task including success criteria
- stimulating the recall of prior learning, making connections to earlier tasks, experience and topics
- presenting the learning scenario, the stimulus and content
- guiding the learner, providing support in the learning process
- eliciting performance of the learner by practice
- providing feedback to the learner in the process
- assessing the performance (several times in the process)
- enhancing retention and transfer

Gagné's model is the basis for instructional design theory which intends to set up a structured learning program [4, 5].

2.3 Personalized Learning and Education

The idea of personalized learning is not new and many educational researchers find it quite obvious that a general approach of teaching all individuals in the same way, as it is done in most forms of schools, leaves room for improvement. In education systems, teachers usually have responsibility for whole groups rather than for individuals. The key issue in personalized learning is the profound knowledge of the individual strength, weaknesses and learning needs. Provided that knowledge, the matching teaching strategies and the required resources to implement these are required. As a further and important factor, the student should be able to orchestrate the curriculum. This is obviously limited in foundational learning but a crucial requirement in advanced learning. Personalized learning allows to take contextual conditions of the learner into account and supports individual interest as well as the coverage of weaknesses [6].

In personalized learning, three main aspects are addressed: instructions that are adapted to the individual learning needs in terms of pace, teaching methods as well as content and learning objectives. Personal competencies are required and assessed as cognitive competency, self-regulating of learning, motivation and social competency [7].

According to the experts' opinion shown in [8], the future higher education will incorporate the personalization of academic learning as well as lifelong learning and multi-institutional study pathways.

Although the advantages of personalized learning seem to be obvious in theory, the practical implementation either requires huge teaching resources or technological support. The Next Generation Learning Challenges (NGLC) initiative supports personalized teaching and a study on the effectiveness was conducted by the RAND Cooperation showing positive results [9].

3 Elearning, Learning Management Systems and Learning Analytics

Learning theories are set up and discussed in natural learning environments. Nevertheless, today learning takes place in scenarios well beyond natural learning environments. Elearning, blended learning, MOOCs, or just the use of online resources in order to look up a topic, watch an explanatory video, participate in a discussion in social media enhances the learning environment and changes the education system.

To keep it simple and focused on the aim of this paper, we consider learning management systems (LMS) as the basis for a online learning system which holds all relevant data. An LMS typically provides a central portal for all users and functions to provide modules, learning units and curricula including, tests, assessment of learner progress, certificates, tutorials, profiles, events, and general content management functions.

Since LMS platforms collect a lot of interesting data, learning analytics systems emerged along with the development of these platforms [10].

Learning analytics is used as a means of quality control of learning, identifying students which need support and data science methods applied to the collected data are used to determine learner behavior and learning strategies. The professional use, structuring and storage of the learner data is a prerequisite for adaptive and personalized learning.

How can we transfer instructional design principles to elearning? This question can be broken down to the instructional events of Gagné. How can we gain attention of the learner? As students are used to short video clips that carry a message, this can be used here as well to draw the students' attention to a feature, a problem, a benefit, an interesting solution in order to draw their attention to the method or learning item to be taught. Given a personalized learning path in an LMS, the learner may get a reference to already solved problems and learning contexts to stimulate recall. Check points and tests are typical components in an LMS which can serve to provide feedback as well as to assess performance repeatedly in the learning process.

4 Future Application Scenarios

Before discussing the following scenarios, the DHBW as higher education institution needs to be introduced since its specific structure and organization is essential for the understanding of the application scenarios. Nevertheless, the proposed solutions can be transferred to a wider range of universities and learning environments. The scenarios are intended to be a basis for discussion for the use of AI, especially XAI and active learning as well as character computing in the domain of elearning.

4.1 DHBW – The Baden-Wuerttemberg Cooperative State University

The Baden-Wuerttemberg Cooperative State University (Duale Hochschule Baden-Württemberg – short: DHBW) is one of the largest higher education institutions in Germany. The DHBW integrates academic studies and on-the-job training in cooperating partner companies. It was the first university in Germany which fully implemented cooperative education. The university has about 34,000 enrolled students and over 9,000 partner companies. The university structure is based on the US State University System and is unique in Germany. Its structure includes the central headquarters in Stuttgart and the local DHBW locations and campuses. The university has nine locations and three campuses. DHBW offers both bachelor and master degree programs.

The special form of education at DHBW is the unique combination of theory and practice. The curricula combine academic skills and work-related expertise. All students are employed at a partner company and after each semester they spend a 12-week training phase at their company which is integrated in the curriculum of the university. Students a taught in small groups of 25–30 persons. The existing learning management system of DHBW was extended during the pandemic and the lecturers are supported by education research centers at every location of DHBW. The curricula of the different locations and majors are coordinated by a central commission such that the education is very similar and comparable over all groups for the basic modules which may be described as the foundational education of the disciplines.

More than 400 groups of students begin their studies every year. With an increasing amount of moodle courses which are set up for every module and an increasing amount of learning units added to the system, a huge learning platform is established to support the studies and build bridges between theory and practice. Students which never physically share a lecture have the chance to connect and establish new forms of education and learning which augment the successful educational model of cooperative education at DHBW.

4.2 Scenario A: XAI and Active Learning Approach to Individualized Learning

Several approaches try to individualize learning. Using a learning management system as a platform allows to assess learner information, preferences and learning behavior beyond the learning module or unit which is supposed to be adapted to the learner. Even though it is the same person, every module is taught in a different context. The context includes the students which are grouped together in the module, groupwork tasks, their interest in the field, the lecturer, the kind of learning material provided, time pressure, etc. Given a sufficiently large dataset, the AI can provide recommendations of learning units, additional material or even choice of an elective module for an individual. The lack of previous observations of a student usually leads to low prediction accuracy and recommender systems fall back to group statistics rather than individual adaptations. The huge teacher and learner network of DHBW provides a good basis for learning algorithms. With about 700 professors and thousands of external lecturers a very good and diverse spectrum of contributions to the learning content is given.

In case the system is enhanced by character computing components, the model includes personality traits, mood, affective states and explicitly includes socio-cultural embeddings. [2, 11] This leads to a much richer basis for conclusions and adaptations to the individual.

Why XAI? When the learning path is adapted to the individual, this can be done by recommendations or automated orchestration of learning items and information hiding in order to reduce the complexity of the presented learning options. In case the learner is surprised by a choice made by the learning system, he or she might question the choice and ask for a reason. The explainable AI then presents the reason for the choice by showing the support for the decision i.e., using a LIME (Local interpretable model-agnostic explanations) [12] algorithm. If the learner agrees with the explanation the learner's curiosity is satisfied. If the learner does not agree, the system allows for interactive model change using active learning approaches [13]. Both measures together are essential for the acceptance of and trust in the system.

4.3 Scenario B: Social Learning

Social learning has many interpretations as a learning theory. In the last years interest in this subject increased as the social interactions of peer learners in online learning courses (MOOCs) were analyzed [14, 15].

Peer learning and learning in groups of students is an important part of education at a university. The outcome strongly depends on the formation of the group. A main aspect of group learning concerns building up self-confidence and social support. By discussing subjects and explaining to others, the group members achieve a better and deeper understanding.

How can a learning management system support groupwork? There are many formal means of supporting groupwork like shared directories or peer assessments hosted on the platform. However, the main issue is to find the right group members to optimize the learning outcome.

This is where character computing may add a new feature. Assuming a system of adaptive orchestration and recommendation as described in scenario A is given, the system has the character information about a learner and the past experience in learning groups as well as the preferred teaching and learning styles and pace. This is a very good basis for a matchmaking service for learners. If the online learning skills and tools are well exploited, the matchmaking is capable of crossing the borders of DHBW locations and campus and for more general learning issues and – as a global extension of a learning system - even the borders of universities and countries.

4.4 Scenario C: Peer Teaching by Example

At DHBW there is another specialty which can be exploited in a community-based learning system. As discussed in Sect. 2, the success of learning depends on motivation of the learner and a good means is to provide the right practical examples to a formal theory. With students coming from 9000 different companies, partly from similar industry branches, they all have their workplace experience which can serve as a knowledge pool.

Given a theoretical concept which is taught at university, one of the instructional events according to Gagné is to stimulate the recall of prior learning and experience, another one is eliciting performance by practice. The task for a student can be to set the concept in the context of his or her workplace and generate an application example. This example can then be shared among the students which helps understanding the theoretical concept by setting an anchor within a known domain of application and interest and thus increase the motivation.

4.5 Scenario D: Virtual Learning Companion

Even though the number of students within die DHBW network is quite large, the perfect companion may be hard to find. In this scenario a virtual learning companion can be implemented. This agent serves as a communication partner which either explains a learning concept or asks for assistance and explanation. As an artificial intelligence agent, it uses the large database of examples, tasks, learning units and even other learners as knowledge base and discusses solutions with the learner. As a virtual character, the agent implements all the facets of character computing to become a perfect match for a human learner.

5 Conclusion

The current growth of online learning and learning environments opens new perspectives on future software supported teaching and learning. Artificial intelligence provides new and interesting enhancements of learning systems and access to large learner data sets opens the potential for individualized learning. Character computing can add another dimension which enables better adaptations of learning content and methods knowing the learner's individual personal, affective, psychological or workplace background as a learning context.

References

1. El Bolock, A., Salah, J., Abdelrahman, Y., Herbert, C., Abdennadher, S.: Character computing. In: Proceedings of the 17th International Conference on Mobile and Ubiquitous Multimedia - MUM 2018, pp. 557–562, November 2018. https://doi.org/10.1145/3282894.3286060
2. Herbert, C., El Bolock, A., Abdennadher, S.: A psychologically driven, user-centered approach to character modeling. In: El Bolock, A., Abdelrahman, Y., Abdennadher, S. (eds.) Character Computing, pp. 39–51. Springer, Cham (2020). https://doi.org/10.1007/978-3-030-15954-2_3
3. Bélanger, P.: Three main learning theories. In: Theories in Adult Learning and Education, pp. 17–34. Verlag Barbara Budrich (2019)
4. Gagne, R.M.: The conditions of learning and theory of instruction (1985)
5. Gagne, R.M., Wager, W.W., Golas, K.C., Keller, J.M., Russell, J.D.: Principles of instructional design, 5th edition. In: Performance Improvement, vol. 44, no. 2, pp. 44–46 (2005). https://doi.org/10.1002/pfi.4140440211
6. OECD, Personalising Education. OECD (2006)

7. Redding, S.: "Enhanced Reader," Personal Competencies in Personalized Learning (2014). moz-extension://d7c37928-065e-e44b-b2ff-ebb2d7f94626/enhanced-reader.html?openApp&pdf=https%3A%2F%2Ffiles.eric.ed.gov%2Ffulltext%2FED5580 63.pdf. Accessed 21 May 2021

8. Ehlers, U.-D.: Future Skills-Future Learning and Future Higher Education (2020)

9. Pane, J., Steiner, E., Baird, M., Hamilton, L., Pane, J.: How Does Personalized Learning Affect Student Achievement? RAND Corporation (2017)

10. Siemens, G.: Learning analytics: the emergence of a discipline. Am. Behav. Sci. **57**(10), 1380–1400 (2013). https://doi.org/10.1177/0002764213498851

11. Reichardt, D.: Affective computing needs personalization—and a character? In: El Bolock, A., Abdelrahman, Y., Abdennadher, S. (eds.) Character Computing, pp. 87–98. Springer, Heidelberg (2020). https://doi.org/10.1007/978-3-030-15954-2_6

12. Ribeiro, M.T., Singh, S., Guestrin, C.: "Why should i trust you?" Explaining the predictions of any classifier. In: Proceedings of the ACM SIGKDD International Conference on Knowledge Discovery and Data Mining, 13–17 August 2016, pp. 1135–1144 (2016). https://doi.org/10.1145/2939672.2939778

13. Settles, B.: Active Learning Literature Survey (2010). http://pages.cs.wisc.edu/~bsettles/pub/settles.activelearning.pdf. Accessed 21 May 2021

14. Grünewald, F., Mazandarani, E., Meinel, C., Teusner, R., Totschnig, M., Willems, C.: openHPI: Soziales und Praktisches Lernen im Kontext eines MOOC. In: DeLFI 2013: Die 11 e-Learning Fachtagung Informatik, pp. 143–154 (2013)

15. Hill, A.J.: UCLA UCLA Electronic Theses and Dissertations Title Social Learning in Massive Open Online Courses: An Analysis of Pedagogical Implications and Students' Learning Experiences (2015). https://escholarship.org/uc/item/6qr7p6rq. Accessed 21 May 2021

Workshop on Deep Learning
Applications (DeLA)

Workshop on Deep Learning Applications (DeLA)

Deep learning is an artificial intelligence (AI) function that imitates the workings of the human brain in processing data and creating patterns for use in decision making. Deep learning is a subset of machine learning in artificial intelligence that has networks capable of learning unsupervised from data that is unstructured or unlabeled. Also known as deep neural learning or deep neural networks.

The objective of the Workshop on Deep Learning Applications is to give an opportunity for researchers to provide further insight into the problems solved at this stage, advantages and disadvantages of the various approaches used, lessons learned, and meaningful contributions to enhance applications based on deep learning. In this sense, the first Workshop on Deep Learning Applications (DeLA) provided a forum for the presentation and discussion of novel research ideas or actual deployments focused on the development of advanced applications based on deep learning.

Organization

Organizing Committee

Dalila Durães	University of Minho, Portugal
Cleber Zanchettin	Northwestern University, USA
Leonardo Matos	Federal University of Sergipe, Brazil
Flávio Santos	University of Minho, Portugal

Program Committee

Ricardo Matsumura Araujo	Federal University of Pelotas, Brazil
Adriano Lorena Inacio de Oliveira	Federal University of Pernambuco, Brazil
Francisco Marcondes	University of Minho, Portugal
Bruno Fernandes	University of Minho, Portugal
Tiago Oliveira	Tokyo Medical and Dental University, Japan
Ângelo Costa	Technical University of Valencia, Spain
Hector Moretón	University of Leon, Spain
Javier Bajo	Technical University of Madrid, Spain
Davide Carneiro	ESTG, Polytechnic Institute of Porto, Portugal
Paulo Novais	University of Minho, Portugal

An Attentional Model for Earthquake Prediction Using Seismic Data

Alana de Santana Correia[(⊠)] [iD], Iury Cleveston[iD],
Viviane Bonadia dos Santos[iD], Sandra Avila[iD], and Esther Luna Colombini[iD]

Institute of Computing, University of Campinas, Campinas, São Paulo, Brazil
{sandra,esther}@ic.unicamp.br

Abstract. Natural disaster prediction is one of the main concerns of authorities globally. Disasters cause large-scale psychological, social, and economic damage; therefore, techniques to predict such events are essential to minimize their impacts. However, despite all efforts to estimate the occurrence of a disaster, making an accurate and robust forecast is a challenging task. In recent years, Deep Learning techniques have innovated several fields by learning the factors that contribute to the phenomena generation; also, biologically inspired concepts such as attention have provided cheap ways to allocate computational resources by consuming only the necessary information to solve the task. This work aims to develop and evaluate a feature-based temporal attentional model to predict the time remaining for an earthquake event by consuming seismic waves from the LANL Earthquake dataset. The proposed models comprehend four distinct architectures based on 1D-CNN, LSTM, and LSTM with self-attention mechanisms. Experimental results indicated that attention plays a vital role in learning temporal relations, with models achieving state-of-the-art results in the task.

Keywords: Earthquake prediction · Deep learning · Attention

1 Introduction

Reducing the risk of natural disasters is a major goal for the United Nations Conference on Sustainable Development (i.e., Rio+20). At least 3.3 million deaths occurred globally due to natural disasters since 1970, and each year, around 226 million people are affected indirectly [3]. Between 2000 and 2010, earthquakes were responsible for 680,000 fatal victims; almost half of them occurred in Haiti. Globally, 102 million people are affected by floods, 37 million by cyclones, hurricanes, typhoons, and 366,000 by landslides [18]. These events drastically impact the population's life and influence several sectors of society. For this reason, natural disaster forecasting is an essential instrument to minimize the devastating impacts of such events.

Commonly, earthquakes are studied by the earth sciences, focusing on three main points: a) when the event will occur, b) where it will occur, and c) what

© Springer Nature Switzerland AG 2021
F. De La Prieta et al. (Eds.): PAAMS Workshops 2021, CCIS 1472, pp. 53–64, 2021.
https://doi.org/10.1007/978-3-030-85710-3_5

will be the impact [1,2]. If these components are known, the disaster risk can be measured early, saving lives and billions of dollars in infrastructure. Although scientific studies advance in this field, interpreting seismic data is still challenging. In this sense, machine learning techniques, such as Deep Learning (DL), have gained prominence as a fundamental tool to help understand seismic information and make increasingly robust predictions. Furthermore, DL techniques can learn the various non-linear factors that contribute to the generation of the observed phenomena, outperforming traditional machine learning (ML) methods [8].

Classic ML algorithms essentially calculate seismic indicators such as Gutenberg Richter b-values, time intervals, earthquake energy, and mean magnitude. In comparison, the most modern DL models can learn several sophisticated features. ML and DL models are both data-driven and work well with medium-magnitude earthquakes, but the results are poor for high-magnitude ones. This occurs mainly due to the scarce data for high-magnitude earthquakes—data-driven models require a large amount of data to provide reasonable predictions [11]. Some DL methods predict major earthquakes by training on them separately, but they still need considerable improvements [12]. One common characteristic of these methods is the analyses of long temporal series of seismic waves, which confers a significant challenge for DL methods.

In the last years, attentional mechanisms were introduced in DL, inspired by biological concepts to deal with large input data and optimize computational resources by dynamically selecting essential information to solve a given task. For temporal tasks, this property is fundamental since the input space becomes intractable for long series, affecting the model's performance significantly. Although attentional concepts are being extensively explored in DL, their main applications are natural language processing and computer vision. Recent surveys in the field indicate that temporal prediction is still a topic that deserves more exploration [13].

Therefore, this work aims to develop and evaluate several earthquake prediction models using the LANL Earthquake Prediction dataset. This dataset was built by the Los Alamos National Laboratory and made available for competition on Kaggle in order to leverage a wide range of knowledge addressing one of the most critical problems in earth science—which usually suffers from a lack of deep learning solutions, mainly due to the scarcity of data. This dataset has challenging features such as long sequences and earthquakes of varying magnitudes, but it has a significant amount of data to build initial DL solutions. These solutions can, via transfer learning, be adapted to work in real-world scenarios.

Specifically, the main contributions of our work are: a) Exploring the classical architectures for temporal series such as 1D Convolutional Neural Network (1D-CNN) [4], and Long Short-term Memory (LSTM) [5,9]; b) Proposing a generic self-attention module for the LSTM-based architectures; c) Evaluating the attentional mechanism impact when plugged in different locations, given that most of the works in the field do not explicitly evaluate the contributions of attention in different points of the architectures; d) Comparing the results of the attentional mechanism with the best results obtained in the competition.

2 Theoretical Background

Convolutional Neural Networks (CNNs) implement convolutional operations to determine the spatial relation between two signals [8]. They are commonly composed of two dimensions (2D-CNN) for computer vision tasks, but 1D CNNs are more appropriate when the signal has only one dimension [6]. Furthermore, 1D CNNs present a significant performance in applications involving temporal sequences analysis, which is our main reason to explore this model. In the same sense, the **Long Short-term Memory (LSTM)** stands out as a particular type of network capable of storing information for a longer time than traditional recurrent networks, diminishing the vanishing gradient problem. Each LSTM cell comprises a hidden and cell state, which controls the information flow by its gates, enabling the cell to remember or forget a specific content [10].

Attentional mechanisms support recurrent neural networks to deal with very long sequences, usually forgotten in traditional models [13]. In this sense, attentional mechanisms provide resource allocation by intelligently selecting the essential part of the information to solve the task at hand. Attention can emerge in two ways: a) **bottom-up attention**, the act of focusing is involuntary and guided by external stimuli to the application; b) **top-down attention**, the cognition and goals voluntarily control the focus [13]. Furthermore, attention can be differentiated based on the restrictions that are imposed on the input information. **Soft attention** defines a continuous distribution of importance among all information elements, whereas **hard attention** defines a discrete subset of importance [13]. There are also **self-attention** mechanisms, a subclass of soft attention that quantify the interdependence between the input elements. Self-attention mechanisms can promote the capture of more distant dependencies compared to CNN and LSTM alone.

3 Related Work

In recent years, machine learning techniques have been used to increase the accuracy of earthquake predictions. Initially, the predictions were made with classical techniques such as support vector machines, decision trees, and shallow neural networks. However, advanced deep learning techniques have increased substantially in the field; notably, LSTMs provided the most efficient architecture for this task [15]. For example, Vardann et al. [14] used LSTMs to predict the magnitude, depth, time, latitude, and longitude of the earthquake, obtaining R^2 (coefficient of determination) results around 59% higher than classical feed-forward neural networks, using the Afghanistan-Tajikistan region private dataset—these were very expressive results at the time. In the same sense, Wang et al. [15] proposed an earthquake prediction model using a spatiotemporal perspective by designing a two-dimensional input LSTM network capable of discovering spatiotemporal relationships between earthquake occurrences, using data gathered from the US Geological Survey (USGS).

Kanarachos et al. [17] proposed a hybrid algorithm using Wavelet Transform, feed-forward neural network, and Hilbert Transformation to detect anomalies during an earthquake, using a private dataset. First, the wavelet decomposition output was passed through a set of stacked neural networks, aiming to learn the signal's temporal structure. The model's output was then compared with the wavelet decomposition output, and the Hilbert transformation was used to detect anomalies in the signal. Recently, Li et al. [16] proposed DLEP (Deep Learning model for Earthquake Prediction), a framework based on CNNs and attention capable of merging explicit features designed by geologists with implicit features extracted through convolutional layers in order to find more accurate predictions for earthquakes events. To test their method, the authors merged the data from eight popular seismic zones: Sichuan Province, Xinjiang Province, Qinghai-Tibet plateau, Shandong-Jiangsu Province, Japan, the Philippines, Chicago, and Los Angeles. However, the dataset has not been made public.

Mousavi et al. [20] proposed an attentional multitask model to simultaneously detect and select phases of an earthquake. The model consists of a deep encoder and three decoders composed of 1D convolutions, bidirectional and unidirectional LSTMs, and transformers with self-attention layers. The encoder consumes seismic signals in the time domain and generates a representation with contextual information about temporal dependencies. Then the decoders use this information to predict the probability that an earthquake signal exists and the probability that the signal is either on the P-phase or S-phase for each point in time. A global attention module at the end of the encoder directs the network's attention to the associated parts of the earthquake signal relevant to each task. This structure generated a network with 372,000 parameters capable of detecting and locating twice as many earthquakes and selecting the phases P and S with precision close to manual selection by human analysts.

4 Methodology

4.1 Dataset

This work uses the **LANL Earthquake Prediction Dataset**[1] to train the models. The dataset is composed of seismic sequences from acoustic waves, which are used to predict the time remaining for the next earthquake. The seismic data is collected in the laboratory from artificially generated earthquakes. Although the data is artificially created, it still provides a challenging task for DL models. Also, when the model is deployed to the real world, it can be used as preventive measures in the face of a disaster situation.

The dataset contains 528,785,170 samples of acoustic waves with their respective time of occurrence. Table 1 presents a sequential sample of the first three points; Fig. 1 illustrates the data referring to the first 81,920 samples of the training set, the acoustic wave is presented in red color; the time to the next earthquake is outlined in blue color. The time remains constant in some parts resulting in a curve composed of several subsequent step functions. This occurs because the signal is sampled at 4 MHz, resulting in 4,096 samples every 12 μs,

---

[1] https://www.kaggle.com/c/LANL-Earthquake-Prediction/data.

Table 1. Sequential samples in the training set. The *accustic_data* corresponds to the seismic wave magnitude, and the *time_to_failure* corresponds to the time remaining until the earthquake event occurs.

acoustic_data	time_to_failure
12	1.4690999832
6	1.4690999821
8	1.469099981

which is the interval between captures. Thus, for every 4,096 samples, the signal is stored and the same remaining time until the earthquake occurrence is assigned. More data and a larger scale demonstrate that the signal is seen as a set of concatenated ramp functions such that an earthquake occurs when the time value reaches zero. Furthermore, we can also observe that the time value reaches zero a few moments after the peaks of greater amplitude.

4.2 Hardware and Metrics

The experiments were performed on an Intel Xeon machine with 16 GB RAM, GPU NVIDIA Tesla K80, and Cuda version 10.0. The results were evaluated using the Mean Absolute Error (MAE) and Mean Squared Error (MSE).

4.3 Architectures

To construct our experiments, we propose four architectures using the following configurations: a) 1D-CNN, b) a classic LSTM, c) LSTM with self-attention in the input layer (LSTM Att-In), and d) LSTM with self-attention in the output layer (LSTM Att-Out).

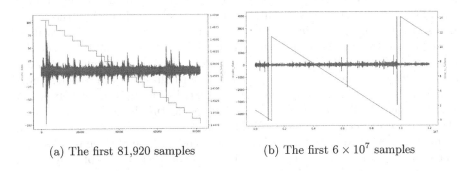

(a) The first 81,920 samples   (b) The first 6×10^7 samples

Fig. 1. Sequential samples of the acoustic wave (red color) and the time remaining for the next earthquake event (blue color). (Color figure online)

The **1D-Convolutional** architecture consists of 8 convolutional layers and one global average pooling 1D (Fig. 2). The first six convolutional layers have 100 channels and a kernel size of 1×10. In addition, there is one 1D max-pooling layer set to 3 to reduce the data dimensionality for every two convolutional layers. Also, a dropout function is set to 0.5 to diminish the overfitting.

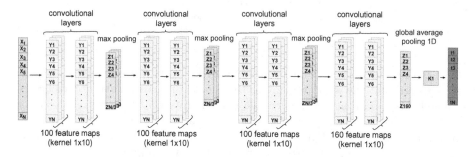

Fig. 2. The 1D-CNN architecture. The model is composed of eight convolutional layers, in which max-pooling operations are employed to reduce the data dimensionality. The output layer uses linear activation.

The **classic LSTM** architecture consists of three LSTM layers with 128 neurons in each one. After that, two fully connected layers with 100 neurons and another with one neuron are employed. This architecture was built incrementally until the MAE in the validation set was satisfactory. Furthermore, both LSTM layers implement dropout with a rate of 30%, and each layer is initialized with the *glorot uniform* algorithm. Except for the last layer that uses linear activation, the others use ReLU activation.

The subsequent architectures employed a generic **self-attention** mechanism, which is fully trainable along with the network and can be included at any point in the LSTM architecture. This mechanism is designed to relate N dimensional temporal data by receiving as input a matrix $I \in \mathbb{R}^{N \times d}$, where N is the series' time steps, in our case defined as 10, and d is the dimension of the features, defined as 13. Our attentional mechanism consists of two permutation modules to invert the data dimension, a dense layer that effectively computes attention and returns an attentional matrix $A \in \mathbb{R}^{N \times d}$ normalized by the softmax function. Finally, the merge module applies a pointwise multiplication between A and the input I. This mechanism is considered feature-based and capable of relating features between elements of different timesteps. When the attentional mechanism is applied to the input layer, the points are the raw temporal series. When the attentional mechanism is applied to the LSTM's output layer, the matrix I represents the last LSTM's latent space vectors. In this sense, for our experiments, we extended the LSTM architecture to include the self-attentional module in the input layer (**LSTM Att-In**), and to the output layer (**LSTM Att-Out**). The proposed architectures are shown in Fig. 3.

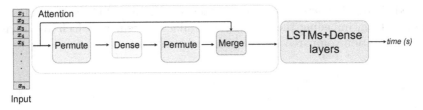

(a) Self-attention in the LSTM's input layer

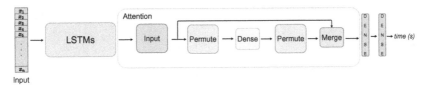

(b) Self-attention in the LSTM's output layer

Fig. 3. LSTM architectures with self-attention mechanisms.

5   Experiments

We executed the experiments independently for each architecture using the RMSProp optimizer [19]. We conducted preliminary tests to define the best optimizer: a) the results provided by the classic Stochastic Gradient Descent (SGD) took a considerable time to converge; b) the results provided by Adam and RMSProp were very similar in terms of quality and computation time. Except for the experiments conducted for the convolutional network, all other experiments were executed with three different learning rate values defined as 0.001, 0.0001, and 0.00005. The training consisted of 300 epochs for the first experiment, 400 for second and third, and 600 for fourth experiment; we have not used early stopping or learning rate decay. For each experiment, the final MAE or MSE was collected for training, validation, and testing.

For the first experiment, we used the 1D-CNN architecture, where 4,096 samples were employed to represent the input space since each seismic sequence has 12 μs. In total, 114,688,000 samples were used, resulting in 40,000 sequences with a size of 4,096. From these 40,000 sequences, we used 28,000 for training, 8,000 for validation, and 4,000 for testing. Thus, the complete training took 4 h, considering 230 epochs and a batch size of 16 samples. The results obtained for the training and validation set are shown in Fig. 4a, where we can observe that the MSE decreases with the number of epochs, reaching a value close to zero. However, the MSE in the validation set was significantly higher, around 15, during most of the training. This final result shows significant overfitting, considering that the model achieved a good fit in training but generalized poorly. Other tests were also performed with a batch size of 128 and 256; however, similar results were obtained. Thus, although the model trained successfully, the MSE remained high for the validation set. We understand that the sequence size adopted directly impacted the results obtained using the 1D-CNN; the sequences are quite long, impeding the learning of significant tremors, which are usually short in duration compared to sequential information.

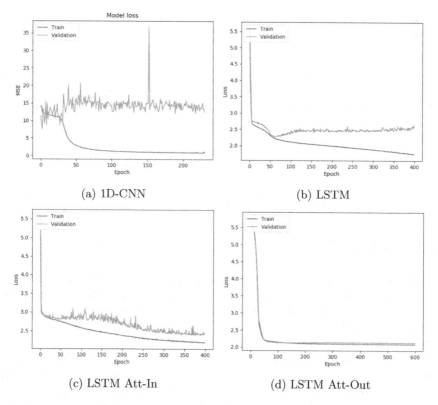

Fig. 4. Training and validation losses. a) 1D-CNN, b) LSTM with learning rate of 0.0001. c) LSTM Att-In with learning rate of 0.0001, d) LSTM Att-Out with learning rate of 0.00005.

Therefore, we performed a second experiment, using a classic LSTM architecture to capture temporal dependencies adequately. The proposed architecture receives as input the seismic sequences and returns the prediction for the time remaining until the next earthquake occurrence. Also, we adopted a simple strategy to extract features from the raw data, aiming to make the input sequences smaller and more representative for the model. We processed the input set in a features extraction step: for every 150,000 points, a 13-dimensional feature vector is extracted to represent the subsequence. The feature extraction step consists of computing statistical metrics such as mean, standard deviation, minimum, maximum, kurtosis, data probability distribution asymmetry, and quantile at 0.01%, 0.05%, 0.95%, and 0.99% of the probability distribution. Also, we computed the maximum, mean, and standard deviation between the absolute values.

After extracting the features, we created a 10-length input subsequence for the LSTM, where each subsequence represents 150,000 points in the original one. The classic LSTM experiments were performed for three different learning rates. Table 2 presents the best results achieved in our experiments for each model.

Table 2. Results for train, validation, and test set based on MAE. The attentional mechanisms provided the lower errors in test.

Model	Learning rate	MAE train	MAE val	MAE test
LSTM	0.001	0.3065	2.6850	2.8635
LSTM	0.0001	1.7730	2.6607	2.7609
LSTM	0.00005	1.6542	3.4571	3.2999
LSTM Att-In	0.001	0.8957	2.8507	2.6757
LSTM Att-In	0.0001	2.1698	2.4597	2.5453
LSTM Att-In	0.00005	2.0888	2.3867	2.7496
LSTM Att-Out	0.001	2.0053	2.1421	2.7272
LSTM Att-Out	0.0001	2.1021	2.0257	2.1453
LSTM Att-Out	0.00005	2.0776	2.1244	**2.1241**

We can observe in Fig. 4b that the classic LSTM model minimized the training loss, indicating proper learning, but with significant overfitting. After epoch 50, the validation loss starts to move away from the training loss, indicating that the model memorizes rather than learning. Despite overfitting, the prediction follows the original series reasonably; in the test set, the model obtained an MAE of 2.7609 with 400 epochs. Thus, the model can predict peaks and valleys of the function as shown in Fig. 5a. The generalization issue is probably caused by the low capability of the LSTM architecture to deal with long-term dependencies between input sequences. Therefore, recognizing earthquake patterns is compromised given the feature representation used.

Consequently, in the third experiment, we tested the effect of adding our self-attentional module directly on the input layer (LSTM Att-In). Our module captures the temporal relationships between the features of 10-length sequences, representing over a million input data. From the results of this experiment, we observed that the MAE diminished compared to the classic LSTM architecture, indicating that the use of self-attention in the input layer brings benefits; training time was not affected by this implementation. Furthermore, we can observe a decrease in overfitting compared to the baseline version in Fig. 4c; however, there was an increase in the loss oscillation for the validation set. Furthermore, the training and validation losses were close to 2, indicating a margin for improvements. Similar to the result found previously, the model can determine the peaks and valleys of the original series, making the prediction closer to the original as shown in Fig. 5b.

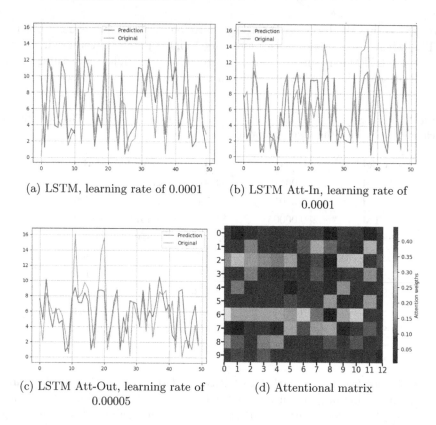

(a) LSTM, learning rate of 0.0001

(b) LSTM Att-In, learning rate of 0.0001

(c) LSTM Att-Out, learning rate of 0.00005

(d) Attentional matrix

Fig. 5. Seismic wave prediction by architecture, and attentional matrix. The attentional matrix lines represent the index of the input data and the columns represent the following features from left to right: mean, standard deviation, minimum, maximum, kurtosis, data probability distribution asymmetry, and quantile at 0.01%, 0.05%, 0.95%, and 0.99%, maximum, mean, and standard deviation between the absolute values.

The attentional matrix produced by the mechanism clearly show that some sequence points from the original data are much more relevant than others for the prediction, as shown in Fig. 5d. For example, the points represented by element 6 in the matrix line are relevant for prediction, as most of its features have high values. Similarly, only feature 8 from point 1 has much relevance for prediction. These relationships of importance between these elements found by the self-attentional mechanism provided the improvements observed.

We performed the fourth experiment to verify whether the architecture's bottleneck would be on the input or on the LSTM output layers. This experiment places the attentional module to weigh the last LSTM's context vector (LSTM Att-Out). The lowest MAE achieved for the test set was 2.12, with a learning rate of 0.00005—which is the lowest value reached in our experiments. Overall, the best MAE was achieved with self-attention implemented in the output layer. We can note that the loss, after epoch 50, quickly stagnated at the value of 2 without oscillations. Unlike all other approaches, we observed that the architecture quickly converged without overfitting in epoch 200. Then, we concluded that our model's bottleneck was in the last LSTM's context vector and that self-attention contributed significantly to generalization and convergence.

We also compared our best results with the best results in the Kaggle competition. The top five MAEs were: 2.26589, 2.29670, 2.29686, 2.29749, 2.29801. These results indicate that our LSTM Att-Out model is performing better than the models classified with the best results at the end of the competition.

6 Conclusion and Future Work

In this work, we developed four architectures to learn the time remaining for earthquake events based on seismic waves. The first model comprehends an 1D-CNN, which results obtained showed that although the loss converged during training, the validation has not shown any minimization. The second model uses three LSTMs layers to improve the temporal dependencies. The results indicated convergence for the training and validation set; however, the MAE for the test set was around 2.76, indicating a margin for improvement. One way to improve the results for time series can be achieved through temporal attentional mechanisms, as they can provide an alternative to capture more distant temporal relations than a 1D convolution filter can achieve. In this sense, two experiments were carried out with self-attention to the input layer and the output layer. The results showed that self-attentional mechanisms provide superior results; the MAE for the test set decreased from 2.76 to 2.12.

For future work, we suggest using end-to-end attention models to improve the results. Transformations such as Fourier or Wavelet can facilitate learning since operating with acoustic data in these domains is easier. Also, we intend to extend the proposed model to a multitasking application of earthquake detection and phase selection. We believe that the multitasking nature of the model coupled with attentional mechanisms can improve the system performance for both tasks since they are complementary. Additionally, hard attention mechanisms on input data can improve model performance and decrease the number of parameters.

Acknowledgment. This study was financed in part by the Coordenação de Aperfeiçoamento de Pessoal de Nível Superior – Brasil (CAPES) – Finance Code 001.

References

1. Rouet-Leduc, B.P.G.: Artificial Intelligence for Earthquake Forecasting (No. LA-UR-19-26395). Los Alamos National Lab. (LANL), Los Alamos, NM (United States) (2019)
2. Corbi, F., et al.: Machine learning can predict the timing and size of analog earthquakes. Geophys. Res. Lett. **46**(3), 1303–1311 (2019)
3. World Bank, & United Nations: Natural hazards, unnatural disasters: the economics of effective prevention. The World Bank (2010)

4. LeCun, Y., Haffner, P., Bottou, L., Bengio, Y.: Object recognition with gradient-based learning. In: Forsyth, D.A., Mundy, J.L., di Gesú, V., Cipolla, R. (eds.) Shape, Contour and Grouping in Computer Vision. LNCS, vol. 1681, pp. 319–345. Springer, Heidelberg (1999). https://doi.org/10.1007/3-540-46805-6_19

5. Sherstinsky, A.: Fundamentals of recurrent neural network (RNN) and long short-term memory (LSTM) network. Physica D **404**, 132306 (2020)

6. Kiranyaz, S., Avci, O., Abdeljaber, O., Ince, T., Gabbouj, M., Inman, D.J.: 1D convolutional neural networks and applications: a survey. Mech. Syst. Signal Process. **151**, 107398 (2021)

7. Rumelhart, D.E., Hinton, G.E., Williams, R.J.: Learning representations by back-propagating errors. Nature **323**(6088), 533–536 (1986)

8. Goodfellow, I., Bengio, Y., Courville, A., Bengio, Y.: Deep Learning, vol. 1, no. 2. MIT Press, Cambridge (2016)

9. Hochreiter, S., Schmidhuber, J.: Long short-term memory. Neural Comput. **9**(8), 1735–1780 (1997)

10. Olah, C.: Understanding LSTM Networks (2015). http://colah.github.io/posts/2015-08-Understanding-LSTMs

11. Al Banna, M.H., et al.: Application of artificial intelligence in predicting earthquakes: state-of-the-art and future challenges. IEEE Access **8**, 192880–192923 (2020)

12. Yang, X., Huang, K., Zhang, R., Goulermas, J.Y.: A novel deep density model for unsupervised learning. Cogn. Comput. **11**(6), 778–788 (2019)

13. Correia, A.D.S., Colombini, E.L.: Attention, please! A survey of Neural Attention Models in Deep Learning. arXiv preprint arXiv:2103.16775 (2021)

14. Bhandarkar, T., Satish, N., Sridhar, S., Sivakumar, R., Ghosh, S.: Earthquake trend prediction using long short-term memory RNN. Int. J. Electr. Comput. Eng. (2088-8708), **9**(2) (2019)

15. Wang, Q., Guo, Y., Yu, L., Li, P.: Earthquake prediction based on spatio-temporal data mining: an LSTM network approach. IEEE Trans. Emerg. Top. Comput. **8**(1), 148–158 (2017)

16. Li, R., Lu, X., Li, S., Yang, H., Qiu, J., Zhang, L.: DLEP: a deep learning model for earthquake prediction. In: 2020 International Joint Conference on Neural Networks (IJCNN), pp. 1–8. IEEE (2020)

17. Kanarachos, S., Christopoulos, S.R.G., Chroneos, A., Fitzpatrick, M.E.: Detecting anomalies in time series data via a deep learning algorithm combining wavelets, neural networks and Hilbert transform. Expert Syst. Appl. **85**, 292–304 (2017)

18. The United Nations Conference on Sustainable Development Secretariat: Disaster Risk Reduction and Resilience Building. Rio de Janeiro, Brazil, p. 4 (2012)

19. Reddy, R.V.K., Rao, B.S., Raju, K.P.: Handwritten Hindi digits recognition using convolutional neural network with RMSprop optimization. In: 2018 Second International Conference on Intelligent Computing and Control Systems (ICICCS), pp. 45–51. IEEE (2018)

20. Mousavi, S.M., Ellsworth, W.L., Zhu, W., Chuang, L.Y., Beroza, G.C.: Earthquake transformer-an attentive deep-learning model for simultaneous earthquake detection and phase picking. Nat. Commun. **11**(1), 1–12 (2020)

Efficient Violence Detection Using Transfer Learning

Flávio Santos[1], Dalila Durães[1(✉)], Francisco S. Marcondes[1], Sascha Lange[2], José Machado[1], and Paulo Novais[1]

[1] Algorithm Center, University of Minho, Braga, Portugal
{flavio.santos,dalila.duraes,francisco.marcondes}@algoritmi.uminho.pt,
{jmac,pjon}@di.uminho.pt
[2] Bosch Car Multimedia, Braga, Portugal
sascha.lange@pt.bosch.com

Abstract. In recent years several applications, namely in surveillance, human-computer interaction and video recovery based on its content has studied the detection and recognition of violence [22]. The purpose of violence detection is to automatically and effectively determine whether or not violence occurs in a short time. So, it is a crucial area since it will automatically enable the necessary means to stop the violence. To quickly solve this problem, we used models trained to solve general activity recognition problems such as Kinetics-400 to learn to extract general patterns that are very important to detect violent behaviour in videos. Our approach consists of using a state of the art pre-trained model in general activity recognition tasks (e.g. Kinetics-400) and then fine-tuning it to violence detection. We applied this approach in two violence datasets and achieved state-of-the-art results using only four input frames.

Keywords: Violence detection · Transfer learning · Action recognition · Deep learning · Surveillance

1 Introduction

Deep learning models applying neural networks. A neural network gets inputs, which are then processed in hidden layers using weights adjusted while training. Then the model exposes a prediction. The weights are adjusted to find patterns to obtain better predictions [3]. The user does not need to define which patterns to look for since the neural network learns independently.

Violence recognition in the video is a unique problem regarding the critical problem of action recognition [12]. So, the recognition of violence itself is a challenging problem, since the concept of violence is subjective [9,31]. We may define violence as any situation or action that may cause physical harm to one or more persons [18,30]. Violence recognition is an essential issue at the application level and the scientific level because it has characteristics that differentiate generic actions.

F. De La Prieta et al. (Eds.): PAAMS Workshops 2021, CCIS 1472, pp. 65–75, 2021.
https://doi.org/10.1007/978-3-030-85710-3_6

We can consider three dimensions (x, y, t) for violence recognition in video, where t is the temporal space variation, x and y is the variation through time. Note that the orientation changes may not be equivalent or symmetrical with the temporal variation and may need to treated space and time asymmetrically. For this, we can consider four different techniques: (i) RGB based [10]; (ii) Keypoints [19]; (iii) Dynamic Image [1]; and (iv) Optical Flow [7].

Detecting violent interaction behaviours can prevent serious problems by reducing the risks of both social instability and personal insecurity [30]. Currently, there are millions of devices in public places, creating enormous pressure on the guards [7]. Hence the importance of automatic detection of events of violence from a large amount of surveillance video data [31].

Performing automated vision-based human violence recognition analysis is an essential task with many applications. However, human behaviour interpretation is still a very complicated situation that cannot be solved with a single approach [20].

The concept of transfer learning is an excellent example of training a model with a set of data and then applying this training model to another dataset and verifying the results obtained, and adjusting the features to better predictions and results. So, one of the advantages of transfer learning is that the number of inputs is higher, and the better are the results obtained.

Our contribution consists of using pre-trained models in general human activity recognition with the Kinetics-400 dataset to solve violence recognition. In this way, it was possible to learn to extract general patterns that are very important to detect violent behaviour in videos. Then, the model was adjusted to detect violence. The fine-tuning step was performed using two different public violence dataset, RWF-2000 [6] and RLVS [25]. Contrary to the common violence recognition approach in the literature, such as [6], our fine-tuned model uses only a few input video frames.

The paper is organized as follows: next section presents the related work with explanations of general video classification, violence recognition on videos, and transfer learning; section III described our framework overview, while section IV, explain the experiments and the results; finally, section V concludes this work with some future directions.

2   Related Work

2.1   General Video Classification

This subsection will explain the different types of architectures that can be applied to video violence recognition. Several datasets can be used for training, but the most used are Kinetics-600 and AVA. The Kinetics dataset is a project that provides a large scale of video clips for human action classification, covering a varied range of human actions. This dataset contains real-world applications with video clips having a duration of around 10 s [4]. Kinetic-600 has 600 different classes, each with 600 videoclips. The AVA dataset densely annotates 80 atomic visual actions in 430 15-minute movie clips. Human actions are noted independently for each person in each video, on keyframes sampled once per second. The dataset also provides bounding boxes around each person. Each person has all its co-occurring actions labelled for a total of 1.6M labels [13]. In some cases, Kinetics-400 are used for pre-trained models. The difference for Kinetics-600 is that this dataset is previous and has only 400 classes, each with 400 videoclips [15].

I3D. I3D is a composition of an inflated 2D ConvNets in 3D. I3D converts image classification models (2D) into 3D ConvNets. This can be done by starting with a 2D architecture and inflating all filters and grouping the kernels - giving them an additional time dimension. The filters are generally square, being transformed into cubic, that is, they change from N × N to N × N × N filters [4,13].

C3D. The 3D ConvNet architecture can better model temporal information due to 3D convolution and 3D grouping operations. ConvNets 3D, convolution and pooling operations are performed through space-time, whereas in 2D ConvNets they are performed only in space. Only ConvNets 3D preserves the input signals' temporal information, resulting in an output volume, unlike 2D ConvNets that lose temporal information from the input signal right after each convolution operation. The same phenomenon applies to 2D and 3D pooling [5,27,28].

Non-local Block. Non-local networks are an efficient, generic and straightforward component for capturing long-range dependencies with deep neural networks in computer vision. Intuitively, a non-local operation calculates the response in one position as a weighted sum of resources at all positions in the input resource maps. The set of positions can be in space, time or space-time, which implies that the operations are applicable for image, sequence and video problems [29].

SlowFast. SlowFast network's architecture can be described as a single flow architecture with two different time rates (slow and fast), which are merged by side connections. The idea is to model two pathways separately, working at low and high temporal resolutions. Thus, the rapid pathway is designed to capture the movement of rapid change, but with less spatial details. The slow pathway is designed to focus on the spatial and semantic domain [11].

ResNet. Residual networks obtain a high performance in the classification and allow deep networks up to more than 1000 layers. Besides, residual networks make use of identity shortcut connections that allow information to flow between layers without attenuation caused by several stacked nonlinear transformations, resulting in improved optimization. Shortcut connections are not blocked, and unprocessed input is always transmitted [14].

X3D. This architecture is a low-computation regime in terms of computation/accuracy trade-off for violence detection on video. Besides, X3D expands a tiny base 2D image architecture into a spatiotemporal one by expanding multiple possible axes. The resulting architecture is referred to as X3D (Expand 3D) for expanding from the 2D space into 3D spacetime domain. The architecture defines a basic set of expansion operations used for sequentially expanding X2D from a tiny spatial network to X3D, a spatiotemporal network, by performing the following operations on temporal, spatial, width and depth dimensions [10]. The original description of the X3D architecture are describe by the authors [10].

2.2   Transfer Learning

Transfer learning is a machine learning technique studied for a long time to solve the different problems of visual categorization. However, in recent years, due to the increase in images, audios and videos on the Internet, they have forced an increase in computational accuracy and efficiency. When traditional machine learning techniques reach their limits, transfer learning is an alternative for visual categorization and can use two approaches. The first approach preserving the original pre-trained network and updating weights based on the new training dataset. The second approach used the pre-trained network for resource extraction and representation, followed by a generic classifier [23]. Our proposed technique for violence recognition falls under the first category.

3   Our Framework Overview

Inductive transfer learning is a common approach in deep learning, for example, computer vision models sometimes are fine-tuned from other models trained on ImageNet [24] and natural language processing models are fine-tuned from language models [8]. Based on these examples, in this work, we propose a fine-tuning generic activity recognition model to detect violence in a video.

An overview of our framework is present in Fig. 1. Initially, it is necessary to obtain a trained model using a general activity recognition dataset, such as Kinetics 400 [15]. Next, we have used fine-tuning this model using a specific violence dataset. We have used a X3D model trained with Kinetics 400 dataset, then we fine-tuned it using both violence dataset RLVS [25] and RWF-2000 [6].

Our hypothesis to use a transfer learning approach to learn a model to recognise violence in video is that a generic activity recognition model can extract some generic features necessary to discriminate if a video has violence or not. Besides, since the pre-trained model already has learned to extract some features to classify videos, it can use less information (frames) from the input videos in the classification and training time.

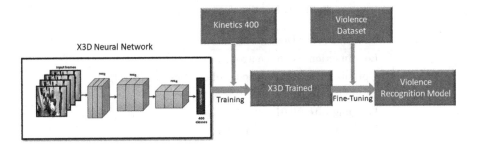

Fig. 1. Our Framework using Transfer Learning Approach.

4   Experiments and Results

This section describe the pre-trained models used to violence video recognition. In addition, we also present the training details and the datasets used in the experiments.

4.1   Models and Training Details

X3D is a family of deep neural networks architectures for efficient video recognition. In [10], they present the X3D versions XS, S, M, L, XL, XXL with 3.6, 3.6, 3.6, 6.08, 11.0, 20.3 millions of parameters, respectively. Although the X3D family present efficient and accurate versions such as M, L, XL and XXL, we have used the pre-trained versions XS and S in our experiments because of its trade-off between the number of parameters, accuracy and number of necessary frames to be processed.

To training both X3D XS and X3D S, we have used stochastic gradient descent [26] with an initial learning rate of 0.01 and a momentum of 0.9. Besides, we set the batch size to 32 input videos.

The model was trained using the cross entropy loss function with the Stochastic Gradient Descent optimizer. We have used the Cosine Annealing [16] learning rate scheduler with an initial learning rate of 0.01. It is important to highlight that every layer with dropout uses a probability of 0.5. Table 1 add more details from the architecture experiments.

4.2   Datasets

The literature presents some datasets for violence recognition in videos, such as The Hockey dataset [2], movie dataset [21], and violent-flow dataset [17]. However, they have some disadvantages in the same background and a low number of videos. Thus, we have chosen to use the Real-Life Videos Situation (RLVS) [25] and Real-World Fighting (RWF-2000) [6] datasets because of their variety of videos.

Table 1. Details of experiments.

Name	Description
Loss function:	Cross entropy
Optimizer:	Stochastic Gradient Descent (SGD)
Dropout rate:	0.5
Learning rate:	0.01
lr scheduler:	Cosine annealing

Real-Life Videos Situation. This dataset consists of 2000 videos divide in two classes: (1) 1000 videos for violence and (2) 1000 videos for non-violence. The violence videos present violence in a huge number of scenarios, such as schools, prison, and street. While the non-violence videos has human activities such as persons playing football, basketball, eating, and swimming.

Real-World Fighting. RWF dataset is composed of 2000 videos collected from the YouTube platform, where 1000 are violent videos and 1000 non-violence videos. All the videos were captured from surveillance cameras in real-world scenes, thus presenting only real situations. Besides, the violent situations in this dataset are not limited, it includes a lot of subjectively violent activities such as fighting, robbery, explosion, shooting, and assault.

Table 2 a comparison between the RWF-2000 and RLVS datasets in terms of characteristics. This two dataset are very similar, but RWF-2000 do not have any audio. For this work, this point is no significant.

Table 2. Comparison of the two datasets.

Dataset	RWF-2000	RLVS
Classes	Violence and non-violence	Violence and non-violence
Avg. size	5 s	5 s
Train	800 videos for each class	800 videos for each class
Validation	200 videos for each class	200 videos for each class
Audio	No audio	Some with audio

4.3 Results and Discussion

This section present all the results achieved in this work and discuss about it. The next two subsections present and discuss the results obtained with RWF-2000 and RLVS datasets, respectively.

RWF-2000. The Table 3 present the results obtained with RWF-2000 dataset. All The results from methods I3D, and P3D were obtained from [6].

Table 3. Results of the proposed approach in this work and others in the literature.

Method	Signal	Accuracy (%)
I3D	RGB	85.75
P3D	RGB	84.50
I3D	OPT	75.50
I3D	OPT + RGB	81.50
P3D	OPT + RGB	87.25
X3D XS (ours)	RGB	81.75
X3D S (ours)	RGB	84.75

From the results, we can see that the I3D present the state-of-the-art results when considering only the RGB signal and the P3D present the general state-of-the-art result. Although our approach does not present state of the art results, it present a competitive result using only few information from the input video because I3D and P3D use 64 frames from the input and our approach uses 4 and 13 frames in X3D XS and X3D S, respectively. Thus, reinforcing our argument that the pre-trained model with general activity recognition dataset learns to extract useful features to build an efficient violence recognition model.

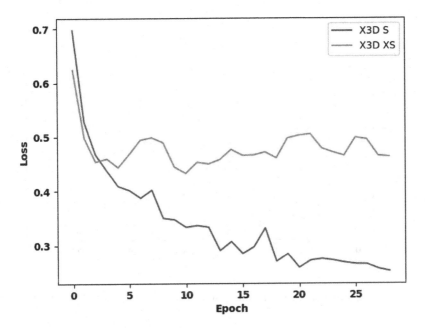

Fig. 2. Curve of the training loss. Using the dataset RWF-2000

Figure 2 present the X3D S and X3D XS loss training curve during the first 30 epochs. We can observe that both curves have almost the same beginning. However, the X3D XS model has stabilized while the X3D S continue decreasing.

RLVS. Table 4 presents the results obtained in the RLVS test set. X3D S and X3D XS achieve better results than M(RLVS), thus our proposed approach has achieved state of the art results on this dataset even using only 4 or 13 input frames.

Table 4. Results of the proposed approach in this work and others in the literature.

Method	Accuracy (%)
M(RLVS) [25]	94.5
X3D XS (ours)	97.5
X3D S (ours)	98.0

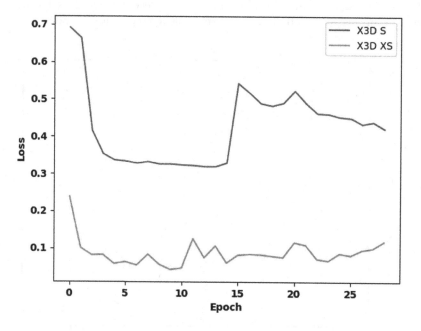

Fig. 3. Curve of the training loss. Using the dataset RLVS.

The Fig. 3 exhibits the X3D S and X3D XS model's training loss curve using the RLVS dataset. In the RLVS case, the difference between both curves is huge when compared to the RWF-2000 (Fig. 2) because both models have very different starts since X3D S achieve a loss of the almost 0.7 in the first epoch while the X3D XS achieve practically 0.25. Although the X3D S has presented a more significant loss than the X3D XS, which shows the best test result. Thus, indicating that the X3D XS model has been overfitting with the training data.

Furthermore, to the experiments with RLVS and RWF-2000 datasets, we joined them and built a new dataset RLVS+RWF-2000 to test our approach. The accuracy achieved with RLVS+RWF-2000 test set using the X3D XS model was 88.13.

5 Conclusion and Future Work

The plan was to use transfer learning to train a model to recognise violence in the video. The global idea was that a generic activity recognition model could extract some generic features necessary to discriminate if a video has or not violence. Furthermore, since the pre-trained model previously has learned to obtain some features to classify videos, it can use fewer frames from the input videos in the classification and training.

It used a X3D model to get a trained model using a general activity recognition dataset, so, it used the Kinetics 400. After that, it refinement this model using both violence dataset RLVS and RWF-2000. It has used stochastic gradient descent [26] with an initial learning rate of 0.01 and a momentum of 0.9 to training both X3D XS and X3D S. Also, it set the batch size to 32 input videos. The results obtained show that it can achieve a state of the art violence recognition model even using only 4 or 13 input frames from video. So, it obtained the general state-of-the-art results for the I3D when considering only the RGB signal and the P3D. Furthermore, it presents a competitive approach using only 4 and 13 frames from the input video in X3D XS and X3D S, respectively. Contrary to I3D and P3D, that use 64 frames. Thus, strengthening our argument that the pre-trained model with general activity recognition dataset learns to extract helpful features to create an efficient violence recognition model.

One of the questions we can do is why transfer learning works for RLVS but not for the RWF-2000 dataset? An answer is that the RWF-200 dataset has the same background and the same people for violence and not violent scenes. Another explanation is the quality of the dataset of RWF-2000 is worse than RLVS.

It intends to do more experiments with this model as future work, transferring the knowledge of a model trained with specific activities rather than with general ones. This is important because some specific activities can contribute most to violence recognition than others. Also, it's possible in future work to train the model with Kinetic-600 to have more activities and verify if some actions caused violence.

Acknowledgment. This work is supported by: European Structural and Investment Funds in the FEDER component, through the Operational Competitiveness and Internationalization Programme (COMPETE 2020) [Project no 039334; Funding Reference: POCI-01–0247-FEDER- 039334].

References

1. Bilen, H., Fernando, B., Gavves, E., Vedaldi, A., Gould, S.: Dynamic image networks for action recognition. In: Proceedings of the IEEE Conference on Computer Vision and Pattern Recognition, pp. 3034–3042 (2016)
2. Cai, Z., Neher, H., Vats, K., Clausi, D.A., Zelek, J.: Temporal hockey action recognition via pose and optical flows. In: Proceedings of the IEEE Conference on Computer Vision and Pattern Recognition Workshops (2019)
3. Carneiro, D., Novais, P., Durães, D., Pego, J.M., Sousa, N.: Predicting completion time in high-stakes exams. Future Gener. Comput. Syst. **92**, 549–559 (2019)
4. Carreira, J., Noland, E., Banki-Horvath, A., Hillier, C., Zisserman, A.: A short note about kinetics-600. arXiv preprint arXiv:1808.01340 (2018)
5. Carreira, J., Zisserman, A.: Quo vadis, action recognition? a new model and the kinetics dataset. In: Proceedings of the IEEE Conference on Computer Vision and Pattern Recognition, pp. 6299–6308 (2017)
6. Cheng, M., Cai, K., Li, M.: Rwf-2000: An open large scale video database for violence detection. arXiv preprint arXiv:1911.05913 (2019)
7. De Souza, F.D., Chavez, G.C., do Valle Jr, E. A., Araújo, A.D. A.: Violence detection in video using spatio-temporal features. In: 2010 23rd SIB-GRAPI Conference on Graphics, Patterns and Images, pp. 224–230. IEEE (2010)
8. Devlin, J., Chang, M.-W., Lee, K., and Toutanova, K. Bert: pre-training of deep bidirectional transformers for language understanding. arXiv preprint arXiv:1810.04805 (2018)
9. Durães, D., Marcondes, F.S., Gonçalves, F., Fonseca, J., Machado, J., Novais, P.: Detection violent behaviors: a survey. In: Novais, P., Vercelli, G., Larriba-Pey, J.L., Herrera, F., Chamoso, P. (eds.) ISAmI 2020. AISC, vol. 1239, pp. 106–116. Springer, Cham (2021). https://doi.org/10.1007/978-3-030-58356-9_11
10. Feichtenhofer, C.: X3d: expanding architectures for efficient video recognition. In: Proceedings of the IEEE/CVF Conference on Computer Vision and Pattern Recognition, pp. 203–213 (2020)
11. Feichtenhofer, C., Fan, H., Malik, J., He, K.: Slowfast networks for video recognition. In: Proceedings of the IEEE International Conference on Computer Vision, pp. 6202–6211 (2019)
12. Gao, Y., Liu, H., Sun, X., Wang, C., Liu, Y.: Violence detection using oriented violent flows. Image Vis. Comput. **48**, 37–41 (2016)
13. Gu, C., et al.: Ava: a video dataset of spatio-temporally localized atomic visual actions. In: Proceedings of the IEEE Conference on Computer Vision and Pattern Recognition, pp. 6047–6056 (2018)
14. He, K., Zhang, X., Ren, S., Sun, J.: Deep residual learning for image recognition. In: Proceedings of the IEEE Conference on Computer Vision and Pattern Recognition, pp. 770–778 (2016)
15. Kay, W., et al. The kinetics human action video dataset. arXiv preprint arXiv:1705.06950 (2017)
16. Loshchilov, I., Hutter, F.: SGDR: stochastic gradient descent with warm restarts. arXiv preprint arXiv:1608.03983 (2016)
17. Mabrouk, A.B., Zagrouba, E.: Spatio-temporal feature using optical flow based distribution for violence detection. Pattern Recogn. Lett. **92**, 62–67 (2017)

18. Marcondes, F.S., Durães, D., Gonçalves, F., Fonseca, J., Machado, J., Novais, P.: In-vehicle violence detection in carpooling: a brief survey towards a general surveillance system. In: Dong, Y., Herrera-Viedma, E., Matsui, K., Omatsu, S., González Briones, A., Rodríguez González, S. (eds.) DCAI 2020. AISC, vol. 1237, pp. 211–220. Springer, Cham (2021). https://doi.org/10.1007/978-3-030-53036-5_23

19. Ren, S., He, K., Girshick, R., Sun, J.: Faster R-CNN: Towards real-time object detection with region proposal networks. IEEE Trans. Pattern Anal. Mach. Intell. **39**(6), 1137–1149 (2016)

20. Ribeiro, P.C., Audigier, R., Pham, Q.C.: Rimoc, a feature to discriminate unstructured motions: application to violence detection for video-surveillance. Comput. Vis. Image Underst. **144**, 121–143 (2016)

21. Rohrbach, A., Rohrbach, M., Tandon, N., Schiele, B.: A dataset for movie description. In: Proceedings of the IEEE Conference on Computer Vision and Pattern Recognition, pp. 3202–3212 (2015)

22. Roman, D.G.C., Chávez, G.C.: Violence detection and localization in surveillance video. In: 2020 33rd SIBGRAPI Conference on Graphics, Patterns and Images (SIBGRAPI), pp. 248–255. IEEE (2020)

23. Sargano, A.B., Wang, X., Angelov, P., Habib, Z.: Human action recognition using transfer learning with deep representations. In: 2017 International Joint Conference on Neural Networks (IJCNN), pp. 463–469. IEEE (2017)

24. Sharif Razavian, A., Azizpour, H., Sullivan, J., Carlsson, S.: Cnn features off-the-shelf: an astounding baseline for recognition. In: Proceedings of the IEEE Conference on Computer Vision and Pattern Recognition workshops, pp. 806–813 (2014)

25. Soliman, M.M., Kamal, M.H., Nashed, M.A.E.-M., Mostafa, Y.M., Chawky, B.S., Khattab, D.: Violence recognition from videos using deep learning techniques. In: 2019 Ninth International Conference on Intelligent Computing and Information Systems (ICICIS), pp. 80–85. IEEE (2019)

26. Sutskever, I., Martens, J., Dahl, G., Hinton, G.: On the importance of initialization and momentum in deep learning. In: International Conference on Machine Learning, pp. 1139–1147 (2013)

27. Taylor, G.W., Fergus, R., LeCun, Y., Bregler, C.: Convolutional learning of spatiotemporal features. In: Daniilidis, K., Maragos, P., Paragios, N. (eds.) ECCV 2010. LNCS, vol. 6316, pp. 140–153. Springer, Heidelberg (2010). https://doi.org/10.1007/978-3-642-15567-3_11

28. Tran, D., Bourdev, L., Fergus, R., Torresani, L., Paluri, M.: Learning spatiotemporal features with 3d convolutional networks. In: Proceedings of the IEEE International Conference on Computer Vision, pp. 4489–4497 (2015)

29. Wang, X., Girshick, R., Gupta, A., He, K.: Non-local neural networks. In: Proceedings of the IEEE conference on computer vision and pattern recognition, pp. 7794–7803 (2018)

30. Zhou, P., Ding, Q., Luo, H., Hou, X.: Violent interaction detection in video based on deep learning. In: Journal of Physics: Conference Series, vol. 844, p. 012044. IOP Publishing (2017)

31. Zhou, P., Ding, Q., Luo, H., Hou, X.: Violence detection in surveillance video using low-level features. PLoS one **13**(10), e0203668 (2018)

A Simple Strategy for Choosing Network Structures in a Object Detection Project with Transfer Learning

Laercio Sartori$^{(\boxtimes)}$ ⓘ, Dalila Durães$^{(\boxtimes)}$ ⓘ, and Paulo Novais$^{(\boxtimes)}$ ⓘ

Algoritmi Centre, University of Minho, Braga, Portugal
pg39391@alunos.uminho.pt, dalila.duraes@algoritmi.uminho.pt,
pjon@di.uminho.pt

Abstract. Compare different network configurations in the early stages of an object detection project can be an interesting approach to identify the one that can provide the best performance and, thus, optimize the investment of time and research efforts for the next steps. In this work we will explore the issue through the study of object recognition applied to a category of items, specifically fruits, where the proposed strategy will be to select a public image dataset of these items and to train some different structures of deep learning networks. We built different combinations of structures composed of pre-trained base networks, in which the upper layers were replaced by new structures, with an increasing degree of complexity. Then will evaluate the results of these pre-trained networks with 25 images of individual fruits obtained on the internet. After we compare the performance between the different structures of networks, it is intended to demonstrate if there is a relationship between the training performance of specific models with the complexity of its upper layers when we apply them to a practical evaluation.

Keywords: Object recognition · Deep learning · Transfer learning

1 Introduction

Object recognition is a widely accepted challenge and has different lines of research with even more diverse results [1]. Different approaches are used to build specialized softwares capable of recognizing objects of different shapes, colors, textures and applications [2]. Such approaches can be distinguished mainly according to the context in which they are applied and according to the computational strategies they use to obtain their results. With this scenario, evaluating whether a given object recognition project is more or less effective than any of the others cannot be limited to just the metrics obtained (accuracy or loss), and it must also be effective within the context in which they are proposed. The disregard of practical results in the context for which a given project was developed

Supported by Algoritmi Centre.

© Springer Nature Switzerland AG 2021
F. De La Prieta et al. (Eds.): PAAMS Workshops 2021, CCIS 1472, pp. 76–87, 2021.
https://doi.org/10.1007/978-3-030-85710-3_7

makes it difficult to fully take advantage of scientific advances beyond the limits of the study environment.

This paper will explore the issue by studying object recognition applied to a category of items, specifically fruits, where the proposed strategy will be to select a public image dataset of these items and train some different structures of deep learning networks.

Accordingly, the remainder of the paper is organized as follows. Section 2 presents a preliminary state of art. Section 3 exhibits the methodology and methods, with the applied strategy, the fruit-360 dataset, and the neural network structures. Section 4 discusses research directions and open problems that we gathered and distilled from our analysis. Finally, Sect. 5 concludes this paper.

2   State of Art

2.1   Object Detection with Deep Learning

Making a computer capable of simulating the behavior of human vision when receiving optical information from the world, converting it, processing it, and obtaining in fractions of a second all its meaning is a great challenge [3]. This challenge gave rise to the research area of Computer Vision that aims, mainly through the use of Deep Learning algorithms, be able to identify, for example, a simple bee on a flower with the same agility and reliability that the human visual system can perform [4].

To perform detection and recognition tasks that can minimally approximate the human visual system, numerous techniques and strategies have been developed, many of them are intrinsically linked and adapted to the context of the problem that is proposed to be solved. The strategies for carrying out the recognition of human actions, for example, are different from those applied in detecting the presence of objects in images, and these are also slightly different from those necessary to make individual recognition of objects in a scene. In addition, the latter can also rely on the identification and differentiation of the instances present in the image.

For object detection and recognition tasks and also for action recognition tasks, there are many deep network structures in use, some of which were made as an evolution of an earlier type that allowed developers to improve them precisely where they were most weak or more inaccurate. As an example, in the analysis carried out on [5] the authors divided the object detection frameworks into two main types. One follows the traditional object detection pipeline, generating region proposals at first and then classifying each proposal into different object categories. The other regards object detection as a regression or classification problem, adopting a unified framework to achieve results directly.

Unfortunately, due to the challenging issues, such as high environment complexity, occlusions, viewpoint changes and high intra-class action variations, the level of accuracy that we can achieve today, although in strong improvement, is still remains a long way to reach what a mature human perception system could do [6, 7].

2.2 Transfer Learning

Although humans have the ability to learn thousands of object's categories in their lives with just a few samples, it is believed that this ability has been achieved by accumulating knowledge over time since birth, which is used to create similar associations that allow us to learn quickly about new objects [8]. So, some models trained on a specific dataset or task can be fine-tuned for a new task even in a different domain, this is a definition of a concept known as transfer learning or domain adaptation. It was very useful when traditional machine learning techniques have reached their limits. The transfer learning concept allows researches to expand their horizon in image recognition. Usually, transfer learning mainly employs two approaches:

- starts from a pre-trained network and updating the weights based on the new training dataset;
- keep the weights from a pre-trained network for feature extraction followed by a classifier algorithm that makes the classifications for the new dataset.

Hence, transfer learning is very useful when the dataset is not sufficient for training the deep learning model from scratch [9].

In practice, the use of the transfer learning technique is an important device used by developers and can even be considered a fundamental strategy to allow the functioning of certain applications, either due to computational capacity restrictions or the need for faster responses. As complex neuronal networks can easily reach tens of millions of parameters, the task of training such networks can take several hours or even several days.

So, it is common to take advantage of network structures with their parameters already defined by previous training to serve as a starting point. For example, in the identification of relevant features that are then taken to some other ML algorithm or even another neural network, faster, capable of extracting some knowledge and make associations with the features received from the already trained block. Furthermore, transfer learning works as a shortcut to saving time or getting better performance. It also allows to obtain equally good results using smaller datasets. Lisa Torrey and Jude Shavlik in their work [10], describe three possible benefits to look for when using transfer learning:

Higher start: the initial skill (before refining the model) on the source model is higher than it otherwise would be.

Higher slope: the rate of improvement of skill during training of the source model is steeper than it otherwise would be.

Higher asymptote: the converged skill of the trained model is better than it otherwise would be.

2.3 TensorFlow and Keras

The widely used python-compatible library, Tensorflow, was chosen to support the development of this work. It is open sourced and ideal for numerical computing what enables the development of large-scale machine and deep learning codes.

It was developed by the Google Brain Team at Google's Machine Intelligence research organization [11] and aim to support researches on machine learning and deep learning projects. By fulfilling the objective of being flexible, efficient, extensible and portable, Tensorflow can be run by devices of different types such as personal computers, smartphones and even large clusters of servers. It also supports the transfer learning process which makes it an important tool in environments with high competition for computational resources, as it eliminates the need to run the entire model in each execution.

We will also make use of Keras [12], an important high-level API, which facilitates the implementation of neural networks. This API will be fundamental for the execution of this work because it will allow to obtain all the neural networks needed with their respective pre-trained weights for the ImageNet images [13].

3 Methodology and Methods

3.1 Applied Strategy

In this work, we will explore the impact that changes in the upper layers of deep learning networks can have on these networks' ability to recognize objects. We will use a public image dataset composed of one category of items, fruits more specifically, where the proposed strategy will be to train some deep learning network structures differentiated mainly by the complexity of their upper layers.

We use pre-trained networks whose their upper layers were replaced by new sets of layers, the weights of the original layers of these networks were frozen so that only the new layers went through the learning process. The objective of this method was to understand how much and how the variation in the complexity of these new layers affects the final result of the object recognition structures used.

3.2 Fruits-360 Dataset

The public dataset selected for this work was the fruits-360 [14,15], a dataset composed of 90,380 images divided into two subsets in a proportion of 75% for training and 25% for testing. Each of these subsets, in turn, originally has a total of 131 different classes of fruits and other vegetables. The construction of this dataset is peculiar because in order to compose the images of a certain class, only a single specimen belonging to it was used. However, this element was arranged in a rotating mechanism that allowed the capture of images of it under different angles and inclinations. The name of the dataset derives directly from this method used for capturing, since we have a complete 360-degree view of each element. Regarding the images, their background was replaced by a standard in white, all of them have the same resolution of 100 × 100 pixels and three-color channels. Yet, this resolution will be slightly reduced in order to be compatible with the entry of pre-trained models loaded from the Keras API.

To train the models, 36 of the original classes of the fruits-360 dataset were selected. The reasons for making this selection are because it contains classes of vegetables that do not fall into the fruit category and, in addition, to optimizing training in terms of time and computational resources. The criteria used to rule out the use of a class were, in addition to the removal of those not belonging to fruits, also the removal of some classes of very similar varieties of the same fruit, and even classes belonging to unusual fruits and not easily found in food retail. Thus, we got the 36 classes that will be used for training the models. Figure 1 shows some samples of the elements in these used classes and Fig. 2 other examples, but these from the removed classes.

Fig. 1. Sample images from fruits classes used for training.

Similar subtypes   Other vegetables (not fruits)   Rambutan   Salak   Cactus Fruit   Unusual fruits

Fig. 2. Sample images from fruits and other vegetables classes not used.

Although the overall percentage of the test subset is 25%, it varies slightly between classes. Considering only for the 36 classes selected for the study, the percentage of test images varies from 24.8% to 25.4%. Further details on it, with information on how the images were captured, processed and a complete list of all the classes and the number of images in each set (train and test) can be found in [14], which is the article prepared by the creators of fruits-360 and that introduce the dataset (Table 1).

Finally, to validate the trained models, a set of images of fruit collected on the internet was used. These images were selected using the Google Images tool and with the sole criterion of having isolated fruits or, if gathered, being of the same species. Then, we built a validation dataset with 25 of these fruit images, belonging to one of the classes used in the training (samples in Fig. 3).

Fig. 3. Sample images from the validation dataset.

Table 1. Dataset's statistics for the 36 selcted classes.

Class name	# Training	# Test	# Total	% Test set	% Total
Apple Braeburn	492	164	656	25,0%	2,7%
Apple Granny Smith	492	164	656	25,0%	2,7%
Apple Red Delicious	490	166	656	25,3%	2,7%
Apricot	492	164	656	25,0%	2,7%
Avocado	427	143	570	25,1%	2,4%
Banana	490	166	656	25,3%	2,7%
Blueberry	462	154	616	25,0%	2,5%
Cantaloupe	492	164	656	25,0%	2,7%
Carambula	490	166	656	25,3%	2,7%
Cherry	738	246	984	25,0%	4,1%
Chestnut	450	153	603	25,4%	2,5%
Clementine	490	166	656	25,3%	2,7%
Cocos	490	166	656	25,3%	2,7%
Corn	450	150	600	25,0%	2,5%
Fig	702	234	936	25,0%	3,9%
Grape White	490	166	656	25,3%	2,7%
Guava	490	166	656	25,3%	2,7%
Kiwi	466	156	622	25,1%	2,6%
Lemon	492	164	656	25,0%	2,7%
Lychee	490	166	656	25,3%	2,7%
Mandarine	490	166	656	25,3%	2,7%
Mango	490	166	656	25,3%	2,7%
Maracuja	490	166	656	25,3%	2,7%
Melon Piel de Sapo	738	246	984	25,0%	4,1%
Mulberry	492	164	656	25,0%	2,7%
Orange	479	160	639	25,0%	2,6%
Peach	492	164	656	25,0%	2,7%
Peach Flat	492	164	656	25,0%	2,7%
Pear Williams	490	166	656	25,3%	2,7%
Physalis	492	164	656	25,0%	2,7%
Pineapple	490	166	656	25,3%	2,7%
Pitahaya	490	166	656	25,3%	2,7%
Pomegranate	492	164	656	25,0%	2,7%
Raspberry	490	166	656	25,3%	2,7%
Strawberry	492	164	656	25,0%	2,7%
Watermelon	475	157	632	24,8%	2,6%
Total	**18 149**	**6 093**	**24 242**	**25,0%**	**100,0%**

3.3 Neural Network Structures

In order to obtain a good variety of results and to be able to minimally carry out the planned comparisons, 25 different structures of neural networks were used. To compose these structures, we used 5 different models, 4 of them available in the keras application package [12], conveniently pre-trained with the images from the public dataset ImageNet [13,16], and 5 different types of upper layers configuration for each one. The construction of these structures follows the diagram in Fig. 4.

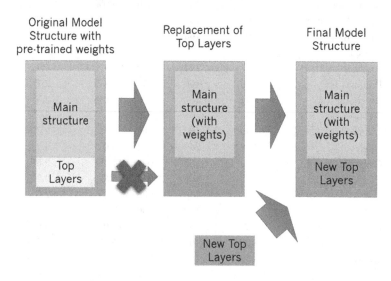

Fig. 4. Construction strategies for the neural network structures.

Additionally, we also use an own model, formed by 4 simple convolutional blocks, each one composed by a depth 32 convolutional layer with a kernel 3×3 followed by a MaxPooling2D layer with a 2×2 size. This model has added at its top the same 5 different top structures, thus completing the 25 structures proposed to be evaluated. The goal of using this very simplified model is to get a reference on how a structure with almost no layer-level complexity would behave during training, compared to the complex and well-established models in the literature.

Due to size limitations, we illustrate in Fig. 5, as a example, only the Own Model structure, with its four convolutional blocks. The structure and composition of the other base models (without ours upper layers) can be found in detail in the reference articles [8,17,18]. For the upper layers added, the Fig. 6 seems to be enough to explain it's structures and purpose.

The new top layer structures used, have different characteristics from each other and an increasing complexity, as can be seen in Fig. 6 which shows how these structures were planned and constructed. As described in the strategy section, the goal in having different types of upper layers is to observe how much of the performance obtained by each base model varies with each upper layer configuration and, if such variation is able to make a given base model more effective than the others. Essentially, the pre-trained models were loaded without their upper layers and had their weights frozen. The new upper layers added to each of these models, contribute to obtain a better customization in the results for the dataset in use. This procedure will allow us to take advantage of the original ability of these networks to extract features from images, while we will also be able to refine the object recognition by training the top layers with such features.

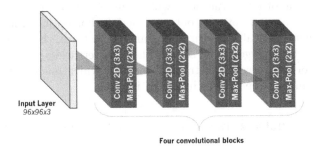

Fig. 5. Structure of the own model.

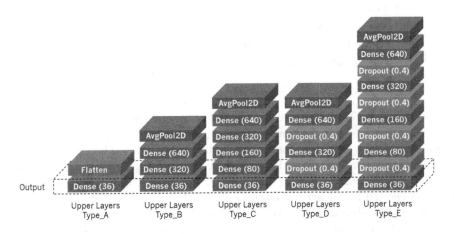

Fig. 6. Structures of the new upper layers added to each base model.

The environment used to run the training and validations codes was made available by the Google Collaboratory platform, where we have the necessary computational resources, namely GPU and RAM, in order to be able to carry out the work in a relatively shorter time.

4   Results and Discussion

To obtain a better comparison between the performance of the various combinations of network and upper layers, the hyper-parameters were kept the same, whenever possible. Although this decision may compromise the achievement of better results in some specific combination, we believe that within the scope of this document, it is a reasonable alternative to be able to make the most egalitarian comparison between the structures. So, they were implemented and trained following this basic parameterization: input_size = $(96 \times 96 \times 3)$, batch_size = 32 and learning rate = 1×10^{-5}.

The loss function used was the categorical-crossentropy, suitable to provide the correct output of our structures, which are configured with Dense layers with 36 neurons using a Softmax output function. For optimization we adopt the ADAM function for all structures. For most structures, the training needed 50 epochs to reach convergence, for some of them. Nevertheless, it was not enough to obtain a good convergence in training metrics, which made it necessary to increase the number of epochs, as indicated in Table 2.

Table 2. Training epochs for each structure.

Model	Upper layers				
	Type_A	Type_B	Type_C	Type_D	Type_E
MobileNetV2	50	50	50	50	100
VGG19	50	50	50	50	100
NasNetMobile	50	50	50	50	100
NasNetLarge	50	50	50	50	150
OwnModel	150	150	500	500	500

According to Table 2, it can be seen that structures with upper layers of Type_E, which has more dropout layers, in general needed more training epochs to be able to converge their metrics then the others types. The same occurred with those structures composed by the Own Model. Still, in this case we believe that the need for more training epochs is due to the fact that this model is not complex enough to extract the features efficiently.

The results obtained after training each of the 25 structures are shown in Table 3. In total, 18 of the 25 structures obtained results above 99% of accuracy in training, while only 9 passed the same level in the test results. Although these results, we can consider that the networks have been properly trained and are ready to recognize the fruits, regardless of where they are in the image, since the images used for learning provide a 360° view of the elements.

In the next step, however, when we applied the models properly trained in fruit recognition to predict the fruit present in each one of the 25 images of the validation dataset, we did not achieve such good results. Although each of the images in the validation dataset has only one type of fruit, the performance of the models in identifying the correct fruit proved to be very deficient, reaching the maximum percentage of correctness of 64%, but with averages below 42% when comparing the results obtained by differentiating only the upper layer used and, got average indices below 54% if we only differentiate the base model (as can also be viewed in Table 3).

An additional comparison performed was through the use of the models with their original structure and weights, without any modification, to identify the images in the validation dataset. The results for this comparison is registered in the last column of Table 3.

Table 3. Training and validation results.

Model	Upper layer	Accuracy	Loss	Val_Accuracy	Val_Loss	Final validation results	Average validation results	Original models' results
MobileNetV2	Type_A	100%	$3,3E-07$	99,36%	$2,2E-02$	44%	53,6%	44,0%
MobileNetV2	Type_B	100%	$6,9E-07$	99,39%	$2,1E-02$	64%		
MobileNetV2	Type_C	100%	$2,1E-07$	99,57%	$1,2E-02$	48%		
MobileNetV2	Type_D	99,74%	$1,3E-02$	99,23%	$2,1E-02$	52%		
MobileNetV2	Type_E	98,72%	$4,4E-02$	98,87%	$4,8E-02$	60%		
VGG19	Type_A	100%	$3,3E-07$	99,26%	$2,5E-02$	48%	48,8%	52,0%
VGG19	Type_B	100%	$2,2E-06$	99,36%	$1,6E-02$	44%		
VGG19	Type_C	100%	$2,1E-05$	99,16%	$4,6E-02$	36%		
VGG19	Type_D	99,78%	$1,0E-02$	99,28%	$2,2E-02$	60%		
VGG19	Type_E	99,01%	$3,1E-02$	99,13%	$3,1E-02$	56%		
NasNetMobile	Type_A	100%	$3,0E-05$	97,01%	$1,3E-01$	40%	36,8%	52,0%
NasNetMobile	Type_B	100%	$2,2E-05$	97,20%	$1,2E-01$	40%		
NasNetMobile	Type_C	100%	$1,0E-04$	96,74%	$1,2E-01$	28%		
NasNetMobile	Type_D	97,55%	$7,4E-02$	95,56%	$1,6E-01$	40%		
NasNetMobile	Type_E	97,75%	$7,6E-02$	96,41%	$1,8E-01$	36%		
NasNetLarge	Type_A	100%	$3,8E-03$	96,46%	$1,4E-01$	28%	36,0%	56,0%
NasNetLarge	Type_B	100%	$1,0E-05$	97,55%	$1,1E-01$	36%		
NasNetLarge	Type_C	99,92%	$3,5E-03$	96,99%	$1,4E-01$	36%		
NasNetLarge	Type_D	97,49%	$7,7E-02$	95,92%	$1,6E-01$	40%		
NasNetLarge	Type_E	98,06%	$6,9E-02$	96,51%	$1,7E-01$	40%		
OwnModel	Type_A	99,96%	$4,6E-03$	95,16%	$3,8E-01$	4%	8,8%	N/A
OwnModel	Type_B	99,69%	$2,5E-02$	93,55%	$3,6E-01$	4%		
OwnModel	Type_C	99,54%	$2,3E-02$	93,14%	$4,2E-01$	16%		
OwnModel	Type_D	93,07%	$2,1E-01$	95,82%	$1,5E-01$	4%		
OwnModel	Type_E	98,60%	$4,2E-02$	96,97%	$1,6E-01$	16%		

5   Conclusions and Future Work

While, in general, the objective is usually to obtain the best absolute results, in this work the focus was to compare the effects of different upper layers on the results of structures, not only between them, but also in comparing their performance with those obtained by the base models in its original structures and already properly trained.

In this way, it was possible to identify that the variation of the upper layers can affect the result of a given base model. Yet, different from what was expected, a proportional or direct relationship was not clearly observed between the complexity of the added upper layers and the increasing of correct predictions in those models. This suggests that this approach, although not guaranteeing better performance in isolation, can serve as a starting point for selecting a better model, with subsequent adjustment of other characteristics and parameters.

Thus, the low performance for the predictions in the validation set and the great difference between these results and the training results, suggest the occurrence of overfitting. Part of this occurrence may be due to the bias that transfer learning techniques can eventually add to the learning of a model and that, when not properly considered, can have a detrimental effect, making it difficult to obtain good results and making conclusions difficult. Note the occurrence of this overfitting may be due to the maintenance of hyperparmetrization of the structures in all training sessions, which may have impaired the ability of the models to generalize their learning. A different hyperparametrization for different networks, acting mainly in the optimization function, can be essential to obtain better results in a future work, where the main motivation is to reach better absolute values and not just the comparison between the performance of different structures.

As a proposal for this work continuation, we suggest to implement modifications, mainly in the structures formed by the base models MobileNetV2 and VGG19, mainly in hyperparametrization, in order to improve the generalization and check if this will really reflect in a better performance for new images predictions. Another proposal would be use some other image dataset, with a greater diversity of elements in the same class, in order to include the natural variations of the appearance of the same specie of fruit in the models' learning. Furthermore, and as described in [19], there are some examples of how to solve problems on transferring learning with negative learning and overfitting, which we will implement in future work.

Acknowledgment. This work has been supported by FCT – Fundação para a Ciência e Tecnologia within the R&D Units Project Scope: UIDB/00319/2020.

References

1. Santos, F., et al.: Modelling a deep learning framework for recognition of human actions on video. In: Rocha, Á., Adeli, H., Dzemyda, G., Moreira, F., Ramalho Correia, A.M. (eds.) WorldCIST 2021. AISC, vol. 1365, pp. 104–112. Springer, Cham (2021). https://doi.org/10.1007/978-3-030-72657-7_10
2. Durães, D., Marcondes, F.S., Gonçalves, F., Fonseca, J., Machado, J., Novais, P.: Detection violent behaviors: a survey. In: Novais, P., Vercelli, G., Larriba-Pey, J.L., Herrera, F., Chamoso, P. (eds.) ISAmI 2020. AISC, vol. 1239, pp. 106–116. Springer, Cham (2021). https://doi.org/10.1007/978-3-030-58356-9_11

3. Toala, R., Gonçalves, F., Durães, D., Novais, P.: Adaptive and intelligent mentoring to increase user attentiveness in learning activities. In: Simari, G.R., Fermé, E., Gutiérrez Segura, F., Rodríguez Melquiades, J.A. (eds.) IBERAMIA 2018. LNCS (LNAI), vol. 11238, pp. 145–155. Springer, Cham (2018). https://doi.org/10.1007/978-3-030-03928-8_12

4. Szeliski, R.: Computer Vision: Algorithms and Applications. Springer, Heidelberg (2010)

5. Zhao, Z.Q., Zheng, P., Xu, S.T., Wu, X.: Object detection with deep learning: a review. IEEE Trans. Neural Netw. Learn. Syst. **30**(11), 3212–3232 (2019)

6. Zhu, F., Shao, L., Xie, J., Fang, Y.: From handcrafted to learned representations for human action recognition: a survey. Image Vis. Comput. **55**, 42–52 (2016)

7. Marcondes, F.S., Durães, D., Gonçalves, F., Fonseca, J., Machado, J., Novais, P.: In-vehicle violence detection in carpooling: a brief survey towards a general surveillance system. In: Dong, Y., Herrera-Viedma, E., Matsui, K., Omatsu, S., González Briones, A., Rodríguez González, S. (eds.) DCAI 2020. AISC, vol. 1237, pp. 211–220. Springer, Cham (2021). https://doi.org/10.1007/978-3-030-53036-5_23

8. Zoph, B., Vasudevan, V., Shlens, J., Le, Q.V.: Learning transferable architectures for scalable image recognition. In: Proceedings of the IEEE Conference on Computer Vision and Pattern Recognition, pp. 8697–8710 (2018)

9. Sargano, A.B., Wang, X., Angelov, P., Habib, Z.: Human action recognition using transfer learning with deep representations. In: 2017 International Joint Conference on Neural Networks (IJCNN), pp. 463–469. IEEE, May 2017

10. Torrey, L., Shavlik, J.: Transfer learning. In: Handbook of Research on Machine Learning Applications and Trends: Algorithms, Methods, and Techniques, pp. 242–264. IGI Global (2010)

11. Abadi, M., et al.: TensorFlow: large-scale machine learning on heterogeneous distributed systems. arXiv preprint arXiv:1603.04467 (2016)

12. Keras API (n.d). https://keras.io/api/applications/

13. ImageNet (n.d.). https://image-net.org/

14. Muresşan, H., Oltean, M.: Fruit recognition from images using deep learning. arXiv preprint arXiv:1712.00580 (2017)

15. Kausar, A., Sharif, M., Park, J., Shin, D.R.: Pure-CNN: a framework for fruit images classification. In: 2018 International Conference on Computational Science and Computational Intelligence (CSCI), pp. 404–408. IEEE, December 2018

16. Deng, J., Dong, W., Socher, R., Li, L.J., Li, K., Fei-Fei, L.: ImageNet: a large-scale hierarchical image database. In: 2009 IEEE Conference on Computer Vision and Pattern Recognition, pp. 248–255. IEEE, June 2009

17. Sandler, M., Howard, A., Zhu, M., Zhmoginov, A., Chen, L.C.: MobileNetV2: inverted residuals and linear bottlenecks. In: Proceedings of the IEEE Conference on Computer Vision and Pattern Recognition, pp. 4510–4520 (2018)

18. Simonyan, K., Zisserman, A.: Very deep convolutional networks for large-scale image recognition. arXiv preprint arXiv:1409.1556 (2014)

19. Pan, S.J., Yang, Q.: A survey on transfer learning. IEEE Trans. Knowl. Data Eng. **22**(10), 1345–1359 (2010). https://doi.org/10.1109/TKDE.2009.191

Workshop on Decision Support, Recommendation, and Persuasion in Artificial Intelligence (DeRePAI)

Workshop on Decision Support, Recommendation, and Persuasion in Artificial Intelligence (DeRePAI)

Decision support systems are applied in different fields to support individuals and groups, as well as to influence human behaviour and decision-making. Decision support systems are expected to facilitate decision-making while enhancing the quality of that decision, whereas recommender systems are expected to facilitate the choice process to maximize the user satisfaction. In decision support and recommendation for groups, it is important to consider the heterogeneity and conflicting preferences of its participants. In addition, decision support and recommendation systems must have strategies for configuring preferences and acquiring user profiles in a nonintrusive (implicit) and time-consuming manner.

On the other hand, the acceptance and effectiveness of the hints and recommendations provided by the system depends on several factors. First, they must be appropriate for the objectives and profile of the user, but also, they must be understandable and supported by evidence (the user must understand why the recommendation is provided and why it is good for him/her). Thus, it is necessary to provide these systems with a mechanism that supports suggestions by means of artificial intelligence. In this way, computational argumentation is a technique that builds upon the natural way humans provide reasons (i.e., arguments) for which a recommendation is suggested and should be accepted. Therefore, a system that uses these technologies must be persuasive to obtain the desired results by influencing human behaviour.

In this workshop, we explored the links between decision-support, recommendation, and persuasion to discuss strategies to facilitate the decision/choice process by individuals and groups. This workshop aims to be a discussion forum on the latest trends and ongoing challenges in the application of artificial intelligence technologies in this area.

Organization

Organizing Committee

João Carneiro	Polytechnic of Porto, Portugal
Jaume Jordán	Universitat Politècnica de València, Spain
Goreti Marreiros	Polytechnic of Porto, Portugal
Stella Heras	Universitat Politècnica de València, Spain

Program Committee

Grzegorz J. Nalepa	AGH University of Science and Technology, Poland
Vicente Julián	Universitat Politècnica de València, Spain
Víctor Sánchez-Anguix	Universitat Politècnica de València, Spain
Juan Carlos Nieves	Umeå University, Sweden
Paulo Novais	Universidade do Minho, Portugal
Carlos Carrascosa	Universitat Politècnica de València, Spain
Javier Palanca	Universitat Politècnica de València, Spain
Andrés Muñoz	Universidad Católica de Murcia, Spain
Ângelo Costa	Universidade do Minho, Portugal
Paula Andrea Rodríguez Marín	Instituto Tecnológico Metropolitano Medellín, Colombia
Floriana Grasso	University of Liverpool, UK
Tiago Oliveira	Tokyo Medical and Dental University, Japan
Patrícia Alves	Polytechnic of Porto, Portugal
Peter Mikulecky	University of Hradec Kralove, Czech Republic
Eva Hudlicka	Psychometrix Associates Blacksburg, USA
Boon Kiat-Quek	National University of Singapore, Singapore
Florentino Fdez-Riverola	University of Vigo, Spain
Hoon Ko	Chosun University, South Korea
Guillaume Lopez	Aoyama Gakuin University, College of Science and Technology, Japan
Ichiro Satoh	National Institute of Informatics Tokyo, Japan

A Hybrid Supervised/Unsupervised Machine Learning Approach to Classify Web Services

Zakieh Alizadeh-Sani[1]([✉]) , Pablo Plaza Martínez[1],
Guillermo Hernández González[3], Alfonso González-Briones[1,2,3] ,
Pablo Chamoso[1,3] , and Juan M. Corchado[1,3,4,5]

[1] BISITE Research Group, University of Salamanca. Edificio Multiusos I+D+i,
37007 Salamanca, Spain
`zakieh@usal.es`
[2] Research Group on Agent-Based, Social and Interdisciplinary Applications
(GRASIA), Complutense University of Madrid, Madrid, Spain
[3] Air Institute, IoT Digital Innovation Hub, Carbajosa de la Sagrada,
37188 Salamanca, Spain
[4] Department of Electronics, Information and Communication,
Faculty of Engineering, Osaka Institute of Technology, Osaka 535-8585, Japan
[5] Pusat Komputeran dan Informatik, Universiti Malaysia Kelantan,
Karung Berkunci 36, Pengkaan Chepa, 16100 Kota Bharu, Kelantan, Malaysia

Abstract. Reusing software is a promising way to reduce software development costs. Nowadays, applications compose available web services to build new software products. In this context, service composition faces the challenge of proper service selection. This paper presents a model for classifying web services. The service dataset has been collected from the well-known public service registry called ProgrammableWeb. The results were obtained by breaking service classification into a two-step process. First, Natural Language Processing(NLP) pre-processed web service data have been clustered by the Agglomerative hierarchical clustering algorithm. Second, several supervised learning algorithms have been applied to determine service categories. The findings show that the hybrid approach using the combination of hierarchical clustering and SVM provides acceptable results in comparison with other unsupervised/supervised combinations.

Keywords: Service classification · API classification · Machine learning · Restful API · NLP · Hierarchical clustering

1 Introduction

Service classification tries to categorize existing service data into a given number of classes. The objective of the service classification problem is to identify the class of a new service. Many researchers have investigated service classification topics in recent decades. This leads to the emergence of various topics in this area.

© Springer Nature Switzerland AG 2021
F. De La Prieta et al. (Eds.): PAAMS Workshops 2021, CCIS 1472, pp. 93–103, 2021.
https://doi.org/10.1007/978-3-030-85710-3_8

In general, classification and annotation of services are the main aspects of service discovery, composition, and management. Some of the works have combined semantic annotations and AI approaches; however, there are two main problems with semantic based approaches:1) Many approaches assume that a set of annotation services is already available. Nevertheless, this assumption can be more challenging in real-world problems. Therefore, it needs much time and a high cost for annotating services. 2)Computational complexity of these techniques is highly dependent on the number of entities (classes, properties, etc.), so it can have the problem of high latency in huge data. Given the mentioned reasons, approaches that use information extraction have been used in this work. Moreover, a series of Artificial intelligence has been conducted on real-world services crawled from a publicly accessible registry. Obtained results show that the hybrid supervised/unsupervised approach improves the classification accuracy of only used supervised classifiers. Moreover, this combination demonstrates efficient performance, which can be using while developing real-time applications.

The structure of the paper is as follows: Sect. 2 reviews the related works. Section 3 presents the proposed approach. Section 4 conducts the available public datasets process of providing the applied dataset in the current study. Section 5 explores the results, and finally, Sect. 6 concludes the study.

2   Related Works

In order to offer services with the same functionality, it is required to extract them from available public service registries. In this regard, a multitude of solutions, such as AI-based [1–4] or semantic-based approaches [5,6], has been proposed by several researchers. The main idea of the semantic web is to represent the knowledge as an ontology base language and then find services using search query [7]. However, in some studies, they have been used semantic approaches for automatic service classification as well [8].

Although the semantic-based approach is better than keyword base searches (UUID) [9], there are some problems in semantic web approaches. A variety of ontology technologies can lead to extra steps such as mapping techniques. The reason for using mappings is that most semantic-based methods use different frameworks of the semantic Web. Moreover, full-automatic annotation can be challenging for the new generation of web services. The new web services almost include less machine-readable structure, which accurate service annotation still needs human supervision.

In general, there are two common implementations of web service design. One is SOAP protocol (Simple Object Access Protocol), and the other is REST (Representational State Transfer). In soap services, SOAP and Web Services Description Language (WSDL) define service descriptions and communication formats between available services. However, REST services contain a set of general web service design which is based on HTTP methods. Over the past decade, most research in service classification has emphasized the use of WSDL features which can include: service name, service documentation, WSDL contents, WSDL schema, WSDL messages, WSDL port types [2,10–12].

Crasso et al. [10] introduced the AWSC model, which has combined text mining and machine learning techniques. A notable point in their work is that they have considered WSDL to include the natural language text and also structured data (Codes). The structured text follows coding conventions such as naming methods, variables, etc. To this end, they have provided some simple rules such as splitting combined developer function naming. For example, service function names such as "sendEmail" will split based on Java function naming, or "send_email" will split when either underlines. Their founding demonstrated that Rocchio algorithms provide better accuracy in comparison to Naïve Bayes.

Some studies utilized ensemble learning. Yuan-jie et al. [2] has investigated SVM and ensemble learning classifiers. Their result has shown that the ensemble learning classification method provided the best accuracy. During applying ensemble classifiers, there are several possibilities to achieve the highest diversity: 1) Different training datasets 2) Different training parameters 3) Different types of classifiers. However, ensemble learning classification has provided better accuracy.

Das et al. [3] have used the QWS (Quality Web Services) dataset for service classification [13], which includes service address and service non-functional parameter. They have used data mining approaches to extract functional service data from service URLs. They have tried random forest, eXtreme gradient boosting, decision tree, and Support Vector Machine(SVM). Their result demonstrated that eXtreme Gradient Boosting has more accurate results. However, QWS includes most traditional web services, which are well-annotated. Also, most of the services in this database are deprecated.

By using intelligent tag recommendations, developers have been able to provide more accurate annotation for their developed services. Shi et al. [4] has introduced tag recommendation for web services that actively learn web service tag recommendation. Their approach has improved multi-labeled service classifications by using active learning.

In general, the AI-based approaches can include 1) Traditional ML algorithms, among which SVM and Naive Bayes algorithms have shown efficient results. 2)Artificial neural networks and fuzzy logic-based approaches 3) Hybrid approaches. Most of the earlier approaches have used traditional ML algorithms. However, the performance of traditional ML learning methods highly depends on the quality of manual feature engineering. Therefore, some works have switched to neural networks and deep learning approaches, which can work without feature engineering. To this end, Y.Yang et al. presented a deep neural network to automatically abstract low-level representation of service description to high-level features without feature engineering and then predict service classification on 50 services categories [14]. However, deep leanings approaches need a massive data-set and can be challenging in real-world interactive service discovery systems. Therefore, the presented model tries to provide the model which can support real-word domain problem.

3   Proposed Approach

The objective of the service classification process is the categorization of service into a fixed number of predefined classes. The proposed approach includes the following steps: 1) providing dataset, 2) NLP pre-processing, 3) clustering, 4) text data Classification, 5) evaluating results. Moreover, several challenges have been recognized in research, most of which are well-known and have popular solutions in text classification (e.g., imbalanced data). Figure 1 demonstrates the big picture of the proposed Model.

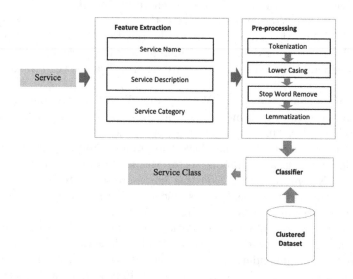

Fig. 1. Hybrid Supervised/Unsupervised Approach to Classify web services

3.1   Feature Extraction

Text feature engineering [15] is one of the common tasks in NLP, which includes some methods for converting text data to numbers: 1) Bag of Words (BOW) which represents documents as the bag of their words. This prepared bag of words can provide methods for converting text to numbers. 2) Word Embedding representing a document by providing impenetrable vectors per word in a vocabulary document. A significant advantage of word embedding is mapping a high-dimensional document to a low-dimensional one. However, the dimension of collected data in the current study is not too big. Therefore, BOW can work well for small data. Additionally, to implement the BOW /TF-IDF (Term

Frequency – Inverse Document Frequency) approach, the most popular python libraries NLTK (Natural Language Toolkit) and Sklearn have used [16].

According to the relevant literature, several feature extractions can be used in the service selection process (Fig. 2). The major features can be extracted from WSDL and REST API descriptions.

WSDL is notably self-described and well-defined, which can help provide more informative service classification features. However, REST Services need extra effort to extract informative features. The reason is why REST supports a greater variety of text data formats.

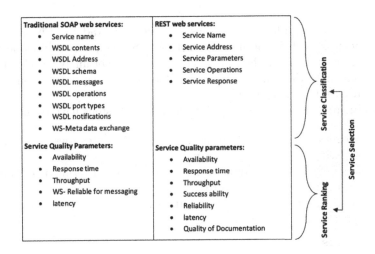

Fig. 2. Some well-known features for Web Services

Service classification is a part of service selection which includes the following stages. At the first stage, Service classification categorizes services based on the same functionality. Then, services with the same functionality will be ranked based on non-functional features. These non-functional features generally include numeric data (e.g., Rating service score, Response time), which can be simply sorted by simple sorting algorithms or Neural network techniques.

3.2 Pre-processing

A service dataset is collected from ProgrammableWeb, which is a real-world public services registry. However, data mining techniques are required to transform collected raw data into informative features. Table 1 demonstrates the raw dataset and provided dataset information.

The collected data is text (service name, description); therefore, first of all, text pre-processing is required before clustering and classification. Text pre-processing has well-known steps which use NLP techniques, including 1) tokenization, 2)lower casing, 3)stop words removal, 4) lemmatization.

Table 1. Raw dataset VS Clustered dataset information

Data	Records	Categories	Train/Test	Preprocess steps
Raw dataset	6535	403	–	–
Clustered Dataset	4645	24	80–20	
				– Select categories with more than 30-rows data – Cluster by hierarchical clustering

There are two significant problems in service metadata. First, services are implemented in different naming methods. Second, most developers use acronyms for implemented class or service names. Accordingly, service names usually do not have the same pattern; therefore, extracting data automatically with a fixed pattern is not feasible.

Moreover, to decrease the categories, the following steps have been applied:

– Select categories with more than 30-row data:(403 categories are decreased to 53 categories)
– Use a bag of words to provide numeric data for the clustering algorithm
– Remove most frequently used words
– Cluster data by hierarchical clustering in order to reduce labeled classes.

3.3 Classifiers

To train a classifier, extracted features in previous steps have been used. Many different machine learning models can be used to train final models (Fig. 1). The main problem is that machine learning algorithms are vulnerable when the dataset is imbalanced. The collected data in this study are sharply skewed, and a significant reason is that web services perform specific tasks that can include a wide range of applications such as database, routing, security, financial services, etc. Therefore, some common applications have more available services. This leads to some service categories which dominate the others. In general, there are some methods for dealing with imbalanced datasets, which are 1) Alter the data 2) Alter the algorithm. In the former, data can be handled by over-sampling minority classes, under-sampling majority classes, or generating data by synthetic samples (SMOTE). This study has selected the second algorithm (Table 2).

4 Dataset

The objective of existing service datasets is to serve service classification and service selection. In the current study, the dataset has been provided, which

Table 2. Available Public Datasets

Title	Year	Desc	Ref
QWS Dataset ver 1.0	2007	This dataset contains nine Quality of Service (QoS) per web service for 365 web services. Moreover, there are two additional attributes: (a) a rank of web services based on our Web Service Relevancy Function (WsRF) and (b) a class that classifies web services based on their overall performance	[13]
QWS Dataset ver 2.0	2008	The dataset includes a set of 2,507 web services and their Quality of Web Service (QWS). The features are Response Time, Availability, Throughput, Success-ability, Reliability, Compliance, Latency, Documentation, Service Name, WSDL Address	[13]
OWLS-TC v3.0 collection	2013	This dataset includes more than 1000 Web service profiles which distributed to seven different domain which are: (Economy, Education, Travel, Communication, Medical, Weapon, and Food)	[18]
programmableweb	2014	includes a set of 24,046 APIs which are annotated by service name, description and link	[17]

represents 6535 real-world web services. The dataset was collected from Programmableweb [17]. This public service registry includes thousands of services from popular providers like Google APIs. Table 2 demonstrates the available dataset.

One of the challenges in existing public datasets is the issue of obsolescence of some services that unfortunately may be out of reach.

Most of the web service repositories have a category field to identify their service functionality. To this end, this work has used the category field as a dataset label. However, the main problem is those categories have too much variety. For example, for 6535 services, it has 503 categories. There are two common approaches to reduce the number of categories: 1)Map all categories to pre-defined categories and join them manually 2)Use automatic approaches to cluster categories and joining them together. The first solution's problem is that maybe two service category names are similar from a human view, but the joined service description text is not similar. Therefore, it can be due to misclassification. On the other hand, the service description text should not be ignored when joining service categories. To solve this problem, this study has selected a hybrid model by combining unsupervised and supervised learning.

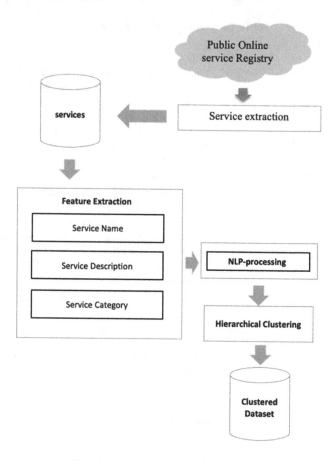

Fig. 3. Process of providing dataset

Therefore, clustering approaches are used for cluster service categories base on their text. Figure 3 demonstrated the process of providing a dataset.

In order to cluster service data, two popular clustering algorithms have been investigated: 1) K-Means clustering, 2) Agglomerative hierarchical clustering. K-Means clustering attempt to partition the dataset into K pre-defined category which subgroups does not have overlap. However, Agglomerative hierarchical clustering does not need pre-defined K as input. Instead, it uses a recursive concept, which can be applied bottom-up or top-down. Both the K-Means algorithm and hierarchical agglomerative clustering have been implemented in this study. Regarding the following reasons, hierarchical agglomerative clustering has been selected:

– Hierarchical clustering does not require specifying the number of clusters.
– Clustering process will be used to cluster collected dataset; therefore, it will occur one time, so, current work does not care about the time complexity of $O(n)$ HAC algorithm or K-Means $O(n)$, also, the dataset is not large.

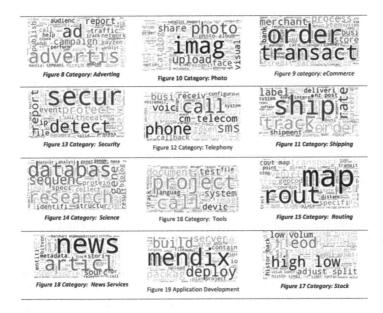

Fig. 4. Word-cloud for Visualizing frequent words in some service categories

- The tree diagram plot (dendrogram) of Hierarchical clustering makes more sense to understand categories that share the same characteristics.

Finger 4 demonstrates word cloud, which visualizes the words in some clustered categories.

5 Results

The results demonstrate that random sampling and SMOTE techniques did not work well in text data. To this end, the current study has selected Alter the algorithm (Table 2). Results reveal that weighted SVM has shown better performance in individual classifiers. This study compares not only different classifiers but also different features engineering has been examined.

Different combinations of feature engineering approaches and the classifier can provide different models. However, some combinations have produced better results, such as BOW/SVM or word embedding/CNN (Table 3).

Table 3. Results

Metric	Multinomial NB	SVM	Random Forest	Gradient Boosting	CNN
Feature Engineering	BOW / TF-IDF	BOW / TF-IDF	BOW / TF-IDF	BOW / TF-IDF	Word-embedding
Accuracy (balanced)	75%	79%	72%	70%	61%
Training time	<1s	<1s	<2s	<4s	<8s

6   Conclusions and Future Works

In the present study, service classification topic research has been conducted in order to identify important topics, approaches, and existing challenges. In addition, the collecting data and implementation of the proposed AI model have been investigated. In fact, service classification is a part of service selection that helps decrease search space. In general, most approaches in service classification fall into ontology-based and AI-based techniques. This study focuses exclusively on AI-based approaches. Moreover, the current research has focused chiefly on service meta-data classification. However, if service codes are also available, topics such as code mining and source code classification need to be investigated. The findings show that most services use REST designs, which are similar to current web technologies. Therefore, in most current service repositories, service descriptions are just in free text format. Consequently, automatic data collection can mainly extract service descriptions, service names, service categories, or URLs at their best. Furthermore, regarding the imbalanced service categories, the hybrid approach has been utilized. Both algorithms, K-Mean and Agglomerative hierarchical, were examined, of which Agglomerative hierarchical performed better. Afterward, baseline elements of text classification have followed which Weighted Support Vector Machines have shown promising results.

Acknowledgments. This research has been supported by the European Union's Horizon 2020 research and innovation programme under grant agreement No. 871177.

References

1. Yang, Y., et al.: ServeNet: a deep neural network for web services classification. In: 2020 IEEE International Conference on Web Services (ICWS), pp. 168–175. IEEE (2020)
2. Yuan-jie, L., Jian, C.: Web service classification based on automatic semantic annotation and ensemble learning. In: 2012 IEEE 26th International Parallel and Distributed Processing Symposium Workshops & PhD Forum, pp. 2274–2279. IEEE (2012)
3. Swami Das, M., Govardhan, A., Lakshmi, D.V.: Classification of web services using data mining algorithms and improved learning model. Telkomnika **17**(6), 3191–3202 (2019)

4. Shi, W., Liu, X., Yu, Q.: Correlation-aware multi-label active learning for web service tag recommendation. In: 2017 IEEE International Conference on Web Services (ICWS), pp. 229–236. IEEE (2017)
5. Alshafaey, M.S., Saleh, A.I., Alrahamawy, M.F.: A new cloud-based classification methodology (CBCM) for efficient semantic web service discovery. Cluster Comput., 1–24 (2021)
6. Liu, J., Tian, Z., Liu, P., Jiang, J., Li, Z.: An approach of semantic web service classification based on Naive Bayes. In: 2016 IEEE International Conference on Services Computing (SCC), pp. 356–362. IEEE (2016)
7. McIlraith, S.A., Son, T.C., Zeng, H.: Semantic web services. IEEE Intell. Syst. **16**(2), 46–53 (2001)
8. Abid, A., Rouached, M., Messai, N.: Semantic web service composition using semantic similarity measures and formal concept analysis. Multimedia Tools Appl. **79**(9), 6569–6597 (2019). https://doi.org/10.1007/s11042-019-08441-z
9. Avancha, S., Joshi, A., Finin, T.: Enhanced service discovery in bluetooth. Computer **35**(6), 96–99 (2002)
10. Crasso, M., Zunino, A., Campo, M.: Awsc: an approach to web service classification based on machine learning techniques. Inteligencia Artificial. Revista Iberoamericana de Inteligencia Artificial **12**(37), 25–36 (2008)
11. Sanchez, C.S., Tello, E.V., De La Rosa, A.G.R., Salazar, H.J., Avendaño, D.E.P.: WSDL information selection for improving web service classification (2017)
12. Sha, S., Qamar, U.: [wip] web services classification using an improved text mining technique. In: 2018 IEEE 11th Conference on Service-Oriented Computing and Applications (SOCA), pp. 210–215. IEEE (2018)
13. QWSdata, Dataset (2007). https://qwsdata.github.io/citations.html. Accessed 2020
14. Yang, Y., Ke, W., Wang, W., Zhao, Y.: Deep learning for web services classification. In: 2019 IEEE International Conference on Web Services (ICWS), pp. 440–442. IEEE (2019)
15. Kadhim, A.I.: Survey on supervised machine learning techniques for automatic text classification. Artif. Intell. Rev. **52**(1), 273–292 (2019). https://doi.org/10.1007/s10462-018-09677-1
16. He, H., Garcia, E.A.: Learning from imbalanced data. IEEE Trans. Knowl. Data Eng. **21**(9), 1263–1284 (2009)
17. Programmableweb, Dataset [16] (2014). https://www.programmableweb.com/api/. Accessed 2020
18. Wsdream, Dataset (2007). https://github.com/wsdream/wsdream-dataset. Accessed 2020

Smart Contracts Based on Multi-agent Negotiation

Ricardo Barbosa[1,2]([✉]) [iD], Ricardo Santos[1] [iD], and Paulo Novais[2] [iD]

[1] CIICESI, Escola Superior de Tecnologia e Gestão, Politécnico do Porto,
Porto, Portugal
{rmb,rjs}@estg.ipp.pt
[2] ALGORITMI Center, University of Minho, Braga, Portugal
pjon@di.uminho.pt

Abstract. Decision-making processes and collaboration scenarios expect users to trust the negotiation process and respective fulfilment of its outcomes. Agents inherit the preferences of the entities that they represent and can engage in negotiation processes to fulfil their goals, or the objectives of a group. When faced with the challenges of multi-agent systems and group decision-making processes and negotiation, the traditional solutions to trust issues are supported by an inclusion of a third-party entity that, consequently, raises new trust challenges. In this work, we propose an alternative solution to this problem, based on a combination of Smart Contracts and blockchain. The immutable and distributed characteristics of these technologies provide a trustworthy support for the negotiation process, including knowledge representation. Additionally, by focusing on the terms used during the negotiation, we can improve Smart Contracts through the automatization of their contractual terms, where their parameters are derived from the output of the negotiation process between agents. This mainly reinforces that negotiation can benefit from the inclusion of Smart Contracts, and vice versa. The proposed model should be independent of protocol, language, and decision processes, however special attention should be addressed to communication, namely to the simplification and generalization of locutions.

Keywords: Negotiation · Smart contracts · Collaboration ·
Multi-agent system

1 Introduction

Traditionally, collaboration is based on trust or a third party that ensures that each participant can fulfil their goals. While trust is defined as a belief that somebody/something is good, sincere, honest, and will not try to harm or trick us, when the social aspect is removed, collaboration can be based on agreeable contracts that bound two entities [28]. From a similar perspective, negotiation is a process where two entities compromise to reach mutually beneficial agreements and agree on a joint decision.

© Springer Nature Switzerland AG 2021
F. De La Prieta et al. (Eds.): PAAMS Workshops 2021, CCIS 1472, pp. 104–114, 2021.
https://doi.org/10.1007/978-3-030-85710-3_9

Whether an agent simulates a machine or product in a manufacturing scenario [30], a vehicle responsible for the transportation of goods and materials, or a person with feelings, personality and mood [24], agents assume the beliefs and preferences and seek the satisfaction through negotiation processes. The current scientific interest in the adoption of autonomous negotiation agents still faces some challenges, and Baarslag et al. [6] identifies three in specific:

1. Necessity for domain knowledge and difficulty of preferences elicitation;
2. Long-term perspective;
3. User trust.

In this work we are focused on providing a solution the user trust issue. While authors reinforce the necessity to incorporate models that can inspire more user trust, they intend to improve of the implications (by integrating Reasoning About Uncertainty into negotiations [29]) rather than the outcome. In our vision, we can address the trust issue by focusing on the outcome of a negotiation. To achieve that, we propose the inclusion of a Smart Contract associated with a blockchain technology, that acts as a knowledge representation, with intention to advance the topic of decentralisation of the decision-making process, and as an alternative to traditional approaches that rely on a third party to enforce the trust of the negotiation terms fulfillment.

The main concern with solutions that rely on a third party, is that we still need to trust on that new entity, which can become a recursive problem. While the complexity increment introduced through the adoption of Smart Contracts and blockchain technologies can be questioned, is our belief that Smart Contracts can be beneficial for the negotiation process, and the reverse is also true. Smart Contracts improve negotiation (and trust) by providing an immutable and distributed registry that can be accessible and interacted by anyone, while providing consensus about the outcome. From a similar perspective, negotiation can improve Smart Contracts through the automatization of the contractual terms by selecting the terms used during the negotiation process and respective outcome.

The remainder of this work is structured as follows. In Sect. 2 we present a background on the technologies and concepts included in this work, with special reference to Smart Contracts and blockchain technology; Sect. 3 describes our proposed solution, including a description of its main components, and further elaboration on the relationship between negotiation outcomes and Smart Contracts; This work concludes (Sect. 4) with a discussion of the proposed solution, its strengths, limitations, and future work paths.

2 Background

You can choose a random event that is a part of your day, and you can find that decision-making processes are a constant presence on our daily life routine. From selecting what clothes to wear, what medicine to prescribe to a patient, to what is going to be next product that is going to boost sales, we can understand the importance of this process [12]. Decisions are based on the will to fulfil previous setted goals, that are mainly displayed because of their attachment to an individual (or a group), becoming a process that can be divided in sub-decisions and tasks [10,23]. When a decision is made, a certain result is going to be produced, and this triggers a necessity for evaluation and understanding regarding the achievement of the objective.

This evaluation process is by itself a challenge task to carry out, since it uses the results (until a decision was made) in the decision-making process [12], to assign a positive or a negative connotation to it [12]. The effectiveness of a decision is an uncertainty, since the process of making a decision can be influenced by the variables used in the process itself. Thus, decision-making process is a very difficult and complex task due to the necessity to consider every factor, each one with a different importance to the final decision [10]. This can be established by assuming a set o variables (e.g. category of decision), previous acquainted knowledge, expectations of specific situations, and personal preferences [10,12].

When we have a decision that must carried out by multiple entities, we are in a presence of a collaboration scenario where each participant work jointly to achieve a common goal (e.g. the development of a product) and the distributed returns are sufficient for all the collaborating parties [20]. This represents a free flow of information between collaborating entities, which provides faster decision-making and enhance the importance of collaboration, while creating new negotiation scenarios.

An agent is described as an entity that senses the environment and acts on it, performing a task continuously, with a strong autonomy, in a shifting environment, while coexisting with other entities and processes. Multi-agent Systems (MAS) aim to provide both principles for construction of complex systems involving multiple agents and mechanisms for coordination of independent agent behaviour [26]. While an agent is any individual entity that is making decisions independently, MAS are a network of agents that work together to solve a specific problem, which implies a certain level of cooperation among the agents involved, that can be explicit by design, or adapted. They adopt the philosophy that a group is better at solving a problem that a single individual, and are a particular type of intelligent systems, where autonomous agents dwell in a world with no control, or persistent knowledge. This infrastructure has been studied as a solution to manage widely distributed systems, in several domains, and aim to provide both principles for construction of complex systems involving multiple agents. MAS, which consists of multiple autonomous agents with distinct goals, are especially suitable for the development of complex and dynamic systems. Agents communicate with each other and with the environment with a focus on understanding the latter and reason upon intelligent models, coordinating their efforts to achieve their goals and the one of the ecosystem where they are inserted in, and negotiating their preferences [2,19].

Originated in 15th century from the French word 'negotiation', negotiation early definition meant "business, trade and traffic" . This term has later given a new meaning and became "to communicate in search of mutual agreement", which resulted in a term shift from "doing business" to "bargain about business". Arguably the most acceptable definition is given as "the process by which a joint decision is made by two or more parties. The parties first verbalize contradictory demands and then move towards agreement by a process of concession making or search for new alternative" [22]. It is a process divided in three phases: (1) pre-negotiation phase; (2) negotiation phase; (3) post-negotiation phase. This process is composed by a negotiation strategy model (e.g., genetic algorithm, time dependent, adaptive, concession, etc.), a utility model (e.g., product function, linear, non-linear, etc.), an opponent model (e.g., stochastic approximation, heuristics, regression analysis, etc.), an acceptance model, a negotiation protocol (e.g., alternative offers, sequential-offer, argumentation, etc.), and an evaluation metric (e.g., number of rounds, pareto-optimality, ANAC scores, etc.) [14].

2.1 Smart Contracts and Blockchain

Following the white paper "Bitcoin: A Peer-to-Peer Electronic Cash System" by Nakamoto [18] blockchain has started its journey to become one of the most popular topics nowadays. The initial association with cryptocurrency accompanied its success, while at the same time intrigued the curiosity of researchers to pursue different scenarios of application [4], whose reach and limitations are still a work in progress [1]. It is described as a generic designation given to transaction persistence protocols, based on different algorithms and cryptographic principles that ensure the integrity and traceability of all transactions within the system, without the need to place trust in a central entity, thereby maintaining it, decentralised and distributed. The successor of the initial blockchain protocols (Blockchain 1.0), whose implementation is restricted to ensuring that a predefined set of validations were respected, is Blockchain 2.0. This new designation is associated with the new generation of blockchain protocol implementations designed since its inception to support the definition of business rules and custom validations through Smart Contracts. As a direct response to the increasing demands from the industry, anxiously expecting a framework that allowed the full exploration of this technology for the most different ends.

Smart contracts were introduced as a concept by Szabo in the 90s [27], whose definition was defined as a computerised transaction protocol that executes the terms of a contract [9]. They differ from traditionally e-contracts, and they are not necessarily contracts, and not necessarily smart [25]. This definition was based on the necessity to translate contractual clauses into code, and embedded into hardware or software that is capable of self-enforce them, resulting in a decrease for the need of a trusted intermediary between transacting parties. In Blockchain, smart contracts are self-enforcing scripts that represent a digital contract [16]. They work as a software protocol that performs an action when certain conditions are met, reducing the amount of human involvement required to create, execute, and enforce a contract. Since there is no necessity for the contract partners to fully trust each other, blockchain, as a distributed system, is suitable for this type of application by removing the intermediary and simplifying trustless protocols between multiple parties [31]. Since then, they have become part of solutions to different problems [7,21,32] and further efforts have been made regarding the tests of its security [3].

3 Proposed Solution

Our proposal pretends to enforce an agreement reached by two (or more) agents during a negotiation process, while addressing the trust issues noted by Baarslag et al. [6]. Similar to the decentralisation of the decision-making process achieved by MAS, we intend to remove the control authority (third party) by making it distributed. To achieve this, we propose the inclusion of Smart Contracts in the negotiation process as an enforcer of the negotiation outcomes.

With Smart Contracts we do not pretend to remove the risk associated with a negotiation and respective agreement outcome, instead, our objective is to allocate the risk so that both parties can clearly understand the terms of the agreement and respective fulfilment scenarios. Regarding the terms, they can be expressed or can be implied, with the latter being associated with a "legal system" or control authority (third party) that decides to reinforce the contract or not. The main problem of delegating a third party to solve the trust issue associated with the negotiation, is that we create a new trust issue because the participants need to trust the third party, believing that it would be impartial and can not be tampered or corrupted by anyone.

We found these trust characteristics and requirements in Smart Contracts, being both immutable (not changing, or unable to be changed[1]) and distributed (to give something out to several people, or to spread or supply something [2]). The analogy here can be expressed in two scenarios: (1) two entities reaching an agreement in a closed room with the presence of a third entity that is responsible to reinforce the terms and outcomes of the contract; (2) two entities reaching an agreement in a public space with thousands of witnesses that can corroborate the terms and respective contract outcomes. In these scenarios, each entity is represented by an agent, and the bilateral negotiations were used to simplify the examples since this approach can be used in applicable in negotiation between multiple agents. Nonetheless, we found scenario two more appellative regarding trust.

While proposing that the reinforcement of a negotiation outcome being performed through Smart Contracts is beneficial to the negotiation and collaboration process between agents, the reverse is also true. We believe that Smart Contracts can be improved through these processes. It is common to argue that Smart Contracts are not really smart, and the 'smartness' associated is a mere sequence of *if ... then ... else* clauses. Instead of proposing major alterations to their structural concepts, we propose the automatization of its terms. The terms that should be expressed in a Smart Contract, can be found during the negotiation process between agents.

---

[1] https://dictionary.cambridge.org/dictionary/english/immutable.
[2] https://dictionary.cambridge.org/dictionary/english/distributed.

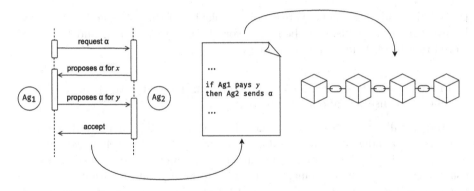

Fig. 1. Interaction between a bilateral Proposal Based Negotiation with AOP outcome between two agents (Ag1 and Ag2) (on the left), a Smart Contract with automatization of its terms (on centre), and a blockchain technology that acts as knowledge representation (on the right).

As result, an example of this concept is illustrated by Fig. 1. On the left we have simple Proposal Based Negotiation using one of the most well-known protocols, the Alternative-Offers Protocol (AOP) [5]. This agreement is then persisted on a Smart Contract (at the centre) whose contract terms are automatically derived from the negotiation process and reflect that if Ag_1 wants α then it should give y to Ag_2 and, consequently, when Ag_2 receives y then it should give α to Ag_1. Finally, on the right, this contract is then stored on a blockchain (to be further discussed in Sect. 3.1). It is important to note that our proposal is independent of protocol, language, and decision process used, and is rather focused on its outcome, meaning that should be applicable for a combination of criteria mentioned previously. Also, considering the lifecycle of a negotiation process ((1)pre-negotiation phase; (2) negotiation phase; (3) post-negotiation phase [14]) the research focus of this work is centred on the negotiation and post-negotiation phase outcomes (namely the resulting agreements and respective contractual terms).

Despise the focus of this work not be addressed to communication or domain language, to achieve the desired automatization of contractual terms, especially when using negotiation techniques like argumentation [15], the locutions need to be simplified, generalized, and become less strict. When in a presence of locutions that are too strict and domain specific, we might lack clarity and dynamism with our contracts. In contrast, if we only have few locutions allowed for negotiation (e.g. propose, accept, reject) then is not possible to request justifications for a given proposal [13].

3.1   Blockchain

As a concept Smart Contracts are not dependent on blockchain (and vice versa) [25], meaning that we should question if there is a justification for the inclusion of blockchain, and consequent increase of complexity of the solution. We strongly believe that this inclusion is beneficial for the overall solution, and by being stored in a blockchain, Smart Contracts:

- Are accessible to everyone;
- Provide interaction with anyone (everyone can interact with them);
- Inherit a consensus about the outcome.

Additionally, regarding trust issues denoted previously, if the outcomes of contract is dependent or can be reinforced by written laws' blockchain can replace the existing "legal system" mainly because this system is not guaranteed in every country or domain. On extreme, it is possible to argue that are situations where the legal systems cannot be fully trusted (mostly because corruption or lack of maturity). Despise the current concerns about the legality of Smart Contracts, they are not the focus of this work. Finally, the contract transaction cost is also low when compared to traditionally adopted solutions.

Blockchain can also act as a knowledge representation that supports the negotiation process, by storing participants and transaction data, providing a shared, immutable, and transparent append-only register for all interactions between all agents in a given network. Despite existing debates regarding the benefits and concerns between public and private blockchains, is possible to achieve the desired results through the adoption of a consortium blockchain (that represents a middle ground between the low trust provided by the public blockchain, and the 'single authority' associated with private blockchains) [17]. This is achieved through a combination of benefits found in private blockchains (like efficiency, transactions, and data access privacy) without consolidation the power in a single entity, which results in a decentralisation of the decision-making process. This unique strategy found in the consortium blockchain is highly beneficial for entities collaboration since it operates under a leadership of a group instead of a single entity.

There is also a possibility to control transactions and general data on the blockchain through network managed permissions. We can also represent each entity (agent) by a public and private profile, which means that blockchain can represent this natural concept associated with agents. As example, agent intentions can be public while preferences remain private. This can prevent the lost of leverage during the negotiation phase.

As for the blockchain technology that should be used, the main condition is the capability of interaction with Smart Contracts, and the blockchain choice should be adapted to each problem context. If we have a context where there is a necessity for transparency and privacy features, it is possible to use Hyperledger Fabric. By being similar to other blockchains, it has a ledger, uses smart contracts, and is a system where the participants can manage their transactions. It differs from not being an open system that allows unknown entities to participate in the network, where each member requires special authorisation and validation to be part of it (closed set of participants) [11].

Is an implementation of a distributed ledger platform for running smart contracts, leveraging familiar and proven technologies, with a modular architecture that allows pluggable implementations of various functions [8]. It has a peculiar architecture called "execute-order-validate", and a distributed application for Fabric consists of two parts:

1. Smart Contract (Chaincode): the central part of a distributed application in Fabric, with special chaincodes existing to manage the blockchain system and maintaining parameters. Chaincode is invoked by an application external to the blockchain, when there is a need to interact with the ledger;
2. An endorsement policy that is evaluated in the validation phase. This policy acts as a static library for the validation of transactions, which can only be parameterised by the chaincode. A typical endorsement policy allows the chaincode to specify the endorsers for a transaction in the form of a set of peers. This set of peers are defined as the smallest set of entities required to endorse a transaction to be valid. To endorse, an entity endorsing peer needs to run the smart contract associated with the transaction and sign its outcome.

With Hyperledger Fabric, a ledger consists of two distinct parts: (1) a world state; (2) and a blockchain. The world state is a database that holds the current values for the ledger state, making it easy to access them, while the blockchain works as a transaction log that registers every change that lead to the current world state. The world state is implemented as a database, providing a rich set of operations for the efficient storage and retrieval of states. When a transaction that implies changes to the world state is submitted, by invoking a smart contract, ends up being committed to the blockchain, where a notification about the validity of the transaction is later sent to its committer.

4   Conclusion and Future Work

With a heterogeneous existence of decision-making problems, collaboration necessities, and negotiation scenarios, we can find a common variable: trust (or the current lack of). When agents negotiate their preferences, trust has been reported as recurrent challenge, and the traditional approaches are based on the existence of a third party that can enforce the fulfilment of the decided terms. The problem with these traditional approaches is that we do not remove a problem of trust, instead we are creating another since there is a necessity to trust the third party, that can quickly become a recursive problem.

Alternatively to search for improvements in the implications of the negotiation process, in this work we have focused on the outcome of the negotiation. We propose the inclusion of a Smart Contract to replace the third party entity and enforce the terms of the agreement (present on the outcome). The immutability and distributed characteristics of this type of digital agreement, when supported by a blockchain technology allow us to propose a solution to the trust issue, while providing a support knowledge representation alternative, and contributing for the decentralisation of decision-making processes.

Despite being an increase in complexity to the solution, the blockchain can also reflect the private and public characteristics of an agent, by keeping their intentions public (for example) while their preferences remain private.

Initially we were expecting only a single side improvement, namely, only for the Smart Contract to benefit the negotiation process. Later, we found that Smart Contracts can also benefit from this process. While Smart Contract can be a clever and marketing wording for this technology, is debatable if they are really a contract, and if they are really smart. Instead of severe alter their behaviour, the terms of a Smart Contract can be automated through the negotiation terms discussed by the agents.

While the focus of this work is oriented to the outcome of the negotiation process, some remarks should be made regarding the communication or domain language. Future work paths should focus on the simplification and generalization of locutions. With rigid and strict locutions we can achieve better performance in complex problems, but we lack the versatility to other problems. In contrast, the over simplification can lead to high diversity but poor performance. It is necessary to find a middle ground that can both benefit the negotiation process, and the automatization of the contractual terms.

Additionally, even if the proposal solution should be applicable with a different combination of negotiation protocols, domain language, decision process, or even blockchain technology (with the requirement that should support Smart Contracts), further experimentations should be performed to understand the impact of the solution considering different domains, contexts, and combination of criteria.

Funding. This work has been supported by FCT—Fundação para a Ciência e Tecnologia within the Project Scope: UIDB/04728/2020.

References

1. Abeyratne, S.A., Monfared, R.P.: Blockchain ready manufacturing supply chain using distributed ledger. Int. J. Res. Eng. Technol. 5(9), 1–10 (2016)
2. Amato, A., Martino, B.D., Scialdone, M., Venticinque, S.: Multi-agent negotiation of decentralized energy production in smart micro-grid. In: IDC (2014)
3. Andesta, E., Faghih, F., Fooladgar, M.: Testing smart contracts gets smarter. In: 2020 10th International Conference on Computer and Knowledge Engineering (ICCKE), pp. 405–412. IEEE (2020)
4. Aste, T., Tasca, P., Di Matteo, T.: Blockchain technologies: the foreseeable impact on society and industry. Computer 50(9), 18–28 (2017)
5. Baarslag, T., Hendrikx, M.J., Hindriks, K.V., Jonker, C.M.: Learning about the opponent in automated bilateral negotiation: a comprehensive survey of opponent modeling techniques. Auton. Agent. Multi-Agent Syst. 30(5), 849–898 (2016)
6. Baarslag, T., Kaisers, M., Gerding, E., Jonker, C.M., Gratch, J.: When will negotiation agents be able to represent us? The challenges and opportunities for autonomous negotiators. In: International Joint Conferences on Artificial Intelligence (2017)

7. Bottoni, P., Gessa, N., Massa, G., Pareschi, R., Selim, H., Arcuri, E.: Intelligent smart contracts for innovative supply chain management. Front. Blockchain **3**, 52 (2020)
8. Cachin, C., et al.: Architecture of the hyperledger blockchain fabric. In: Workshop on Distributed Cryptocurrencies and Consensus Ledgers, vol. 310 (2016)
9. Christidis, K., Devetsikiotis, M.: Blockchains and smart contracts for the internet of things. IEEE Access **4**, 2292–2303 (2016)
10. Dean, J.W., Sharfman, M.P.: Does decision process matter? A study of strategic decision-making effectiveness. Acad. Manag. J. **39**(2), 368–396 (1996). https://doi. org/10.2307/256784
11. Dib, O., Brousmiche, K.L., Durand, A., Thea, E., Hamida, E.B.: Consortium blockchains: overview, applications and challenges. Int. J. Adv. Telecommun. **11**(1 & 2), 51–64 (2018)
12. Hamilton, J.G., et al.: What is a good medical decision? A research agenda guided by perspectives from multiple stakeholders. J. Behav. Med. **40**(1), 52–68 (2017). https://doi.org/10.1007/s10865-016-9785-z
13. Jin, Y., Geslin, M.: A study of argumentation-based negotiation in collaborative design. Artif. Intell. Eng. Design Anal. Manuf.: AI EDAM **24**(1), 35 (2010)
14. Kiruthika, U., Somasundaram, T.S., Raja, S.K.S.: Lifecycle model of a negotiation agent: a survey of automated negotiation techniques. Group Decis. Negot. **29**(6), 1239–1262 (2020). https://doi.org/10.1007/s10726-020-09704-z
15. Kraus, S.: Automated negotiation and decision making in multiagent environments. In: Luck, M., Mařík, V., Štěpánková, O., Trappl, R. (eds.) ACAI 2001. LNCS (LNAI), vol. 2086, pp. 150–172. Springer, Heidelberg (2001). https://doi.org/10. 1007/3-540-47745-4_7
16. Lin, I.C., Liao, T.C.: A survey of blockchain security issues and challenges. IJ Netw. Secur. **19**(5), 653–659 (2017)
17. Mingxiao, D., Xiaofeng, M., Zhe, Z., Xiangwei, W., Qijun, C.: A review on consensus algorithm of blockchain. In: A review on consensus algorithm of blockchain. In: 2017 IEEE International Conference on Systems, Man, and Cybernetics (SMC), pp. 2567–2572 (2017). https://doi.org/10.1109/SMC.2017.8123011
18. Nakamoto, S.: Bitcoin: A peer-to-peer electronic cash system. Bitcoin **4** (2008). https://bitcoin.org/bitcoin.pdf
19. Okumura, M., Fujita, K., Ito, T.: An implementation of collective collaboration support system based on automated multi-agent negotiation. In: Ito, T., Zhang, M., Robu, V., Matsuo, T. (eds.) Complex Automated Negotiations: Theories, Models, and Software Competitions. SCI, vol. 435, pp. 125–141. Springer, Heidelberg (2013). https://doi.org/10.1007/978-3-642-30737-9_8
20. Oliver, A.L.: On the duality of competition and collaboration: network-based knowledge relations in the biotechnology industry. Scand. J. Manag. **20**(1), 151–171 (2004). https://doi.org/10.1016/j.scaman.2004.06.002. Different Perspectives on Competition and Cooperation
21. Omar, I.A., Jayaraman, R., Salah, K., Debe, M., Omar, M.: Enhancing vendor managed inventory supply chain operations using blockchain smart contracts. IEEE Access **8**, 182704–182719 (2020)
22. Pruitt, D.G.: Introduction: an overview of negotiation. In: Pruitt, D.G. (ed.) Negotiation Behavior, pp. 1–17. Academic Press (1981). https://doi.org/10.1016/B978-0-12-566250-5.50006-9

23. Santos, R., Marreiros, G., Ramos, C., Bulas-Cruz, J.: Argumentative agents for ambient intelligence ubiquitous environments. In: Proceedings of Artificial Intelligence Techniques for Ambient Intelligence. ECAI'08 – 18th European Conference on Artificial Intelligence (2008)

24. Santos, R., Marreiros, G., Ramos, C., Neves, J., Bulas-Cruz, J.: Personality, emotion, and mood in agent-based group decision making. IEEE Ann. Hist. Comput. **26**(06), 58–66 (2011)

25. Schmitz, A.J.: Making smart contracts 'smarter' with arbitration. American Arbitration Association website (2020, forthcoming)

26. Stone, P., Veloso, M.: Multiagent systems: a survey from a machine learning perspective. Auton. Robots **8**, 345–383 (2000). https://doi.org/10.1023/A:1008942012299

27. Szabo, N.: Smart contracts: building blocks for digital markets. EXTROPY: J. Transhumanist Thought (16) **18**(2) (1996)

28. Tschannen-Moran, M.: Collaboration and the need for trust. J. Educ. Adm. (2001)

29. Vente, S., Kimmig, A., Preece, A., Cerutti, F.: The current state of automated negotiation theory: a literature review. arXiv e-prints, p. arXiv-2004 (2020)

30. Wang, S., Wan, J., Zhang, D., Li, D., Zhang, C.: Towards smart factory for Industry 4.0: a self-organized multi-agent system with big data based feedback and coordination. Comput. Netw. **101**, 158–168 (2016). https://doi.org/10.1016/j.comnet.2015.12.017

31. Wüst, K., Gervais, A.: Do you need a blockchain? In: 2018 Crypto Valley Conference on Blockchain Technology (CVCBT), pp. 45–54 (2018)

32. Yao, Y., Kshirsagar, M., Vaidya, G., Ducrée, J., Ryan, C.: Convergence of blockchain, autonomous agents, and knowledge graph to share electronic health records. Front. Blockchain **4**, 13 (2021)

Recommending Metadata Contents for Learning Objects Through Linked Data

André Behr[1]([✉])([iD]), Armando Mendes[1,2]([iD]), Paulo Trigo[5]([iD]), José Cascalho[1,2]([iD]), Hélia Guerra[1,3]([iD]), Ana Costa[1,4]([iD]), Manuela Parente[1,4]([iD]), Andrea Botelho[1,4]([iD]), and Rosa Vicari[6]([iD])

[1] FCT, University of the Azores, Ponta Delgada, Portugal
[2] GRIA and LIACC, Ponta Delgada, Portugal
[3] NIDeS and Centro Algoritmi, Ponta Delgada, Portugal
[4] CIBIO and InBIO, Ponta Delgada, Portugal
[5] ISEL and GuIAA, Lisbon, Portugal
[6] Federal University of Rio Grande do Sul, Porto Alegre, Brazil

Abstract. Attach metadata to digital objects effectively underlies the development of high-quality services in systems. This work explores how the metadata of a learning object represented as linked data, in a brand new repository, can be a facilitator to a more complete catalog and search with contents recommendations. The proposed approach underlies in DBpedia Spotlight for unstructured text annotation to deliver recommendations at the learning object cataloging phase and GEMET, a marine domain thesaurus, to expand marine searching terms. Each learning object is described with OBAA metadata as a set of triples stored in Resource Description Framework format to deliver interoperability and Linked Data compatibility.

Keywords: Linked Data · Metadata recommendations · Learning Objects

1 Introduction

Nowadays, the volume of data has been increasing at an unprecedented rate from heterogeneous sources. With the use of Artificial Intelligent and Big Data

This work is financed by the FEDER in 85% and by regional funds in 15%, through the Operational Program Azores 2020, within the scope of the SEA-THINGS Learning Objects to Promote Ocean Literacy project ACORES-01-0145-FEDER-000110. This study was also supported in part by the Coordenação de Aperfeiçoamento de Pessoal de Nível Superior - Brazil (CAPES) - Finance Code 001. This work was partially funded by FEDER funds through the Operational Programme for Competitiveness Factors - COMPETE and by National Funds through FCT - Foundation for Science and Technology under the UID/BIA/50027/2020 and POCI-01-0145-FEDER-006821, by funding the CIBIO/InBIO.

© Springer Nature Switzerland AG 2021
F. De La Prieta et al. (Eds.): PAAMS Workshops 2021, CCIS 1472, pp. 115–126, 2021.
https://doi.org/10.1007/978-3-030-85710-3_10

technologies, this huge amount of data supports the emergence of various service providers in Smart Cities [1].

Big Data is usually depicted as a set of five "Vs": volume, velocity, variety, value, and veracity. The variety aspect is usually related to data itself and different representation formats, terms of correctness, underlying conceptualizations or data models, temporal and spatial dependencies. This leads to problems related to data integration that is attached to the Semantic Web and Linked Data (LD) ideas [10].

Shadbolt *et al.* [16] define the Semantic Web as a Web of actionable information derived from data through a semantic theory for symbol interpretation. The semantic theory provides some kind of "meaning" through logical connections of terms to provide interoperability between systems. The authors argue that a large quantity of interlinked data should outline the Semantic Web. Also, the data have to be standardized to be reach and manageable by intelligent tools or agents, both humans and machines.

Linked Data is a subfield of the Semantic Web. It addresses aspects for good practices in how to publish and link data sets on the Web. Resource Description Framework (RDF) represents data and encodes it in triples (subject, predicate, and object), providing a minimalist representation of knowledge on the Web [4].

The Linking Open Data Project[1] has been consolidating the Linked Data principles, converting and publishing data in RDF from data sets under open licenses. DBpedia is the core node of this project that extracts data from Wikipedia and shares it in RDF triples that are commonly referenced in other data sets, generating the so-called Linked Open Data cloud.

Some kinds of Recommender Systems have been applying Linked Data as a powerful information source to boost its predictivity. LD-based approaches already have presented good results in terms of accuracy and ranking [6,13,18].

However, the search and recommendation services are affected when there are no precise metadata. And considering a broad scope, the lack of high-quality metadata can burden the automatizing of a repository quality control process [17].

This work explores how to represent Learning Objects (LOs) metadata as Linked Data to provide useful information both to humans and machines. This kind of LO repositories can be considered Linked Data end-points, providing integration at the semantic level. Additionally, they can deliver enhanced suggestions to catalog and query functionalities. The repository used in this work, the Re-Mar, is in the final stage of development. Since it has a small amount of LOs, recommendations based on LOs and users are not applied yet on it. We enable guidance in a previous step, support metadata cataloging with suggested contents. In this way, provide more correct results and LO recommendations to users are expected in the future. We also explore LD to related terms in the search.

---

[1] https://www.w3.org/wiki/SweoIG/TaskForces/CommunityProjects/ LinkingOpenData.

This paper follows with presenting and discussing related works. In the next section, a Linked Data description for LOs with the Agent-based Learning Objects (OBAA) metadata. Further, a learning object repository (Re-Mar) contextualizes this work and then aspects related to how LO as Linked Data can deliver content recommendations to users on metadata authoring over such repository aggregated data. In the end, the conclusion and future works are proposed.

2 Related Work

According to a survey made by Pereira *et al.* [15], the use of Linked Data in education has three main objectives: (i) availability of educational data as Linked Data, (ii) integration and interoperability of educational data and systems, and (iii) Linked Data consumption for different educational purposes. The authors also argue that using metadata standards in educational resource repositories could be a facilitator in providing learning objects as Linked Data and establishing interoperability among different repositories.

Nahhas *et al.* [12] summarize the Linked Data lifecycle that has been employed by several institutions: (i) raw data collection, (ii) ontologies reuse and extension if needed to define the vocabulary model, (iii) extract and/or generate RDF data sets, (iv) internal and external data interlinkage, (v) store RDF data sets and provide SPARQL endpoint, (vi) explore RDF data to develop applications and services, and (vii) provide optimized and quality data. Linked Data can be combined with Learning Analytics and Data Mining to provide useful personalization regarding learning materials and interdisciplinary connections.

There are some efforts to generate RDF for metadata automatically. We can cite a framework [9] to create RDF from real-time Web data extracted from multiple repositories and works based on OAI-PMH for legacy repositories [3,11]. Otherwise, an OBAA metadata generation tool is proposed in [2], it is supported by application profiles and educational metadata ontologies for data consistency but in a non-automatic way.

The Center for Expanded Data Annotation and Retrieval (CEDAR) [7] has been developing tools and services where it is possible to author metadata and submit them to repositories. Services can be divided into two functional groups. One for metadata repository services, with storage and management for templates and metadata. And the other to metadata enrichment and submission services that are related to this work. The service provides metadata semantically enriched from BioPortal ontology terms and JSON-LD (an RDF serialization). It also provides a value recommender service based on previous values that compose a ranked list of suggested values.

RDF data can be considered as a source for recommendations and queries. BROAD-RSI [14] is an educational recommender system based on social network profiles of users that searches in different repositories (Linked Data, Learning Objects, and videos). For Linked Data, DBpedia and Open University (for specific educational goals) content sources were used. Among DBpedia available properties, they employed *dbpedia-owl:abstract, foaf:isPrimaryTopicOf, dbpedia-owl:wikiPageExternalLink, dbpedia-owl:academicDiscipline, dbpprop:discipline Of, dbpedia-owl:literaryGenre, dcterms:subject,* and *dbpprop:hasPhotoCollection* to user's learning process. For example, a brief topic explanation, links to conferences, journals, and other sites that are associated with the topic of interest. They also employ a Computer Science taxonomy based on the Association for Computing Machinery (ACM) classification system for query enhancement through narrower terms. In [19], user reviews are explored for generating recommendations to items through semantic annotation to deliver useful and non-trivial information to related items. DBpedia and Wikidata can be used to discover other resources connected with the annotated entities.

Considering the related works, we follow the guidelines presented in [15] and [12] to share LOs as Linked Data for different kinds of educational consumption. The work of Pereira *et al.* [14] is the most similar approach, but our work differs in applying a different domain thesaurus and representing LOs as Linked Data since the beginning.

3   OBAA Metadata to Describe LOs as Linked Data

Learning objects can be defined as digital artifacts that support learning and may be reused over time [21]. Learning object repositories organize LO collections to their retrieval, usually supported by metadata. As a repository grows, it is important to keep providing quality services, such as searching and recommendation.

The OBAA proposal [20] is one of the metadata standard efforts to describe learning objects effectively for well-founded services. It is compliant with IEEE-LOM metadata, but extends it in several ways, such as to support interoperability among platforms and relations with different learning content types, interactions, and didactic strategies. Besides that, it attaches accessibility for users and segmentation for objects.

Furthermore, OBAA can be transposed into Linked Data and ontologies to describe LOs and be compatible with the Semantic Web. Individuals can represent LOs' metadata categories and subcategories, and data properties store metadata values [3]. Figure 1 shows how a metadata fragment in stated XML format can be described as Linked Data concepts, where a contributing individual (subject) is linked with entity and role (predicates) data properties to its values (objects). Subjects and predicates are RDF Uniform Resource Identifier (URI) references, and objects can be an RDF URI reference or a literal value. In this way, several individuals can be interlinked, forming an RDF graph, representing the entire LO metadata.

Each LO RDF graph can be connected with other LO RDF graphs to expand knowledge representation. It can be a direct relation (concrete link/predicate), such as to indicate a reference, requirement, or version through the LOs lifecycles. Besides that, it can be a shared concept (but with no explicit link/predicate), a common author or organization, keyword, knowledge area, LO type, as examples.

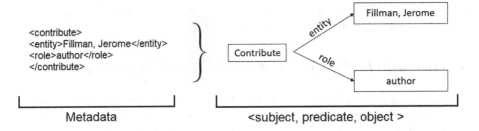

Fig. 1. LO XML metadata fragment to Linked Data concepts.

These LO connections lead to a local knowledge graph that can be queried to provide recommendations for users.

Figure 2 shows how small triples of LOs can be interconnected, generating an extended RDF graph for searching. Blue circles represent individuals for metadata (sub)categories that are interconnected with object properties. Green dotted lines depict direct connections and red dotted lines represent a shared concept that interlinks LOs.

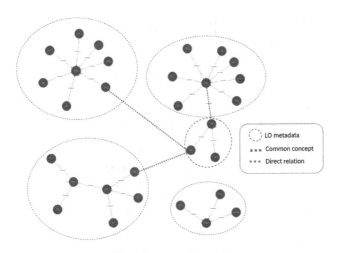

Fig. 2. LO RDF graphs interconnections.

These local data could be interlinked with external data. For example, keywords can be associated with DBpedia concepts, interlinking a repository with the Linked Open Data cloud. These recurrent data connection lead to an extended knowledge graph (almost a global database) that can be queried to combine some useful information.

On the other hand, learning object repositories can afford storage for all these LO representations in a local triplestore to provide end-point access for intelligent tools and agents. Besides that, it can support SPARQL queries to navigate in this interconnected network.

4   Towards Linked Data at Re-Mar LO Repository

The Repository of Marine Learning Objects (Re-Mar) intends to provide aspects of LO authoring, recommendations, usage, and searching supported by agent-based tools and ontologies. It is one of the goals of the multidisciplinary SeaThings[2] project that aims to provide a learning object repository related to ocean subjects to students and teachers.

Re-Mar is a brand new repository that corroborates with Open Data through Creative Commons (CC) licenses. This kind of license ensures credits for authors by reusing and sharing LOs with the same license. At Re-Mar, all the LOs must be shared with CC BY-SA[3] and CC BY-NC-SA[4] URIs.

Figure 3 depicts the aimed infrastructure architecture for Re-Mar that follows the MILOS [8] proposal. It is a three-layered architecture composed of Ontologies, Agents, and Interface Facilities.

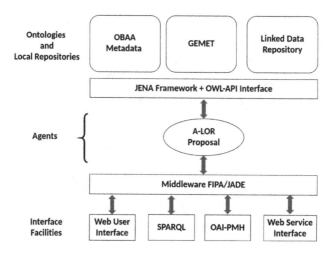

Fig. 3. Overview of Re-Mar infrastructure architecture.

The Ontology level provides the specification of knowledge that will be shared among the intelligent agents. For example, ontologies for the OBAA metadata, learning domain, and curricular structure can be attached. Aside from the OBAA metadata ontology used to describe LO metadata as RDF triples to store it in a

---

[2] https://fgf.uac.pt/en/content/sea-things-objetos-de-aprendizagem-para-promover-literacia-oceanica.

[3] http://creativecommons.org/licenses/by-sa/4.0/.

[4] http://creativecommons.org/licenses/by-nc-sa/4.0/.

Linked Data repository, Re-Mar reuses the GEMET (GEneral Multilingual Environmental Thesaurus)[5] that was extended and improved by including regional terms and concepts with the help of a team of Biologists fully integrated into the project.

Interface and Facilities represent some applications and services that can consume the learning object repository. It can be done by Virtual Learning Environments (VLE), Learning Object Repositories (LORs), web servers, and other services, for example. This level interacts directly with the Agents level. This communication is provided by JADE middleware under the standard FIPA for message exchange.

At the center layer, it is an Active-Learning Object Repository (A-LOR) proposal that will be a set of Agents to deliver functionalities to the repository, such as analytics, recommendation, interface, and management aspects, to share LOs more actively so that they could collaborate to reconfigure metadata itself.

The next section will depict how Linked Data can be applied at Re-Mar to catalog and search aspects. These aspects will be later incorporated in the Agent layer.

5   Linked Data Enhancement for LOs

The advent of Big Data has generated a lot of unstructured and semi-structured data. Some tools can assist with these diversities of data to mitigate this drawback in common knowledge representation. DBpedia Spotlight [5] is one of such tools, it automatically annotates mentions of DBpedia resources in unstructured text, linking it to the Linked Open Data cloud through DBpedia.

Learning object repositories can incorporate this tool at the submission step, where the user usually has to fill some metadata fields. The main idea is to detect DBpedia resources from unstructured text, as in title and description form sections, through an API call. From this, a list of identified resources can be used as content recommendations to automatic fill some form sections, as learning object type and keywords, using a simple match or a regular expression. The user is free to edit or add some content and fill the other input form sections. Last, the system can identify new resources provided by the user and store the metadata in triples.

Figure 4 illustrates a sample text filled by the user in a section form that can provide three DBpedia resources. With this concept annotation, it is also possible to generate some recommendations for LO metadata cataloging that users may accept or change. Then, the system can present the LO type (Fig. 5) and furnish keywords (Fig. 6) suggestions at the cataloging phase. Beyond that, other improved Linked Data recommendations can be provided by analyzing the LO text file submitted.

---

[5] https://www.eionet.europa.eu/gemet/en/exports/rdf/latest.

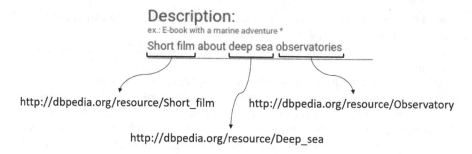

Fig. 4. Linked Data concepts from unstructured data.

Learning object type(s): *

☐ Questionary	☐ Problem	☐ Test	☐ Question statement
☐ Class plan	☐ Field outing	☐ Laboratory experience	☐ Script
☐ Book	☐ Infography	☐ Web page	☐ Theatrical / dramatized text ☐ Narrated text
☑ Video documentary	☐ Filmed demonstration	☐ Recorded or filmed lesson	
☐ Game	☐ Simulation		

Add other type _____   Add

Fig. 5. LO type recommendation with Linked Data concepts.

Each input form section is related to an RDF individual (subject) and data properties (predicates) to knowledge representation. For the example mentioned above, there are two individuals, one representing the general metadata and the other the educational metadata. The general individual will be linked with one *description* and two *keyword* data properties. The *description* data property stores the unstructured text "Short film about deep-sea observatories" and two *keyword* data properties stores DBpedia URIs: "http://dbpedia.org/resource/Deep_sea" and "http://dbpedia.org/resource/Observatory". The educational individual will be linked with a *learningResourceType* data property that will store the "http://dbpedia.org/resource/Short_film" URI.

After the LO submission, all the triples are created in the same way from the form fields, generating a set of individuals, properties, and values (literals or URIs) related to the LO. The user can view the LO metadata and can access DBpedia links to navigate in the RDF graph to other concepts. For keywords, it also possible to embed the DBpedia text abstract to the related resource for explanation accessing the *dbpedia-owl:abstract* property.

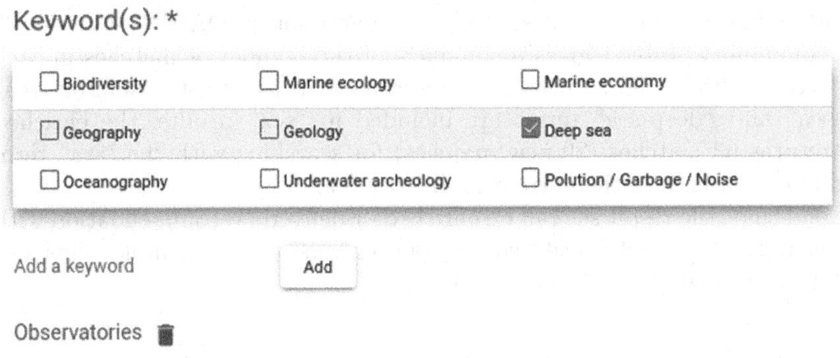

Keyword(s): *

☐ Biodiversity	☐ Marine ecology	☐ Marine economy
☐ Geography	☐ Geology	☑ Deep sea
☐ Oceanography	☐ Underwater archeology	☐ Polution / Garbage / Noise

Add a keyword   **Add**

Observatories 🗑

Fig. 6. Keywords recommendation with Linked Data concepts.

In the Re-Mar searching context, GEMET thesaurus (see Fig. 3) can provide marine-related terms to expand searching and retrieve more LOs. For example, if a user queries for "Sea", it is possible to use SPARQL to navigate in GEMET to suggest other terms. Figure 7 depicts SPARQL queries to "sea" that returns the following terms:

- (a) narrow terms:
  - "deep sea"
  - "deep-sea"
  - "ocean"
  - "open sea"
  - "seagrass"
- (b) related terms:
  - "sea resource"
  - "protected marine zone"
  - "marine protected area"

```
PREFIX skos: <http://www.w3.org/2004/02/skos/core#>
SELECT ?narrower_term ?term
WHERE {
?term skos:prefLabel \"sea\"@en .
?term skos:narrower ?narrower .
?narrower skos:prefLabel ?narrower_term .
FILTER (lang(?narrower_term) = \"en\")
}
```
(a)

```
PREFIX skos: <http://www.w3.org/2004/02/skos/core#>
SELECT ?related_term ?term
WHERE {
?term skos:prefLabel \"sea\"@en .
?term skos:related ?related .
?related skos:prefLabel ?related_term .
FILTER (lang(?related_term) = \"en\")
}
```
(b)

Fig. 7. SPARQL queries for getting (a) narrower terms and (b) related terms.

To better understand the impact of using this approach in the search, we exemplify with a community repository, the Department of Oceanography and Fisheries at the Azores University institutional repository and how the extended query addresses to gain in results. Taking into account an OAI-PMH retrieval[6] in this community, Table 1 gives a summary of the number of matches in each search term for the title, subject, and description metadata. Considering that "deep sea" and "deep-sea" terms are included in "sea" results, the enriched search returns 93 matches (29 new matches) for searching with the "sea" term instead of 64 matches in the current repository search.

Beyond that, the result set can be enriched or deliver a recommendation with direct related LOs, by reference, requirement, or version, for example. This also can be done through an SPARQL query.

Table 1. The number of matches for a "sea" query in the title, subject, and description metadata. *As "sea" is a substring in "deep sea" and "deep-sea", its matches are included in a query without LD

Term	# of matches for a "sea" query	
	Without LD	With LD
Sea	64	64
Ocean	0	26
Deep sea	6*	6
Deep-sea	31*	31
Marine protected area	0	3
Total	64	93

6   Conclusion

Provide quality metadata is an important issue for learning object repositories. It supports well-provided services, such as recommendation and search. Interlinked and structured data boost information retrieval and the production of new data by reuse both for humans and machines. Moreover, heterogeneous entities can work in a collaborative way aggregating the Linked Data.

This work presented how to employ Linked Data to support content recommendations and queries in a learning object repository called Re-Mar. It is expected that the suggested metadata might improve search results and support intelligent agents in how to catalog metadata properly. Learning objects are described as a composition of individuals and properties that can be represented as a set of triples to deliver a syntactic description that further can support ontologies to get knowledge inference and semantic description.

Future works are expected to interlink the metadata of OBAA with IEEE-LOM at the Linked Open Data cloud, explore the repository with linked data end-points in a federated search, and evaluate the expanded queries results with

---

[6] http://repositorio.uac.pt/oaiextended/request?verb=ListRecords& metadataPrefix=oai_dc&set=com_10400.3_10 Accessed in 2021/05/25.

the repository users. Besides that, the project intends to incorporate these functionalities in intelligent agents in the repository architecture. Last, when the repository would have a good amount of learning objects, it is expected to apply algorithms for learning object recommendations.

References

1. Allam, Z., Dhunny, Z.A.: On big data, artificial intelligence and smart cities. Cities **89**, 80–91 (2019)
2. Behr, A., Primo, T.T., Vicari, R.: Obaa-leme: a learning object metadata content editor supported by application profiles and educational metadata ontologies. In: Anais dos Workshops do Congresso Brasileiro de Informática na Educação, vol. 3, p. 455 (2014)
3. Behr, A.R.: Uma abordagem para promover reuso e processamento de inferências em ontologias de metadados educacionais. Master's Thesis (2016)
4. Bizer, C., Heath, T., Berners-Lee, T.: Linked data: the story so far. In: Semantic Services, Interoperability and Web Applications: Emerging Concepts, pp. 205–227. IGI global (2011)
5. Daiber, J., Jakob, M., Hokamp, C., Mendes, P.N.: Improving efficiency and accuracy in multilingual entity extraction. In: Proceedings of the 9th International Conference on Semantic Systems (I-Semantics) (2013)
6. Di Noia, T., Magarelli, C., Maurino, A., Palmonari, M., Rula, A.: Using ontology-based data summarization to develop semantics-aware recommender systems. In: Gangemi, A., et al. (eds.) ESWC 2018. LNCS, vol. 10843, pp. 128–144. Springer, Cham (2018). https://doi.org/10.1007/978-3-319-93417-4_9
7. Egyedi, A.L., et al.: Embracing semantic technology for better metadata authoring in biomedicine. In: (SWAT4LS) (2017)
8. Gluz, J.C., Vicari, R.M., Passerino, L.M.: An agent-based infrastructure for the support of learning objects life-cycle. In: Cerri, S.A., Clancey, W.J., Papadourakis, G., Panourgia, K. (eds.) ITS 2012. LNCS, vol. 7315, pp. 696–698. Springer, Heidelberg (2012). https://doi.org/10.1007/978-3-642-30950-2_126
9. Govathoti, S., Babu, M.P.: An implementation of a new framework for automatic generation of ontology and RDF to real time web and journal data. Int. J. Comput. Sci. Inf. Secur. (IJCSIS) **16**(1) (2018)
10. Hitzler, P., Janowicz, K.: Linked data, big data, and the 4th paradigm. Semantic Web **4**(3), 233–235 (2013)
11. Medina, M.A., Sánchez, J.A., Cervantes, O., Benitez, A., de la Calleja, J.: LOD4AIR: a strategy to produce and consume linked open data from OAI-PMH repositories. In: 2017 International Conference on Electronics, Communications and Computers (CONIELECOMP), pp. 1–8. IEEE (2017)
12. Nahhas, S., Bamasag, O., Khemakhem, M., Bajnaid, N.: Added values of linked data in education: a survey and roadmap. Computers **7**(3), 45 (2018)
13. Natarajan, S., Vairavasundaram, S., Natarajan, S., Gandomi, A.H.: Resolving data sparsity and cold start problem in collaborative filtering recommender system using linked open data. Expert Syst. with Appl. **149**, 113248 (2020)
14. Pereira, C.K., Campos, F., Ströele, V., David, J.M.N., Braga, R.: Broad-RSI-educational recommender system using social networks interactions and linked data. J. Internet Serv. Appl. **9**(1), 1–28 (2018)

15. Pereira, C.K., Siqueira, S.W.M., Nunes, B.P., Dietze, S.: Linked data in education: a survey and a synthesis of actual research and future challenges. IEEE Trans. Learn. Technol. **11**(3), 400–412 (2017)
16. Shadbolt, N., Hall, W., Berners-Lee, T.: The semantic web revisited. Intell. Syst. IEEE **21**(3), 96–101 (2006)
17. Tavakoli, M., Elias, M., Kismihók, G., Auer, S.: Metadata analysis of open educational resources. In: LAK21: 11th International Learning Analytics and Knowledge Conference, pp. 626–631 (2021)
18. Vagliano, I., Monti, D., Morisio, M.: Semrevrec, : A recommender system based on user reviews and linked data. In: RecSys Posters (2017)
19. Vagliano, I., Monti, D., Scherp, A., Morisio, M.: Content recommendation through semantic annotation of user reviews and linked data. In: Proceedings of the Knowledge Capture Conference, pp. 1–4 (2017)
20. Vicari, R.M., Ribeiro, A., da Silva, J.M.C., Santos, E.R., Primo, T., Bez, M.: Brazilian proposal for agent-based learning objects metadata standard - OBAA. In: Sánchez-Alonso, S., Athanasiadis, I.N. (eds.) MTSR 2010. CCIS, vol. 108, pp. 300–311. Springer, Heidelberg (2010). https://doi.org/10.1007/978-3-642-16552-8_27
21. Wiley, D.A.: Learning object design and sequencing theory. Ph.D. Thesis, Brigham Young University (2000)

Using Machine Learning to Predict the Users Ratings on TripAdvisor Based on Their Reviews

João Carneiro[1]([✉]) [iD], Jorge Meira[1,2] [iD], Paulo Novais[3] [iD], and Goreti Marreiros[1] [iD]

[1] GECAD – Research Group on Intelligent Engineering and Computing for Advanced Innovation and Development, Institute of Engineering, Polytechnic of Porto, 4200-072 Porto, Portugal
`{jrc,janme,mgt}@isep.ipp.pt`
[2] CITIC – Centro de Investigación en Tecnologías de la Información y las Comunicaciones, University of A Coruña, 15071 A Coruña, Spain
[3] ALGORITMI Centre, University of Minho, 4800-058 Guimarães, Portugal
`pjon@di.uminho.pt`

Abstract. Argumentation-based dialogue models have shown to be appropriate for decision contexts in which it is intended to overcome the lack of interaction between decision-makers, either because they are dispersed, they are too many, or they are simply not even known. However, to support decision processes with argumentation-based dialogue models, it is necessary to have knowledge of certain aspects that are specific to each decision-maker, such as preferences, interests, limitations, among others. Failure to obtain this knowledge could ruin the model's success. In this work, we intend to facilitate the acquiring information process by studying strategies to automatically predict the tourists' preferences (ratings) in relation to points of interest based on their reviews. We explored different Machine Learning algorithms (Logistic Regression, Random Forest, Decision Tree, K-Nearest Neighbors and Recurrent Neural Networks) and Natural Language Processing strategies to predict whether a review is positive or negative and the rating assigned by users on a scale of 1 to 5. The experiments carried out showed that the developed models can predict with high accuracy whether a review is positive or negative but have some difficulty in accurately predicting the rating assigned by users.

Keywords: Machine learning · Natural language processing · Sentiment analysis · Argumentation-based dialogues · Tourism · TripAdvisor

1 Introduction

Argumentation-based dialogue models are extremely useful in contexts where a group of agents is intended to find solutions for complex decision problems using negotiation and deliberation mechanisms [1–3]. In addition, they allow human decision-makers to understand the reasons that led to a given decision (enhancing the acceptance of decisions) and to define mechanisms for intelligent explanations [4, 5]. These models receive the decision-makers' preferences as input (for instance, regarding criteria and

© Springer Nature Switzerland AG 2021
F. De La Prieta et al. (Eds.): PAAMS Workshops 2021, CCIS 1472, pp. 127–138, 2021.
https://doi.org/10.1007/978-3-030-85710-3_11

alternatives) that are typically used to model the agents that represent them [6]. However, obtaining these preferences is not a simple process: first, in the contemporary and highly dynamic world in which we live, it is less and less comfortable for decision-makers to answer questionnaires and second, it is sometimes difficult to express preferences through questionnaires [7, 8]. To facilitate this task, strategies that aim to automatically identify the users' preferences have been proposed. One of those strategies consists in using Machine Learning (ML) algorithms and Natural Language Processing (NLP) to automatically extract from a text corpus the users' opinion through different strategies such as: text wrangling and pre-processing, named entity recognition and sentiment analysis [9, 10]. However, there are many algorithms and strategies that can be applied. Therefore, it is mandatory to develop specific procedures according to the application topic, to achieve the best results.

In this work, we studied the problem previously described under the topic of group recommendation systems, more specifically in the context of tourism, in which there has been an increased interest in the development of technologies capable of making recommendations according to the interests of each group member. We assumed as habitual that users/tourists express their opinions regarding Points of Interest (POI) on social networks (such as, TripAdvisor, Facebook or Booking.com) and we intend to take advantage of that to automatically predict their preferences non-intrusively. For this, we used a public dataset (available in Kaggle) and applied the development lifecycle for intelligent systems using concepts of NLP defined in [11]. More specifically, we developed forecast models using 5 ML algorithms (Logistic Regression, Random Forest, Decision Tree, K-Nearest Neighbors and Recurrent Neural Networks), using each of them both as a classification and regression methods. In addition, we used NLP to extract more knowledge from the users reviews and various libraries of Sentiment Analysis (Vader, TextBlob and Flair) to find those that best fit this context.

The rest of the paper is organized in the following order: the methodology is presented in the next Section and in the last Section some conclusions are put forward alongside with suggestions of work to be done hereafter.

2 Methods

In this Section, we describe the methodology in detail. We start by enlightening the problem that we intend to address. Next, we justify the choice of the dataset, carry out its analysis, cover preprocessing and feature engineering. Finally, we approach the used computational techniques and describe the tests and results obtained.

2.1 Understand the Problem Statement

The problem we want to overcome is to predict, non-intrusively and with a high level of accuracy, how much a tourist likes/dislikes a given POI. Subsequently, we intend to use the predicted preferences to model intelligent agents that represent tourists in a group recommendation system, who seek to jointly decide (using an argumentation-based dialogue model) and recommend to the group of tourists the set of POI to visit. For this, we chose to use the reviews that tourists write in social media (TripAdvisor) to predict their preferences.

2.2 Collect Dataset

The chosen dataset was selected based on 2 criteria: it needed to be a public dataset and should best represent the context in which this work intends to be applied. Therefore, a dataset available at Kaggle[1] and which is composed by more than 20 thousand hotel reviews extracted from TripAdvisor was selected. The fact that there already are many works that use this dataset allowed us to know beforehand that it would be very difficult to get good results, since, for example, for 5-class problem the presented accuracy of the large majority varies between 30% and 60%.

2.3 Analyze Dataset, Preprocessing and Feature Engineering

The dataset is composed by the attributes "Review" and "Rating". Table 1 shows some examples of the type of records that make up the dataset. The "Rating" is between 1 and 5, where 1 is the worst and 5 is the best possible evaluation.

Table 1. Small example of the used dataset.

Review	Rating
nice hotel expensive parking got good deal sta…	4
ok nothing special charge diamond member hilto…	2
nice rooms not 4* experience hotel monaco seat…	3
unique, great stay, wonderful time hotel monac…	5
great stay great stay, went seahawk game aweso…	5

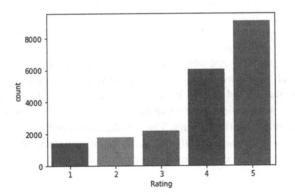

Fig. 1. Distribution by "Rating".

---

[1] https://www.kaggle.com/andrewmvd/trip-advisor-hotel-reviews.

The dataset consisted of 20491 records and 2 columns, and it did not have any missing data. Figure 1 shows the distribution by "Rating". As it is possible to verify, the dataset is quite unbalanced, with many more records with positive evaluation (Rating 5: 9054; Rating 4: 6039) than with negative evaluation (Rating 2: 1793; Rating 1:1421). Furthermore, the number of records with intermediate evaluation is also much lower than the number of records with positive evaluation (Rating 3: 2184).

To study possible correlations between the "Review" and the assigned "Rating", we created 3 new attributes: "Word_Count", "Char_Count" and "Avera-ge_Word_Length". The "Word_Count" stands for the number of words used in the "Review", the "Char_Count" stands for the number of characters used in the "Review" and the "Average_Word_Length" stands for the average size of the words used in the "Review". The "Average_Word_Length" did not show statistical relevance, but we found that the most negative reviews tended to be composed of more words than the most positive reviews (Fig. 2), which made us believe that the attribute "Word_Count" would be very relevant for the creation of the model.

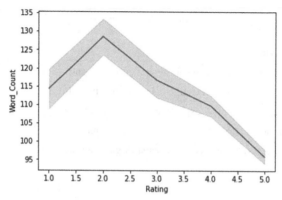

Fig. 2. Correlation between the average number of words in the "Review" with the assigned "Rating".

In the next step, we analyzed which words were most used in the reviews. In addition, we analyzed which words were most used in negative reviews (Rating 1 and 2) and in positive reviews (Rating 3, 4 and 5). We found that many of the most used words were the same, both in positive and in negative reviews. In Table 2 are presented the most used words considering all the reviews. The fact that many of the most used words are the same, in both positive and negative reviews, made us wonder if eliminating these words would be a good strategy in creating the model.

Table 2. List of the most used words in reviews.

Word	#	Word	#	Word	#	Word	#	Word	#
hotel	42079	not	30750	room	30532	great	18732	n't	18436
staff	14950	good	14791	did	13433	just	12458	stay	11376
no	11360	rooms	10935	nice	10918	stayed	10022	location	9515
service	8549	breakfast	8407	beach	8218	food	8026	like	7677
clean	7658	time	7615	really	7612	night	7596	...	...

Then we use some libraries to perform sentiment analysis. We applied 3 different libraries: Textblob, Vader and Flair. Textblob and Vader presented similar results, while Flair did not obtain results that correlated with the "Rating". With Textblob we got 2 new attributes (Polarity and Subjectivity) and with Vader we got 3 new attributes Positive_Sentiment, Negative_Sentiment and Neutral_Sentiment. Figure 3 presents the density of the "Polarity" attribute obtained with Textblob. We found that the "Polarity" is mostly positive, which makes sense since, as we saw earlier, most reviews are also positive.

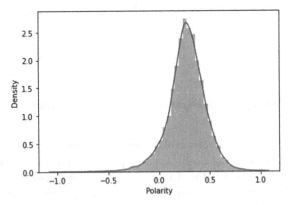

Fig. 3. Density of the "Polarity" attribute obtained with Textblob.

Figure 4 presents the correlation between "Polarity" and "Rating". We can see that the polarity rises as the rating increases, which clearly demonstrates the existence of correlation. However, we also found that the boxplots of each rating level are superimposed, which is a strong indicator of the difficulty in achieving success in creating classification models. In addition, we verified the existence of many outliers, which may not actually be, as is the case for "Rating" equal to 1, in which we verified the existence of many records with polarity between -1 and -0.65. Figure 5 presents the correlation between "Subjectivity" and "Rating". As we can see, does not seem to exist any kind of correlation between subjectivity and rating.

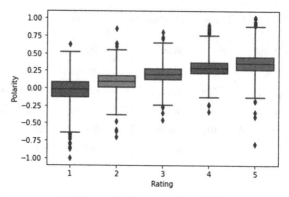

Fig. 4. Correlation between "Polarity" and "Rating".

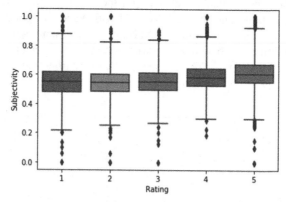

Fig. 5. Correlation between "Subjectivity" and "Rating".

To create a more simplified version of the assessment made by tourists, we generated a new attribute called "Sentiment" with a value equal to 1 for records where the "Rating" was equal to or greater than 3 and with a value equal to 0 for records where the "Rating" was less than 3. This attribute will allow us to distinguish positive ratings from negative ratings.

We also carried out important preprocessing activities that allowed us to prepare the dataset and discover some important aspects. First, we put all the corpus in lowercase. Then, we tokenize all the corpus and performed the lemmatization and removed all the punctuation. In addition, we used other techniques that did not allow us to obtain better results, such as: removing stopwords, stemming and considering only the characters of the alphabet. Finally, we used the MinMaxScaler to normalize the data.

2.4   Computational Techniques

Considering the objective of this work, we believed that it would be important to test the results that would be possible to obtain with different algorithms, both as classification methods and as regression methods. We anticipated that if algorithms as classification methods failed due to previously identified limitations that algorithms as regression methods could be an acceptable alternative in the context of the objective of this work. The algorithms used were: Logistic Regression, Random Forest, Decision Tree, K-nearest neighbors and Bidirectional Long/Short -Term Memory. The first 4 used the Scikit-learn library and the last one used the Keras library.

2.5 Tests and Evaluation

Several experiments were carried out with the selected algorithms to tune parameters for optimization. However, no significant differences were found, ending up with the default configuration in the used libraries. To improve the estimated performance of the ML models we performed cross validation with 5 repetitions.

We defined 6 different scenarios to create models. In the first 3 scenarios (#1, #2 and #3) the set of most used words that did not express feeling were removed (hotel, room, staff, did, stay, rooms, stayed, location, service, breakfast, beach, food, night, day, hotel, pool, place, people, area, restaurant, bar, went, water, bathroom, bed, restaurants, trip, desk, make, floor, room, booked, nights, hotels, say, reviews, street, lobby, took, city, think, days, husband, arrived, check and told) and in the other 3 (#4, #5 and 6) all words were kept.

For all scenarios we used the TfidfVectorizer class from the Scikit-learn library to transform the "Review_new" feature to feature vectors and we defined max_features equal to 5000. In addition, in scenarios #1 and #4 the features considered were: "Review_new", "Polarity", "Word_Count", "Char_Count", "Average_Word_Length", "Positive_Vader_Sentiment" and "Negative_Vader_Sentiment"; in scenarios #2 and #5 the features considered were: "Review_new" and "Polarity"; and in scenarios #3 and #6 only the feature "Review_new" was considered. Each algorithm was applied to each scenario with both the classification method and the regression method. Finally, all combinations were applied to a 5-class problem (Y = "Rating") and a 2-class problem (Y = "Sentiment").

Figure 6 presents the results obtained with the 5 algorithms for each of the scenarios defined with the classification method for the 5-class problem (Y = "Rating"). As can be seen, the Logistic Regression algorithm obtained the best results for all scenarios, with an accuracy always higher than 0.6, followed by the Random Forest algorithm. The other 3 algorithms obtained considerably lower results, and in the case of the BiLSTM algorithm the results were very weak, as it classified all cases with a "Rating" of 4.

Since scenario 4 was the one that allowed achieving the best results, in terms of accuracy, Table 3 presents Precision and Recall for each of the algorithms in scenario 4 with the classification method for the 5-class problem. We verified that the Logistic Regression and Random Forest algorithms present interesting results. It is possible to verify that relatively high values were obtained for the extreme cases ("Rating" = 1 and "Rating" = 5), but the quality is quite low in the classification of intermediate values.

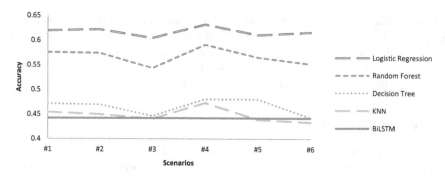

Fig. 6. Algorithms accuracy for the classification method (Y = "Rating").

Table 3. Precision and Recall for scenario 4 with the classification method (Y = "Rating").

	Precision					Recall				
	L 1	L 2	L 3	L 4	L 5	L 1	L 2	L 3	L 4	L 5
Logistic regression	0,66	0,47	0,46	0,53	0,72	0,65	0,40	0,27	0,52	0,82
Random forest	0,63	0,48	0,42	0,47	0,64	0,70	0,27	0,04	0,39	0,90
Decision tree	0,49	0,33	0,23	0,39	0,62	0,50	0,32	0,23	0,39	0,62
KNN	0,37	0,20	0,19	0,40	0,64	0,60	0,22	0,18	0,31	0,67
BiLSTM	0	0	0	0,29	0	0	0	0	1	0

Figure 7 presents the results obtained with the 5 algorithms for each of the scenarios defined with the classification method for the 2-class problem (Y = "Sentiment"). As can be seen, the results were quite good. Once again, the Logistic Regression and Random Forest algorithms obtained the best results, with the Logistic Regression algorithm showing an accuracy very close to 0.95. Decision Tree and K-Nearest Neighbors algorithms obtained reasonable results mainly in scenarios where more features were considered. The BiLSTM algorithm returned the worst results.

Table 4 presents Precision and Recall for each of the algorithms in scenario 4 with the classification method for the 2-class problem. The results presented by the Logistic Regression algorithm are quite solid. It is verified that the Recall for L 1 (Sentiment = 0) is lower than desirable, but this is probably explained by the dataset being unbalanced.

The next experiences concern the application of the algorithms to the previously presented scenarios with the regression method. Figure 8 presents the Mean Absolute Error obtained with the 5 algorithms for each of the scenarios defined with the regression method for the 5-class problem (Y = "Rating"). As it turns out most algorithms got bad results. However, the Random Forest algorithm presented very interesting results, obtaining a Mean Absolute Error of 0.69 in scenario 4 (which is quite good considering the problem in question).

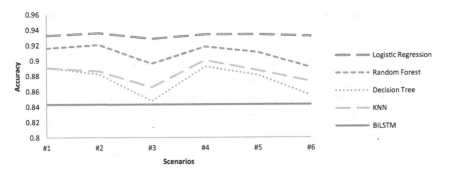

Fig. 7. Algorithms accuracy for the classification method (Y = "Sentiment").

Table 4. Precision and Recall for scenario 4 with the classification method (Y = "Sentiment").

	Precision		Recall	
	L 1	L 2	L 1	L 2
Logistic regression	0,849624	0,946389	0,702736	0,976846
Random forest	0,873541	0,922977	0,558458	0,98495
Decision tree	0,657431	0,934858	0,649254	0,937022
KNN	0,735152	0,923111	0,569652	0,96179671
BiLSTM	0	0,843061	0	1

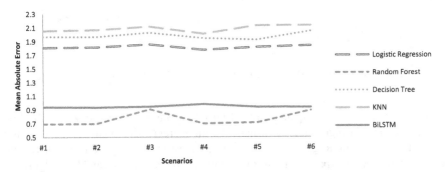

Fig. 8. Algorithms Mean Absolute Error for the regression method (Y = "Rating").

Table 5 presents Mean Squared Error, Root Mean Square Error and Mean Absolute Error for each of the algorithms in scenario 4 with the regression method for the 5-class problem. Once again, it is possible to verify that the Random Forest algorithm obtained very good results, unlike the other algorithms. Although the BiLSTM algorithm seems to give reasonable results, this only happens due to the fact that it always generates the same output and most reviews are positive.

Table 5. Mean squared error, root mean square error and mean absolute error for scenario 4 with the regression method (Y = "Rating").

	Mean squared error	Root mean square error	Mean absolute error
Logistic regression	4,140872	2,034913	1,77198
Random forest	0,733771	0,856604	0,694623
Decision tree	8,018544	2,831703	1,942417
KNN	5,818965	2,412253	2,007092
BiLSTM	1,522414	1,233862	0,978359

Figure 9 presents the Mean Absolute Error obtained with the 5 algorithms for each of the scenarios defined with the regression method for the 2-class problem (Y = "Sentiment"). We verified that in this case all algorithms, with the exception of the BiLSTM algorithm, obtained very good results.

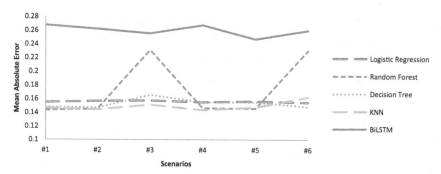

Fig. 9. Algorithms Mean Absolute Error for the regression method (Y = "Sentiment").

Table 6 presents Mean Squared Error, Root Mean Square Error and Mean Absolute Error for each of the algorithms in scenario 4 with the regression method for the 2-class problem. The Logistic Regression algorithm again presents very good results that were consistent across all experiments. In this scenario, the K-nearest neighbors algorithm also presented interesting results.

Table 6. Mean squared error, root mean square error and mean absolute error for scenario 4 with the regression method (Y = "Sentiment").

	Mean squared error	Root mean square error	Mean absolute error
Logistic regression	0,097812	0,312749	0,154837
Random forest	0,07346	0,271034	0,146088
Decision tree	0,154987	0,393684	0,154987
KNN	0,095474	0,308988	0,143406
BiLSTM	0,132327	0,363768	0,267391

3   Conclusions and Future Work

This work aimed to study strategies to automatically predict tourists' preferences regarding tourism points of interest. The method consisted in using Machine Learning algorithms and Natural Language Processing techniques on reviews that tourists make on TripAdvisor® to predict their assigned ratings. The chosen dataset had a lot of issues making it difficult to get better results (the top 3 were: being unbalanced, having comments that were not about the POI and having comments with very poor writing quality). Since it is a public dataset, we already knew it would be extremely challenging because most existing works present accuracy rates between 30% and 60%. However, we decided to use this dataset as it is a good example of the reality and type of problems that exist in the context of the topic of this work.

The work carried out allowed us to find important conclusions. First, the inclusion of sentiment analysis had a much smaller positive impact than expected. Furthermore, it was possible to notice that, for this dataset, the Vader and TextBlob models obtained a good correlation with the ratings associated with comments while Flair did not. Second, although negative comments are usually longer, the inclusion of the "Word_Count" attribute did not prove to be relevant. Third, the Logistic Regression algorithm proved to be, for classification, the one that achieved a greater accuracy, while the Random Forest algorithm, for regression, proved to be the one that obtained the smallest error. Finally, the Bidirectional LSTM algorithm obtained very poor results for both classification and regression, most likely because the dataset was not large enough. Finally, the conducted study showed that there is a much greater difficulty in predicting intermediate levels, which can have different explanations. If on the one hand, the dataset may not be sufficiently representative, for example in comments with a level 3 rating, on the other hand, the fact that people are different can also have a big impact on a scale from 1 to 5, i.e., the same words have different meanings/weights for different people and people who evaluate a POI with the same rating may express it in a completely different way.

As future work, we intend to replicate this study with a much larger dataset and in which comments/evaluations are about different points of interest. Furthermore, we intend to test with a balanced dataset. Finally, we intend to create a model to identify only those tourists who really like or dislike a particular point of interest, in which the main objective is not to identify everyone, but fundamentally not to fail those who are identified in those conditions.

Acknowledgments. This work was supported by the GrouPlanner Project under the European Regional Development Fund POCI-01–0145-FEDER-29178 and by National Funds through the FCT – Fundação para a Ciência e a Tecnologia (Portuguese Foundation for Science and Technology) within the Projects UIDB/00319/2020 and UIDB/00760/2020.

References

1. Carneiro, J., Martinho, D., Marreiros, G., Jimenez, A., Novais, P.: Dynamic argumentation in UbiGDSS. Knowl. Inf. Syst. **55**(3), 633–669 (2017). https://doi.org/10.1007/s10115-017-1093-6
2. Carneiro, J., Martinho, D., Marreiros, G., Novais, P.: Arguing with behavior influence: a model for web-based group decision support systems. Int. J. Inf. Technol. Decis. Making **18**, 517–553 (2019)
3. Carneiro, J., Alves, P., Marreiros, G., Novais, P.: A multi-agent system framework for dialogue games in the group decision-making context. In: Rocha, Á., Adeli, H., Reis, L., Costanzo, S. (eds.) New Knowledge in Information Systems and Technologies, vol. 930, pp. 437–447. Springer, Heidelberg (2019). https://doi.org/10.1007/978-3-030-16181-1_41
4. Thimm, M.: Strategic argumentation in multi-agent systems. KI-Künstliche Intelligenz **28**, 159–168 (2014). https://doi.org/10.1007/s13218-014-0307-2
5. McBurney, P., Parsons, S.: Dialogue games for agent argumentation. In: Simari, G., Rahwan, I. (eds.) Argumentation in Artificial Intelligence, pp. 261–280. Springer, Heidelberg (2009). https://doi.org/10.1007/978-0-387-98197-0_13
6. Carneiro, J., Andrade, R., Alves, P., Conceição, L., Novais, P., Marreiros, G.: A consensus-based group decision support system using a multi-agent MicroServices approach. In: Proceedings of the 19th International Conference on Autonomous Agents and MultiAgent Systems, pp. 2098–2100 (2020)
7. Carneiro, J., Alves, P., Marreiros, G., Novais, P.: Group decision support systems for current times: overcoming the challenges of dispersed group decision-making. Neurocomputing **423**, 735–746 (2021)
8. Carneiro, J., Saraiva, P., Conceição, L., Santos, R., Marreiros, G., Novais, P.: Predicting satisfaction: perceived decision quality by decision-makers in web-based group decision support systems. Neurocomputing **338**, 399–417 (2019)
9. Sun, S., Luo, C., Chen, J.: A review of natural language processing techniques for opinion mining systems. Inf. fusion **36**, 10–25 (2017)
10. Chen, X., Xie, H., Cheng, G., Poon, L.K., Leng, M., Wang, F.L.: Trends and features of the applications of natural language processing techniques for clinical trials text analysis. Appl. Sci. **10**, 2157 (2020)
11. Thanaki, J.: Python Natural Language Processing. Packt Publishing Ltd., Birmingham (2017)

Comparison of Predictive Models with Balanced Classes for the Forecast of Student Dropout in Higher Education

Vaneza Flores[1] , Stella Heras[2(✉)] , and Vicente Julián[2]

[1] National University of Moquegua (UNAM), Moquegua, Peru
vfloresg@unam.edu.pe
[2] Valencian Research Institute for Artificial Intelligence (VRAIN),
Universitat Politécnica de Valéncia (UPV), Valencia, Spain
{stehebar,vjulian}@upv.es

Abstract. Based on the premise that university student dropout is a social problem in the university ecosystem of any country, technological leverage is a way that allows us to build technological proposals to solve a poorly met need in university education systems. Under this scenario, the study presents and analyzes eight predictive models to forecast university dropout, based on data mining methods and techniques, using WEKA for its implementation, with a dataset of 4365 academic records of students from the National University of Moquegua (UNAM), in Peru. The objective is to determine which model presents the best performance indicators to forecast and hence prevent student dropout. The aim of the study is to propose and compare the accuracy of eight predictive models with balanced classes, using the SMOTE method for the generation of synthetic data. The results allow us to confirm that the predictive model based on Random Forest is the one that presents the highest accuracy and robustness.

Keywords: University dropout · Predictive model · Data mining · SMOTE

1 Introduction

The phenomenon of university student dropout has been a research topic for several decades [9]. At present, this problem has become more important due to the negative effects caused by COVID-19. With the pandemic, university dropouts have risen, as reported by UNESCO, with around 23.4 million students dropping out of a university in Latin America and the Caribbean regions [28]. However, according to [22] and [8] there is no general consensus on the definition of dropout in relation to university studies. Following Tinto's theory [38], desertion is defined as the procedure carried out by the university student when he/she voluntarily or forcibly abandons the studies, due to negative or positive influence of internal or external factors.

© Springer Nature Switzerland AG 2021
F. De La Prieta et al. (Eds.): PAAMS Workshops 2021, CCIS 1472, pp. 139–152, 2021.
https://doi.org/10.1007/978-3-030-85710-3_12

The deficient detection of the dropout of students in higher education is an important problem for the managers of the world's universities [7,21,27]. The situation is exacerbated in countries with low cultural and economic levels and hence, counteracting the consequences of university student dropout is studied worldwide [36,37]. Consequently, research has emerged in various areas such as psychology, economics, sociology, health, education, computer science and others, where it is clearly evident that there is a significant number of students who drop out from these type of university degrees. Many studies establish that the critical point where student dropout is manifested is in the first year of university studies [13,26,29]. However, student dropout is a phenomenon that can manifest itself in any academic period [6,32], for which corrective and preventive measures should be proposed aimed at university retention.

Dropout, typified as a social problem in the university ecosystem, has negative effects in the socio-economic, institutional, academic and individual environment [28]. In this sense it is necessary to have adequate tools that allow the detection of student dropout in higher education institutions. Therefore, taking technology as an ally for solving student dropout problems and considering the excessive volume of data administered by computer systems in universities, our approach is framed in a technological solution based on Educational Data Sciences (EDC) [30,31], specifically in Educational Data Mining (EDM) [17], a discipline widely studied by researchers to address the analysis of education and learning in university students such as in [1,5,19,33].

In this work, several methods and EDM techniques are applied and evaluated for the construction of a predictive model that allows predicting student dropout at the National University of Moquegua (UNAM), a university licensed by the Superintendency of National University Education (SUNEDU) in Peru. The model uses a dataset of 4,365 student academic records, from 2008 to 2019, provided by the Directorate of Academic Affairs and Services (DASA) of the UNAM. The techniques correspond to the classification of Decision Trees, Decision Rules and Bayesian Networks, using WEKA as a Data Mining (DM) tool.

There are other authors that have investigated the application of these techniques to detect dropout risks. Section 3 shows how our model outperforms these proposals. In addition, when these predictive models are built with real data from the university ecosystem, it has been observed that the classes are unbalanced. Thus, researchers recommend carrying out the adequate balancing of the classes as future work [15], but few follow this approach [24]. This study implements this recommendation and applies the *SMOTE* algorithm for class balancing with synthetic data.

The rest of the paper is structured as follows: in Sect. 2 the proposal of the model is developed using the first three phases of the CRISP-DM methodology (Cross Standard Process of Data Mining)[1], which basically defines the DM objectives aligned to the institutional objectives of the UNAM, and the preparation of the data that will be supplied to the DM model; in Sect. 3, several models

---

[1] https://www.the-modeling-agency.com/crisp-dm.pdf.

based on DM are implemented and evaluated; finally, in Sect. 4 conclusions and future work are proposed.

2   Predictive Model

For this study, three DM techniques (Decision Trees, Decision Rules and Bayesian Networks) and eight classification algorithms were applied to create the predictive models. These algorithms have been reported as suitable for this type of classification problem in the literature. The description of the algorithms is shown in Table 1.

Table 1. Algorithms definition

DM technique	Algorithm	Description
Decision trees	Random forest	Builds a forest of trees in a random way, where each tree created is generated from a set of sample data taken at random. Likewise, each node is created randomly, prioritizing the elements that report a better grouping of the data contained in the sample [23]
	Random tree	Builds a tree based on the randomly chosen K attributes at each node, with no pruning performed for this action. You can calculate the estimate of the probabilities of the class aligned to a retention set [14]
	J48	Also known as C4.5 decision tree. It compares classification algorithms for the predictions, generating a pruned or unpruned decision tree [35]
	REP tree	Builds a tree containing K randomly selected attributes for each node of the tree without pruning [14]
Decision rules	JRIP	Builds a rule with the Ripper algorithm, including heuristic global optimization of the rule set [11]
	OneR	Builds a rule and uses a 1R classifier, uses the minimum error attribute for the predictive process, and then the numerical attributes are discretized [16]
Bayesian Networks	Bayes Net	Builds a Bayesian Network using various search algorithms and quality measures. It provides data structures (network structure, conditional probability distributions, etc.) and learning algorithms of the Bayes Network such as K2 and B [14]
	Naive Bayes	Builds the Naive Bayes probabilistic classifier. This classifier can use core density estimators of the analyzed data, in order to improve performance if the normality assumption is very incorrect. In some cases, numerical attributes are handled after a supervised discretization process [14]

In addition, SMOTE (Synthetic Minority Oversampling Method), a technique proposed by Chawla [10], is used to generate new instances of the minority class through the interpolation of the values of the minority instances closest to a given class. The set of data created is also known as synthetic data [10,20,25]. With this technique, we are able to solve the problem of data imbalance, which consists in the predominance of certain values in the data and the scarcity or absence of others, which makes it difficult or impossible to extract information or the objective analysis of the model. Synthetic data is generated in two steps: 1) calculate the value of the difference between each minority data point and its closest neighbor; and 2) the result is multiplied by a random number between 0 and 1, and the result is added to the sample considered to generate the synthetic pattern.

To build our model, we develop in this section phases 1 to 3 of the CRISP-DM Methodology (a standard process model for data mining) [41], where the objectives of the DM project are designed in line with the institutional objectives of the university, the collection and the understanding of the collected data is framed in the objectives of DM, and the process of preparing the data is carried out so that data can be used as a supply in the models based on DM techniques.

2.1 Phase 1: Business Understanding

The objectives and requirements of the DM project are proposed from the perspective of university strategic planning, in order to predict student dropout at UNAM. The main outputs of this process resulting from the generic tasks of the CRISP-DM methodology are:

Determining Business Objectives. The UNAM presented in its Educational Model for the year 2020 the following institutional strategic objectives: 1) Improve academic training for university students; 2) Promote formative, scientific, technological and humanistic research in the university community; 3) Strengthen institutional management; 4) Improve cultural outreach and social projection activities; and 5) Implement risk management. Objective 1 is selected, since it well aligned to the problem of university student dropout. Starting from the premise that academic performance is the result of an educational process or academic training, likewise, the factors that negatively influence academic performance put at risk the permanence of the university student or the delay in their studies [2,18,40]. Therefore, student dropout is closely related to the academic training given at a university.

Determining DM Project Objectives. The proposed objectives are:

- General objective (GO): To propose a predictive model based on DM techniques that allows, from the input data, to detect student dropout at UNAM.
- Specific objective 1 (SO1): Determine the factors prior to the student's admission to university that explain student dropout at UNAM.
- Specific objective 2 (SO2): Determine the factors of the student's university academic context that explain student dropout at UNAM.

- Specific objective 3 (SO3): Determine the student's social factors that explain student dropout at UNAM.
- Specific objective 4 (SO4): Train a predictive model based on DM to detect student dropout at UNAM.

2.2 Phase 2: Data Understanding

In this phase, an analytical work process is carried out. The objective is to start the exploration of the data of the UNAM academic system. The recognition of the attributes required for the construction of the dataset aimed at student dropout is organized into three categories: factors prior to university admission, factors of the university academic context, and the social factors of the students.

Gathering Initial Data. As a starting point, the theoretical model of Díaz [12] has been considered to have a mapping of the possible factors associated with university dropouts. However, knowing the limitations in the data registration of UNAM students, only three factors associated with dropout have been considered, as proposed in [4, 13, 15, 21, 24, 34, 39].

- Social factors: Gender; Marital status; Age; Economic dependency, and Place of birth.
- Factors prior to university admission: Type of educational institution of origin; Location of the educational institution of origin; University admission modality; University entrance note; Choice of area of university studies; and Place of birth.
- Academic factors: Degree; Curriculum plan; Subsidiary; Semesters in progress (for students); Semester of graduation (for graduates); Semesters of permanence; Last student average; Average of graduation; Repetition by number of courses; and Re-entry to another degree at the same university.

Of these 21 attributes requested to the UNAM's Directorate of Academic Affairs and Services (DASA) to perform this study, only 15 were obtained, in some cases with more than 80% incomplete or missing data. The information provided contained the record of the admitted students, current students, and graduates of the UNAM, from 2008 to 2019. Each of the records was anonymized to fulfill privacy requirements.

Dataset Description. The description of the data is presented in Table 2, where the attributes provided by DASA are detailed. Note that some of these data were not initially requested, but still used to generate new useful attributes for the design of the predictive model.

Table 2. UNAM dataset description

ID	Attribute	Description
1	Registration number	Number generated to identify students and observe privacy requirements
2	Gender	Gender of the student
3	Date of birth	Student's date of birth
4	Marital status	Marital status of the student (many records appear incomplete)
5	Degree	Study program chosen by the student
6	Faculty	Faculty where the study program chosen by the student is taught
7	Curricular plan	Curricular plan of the study program
8	Student class	If the student dropped out or is continuing with his/her university studies
9	Curriculum change	Data for the year in which the enrollment change was made (if any)
10	Current branch of studies	Current area where the student is enrolled
11	Admission campus	Campus where the student entered
12	Mode of admission	Type of admission to the university through the ordinary or extraordinary admission process
13	Country	Country where the university student was born
14	Department	Department where the university student was born
15	Province	Province where the university student was born
16	District	District where the university student was born
17	School	Educational institution where he/she finished secondary school
18	District of the school	District where the school is located
19	Type of school	The type of the secondary school (public or private)
20	Year of completion of secondary studies	Year in which secondary studies are completed
21	Admission campus code	Code that indicates the university entrance campus
22	Description of the campus entry code	Describes the campus (Moquegua, Ilo and Ichuña) in relation to the code entered
23	Semester entrance	Semester of entrance to the university
24	Semester of last registration	Semester of last registration
25	Semester of graduation	Semester of university graduation
26	Last accumulated average	Average cumulative grade of the student

2.3   Phase 3: Data Curation

In this phase, the dataset provided in the previous phase was used to perform the selection of relevant data, aligned to the identified problem, to be used later in phase 4 as input for the data mining techniques. The goal in this phase is to get a curated dataset. For this purpose, the WEKA tool was used, which allowed data cleaning activities, elimination of incomplete records, actions to complete missing data and, finally, the construction of the target class, which in our case is called the *Student State*.

Data Construction. This action entails the creation of several attributes (School Egress Age, Admission Year, Admission Semester, Semesters Of Permanence, Admission Age, Years Between Exit From College To Admission To University, And New Application) from the additional data provided by DASA.

We proceeded to eliminate 21 instances that corresponded to transient students coming from national or foreign student mobility programmes, so the dataset was reduced to 4344 instances. The attribute Registration number was removed, since it does not provide useful information for the construction of the predictive model, reducing the number of attributes to 25.

The dataset was normalised in a standard numerical format for the 25 attributes. Additionally a data dictionary was designed to identify those attributes that presented a numerical category (e.g. Gender, Marital Status, Degree, Faculty). Missing data, or those with inconsistent or incomplete information, were curated with an empty value.

It was identified that the attribute Student class contained information to build the target class, which we named Student State, setting two tags: Not dropout and Dropout.

In general, few missing data were detected. However, for the attributes with these anomalies, the fields were filled with the average value of the attribute.

Data Integration. The dataset shown an imbalance of the Student State attribute (target class), (2113 "Not Dropout" vs 947 "Dropout"). As a corrective measure, the SMOTE algorithm was applied to generate synthetic data that allows balancing both classes. As result, 4756 student records were obtained. With this new dataset the classifiers for the creation of the predictive model (phase 4) were implemented.

Data Formatting. As a result of the previous steps, the dataset for data analysis was obtained. Based on this process, actions were carried out to order the instances and attributes, configuration of the attribute value labels, standardize the values to a numerical format, elimination of commas, quotation marks and a colon in the analyzed fields, activities which favor the correct development of the modeling processes, obtaining as a result a subset of 18 selected attributes for the construction of the predictive model, as shown in Table 3.

Table 3. Attributes selected and grouped in the factors associated with student dropout

Factors associated with student dropout	Name of the selected attribute
Factors prior to university admission	1. School type
	2. College graduation age
	3. Entry Mode
	4. Faculty
	5. Years Between Leaving College to Entering University
Factors of the academic context	6. School type
	6. Year of Admission
	7. Semester Admission
	8. Campus Admission
	9. Current Campus Studies
	10. Degree
	11. Curriculum Plan
	12. Curriculum Change
	13. Last Accumulated Average
	14. Semesters of Permanence
	15. New Application
Social factors	16. Gender
	17. Age of Admission
Target Class	18. Student State

3   Model Evaluation

Continuing with the CRISP-DM methodology, in this section phases 4, 5 and 6 are developed. The purpose is to find the most appropriate modeling technique for the DM project that solves the institutional and DM objectives set out in phase 1, to later be deployed in the UNAM.

3.1   Phase 4: Modelling

To develop the predictive model for the UNAM, we used 8 DM techniques, among those proposed in the literature. The purpose is to validate previous results, that report the best indicators of accuracy, performance and robustness compared to those that are less used or recommended. The DM techniques used are: Decision Trees (Random Forest, Random Tree, J48 and REP Tree), Decision Rules (JRIP, OneR), and Bayesian Networks (Bayes Net, Naive Bayes). Once our model was trained, we performed a cross-validation test using WEKA, a tool widely used to train DM classifiers. Stratified cross-validation (10%) with 10 folds was performed. We got the classification results provided in Table 4, with the accuracy, true and false positives and precision values.

3.2   Phase 5: DM Techniques Evaluation

Analyzing the performance measures of the eight predictive models with the parameters accuracy, area under the ROC curve (AUC), and the percentage of correctly classified instances (ICC), Table 4 shows that the best accuracy result was obtained by the Random Forest algorithm with a value of 0.97, which indicates that the predictive model performed a correct classification of 4,604 records out of a total of 4,756 instances, being OneR the one that got the wrost result.

Table 4. DM techniques evaluation

Algorithms	ICC (%)	ROC Area	Dropout	TP	FP	Precision	Accuracy
Random forest	**96.78**	**0.99**	Not Dropout	0.96	0.03	0.97	**0.97**
			Dropout	0.97	0.04	0.96	
Random tree	93.06	0.95	Not dropout	0.92	0.05	0.95	0.93
			Dropout	0.95	0.08	0.91	
J48	95.63	0.98	Not dropout	0.95	0.03	0.96	0.96
			Dropout	0.96	0.05	0.95	
REPTree	95.40	0.98	Not dropout	0.95	0.04	0.96	0.95
			Dropout	0.96	0.05	0.95	
JRIzP	94.74	0.96	Not dropout	0.94	0.04	0.96	0.95
			Dropout	0.96	0.06	0.94	
OneR	79,00	0.79	Not dropout	0.74	0.16	0.82	0.79
			Dropout	0.84	0.26	0.76	
Bayes Net	89.40	0.96	Not dropout	0.92	0.14	0.87	0.89
			Dropout	0.86	0.07	0.92	
Naive Bayes	89.47	0.96	Not dropout	0.92	0.13	0.87	0.89
			Dropout	0.86	0.07	0.92	

Regarding the ROC area, Random Forest obtained a 0.993, the best value of the ROC Area, in contrast with OneR with a value of 0.79. The scientific literature indicates that the best value is the one with a tendency to 1. This result allowed to qualify the predictive model as a predictive proposal with greater capacity to discriminate against students with a dropout profile. Likewise, it supports the quality of the entry values.

Finally, for the percentage of correctly classified instances (ICC), Random Forest obtained a value of 96.78%, in contrast is OneR with a value of 79.00%. This result is interpreted as the ability or robustness of the Random Forest algorithm to correctly classify the instances in the dataset.

For the selection of the best attributes, five attribute selection algorithms implemented in Weka were used[2] and for the evaluation of the attribute quality to discriminate the target class, the Ranker attribute search method was

---

[2] Attribute selection algorithms used: OneR Attribute Evaluation, Relief Factor Attribute Evaluation, Info Gain Attribute Evaluation, Gain Ratio Attribute Evaluation, and Symmetrical Uncertainty Attribute Evaluation.

used. These algorithms remove those attributes that are irrelevant or have little influence on the target class (output variable) of the predictive model. The results reported that all attributes of the factors associated with student dropout appeared with a frequency greater than 2 in the results of the selection algorithms, specifically, in all five selection algorithms. Therefore, it was concluded that all attributes from Table 3 had a significant impact on student dropout from UNAM and were 100% relevant to predict the state (Dropout/Not dropout) of the target class (Student State) of the predictive model.

Finally, Table 5 compares the performance of our models with those trained in other previous related work (results as published by the authors), illustrating the improvement achieved with the application of our SMOTE balancing technique.

Table 5. Comparison of our model with other related work

Authors	Evaluated techniques	Best technique	Balances data (Y/N)	Dataset size	Accuracy	ROC Area	ICC (%)
Flores, Heras y Julián (our model)	Random forest, random tree, J48, REP tree, JRIP, OneR, Bayes Net, Naive Bayes	Random forest	Y	4365	0.97	0.99	96.78
Behr et al. (2020) [4]	Random forest	Random forest	N	17910	–	0.86	–
Beaulac and Rosenthal (2019) [3]	Random forest	Random forest	N	38842	0.79	–	–
Solis et al. (2018) [34]	Random Forest, Neural networks, SVMs, logistic regression	Random forest	N	80527	–	–	91.00
Hernández-Leal et al. (2018) [15]	Random tree, J48, REP tree, JRip, OneR	J48	N	655	–	–	95.43
Maya et al. (2017) [21]	Multilayer perceptron, random forest, J48, random tree	Random forest	N	670	0.88	–	85.5
Miranda y Guzmán (2017) [24]	Neural networks, Decision trees, Bayesian Nets	Decision trees	Y	9195	–	0.74	82
Torres et al. (2016) [39]	Random forest, ZeroR, J48, simple CART, Naive Bayes, Bayes Net, multilayer perceptron	Random forest	N	5547	0.89	0.91	–
Eckert y Suénaga (2015) [13]	J48, Bayes Net (TAN), OneR	J48	N	855	0.79	–	80.23

3.3 Phase 6: Exploitation and Deployment

Once the predictive model has been created and validated to predict student dropout at UNAM, the knowledge derived from the model must be deployed. In this phase the decision maker at the university can take actions based on the data obtained. For example, if the record of a student who is currently in the academic semester is entered and the model predicts his/her dropout, the profile obtained (characteristics) is analyzed to implement active retention protocols. Additionally, actions must be taken to monitor and maintain the model. One of the advantages of this action is to have a baseline for each academic period on the subject of dropping out and to control the goals achieved at the end of the academic year. Additionally, sharing with the university community the results obtained by applying the predictive model could comfort the student by feeling sure that their academic performance is being monitored for activate retention strategies that help them lead a good track record and progress in their studies.

4 Conclusion and Future Work

This paper shows that training a predictive model based on DM with a dataset with attributes that characterize students from higher education studies allows detecting student dropout at UNAM. Eight classification algorithms (Random Forest, Random Tree, J48, REPTree, JRIP, OneR, Bayes Net and Naive Bayes). Subsequently, performance measures were used (accuracy, ROC area, ICC) to evaluate the models. The results show that Random Forest is the best classification algorithm to detect student dropout at UNAM, outperforming the results obtained in related works.

For the construction of predictive models based on classification algorithms (DM techniques), an adequate balancing of the dataset was carried out, allowing to match the target class (Student State) and obtain classification results with greater accuracy. For this case, the SMOTE algorithm was used. The process allowed to match the two labels of the target class in a dataset, generating a synthetic data to standardize the class in two groups (Dropout/Does not dropout).

As current and future work, a more comprehensive comparison of predictive models using other Neural Networks techniques is being carried out with the dataset UNAM's DASA dataset (i.e. Logistic regression, Support vector machines and Nearest neighbor) to know the accuracy, performance and robustness of their results for this specific problem. Furthermore, we plan to analyse the extent to which student characteristics lead to dropout (e.g. whether there is a dominant gender in dropout or whether there are degrees more prone to dropout).

Acknowledgements. This work is partially supported by the Spanish Government project TIN2017-89156-R, and the Valencian Government project PROMETEO/2018/002. The research was developed thanks to the support of the National University of Moquegua, which provided the information for the creation of the dataset.

References

1. Abe, K.: Data mining and machine learning applications for educational big data in the university. In: 2019 IEEE International Conference on Dependable, Autonomous and Secure Computing, International Conference on Pervasive Intelligence and Computing, International Conference on Cloud and Big Data Computing, International Conference on Cyber Science and Technology Congress (DASC/PiCom/CBDCom/CyberSciTech), pp. 350–355. IEEE (2019)
2. Arias-Gómez, D., Durán-Aponte, E.: Persistencia académica en un programa de nivelación universitario venezolano: caso universidad simón bolívar. Rev. Digit. de Inv. en Docencia Universitaria 11(2), 289–307 (2017)
3. Beaulac, C., Rosenthal, J.S.: Predicting university students' academic success and major using random forests. Res. High. Educ. 60(7), 1048–1064 (2019)
4. Behr, A., Giese, M., Theune, K., et al.: Early prediction of university dropouts-a random forest approach. Jahrbücher für Nationalökonomie und Statistik, 1(ahead-of-print) (2020)
5. Bharara, S., Sabitha, S., Bansal, A.: Application of learning analytics using clustering data mining for students' disposition analysis. Educ. Inf. Technol. 23(2), 957–984 (2018)
6. Carvajal, C.M., González, J.A., Sarzoza, S.J.: Variables sociodemográficas y académicas explicativas de la deserción de estudiantes en la facultad de ciencias naturales de la universidad de playa ancha (chile). Formación universitaria 11(2), 3–12 (2018)
7. Castillo-Sánchez, M., Gamboa-Araya, R., Hidalgo-Mora, R.: Factores que influyen en la deserción y reprobación de estudiantes de un curso universitario de matemáticas. Uniciencia 34(1), 219–245 (2020)
8. Castro, Y.G., Durán, O.M., Zamudio, M.T.: Riesgos de deserción en las universidades virtuales de colombia, frente a las estrategias de retención. Libre Empresa 14(2), 177–197 (2017)
9. Castro-Montoya, B.A., Lopera-Gómez, C.M., Manrique-Hernández, R.D., Gonzalez-Gómez, D.: Modelo de riesgos competitivos para deserción y graduación en estudiantes universitarios de programas de pregrado de una universidad privada de medellín (colombia). Formación universitaria 14(1), 81–98 (2021)
10. Chawla, N.V., Bowyer, K.W., Hall, L.O., Kegelmeyer, W.P.: Smote: synthetic minority over-sampling technique. J. Artif. Intell. Res. 16, 321–357 (2002)
11. Cohen, W.W.: Fast effective rule induction. In: Machine Learning Proceedings 1995, pp. 115–123. Elsevier (1995)
12. Díaz Peralta, C.: Modelo conceptual para la deserción estudiantil universitaria chilena. Estudios Pedagógicos (Valdivia) 34(2), 65–86 (2008)
13. Eckert, K.B., Suénaga, R.: Análisis de deserción-permanencia de estudiantes universitarios utilizando técnica de clasificación en minería de datos. Formación Universitaria 8(5), 03–12 (2015)
14. Frank, E., Hall, M.A., Witten, I.H.: The WEKA workbench. Morgan Kaufmann (2016)
15. Hernández-Leal, E.J., Quintero-Lorza, D.P., Escobar-Naranjo, J.C., Ramírez-Gómez, J.S., Duque-Méndez, N.D.: Educational data mining for the analysis of student desertion. Learn. Anal. Latin Am. 2018(2231), 51–60 (2018)
16. Holte, R.C.: Very simple classification rules perform well on most commonly used datasets. Mach. Learn. 11(1), 63–90 (1993)

17. Huebner, R.A.: A survey of educational data-mining research. Res. High. Educ. J. **19** (2013)
18. Kinsumba, P.A., Fernández, R.L., Alonso, M.J.B.: Análisis de factores relacionados con el éxito académico en la universidad agostinho neto. Luz **16**(3), 4–15 (2017)
19. Kurdi, M.M., Al-Khafagi, H., Elzein, I.: Mining educational data to analyze students' behavior and performance. In: 2018 JCCO Joint International Conference on ICT in Education and Training, International Conference on Computing in Arabic, and International Conference on Geocomputing (JCCO: TICET-ICCA-GECO), pp. 1–5. IEEE (2018)
20. Maciejewski, T., Stefanowski, J.: Local neighbourhood extension of smote for mining imbalanced data. In: 2011 IEEE Symposium on Computational Intelligence and Data Mining (CIDM), pp. 104–111. IEEE (2011)
21. Maya, N.E.R., Alfaro, A.J.J., Hernandez, L.A.R., Carranza, B.A.S., Garduno, J.K.R.: Data mining: a scholar dropout predictive model. In: 2017 IEEE Mexican Humanitarian Technology Conference (MHTC), pp. 89–93. IEEE (2017)
22. Merlino, A., Ayllón, S., Escanés, G.: Variables que influyen en la deserción de estudiantes universitarios de primer año. construcción de índices de riesgo de abandono/variables that influence first year university students' dropout rates. construction of dropout risk indexes. Actualidades Investigativas en Educación **11**(2) (2011)
23. Meza-Obando, F.: Estimating the redshift of galaxies from their photometric colors using machine learning methods. A first approach to Acoustic Characterization of Costa Rican Children's Speech
24. Miranda, M.A., Guzmán, J.: Análisis de la deserción de estudiantes universitarios usando técnicas de minería de datos. Formación Universitaria **10**(3), 61–68 (2017)
25. Moreno, J., Rodríguez, D., Sicilia, M., Riquelme, J., Ruiz, R.: SMOTE-I: mejora del algoritmo SMOTE para balanceo de clases minoritarias. Actas de los Talleres de las Jornadas de Ingeniería del Software y Bases de Datos **3**(1) (2009)
26. Muñoz-Olano, J.F., Hurtado-Parrado, C.: Effects of goal clarification on impulsivity and academic procrastination of college students. Rev. Latinoamericana de Psicología **49**(3), 173–181 (2017)
27. Parrino, M.C.: Aristas de la problemática de la deserción universitaria (2005)
28. Pedró, F.: Covid-19 y educación superior en américa latina y el caribe: efectos, impactos y recomendaciones políticas. Análisis Carolina **36**(1), 1–15 (2020)
29. Pérez, A.M., Escobar, C.R., Toledo, M.R., Gutierrez, L.B., Reyes, G.M.: Prediction model of first-year student desertion at universidad bernardo o' higgins (ubo). Educ. Pesqui. **44**, e172094–e172094 (2018)
30. Proaño, J.P.Z., Villamar, V.C.P.: Systematic mapping study of literature on educational data mining to determine factors that affect school performance. In: 2018 International Conference on Information Systems and Computer Science (INCIS-COS), pp. 239–245. IEEE (2018)
31. Raju, R., Kalaiselvi, N., Divya, I., Selvarani, A., et al.: Educational data mining: A comprehensive study. In: 2020 International Conference on System, Computation, Automation and Networking (ICSCAN), pp. 1–5. IEEE (2020)
32. Ruiz-Ramírez, R., García-Cué, J.L., Pérez-Olvera, M.A.: Causas y consecuencias de la deserción escolar en el bachillerato: Caso universidad autónoma de sinaloa. Ra Ximhai **10**(5), 51–74 (2014)
33. Shrestha, S., Pokharel, M.: Machine learning algorithm in educational data. In: 2019 Artificial Intelligence for Transforming Business and Society (AITB), vol. 1, pp. 1–11. IEEE (2019)

34. Solís, M., Moreira, T., Gonzalez, R., Fernandez, T., Hernandez, M.: In: Perspectives to predict dropout in university students with machine learning, pp. 1–6. IEEE (2018)
35. Suca, C., Córdova, A., Condori, A., Cayra, J., Sulla, J.: Comparación de algoritmos de clasificación para la predicción de casos de obesidad infantil. Universidad Nacional de San Agustín, Perú (2016)
36. Taylor, J.D., Miller, T.K.: Necessary components for evaluating minority retention programs. NASPA J. **39**(3), 266–283 (2002)
37. Thompson, P.: Deserción universitaria. análisis de los egresados de la carrera de administración. cohorte 2011–2016. Población y Desarrollo (45), 107–112 (2017)
38. Tinto, V.: Dropout from higher education: a theoretical synthesis of recent research. Rev. Educ. Res. **45**(1), 89–125 (1975)
39. Torres, C.Z., Ramos, C.A., Moraga, J.L.: Estudio de variables que influyen en la deserción de estudiantes universitarios de primer año, mediante minería de datos. Ciencia Amazónica (Iquitos) **6**(1), 73–84 (2016)
40. Vilalta Alonso, J.A., Becerra Alonso, M.J., Lau Fernández, R.: El éxito académico en el primer año de la carrera de ingeniería industrial y su vínculo con factores académicos previos. Páginas de Educación **13**(1), 42–57 (2020)
41. Wirth, R., Hipp, J.: CRISP-DM: towards a standard process model for data mining. In: Proceedings of the 4th International Conference on the Practical Applications of Knowledge Discovery and Data Mining., vol. 1. Springer-Verlag London, UK (2000)

Causal Interventions and Argumentation-Based Frameworks: Formalization of "What If" Scenarios

Esteban Guerrero[(✉)] [iD]

Department of Computing Science, Umeå University, Umeå, Sweden
esteban@cs.umu.se

Abstract. Argumentation-based frameworks are used as a decision-making mechanism for software agents. This paper aims to investigate how a formal argumentation framework is affected when the underlying causal relationships of its theory is modified in counterfactual situations, the so-called *"what if"* scenarios. In contrast to previous approaches where *causality* relationships were derived from static probabilistic distributions, we address scenarios where causal models are intervened. Two novel contributions in the synergy between argumentation and causal theories are presented: 1) we characterize interventions and their consequences in causal argumentation frameworks; and 2) we introduce an account of the so-called *sequential interventions* that give a characterization of manipulations on time.

Keywords: Causal theory · Argumentation theory · Counterfactuals

1 Motivation

"What if I increase my physical activity?" can be one of the most common questions that most middle-aged adults ask themselves to speculate (dream) about their health condition. *Causal models* are mathematical objects that provide interpretations of queries such as the earlier "what if..." in a specific domain. Briefly, variables of a causal model have causal effects on others, such effect is modeled by a set of *structural equations* that represent a distinct mechanism (or law) in the world, which can be modified by *external actions* without altering the others [11]. Such structural equations when represented in a formal language (*e.g.* first-order dynamic logic [12] etc.), they fulfill a set of *axiomatizations* [7] useful for designing reasoning mechanisms about causality. Indeed, the use of direct mappings from structural causal equations to propositional languages as knowledge representation is not new (*e.g.* [17]). In the *formal argumentation theory* (as a computational decision-making approach) literature, the use of mappings from structural causal representations to knowledge representations, although common (*e.g.* [16]), has not rigorously considered the formal treatment of causal models dynamics, particularly in *causal interventions* the so-called *counterfactuals* (i.e. "what if..." scenarios). The conception and use of a causal relationship

© Springer Nature Switzerland AG 2021
F. De La Prieta et al. (Eds.): PAAMS Workshops 2021, CCIS 1472, pp. 153–164, 2021.
https://doi.org/10.1007/978-3-030-85710-3_13

as a probabilistic distribution have substantial research in the argumentation theory literature (*e.g.* [13]). However, during an intervention the underlying probabilistic distribution changes, and individual probabilities for those intervened variables are non-identifiable neither estimable from frequency data alone [24]. In practice, such probabilistic argumentation frameworks capturing causal relationships may not be successful in the characterization of interventions. An additional problem arises when a variable with a non-identifiable causal interpretation (*i.e.* not sufficient evidence) is added to such mapping, but it has a deductive contradictory interpretation (*e.g.* $\alpha \equiv \neg\beta$). The solution for this problem from a causal theory perspective is straightforward (see [24]), however, from the *deductive systems* perspective it requires a computational mechanism to handle potential inconsistencies among mapped variables.

This paper aims to provide a first characterization of the effects of causal models interventions on argumentation frameworks. We provide a general account of the behavior of causal argumentation frameworks under different counterfactual situations, such as *sequential interventions*, which are continuous modifications of the underlying causal model in several variables.

We depart from general axiomatizations of causal models [7] and from a structural argumentation theory perspective of *deductive systems* (see [9]), and we propose a *causal argumentation framework* to investigate interventions. In summary, in addition to our framework, two technical contributions are presented: 1) a characterization of interventions specifying different non-addressed issues impacting argumentation frameworks, and 2) we provide an account of sequential interventions, which provides a characterization of manipulations on time. Finally, we exemplify our theoretical findings using statistical data from a large database (more than 12 million of registers) of human activity behavior in northern Sweden [18].

This paper introduces a causal argumentation framework in Sect. 2, then in Sect. 3 we present how interventions impact an argumentation framework. We exemplify our contributions in Sect. 4, and we provide a technical discussion in Sect. 5. Conclusions and future work is presented in Sect. 6.

2   Framework to Build Consistent Causal Scenarios

In this section, a framework to formalize the concept of a "what if"-scenario in terms of structural argumentation theory.

We start with a mapping function between a causal model defined as a tuple $M = \langle U, V, F \rangle$, and a propositional language $\mathcal{L}$, which allows us to form a theory Σ where atoms of the form x_1, y_1 can build complex structures (statements) about a particular causal hypothesis using basic operations: $\wedge$ (conjunction), $\neg$ (negation) and $\vdash$ (logical inference). We denote a mapped variable from a structural equation in M to a Σ with the character (*). Additionally, we use the symbol $\vdash_c$ to represent a causal entailment that fulfills a set of axioms [7]. More formally, let $M = \langle U, V, Fx \rangle$ be a causal model. Our mapping $\mathcal{M}$ is a tuple $\langle \Sigma, P \rangle$ where $\Sigma \subseteq U^* \cup V^*$ and P is a probabilistic function defined over the domain of M.

In scenarios where additional variables are added with no-causal evidence but a speculative or hypothesized relationship of deduction is presented, we can use formal argumentation to build structures with a *support-conclusion* form. We call those argument-based structures *causal argumentation-based hypothesis* *chyps* that are tuples $chyp = \langle \underbrace{S}_{support}, \underbrace{\sigma, P_{\sigma'}}_{conclusion} \rangle$.

Definition 1 (Causal argument-based hypotheses). *Let us consider a $\mathcal{M}$ framework with $S \subseteq \Sigma$ and $\sigma \in \Sigma$. A causal argumentation-based hypothesis is the tuple $chyp = \langle S, \sigma, P_{\sigma'} \rangle$ in which the following conditions holds:*

1. *S is consistent*
2. *$S \vdash \sigma$*
3. *$S \vdash_c \sigma$; and*
4. *$\nexists S' \subset S$ such that $S' \vdash \sigma$*
5. *$P_{\sigma'}$ is the conditional probability between S and σ*

Where S is called support and the tuple $(\sigma, P_{\sigma'})$ is the conclusion. Condition 3 and 4 ensure that σ is caused and deductively inferred from a support S.

A *chyp* is a minimal specification of the causal behavior of a mapped variable in a causal model, containing its inference entailment nature, and the evidence supporting a deductive conclusion with its associated probability distribution $P_{\sigma'}$. Let us denote $Ch(\Sigma)$, the set of all causal hypotheses built from Σ. *chyp* structures can have logical *incompatibilities* that leads us to the notion of *chyp* attack:

Definition 2. *Let $chyp_1, chyp_2 \in Ch$ be two chyps, we say that $chyp_1$ attacks $chyp_2$iff. i) $\exists \sigma \in Supp(chyp_2)$ s.t. $\sigma \equiv \neg Conc(chyp_1)$, and/or ii) $Conc(chyp_2) \equiv \neg Conc(chyp_1)$.*

We use a function $att(chyp_a, chyp_b)$ that represents any type (i or ii) of attack from $chyp_a$ to $chyp_b$. A graph with *chyps* as nodes, and attack relationships as edges will be called a *causal argumentation framework*.

Definition 3 (Causal argumentation framework). *A causal argumentation framework $CAF = (Ch, \rightarrow, \mathcal{P})$, where the arrow $\rightarrow \subseteq Ch \times Ch$ represents all the attack relationships in a CAF, and $\mathcal{P}$ is the underlying probabilistic evidence supporting the causal model.*

In formal argumentation literature, *argumentation semantics* are patterns of selection for obtaining winner arguments from a graph composed by arguments and attack relationships. We use in this paper those argumentation semantics proposed by Dung in [5] to select "strong" *chyps* from a CAF graph. We use a function SEM that represents the application of Dung's semantics to a CAF, i.e. $SEM(CAF) = \mathcal{E} = \{Ext_1, \ldots Ext_l\}$, which returns a set of l non conflicting sets of structures called *extensions*, i.e. $\mathcal{E} = \{\{chyp_1, \ldots, chyp_i\}, \ldots, \{chyp_j, \ldots, chyp_k\}\}$. SEM is based on the so-called *admissible sets*, i.e., $\nexists a, b \in \mathcal{E}$

such that a attacks b, we say that $\mathcal{E}$ is an *admissible set* iff $\mathcal{E}$ defends all its elements; $\mathcal{E}$ is a *preferred* extension iff $\mathcal{E}$ is a maximal; and we say that $\mathcal{E}$ is a *stable* extension iff $\forall a \in \mathcal{I}\backslash\mathcal{E}, \exists b \in \mathcal{E}$ such that $\nexists\, b$ attacks a.

A violation of conditions 3 and 4 in Definition 1 can lead to a deductive correlation without causation. Then, we can say that the support and conclusion in a *chyp* structure have deductive and causal correlation.

Proposition 1 (Deductive correlation and causation). *The support and conclusion in chyp-like structures are deductively and causally correlated.*

Proposition 1 is narrowed to those argument-based structures built following Definition 1.

3   Effects of Causal Interventions in Argumentation Frameworks

A *"what if"*-scenario is a *manipulation* in M, noted as $do(X = x)$ an intuitively reads: if I do x the variable X. Such interventions produce changes in the *children's* conditional probabilities of the intervened variable: $P(Y = y|do(X = x)) = \prod_{pa_X} P(y|x, pa_X)P(pa_X)$ where pa_X is the set of all parents of variables in X.

A causal intervention impacts a CAF in two ways: 1) it may introduce new relations of (deductive or causal) attacks between *chyp*s, and 2) the underlying probability distribution changes given the intervention (variables affected by a counterfactual manipulation are those *descendants* of such manipulated variable). We denote an *intervened* CAF as CAF_x w.r.t. a $x \in M_x$, which is the manipulated model M by x. Therefore, the computation of individual probabilities of argument structures from childrens' variables are different compared with a pre-intervention CAF.

Proposition 2 (Probability independent argument structures). *During an intervention of a causal model, individual probabilities of the intervened variable's parents are not affected, therefore probabilities of argument-based structures linked to those parents are invariant and definable.*

Even when a causal model follows a Markov characteristic individual probabilities of *chyps* are non-identifiable [20], then maximum and minimum boundaries ($\bar{P} = [P_{min}, P_{max}]$) of the causal inference can be defined for those argument-based children affected by the intervention (see [21,24] for more details).

Definition 4 (Intervened causal hypotheses). *During an intervention $do(\sigma = \omega)$, the probability of the intervened model is given by $\bar{P}_\omega = [P_{min}, P_{max}]$, then a causal intervened hypothesis is defined as $chyp_\omega = \langle S, \sigma, \bar{P}_\omega \rangle$.*

In an intervened causal hypothesis, it is stated that its causal probability is given by $\bar{P}_\omega$ where it is possible to guarantee the existence of bounds for computing such limits.

Proposition 3. *Let CAF_x be an intervened causal argumentation framework, the individual probability of every $chyp \in CAF_x$, may not be estimable from frequency data alone.*

A straightforward consequence for argument-based structures during an intervention, is that probability of those structures associated to the intervened variables' parents are not affected.

Corollary 1. *In a CAF_x the probability of argument-based structures associated to the intervened variable's parents is not affected and it is identifiable.*

Regarding intervened causal hypotheses (Definition 4), $\bar{P}$ can be seen also as a degree of uncertainty.

Definition 5 (Uncertainty probability range). *Let $\bar{P} = [P_{min}, P_{max}]$ where $P_{min/max} \in \mathbb{R}[0,1]$, be a range of probabilities of a chyp. A function $\mathsf{Unc} : \bar{P} \to [0,1]$ returns a measurement of uncertainty for the range $\bar{P}$.*

Intuitively, the larger the probability range, the larger the uncertainty and Unc closer to 1. In a pre-intervention scenario, where the probability distribution of the causal model follows: $\sum P = 1$, probabilities of every *chyp* are definite, and $\mathsf{Unc} = 1$.

We can hypothesize that for all argument-based structure where causal models are mapped to a propositional language to build arguments, during an intervention, the underling probability distribution associated to the argumentation framework changes, therefore a re-computation of individual probabilities is necessary.

Proposition 4 (Change in probability distribution of argumentation frameworks). *Let CAF and CAF_x be a causal argumentation framework and its intervened version when X is manipulated. The probability distributions associated to CAF and CAF_x are different, then for every causal argument structure except its parents, a re-computation of individual probabilities are necessary.*

In *sequential interventions* [22] (*e.g.* $do(X = x)$ then $do(Y = y)$ and $X, Y \in M$), we can prove that the joint effect of sequential interventions in a CAF is the same as if we perform individual interventions successively.

Proposition 5 (Sequential interventions in CAFs). *Let $X, Y \in M$ be two variables in the causal model M, and let CAF_{X*} and CAF_{Y*} two interventions in X, Y respectively. The set of extensions in a sequential intervention $CAF_{X*,Y*}$ is the same as a joint effect of separated interventions CAF_{X*} then CAF_{Y*}, or conversely, iff the set of causal hypotheses of pre-intervention CAF remains invariable.*

The relevance of Proposition 5 can be seen when different interventions are applied in distinct time points in the same CAF.

3.1 Defeat Status During an Intervention

A *chyp* is defeated by other when the support is compromised. In previous approaches ([3,13] among others), a probability level associated to a belief degree of the argument (or argument structure) has been used as a method to decide a "winner" in such ties. However, in causal argumentation frameworks, during an intervention a probability range ($\bar{P} = [0,1]$) is associated to a *chyp* rather individual probabilities, then the defeat status can be given by a level of uncertainty of the probability range, in other words, the wider the probability range is, the larger the causal uncertainty associated to a *chyp* will be, and the most compromised support of such *chyp*.

Proposition 6 (Defeat considering causal uncertainty). *Let* CAF_x *an intervened causal argumentation framework where* $chyp_a = \langle S, \sigma, \bar{P}_\sigma \rangle$, $chyp_a = \langle S, \phi, \bar{P}_\phi \rangle \in Ch$ *are two argument-based causal hypotheses. We say that* $chyp_a$ *defeats* $chyp_b$ *iff.* $\mathsf{Unc}(\bar{P}_\phi) > \mathsf{Unc}(\bar{P}_\sigma)$ *and* $\mathsf{Conc}(chyp_a) \equiv \neg\mathsf{Conc}(chyp_b)$.

4 Examples and Experiments

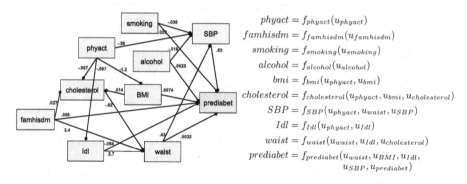

$$phyact = f_{phyact}(u_{phyact})$$
$$famhisdm = f_{famhisdm}(u_{famhisdm})$$
$$smoking = f_{smoking}(u_{smoking})$$
$$alcohol = f_{alcohol}(u_{alcohol})$$
$$bmi = f_{bmi}(u_{phyact}, u_{bmi})$$
$$cholesterol = f_{cholesterol}(u_{phyact}, u_{bmi}, u_{cholesterol})$$
$$SBP = f_{SBP}(u_{phyact}, u_{waist}, u_{SBP})$$
$$Idl = f_{Idl}(u_{phyact}, u_{Idl})$$
$$waist = f_{waist}(u_{waist}, u_{Idl}, u_{cholesterol})$$
$$prediabet = f_{prediabet}(u_{waist}, u_{BMI}, u_{Idl}, u_{SBP}, u_{prediabet})$$

Fig. 1. (Left) Causal model of prediabetes factors for Swedish population. (Right) Estructural equations for the causal model.

We exemplify and test our framework using real-world causal models obtained from a large database of human activity behavior in northern Sweden [19]. We use as a case scenario an investigation to determine the prevalence and risk factors for *prediabets*. The causal graph presented in Fig. 1 has different endogenous variables: systolic blood pressure - *SBP* (high, normal, low), *cholesterol* (high, normal, low), physical activity - *phyact* (high, normal, low), *alcohol* consumption (high, normal, low), *smoking* (yes, no), family history - *famhisdm* (yes, no), body mass index - *bmi* (high, normal, low), and *waist* measurement (high, normal, low). As usual in causal models, *disturbances* noted as $u_x \in U$ are understood to govern the uncertainties associated with the causal relationships [7], *e.g.*

$u_{alcohol}$. Based on such causal model $\mathcal{M}$, some structural equations are derived (see Fig. 1), which can be mapped to a propositional language forming a theory as is presented in 1. The mapping to classical logic dismisses the uncertainty u_x, that could be captured by other underlying languages such as *extended logic programs* [8], among others.

$$
\left\{
\begin{array}{c}
phyact. \\
famhisdm. \\
smoking. \\
alcohol. \\
u_{smoking} \vdash_c SBP \\
u_{smoking} \vdash_c prediabet \\
u_{phyact} \vdash_c bmi \\
u_{phyact} \wedge u_{bmi} \vdash_c u_{cholesterol} \\
u_{phyact} \wedge u_{waist} \wedge u_{alcohol} \wedge u_{smoking} \vdash_c u_{SBP} \\
u_{phyact} \vdash_c ldl \\
u_{famhisdm} \wedge u_{ldl} \wedge u_{cholesterol} \vdash_c waist \\
u_{waist} \wedge u_{BMI} \wedge u_{ldl} \wedge u_{smoking} \wedge u_{SBP} \vdash_c prediabet
\end{array}
\right\} \tag{1}
$$

chyps

A number of *chyps* are built from the theory 1, see Ch. Each $chyp \in Ch$ represents a deductive and causal hypothesis about the variables involved in prediabetes, and jointly, the Ch set provides a view of all the information related to such disease before any intervention is performed.

$$
Ch = \left\{
\begin{array}{c}
chyp_1 = \langle \top, phyact, P_{phyact} \rangle \\
chyp_2 = \langle \top, famhisdm, P_{famhisdm} \rangle \\
chyp_3 = \langle \top, smoking, P_{smoking} \rangle \\
chyp_4 = \langle \top, alcohol, P_{alcohol} \rangle \\
chyp_5 = \langle \{u_{phyact} \vdash_c bmi\}, bmi, P_{bmi} \rangle \\
chyp_6 = \langle \{u_{phyact} \wedge u_{bmi} \vdash_c u_{cholesterol}\}, cholesterol, P_{cholesterol} \rangle \\
chyp_7 = \langle \{u_{phyact} \wedge u_{waist} \wedge u_{alcohol} \wedge u_{smoking}) \vdash_c u_{SBP}\}, SBP, P_{SBP} \rangle \\
chyp_8 = \langle \{u_{phyact} \vdash_c ldl\}, ldl, P_{ldl} \rangle \\
chyp_9 = \langle \{u_{famhisdm} \wedge u_{ldl} \wedge u_{cholesterol} \vdash_c waist\}, waist, P_{waist} \rangle \\
chyp_{10} = \langle \{u_{waist} \wedge u_{BMI} \wedge u_{ldl} \wedge u_{smoking} \wedge u_{SBP} \vdash_c prediabet\}, prediabet, P_{prediabet} \rangle
\end{array}
\right\}
$$

The selection of consistent *chyps* from Ch using SEM without intervention is straightforward and omitted in this paper. However, when a causal intervention is performed in $\mathcal{M}$, the set Ch changes given that the entailment $\vdash_c$ is affected, which impacts the *chyp* Definition 1.

Interventions

Now, let us suppose that we provide $\mathcal{M}$ to a person (user) as a graphical tool for reflecting about her/his health regarding prediabetes. We can assume also that the person is interested on creating new future scenarios, for example she/he asks her/himself: *"what if I do more physical exercise?"*, then such intervention in *phyact* impacts the causal model as is presented in Fig. 2.

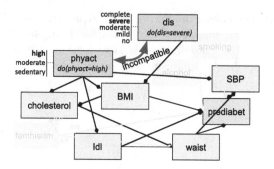

Fig. 2. Interventions in variables *phycat* and *dis*.

As we can see in Fig. 2, some variables such as *smoking, alcohol* and *famhisdm* are "removed" from the model given the intervention. Such change affects the generation of *chyps* and what can be derived from a CAF. Let us complement this example presenting how our framework deals with new information that has not enough evidence to justify causality, but health care professionals have hypotheses that it is related to prediabetes. Let us assume that we add information about a *physical disability* (*dis*) as variable linked to *BMI* (see Fig. 2 variable *dis*). In this new scenario, a clear incompatibility is formed between *phyact* and *dis*, which leads to the following set of *chyps*:

$$Ch' = \left\{ \begin{array}{c} chyp_1 = \langle \top, phyact, P_{phyact} \rangle \\ chyp_5 = \langle \{u_{phyact} \vdash_c bmi\}, bmi, P_{bmi} \rangle \\ chyp_6 = \langle \{u_{phyact} \wedge u_{bmi} \vdash_c u_{cholesterol}\}, cholesterol, P_{cholesterol} \rangle \\ chyp_8 = \langle \{u_{phyact} \vdash_c Idl\}, Idl, P_{Idl} \rangle \\ chyp_{10} = \langle \{u_{waist} \wedge u_{BMI} \wedge u_{Idl} \wedge u_{smoking} \wedge u_{SBP} \vdash_c prediabet\}, \\ prediabet, P_{prediabet} \rangle \\ chyp_{11} = \langle \top, dis, P_{dis} \rangle \\ chyp_12 = \langle \{u_{dis} \vdash_c bmi\}, bmi, P_{bmi} \rangle \end{array} \right\}$$

In this example, although simple but informative, we can see that when $SEM()$ is applied to the CAF formed by Ch' and $\rightarrow = \{att(chyp_1, chyp_11)\}$ we will have at least two alternatives (in the case of using a credulous SEM) that are causal and deductively consistent.

5   Discussion and Related Work

Interventions in causal models is active research topic in artificial intelligence considering their potential to generate scenarios. In those manipulations, it is expected a high level of uncertainty due the lack of complete information. In general, the conditional probability of a counterfactual sentence "If it were A then B", given evidence e, can be computed in three steps [21]: 1) Abduction: update $P(u)$ by the evidence e, to obtain $P(u|e)$. 2) Action: modify M by the action $do(A)$, where A is the antecedent of the counterfactual, to obtain the submodel M_A. And 3) Deduction: use the updated probability $P(u|e)$ in conjunction with M_A to compute the probability of the counterfactual consequence B. In this paper, we confine our attention to the third step to build consistent scenarios of counterfactuals. We propose a characterization of one particular type of interventions, however other types of such manipulations are well-known (see [20,24]), which are part of our future work. In the formal argumentation theory, the generation of consistent scenarios from argument-based structures is a "natural" procedure, and a number of theoretical and practical approaches have been proposed (see [10] among many others). Probabilistic argument-based approaches, *i.e.* the use of a probabilistic distribution linked to individual arguments or other parts of an argumentation framework, has a well-known and solid foundations (see for example [6,13]). Despite all these efforts, the investigation of interventions in argumentation frameworks has been disregarded. Recently, causal analysis based on directed graphs has been revisited in [17], however changes in the probability distribution due to causal manipulations was not considered. In fact, it seems that changes in the underlying probabilistic distribution is not accounted in the argumentation literature. On the other hand, we depart from acknowledging distribution changes, and how those modifications impact in the argumentation framework (see Proposition 4 and Proposition 3). A novel contribution of our proposal is the analysis of sequential interventions (Proposition 5), which is captured by our framework. Interestingly, is that time sequential interventions, *i.e.* time varying treatments scenarios (see [4]) can be also described using our framework. We believe that this is key for real-world applications, being part of our future work.

5.1   Causality and Probability in Argumentation Theory

When the underlying causal model fulfills a Markov condition in a pre-intervention situation, the treatment of probabilities follows *syntactically* a *constellation approach* [14], where P is used to generate a probability distribution over full CAF graph. However, during an intervention as we saw such distribution changes. In this paper, we proposed a characterization of one particular type of interventions, however other types of such manipulations are well-known, which are part of our future work.

   In non-intervened models, the probability distribution in our framework has a causal interpretation, meaning that in $chyp_a = \langle S, \sigma, P_{\sigma'} \rangle$ there are causal evidence $P_{\sigma'}$ to support that S causes σ. In this setting, the probability in every $chyp$ is *semantically* different to the main stream analysis of probability distribution in the argumentation theory literature (see [13] as an example). However, *syntactically* we can use the state-of-the-art to obtain new properties. For example, if we consider that in a pre-intervention of a CAF for each $att(chyp_a, chyp_b) \in \rightarrow$, and if $P(chyp_a) > 0.5$, then $P(chyp_b) \leq 0.5$. Therefore, we can propose what could be causally rational, extending constellation approaches of probabilistic argumentation:

Proposition 7 (Causal probability of CAF under intervention). *Let* $P(v_1, \ldots, x, \ldots, v_l)$ *be a probability distribution from a Markovian model M, linked to causal argumentation framework* $CAF = (Ch, \rightarrow, \mathcal{P})$. *During an intervention of a variable X, the probability distribution of* CAF_x *is rational.*

Proposition 7 says that if the probability distribution in a CAF is rational, *i.e.* $P = 1$, then, in an intervention such as CAF_x, then the rationality is preserved, and every *chyp* will have a rational causal probabilistic level, for example:

- $P(chyp_x) = 0$ represents that S does not cause σ with certainty.
- $P(chyp_x) < 0.5$ represents that S does not cause σ to some degree.
- $P(chyp_x) = 0.5$ represents that S does not cause σ, neither S causes σ.
- $P(chyp_x) > 0.5$ represents that S causes σ to some degree.
- $P(chyp_x) = 1$ represents that S causes σ with certainty.

This treatment of causality can be used for defining a defeat relationship in pre-intervention that is straightforward, and we refer to the reader to general probabilistic approaches on argumentation theory (see for example [13]).

We can extend the same analysis of causal probability to sets of causal hypotheses, for example considering $G \subseteq Ch$ in a $CAF_x = (Ch, \rightarrow, \mathcal{P})$, when $P(G) = 1$ we say that doing x, a variable $y \in G$ is certainly caused by such intervention.

Proposition 8. *In a pre-intervention* CAF *we have that* $\sum_{G \subseteq CAF} P(G) = 1$.

Similarly, we can analyze the case of an intervention:

Proposition 9. *During an intervention to a causal argumentation framework* CAF_x, *the total probability distribution is* $\sum_{G' \subseteq CAF_x} P(G') \leq 1$.

6   Conclusion

Our framework takes as *input*: structural equations from a causal model, a set of variables that it is known may conflict during an intervention (potential attacks), and one or several specific variables to intervene. Then, our framework generates as output consistent and causal sets of argument-based structures that we call *chyps*. We use sets of *chyps* to define consistent and causal scenarios. Our contributions are aligned to the probabilistic formal argumentation literature, specifically those approaches considering causal models as underlying representations. We propose novel mechanisms describing the nature of causal interventions and their impact on argumentation frameworks. We believe that theoretical and empirical work on interventions in the formal argumentation field is important and under development. We report in this paper the ongoing work on the implementation of our theoretical framework, and we present an initial prototype design that will be tested using a real-world scenario in the Northern Sweden. We reported a system to implement our framework. The design of this tool considers interventions as direct manipulations of variables from a user interface.

Naturally, the user interface representation (the star in Fig. 3) is an oversimplification of the underlying causal model. In [15], it is presented the methodology to select representative variables that a user may consider relevant. For the implementation of STAR-C platform, we take advantage of the Tweety argumentation library [23], and we used a causal reasoning library DoWhy [1] to obtain probability distributions. Our current work is the design of graphical representations to provide intuitive reading to sets of *chyps* (see Fig. 3).

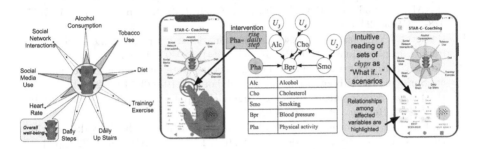

Fig. 3. Proposed user interface to capture interventions directly from users, where a dragging movement of a value in a variable (peaks in the star) starts our causal-argumentation framework process. Part of the STAR-C project in Sweden

Our future work will be focused on three aspects: 1) the fulfillment of abstract axioms from deductive systems [2,9] and causal inference [7]; and 2) the exploration of sequential and time-related interventions considering probabilistic argumentation frameworks.

Acknowledgment. Research was supported by Forte, the Swedish Research Council for Health, Working Life and Welfare, which supports the STAR-C project during 2019–2024 (Dnr. 2018-01461).

References

1. DoWhy: A Python package for causal inference. https://github.com/microsoft/dowhy
2. Amgoud, L.: Postulates for logic-based argumentation systems. Int. J. Approx. Reason. **55**(9), 2028–2048 (2014)
3. Amgoud, L., Cayrol, C.: Inferring from inconsistency in preference-based argumentation frameworks. J. Autom. Reason. **29**(2), 125–169 (2002)
4. Arjas, E., Parner, J.: Causal reasoning from longitudinal data. Scand. J. Stat. **31**(2), 171–187 (2004)
5. Dung, P.M.: On the acceptability of arguments and its fundamental role in non-monotonic reasoning, logic programming and n-person games. Artif. Intell. **77**(2), 321–357 (1995)
6. Gabbay, D.M., Rodrigues, O.: Probabilistic argumentation: an equational approach. Log. Univers. **9**(3), 345–382 (2015)

7. Galles, D., Pearl, J.: Axioms of causal relevance. Artif. Intell. **97**(1–2), 9–43 (1997)
8. Gelfond, M., Lifschitz, V.: Classical negation in logic programs and disjunctive databases. New Gener. Comput. **9**(3–4), 365–385 (1991)
9. Guerrero, E., Nieves, J.C., Lindgren, H.: Semantic-based construction of arguments: an answer set programming approach. Int. J. Approx. Reason. **64**, 54–74 (2015)
10. Guerrero, E., Nieves, J.C., Sandlund, M., Lindgren, H.: Activity qualifiers in an argumentation framework as instruments for agents when evaluating human activity. In: Demazeau, Y., Ito, T., Bajo, J., Escalona, M.J. (eds.) PAAMS 2016. LNCS (LNAI), vol. 9662, pp. 133–144. Springer, Cham (2016). https://doi.org/10.1007/978-3-319-39324-7_12
11. Halpern, J.Y., Pearl, J.: Causes and explanations: a structural-model approach. Part II: Explanations. Br. J. Philos. Sci. **56**(4), 889–911 (2005)
12. Harel, D.: First-Order Dynamic Logic. Lecture Notes in Computer Science, vol. 68. Springer, Heidelberg (1979). https://doi.org/10.1007/3-540-09237-4
13. Hunter, A.: A probabilistic approach to modelling uncertain logical arguments. Int. J. Approx. Reason. **54**(1), 47–81 (2013)
14. Li, H., Oren, N., Norman, T.J.: Probabilistic argumentation frameworks. In: Modgil, S., Oren, N., Toni, F. (eds.) TAFA 2011. LNCS (LNAI), vol. 7132, pp. 1–16. Springer, Heidelberg (2012). https://doi.org/10.1007/978-3-642-29184-5_1
15. Lindgren, H., et al.: The Star-C Intelligent Coach: A Crossdisciplinary Design Process of a Behaviour Change Intervention in Primary Care. Prague, Czech Republic (2020, in press)
16. Morveli-Espinoza, M., Nieves, J.C., Augusto Tacla, C.: Towards an imprecise probability approach for abstract argumentation. In: 24th European Conference on Artificial Intelligence (ECAI 2020), Including 10th Conference on Prestigious Applications of Artificial Intelligence (PAIS 2020), Virtual, 29 August–8 September 2020, pp. 2921–2922. IOS Press (2020)
17. Morveli-Espinoza, M., Nieves, J.C., Tacla, C.A.: An imprecise probability approach for abstract argumentation based on credal sets. In: Kern-Isberner, G., Ognjanović, Z. (eds.) ECSQARU 2019. LNCS (LNAI), vol. 11726, pp. 39–49. Springer, Cham (2019). https://doi.org/10.1007/978-3-030-29765-7_4
18. Ng, N., et al.: Sustainable behavior change for health supported by person-tailored, adaptive, risk-aware digital coaching in a social context: study protocol for the STAR-C research programme. Front. Public Health **9**, 138 (2021)
19. Norberg, M., Wall, S., Boman, K., Weinehall, L.: The Västerbotten Intervention Programme: background, design and implications. Glob. Health Action **3**(1), 4643 (2010)
20. Pearl, J.: Causal diagrams for empirical research. Biometrika **82**(4), 669–688 (1995)
21. Pearl, J.: Probabilities of causation: three counterfactual interpretations and their identification. Synthese **121**(1–2), 93–149 (1999)
22. Pearl, J.: An introduction to causal inference. Int. J. Biostat. **6**(2), 1643–1662 (2010)
23. Thimm, M.: The Tweety library collection for logical aspects of artificial intelligence and knowledge representation. Künstl. Intell. **31**(1), 93–97 (2017)
24. Tian, J., Pearl, J.: Probabilities of causation: bounds and identification. Ann. Math. Artif. Intell. **28**(1–4), 287–313 (2000)

Defining an Architecture for a Remote Monitoring Platform to Support the Self-management of Vascular Diseases

Ana Vieira[1]([⊠]) [iD], João Carneiro[1] [iD], Luís Conceição[1] [iD], Constantino Martins[1] [iD], Julio Souza[2] [iD], Alberto Freitas[2] [iD], and Goreti Marreiros[1] [iD]

[1] GECAD – Research Group on Intelligent Engineering and Computing for Advanced Innovation and Development, Institute of Engineering, Polytechnic of Porto, Porto, Portugal
{aavir,jrc,msc,acm,mgt}@isep.ipp.pt
[2] CINTESIS – Center for Health Technology and Services Research, Porto, Portugal
{juliobsouza,alberto}@med.up.pt

Abstract. The aging of the worldwide population has led to a growing prevalence of vascular diseases, negatively impacting national healthcare systems and patients. The application of information technologies in the health sector has the potential to allow the remote monitoring of patients and the personalization of healthcare. This work proposes the architecture for a remote monitoring platform that supports the self-management of vascular diseases in the context of the Inno4Health project, with the goal of stimulating the innovation in the continuous monitoring of the patients' health. The platform aims to support health professionals and patients with vascular diseases through the continuous monitoring of their health condition and presentation of monitoring reports. Self-management tools will be provided to patients through the presentation of personalized recommendations adapted to their current health condition. By doing so, we believe it will be possible to improve the patients' self-management of their disease as well as decrease the risk of disease-related complications.

Keywords: mHealth · Personalized healthcare · Vascular diseases · Remote monitoring

1 Introduction

As the worldwide population ages at an unprecedented rate, there is a growing prevalence of vascular diseases [1, 2], such as Intermittent Claudication, Venous Ulcers and Diabetic Foot Ulcers. Intermittent Claudication is a debilitating condition with higher prevalence in patients with ages above 60 years old [3]. Venous Ulcers are the last stage of Chronic Venous Disease and are often underdiagnosed [2], being more frequent among women and affecting more than 23% of the adult population [4]. Diabetic Foot Ulcers are the most frequent complications of diabetes, with around 25% of the diabetic patients developing this condition with disease's progression [5]. These diseases can negatively impact the quality of life, and due to their severity, they involve frequent monitoring

© Springer Nature Switzerland AG 2021
F. De La Prieta et al. (Eds.): PAAMS Workshops 2021, CCIS 1472, pp. 165–175, 2021.
https://doi.org/10.1007/978-3-030-85710-3_14

by the physicians and regular hospitalizations [6, 7], causing an impact not only on the national healthcare systems but also for patients who may not be able to afford the costs of the treatments. Several studies have shown that the continuous monitoring of patients with these pathologies results in an improvement of their clinical condition [6, 8, 9], being imperative the development of intelligent solutions that allow the remote monitoring of patients with vascular diseases.

Although the application of information technologies in the health sector has resulted in innovative solutions for the remote monitoring and the personalization of healthcare, these are still rarely applied towards the healthcare of patients with vascular diseases [10]. Recent studies have sought the personalization of the patients with vascular diseases' healthcare [11–13]. A smartphone application was developed by the authors in [11] to remotely track the progression of the patient's peripheral arterial disease as well as to monitor the daily activity of the patient, such as physical therapy performed or medication taken. A smartwatch-based service for the monitoring of patients with peripheral arterial disease, WalkCoach, was proposed in [12]. The service intends to assist patients in their home exercise therapy and is composed by a smartwatch and a mobile application. The smartwatch monitors the patient's activity, such as the physical exercise performed during the day, and the mobile application provides information about the patient's daily progress as well as the exercise program assigned. The mobile application also allows the patient the control over parameters such as the start and end times of the exercise including its duration. The authors in [13] proposed a smartphone application, YORwalK, to promote the exercise in patients with peripheral arterial disease. The application has as main features the presentation of the patient's daily activity, such as the number of steps walked, the six-minute walking test, an exercise that has the duration of six minutes and helps the application to determine the pain free walking distance, and the presentation of weekly and monthly reports regarding the patient's progress and current status. Overall, the proposed solutions focus mainly on monitoring the patient's daily activity and on the presentation of physical exercises to be performed, lacking functionalities concerning the self-management of the disease. Additionally, the solutions did not present interfaces aimed to support the physician in the clinical decision-making.

Related works in the topic of remote monitoring through non-invasive sensors and personalization of care have resulted in high quality solutions. The authors in [14] present a solution to support the elderly community in their home environment through remote monitoring. The solution, UserAccess, is an evolution of a previous platform named iGenda, that provides intelligent event management and consists of a platform that receives events from its users and schedules them according to information such as their importance. The aim of the UserAccess is to deliver information concerning the care receivers to caregivers. UserAccess collects data throughout the day using several body and home sensors, as well as mobile devices, and provides it to the care receiver. The information can be medical oriented, for formal caregivers, or notifications regarding the receiver's status and warnings from the home sensors, for informal caregivers. UserAccess also uses the iGenda platform in order to schedule events, such as medical appointments. In [15] it is presented a platform that uses a wearable sensor, an Emotional Smart Wristband, to detect the current emotional status of the user. This solution is integrated in the iGenda platform, and is capable of scheduling events, such as tasks to be performed, according to the user's current emotional status. The article [16] presents PHAROS, a system that promotes the active ageing of elderly people through the suggestion and monitoring of physical activities to perform in their homes. The solution is composed by a social robot that processes visual input in order to identify the exercise being performed as well as the user's performance, and a recommendation system that analyses the collected data during the physical activity and suggests exercise programs adequate to the user's performance. The authors in [17] present a personal assistant, ME^3CA, that provides personalized exercise programs for elderly people at home. In order to collect the data regarding the user, the proposed system has several wearable sensors, that collect different physiological signals, as well as environmental sensors. The system has a set of decision-making algorithms that are able to measure the emotional state of the user and their performance during the activity to improve future recommendations. From a general standpoint, the solutions presented in the literature have a high level of quality and are able to support the users by remotely monitoring their home environment. However, the majority are specifically designed for the care of elderly people at home and are not able to assist and monitor them in exterior settings. Furthermore, if the user has a medical condition, such as a vascular disease, the proposed solutions do not provide specific support to it, such as tools for the disease's self-management, monitor of disease-related parameters, prediction of disease-related risk, among others.

The main goal of the Inno4Health[1] project is to stimulate the innovation in the continuous monitoring of health and fitness conditions in healthcare and in sports settings. In sports settings, the developed technology will be used to continuously assess the athletes' fitness and health in order to provide information to coaches and athletes and to help them optimize their performance during competitions. In healthcare settings, the continuous monitoring of the health of patients will provide information to both patients and physicians regarding the ability to prevent, to prepare or to recover from invasive medical interventions. In order to accomplish the proposed goal, the Inno4Health project will create innovative wearable monitoring sensors, that will allow the continuous monitoring of patients and athletes, and artificial intelligence techniques will be used in order to develop a set of algorithms for the assessment of the athletes' and patients' health and fitness conditions. Mobile applications and dashboards will also be developed in order to display the generated insights and other information to patients, physicians, athletes, and coaches. The Inno4Health project is composed by a consortium of several industrial leaders in health and sports domains, security, privacy, as well as academic, clinical and sports partners from seven countries, including Portugal. The Portuguese use case is focused on the healthcare, more specifically on the vascular diseases' domain. To accomplish this use case, the Portuguese consortium will develop a set of intelligent services that enable the remote monitoring and smart coaching of patients with vascular diseases. Innovative non-invasive wearable sensors will be developed in order to continuously monitor the patients' health and several intelligent algorithms will be implemented with the aim of generating meaningful insights that will support both patients and health professionals.

---

[1] Web page of the project: https://inno4health.eu/.

This paper proposes an architecture for a remote monitoring platform to support the self-management of vascular diseases, such as Intermittent Claudication, Venous Ulcers, and Diabetic Foot. The platform differs from related systems proposed in the literature by providing personalized support to patients with vascular diseases and their health professionals through the continuous monitoring at home as well as in external environments. The platform will be developed in the context of the Portuguese use case of the Inno4Health project and aims to remotely monitor the patient's health condition throughout their daily life using non-invasive wearable sensors. It is also intended to provide patients self-management tools through the presentation of personalized recommendations about behaviors to adopt and tasks to perform, as well as provide their treating physicians monitoring reports and assistance in the decision-making, through the prediction of the risk of disease-related complications, among others.

The remainder of the paper is structured as follows. Section 2 presents the proposed architecture for the remote monitoring platform, Sect. 3 explores possible perspectives of artificial intelligence techniques to be implemented in the solution, and in the last section, Sect. 4, conclusions are taken and future work to be performed is presented.

2 Proposed Architecture

The growing prevalence of vascular diseases is negatively impacting both patients and healthcare providers. These diseases can lead to a mobility loss [18, 19] and, due to their severity, require frequent follow-ups and regular hospitalizations. The extensive monitoring of the patient's health condition is typically only performed in healthcare settings, being difficult to monitor the patient's condition outside of them. The need of constant monitoring of patients with vascular diseases has led to a growing burden not only on the national healthcare systems but also on patients who may not be able to afford the treatments.

In order to address the current challenges and burdens in the healthcare of patients with vascular diseases we propose an architecture of a remote monitoring platform. The continuous monitoring of the patient will be performed through innovative non-invasive wearable sensors. This platform intends to generate meaningful insights regarding the patient's health condition, which in turn will be used to assist both patients and health professionals. Patients will be supported in the self-management of their disease through the presentation of personalized recommendations regarding their current health condition and behaviors to adopt in order to improve it. Health professionals will be presented monitoring reports concerning the patient's health condition and will be given assistance in the clinical decision-making.

Figure 1 presents the proposed architecture for the platform. The main users of the platform will be the Patient, who will wear the monitoring sensors and will provide clinical data through the interaction with the mobile application, and the Health Professional, who will have access to the patient's health condition and insights generated by the platform and will be assisted in the clinical decision-making through a web application.

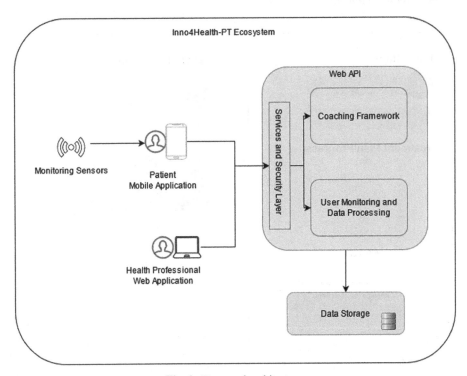

Fig. 1. Proposed architecture.

Monitoring Sensors will be used to monitor the patient's health condition throughout the day. Since the platform will comprise the monitoring of three types of vascular diseases (intermittent claudication, venous ulcers, and diabetic foot ulcers), two types of wearable monitoring sensors will be used in the platform. An insole sensor and a patch will be used by patients in order to monitor variables such as the walking distance, speed, heart rate, among others. The sensors will then connect to the patient's mobile application to transfer the collected data.

The patient will interact with the platform through a mobile application. This application will be used to obtain the clinical data collected through the monitoring sensors and will present insights about the patient's current health condition and personalized recommendations about activities to perform and behaviors that the patient needs to adopt to improve their health. Figure 2 presents an example of two interfaces of the patient's mobile application.

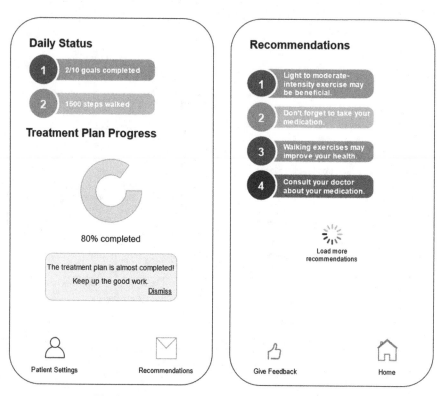

Fig. 2. Example of the mobile application's interfaces

A Web Application will be provided to health professionals, in order to allow the visualization of the patient's health condition and to support the professional in the clinical decision making. Examples of the support in the clinical decision-making are the prediction of the patient's readiness for surgery, possible reactions to medical interventions, the recommendation of medication to prescribe to the patient, and the presentation of the current condition of the patient. Figure 3 presents an example of an interface for the presentation of the monitoring reports.

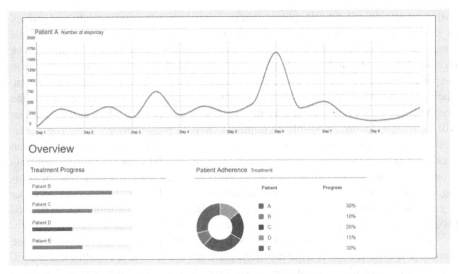

Fig. 3. Example of an interface for visualization of patient-related data

The web application will also be used by the health professional to insert knowledge regarding the rules that will be used to generate personalized recommendations that will be presented to the patients, clinical guidelines used in the treatment of patients, as well as data on the patient's health condition progression. Figure 4 presents an example of an interface for the definition of a new rule in the web application.

Create New Rule

Identifier	Rule BMI
Insert associated variables	× Healthy × BMI
BMI	>= 25
Healthy	No
Recommendation Text	Light to moderate-intensity exercise may be beneficial

Create Rule

Fig. 4. Example of an interface of the Web Application

The Web API is the main component of the proposed architecture, being composed by the Services and Security Layer, Coaching Framework, and User Monitoring and Data Processing. The Services and Security Layer will serve as a gateway between the Web API and external services, such as mobile and web applications. This layer will expose a set of services to acquire the patient's clinical data, information inserted by the health professional and provide the generated insights regarding the patient's health condition and personalized recommendations. Since health-related data is sensitive data, this layer will also contain a security component that will ensure the integrity, security, and privacy of all data. The Coaching Framework will provide a set of intelligent services for the smart coaching of patients. Through the Services and Security Layer, the framework receives data which will be used to generate personalized recommendations adequate to the patient's health condition. To do so, the framework will have a Rule-Based System. The rules available in the framework will be based on clinical guidelines defined by the health professionals and will specify the conditions associated to the clinical data that will be used to identify possible recommendations to present to the user. The generated recommendations will be sent to the Services and Security Layer and will be then presented to the patient through the mobile application. The User Monitoring and Data Processing component will gather all patient-related data collected through the monitoring sensors and will use a set of artificial intelligence techniques to process it in order to generate meaningful insights regarding the patient's health condition. The generated insights will be used to assist the health professional in the clinical decision-making.

The Data Storage will contain the information concerning the patient, such as the clinical data obtained through the monitoring sensors and interactions with the platform. It will also contain all the knowledge used in the data processing, such as guidelines used in the generation of personalized recommendations and knowledge inserted by health professionals.

3 Possible Perspectives

As the Inno4Health project is at an early phase of execution, the proposed platform's components have not yet been developed. Therefore, in this section possible artificial intelligence techniques to be employed in the data processing components of the architecture, such as the Coaching Framework and the User Monitoring and Data Processing, proposed in the Fig. 1 will be explored.

For the Coaching Framework, as mentioned above, a Rule-Based System will be implemented with the aim of generating personalized recommendations adequate to the patient's current health condition. The Rule-Based System will be developed using JBoss Drools, an open-source rule engine framework. This framework presents many advantages, such as intuitive language, that non-developers such as health professionals can easily understand, easy integration with web services [20]. The framework is easily scalable, in the sense that it is possible to add new rules without changing the rules previously added. The rules used by the system will use as a base knowledge inserted by the health professionals in the Web Application component of the platform as well as previously defined clinical guidelines used in the treatment of patients with vascular diseases. Figure 5 presents an example of a rule in the Drools format that will be used in the generation of personalized recommendations.

```
rule "Weight Loss"
when
    variable0:Variable(Name == "BMI", Value >= "25")
    variable1:Variable(Name == "Healthy", Value == "No")
then
    recommendation.setRecommendation("Light to moderate-intensity
    exercise may be beneficial.");
end
```

Fig. 5. Rule example

However, if the patient does not present sufficient data (in cases where the patient is still new to the platform) the system will not be able to accurately generate recommendations. In order to address this issue, it will be necessary to employ another technique in the Coaching Framework. Case-Based Reasoning (CBR) can be used to address the issue of missing data, since it can be used to identify possible recommendations to present to the patient based on their similarity to other patients. Health professionals will validate the recommendations generated by CBR in order to ensure the presentation of adequate recommendations to the patient. Reinforcement Learning will also be implemented in this component in order to improve the accuracy of the generated recommendations. For that, the patient's feedback regarding each of the presented recommendations will be considered. This will allow the system to understand which recommendations the patient thought that were useful and that helped to improve their motivation to adopt healthy behaviors.

For the User Monitoring and Data Processing component of the remote monitoring platform, artificial intelligence techniques will be implemented in order to generate insights concerning the patient's health condition. The implementation of classification techniques, such as Decision Trees or Naïve Bayes, and clustering techniques, such as K-Means, may provide important information about the diagnostic of the patient's current health condition and the prediction of the risk of disease-related complications and possible reactions to medical interventions. With a comprehensive understanding of the health condition and the prediction of risks associated to the disease it will be possible to provide strong insights regarding the patient's health condition to the health professional.

For the representation of patient-related data used and knowledge generated by both Coaching Framework and User Monitoring and Data Processing components, ontologies will be used. This technique allows the creation of a knowledge base with facts about the patient and as mentioned in [21], one of the main advantages of this technique is that it allows the management of a substantial number of clinical guidelines. Therefore, ontologies will be implemented in the platform with the aim of creating a knowledge base that comprises patient-related data, knowledge used and generated in the data processing components, as well as clinical guidelines that will be used to assess the patient's health.

4   Conclusions and Future Work

The growing prevalence of vascular diseases in the worldwide population and their severity has led to an overload of the national healthcare systems, as well as an economic burden of the patients. The development of innovative technological solutions for the remote monitoring and self-management of the disease is essential to address the current challenges in the healthcare of patients with vascular diseases.

In this work it is presented an architecture for a remote monitoring platform to support the self-management of vascular diseases to be developed in the context of the Portuguese use case of the Inno4Health. The Portuguese use case aims to stimulate the innovation in the continuous monitoring in health settings by developing a set of intelligent services that enable the remote monitoring and smart coaching of patients with vascular diseases. By using non-invasive monitoring sensors, the proposed platform will continuously monitor the patient's health condition throughout their daily life and will allow the self-management of the disease through the presentation of information regarding their diseases, among personalized recommendations concerning healthy lifestyle behaviors to adopt and activities to perform. The platform will also support the health professional in the clinical decision-making through the display of meaningful insights generated during the processing of the patient-related data, such as the patient's current condition, prediction of possible reactions to medical interventions, among others.

As future work we intend to develop the Coaching Framework component of the proposed platform. Specifically, we intend to implement the Rule-Based System in order to generate personalized recommendations based on the patient's health. In order to improve the accuracy of the generated recommendations, Case-Based Reasoning and Reinforcement Learning will also be implemented. The generated recommendations will be posteriorly validated by the health professionals to ensure the adequacy of the recommendations.

Acknowledgements. This research work was developed under the project Inno4Health (EUREKA-ITEA3: 19008; POCI-01-0247-FEDER-069523) and by National Funds through FCT (Fundação para a Ciência e a Tecnologia) under the project UIDB/00760/2020. Ana Vieira is supported by national funds through FCT Ph.D. studentship with reference UI/BD/151115/2021.

References

1. Song, P., et al.: Global, regional, and national prevalence and risk factors for peripheral artery disease in 2015: an updated systematic review and analysis. Lancet Glob. Health **7**(8), e1020–e1030 (2019)
2. Nicolaides, A.N., Labropoulos, N.: Burden and suffering in chronic venous disease. Adv. Ther. **36**(Suppl. 1), 1–4 (2019)
3. Norgren, L., Hiatt, W.R., Dormandy, J.A., Nehler, M.R., Harris, K.A., Fowkes, F.G.: Inter-society consensus for the management of peripheral arterial disease (TASC II). J. Vasc. Surg. **45**(Suppl. S), S5–S67 (2007)
4. Rajathi, V., Bhavani, R., Jiji, W.: Varicose ulcer (C6) wound image tissue classification using multidimensional convolutional neural networks. Imaging Sci. J. **67**, 1–11 (2019)

5. Abbott, C.A., et al.: Innovative intelligent insole system reduces diabetic foot ulcer recurrence at plantar sites: a prospective, randomised, proof-of-concept study. Lancet Digit. Health **1**(6), e308–e318 (2019)

6. McDermott, M.M.: Exercise training for intermittent claudication. J. Vasc. Surg. **66**(5), 1612–1620 (2017)

7. Kelechi, T.J., Johnson, J.J., Yates, S.: Chronic venous disease and venous leg ulcers: an evidence-based update. J. Vasc. Nurs. **33**(2), 36–46 (2015)

8. Mulligan, E.P., Cook, P.G.: Effect of plantar intrinsic muscle training on medial longitudinal arch morphology and dynamic function. Man Ther. **18**(5), 425–430 (2013)

9. Sartor, C.D., et al.: Effects of strengthening, stretching and functional training on foot function in patients with diabetic neuropathy: results of a randomized controlled trial. BMC Musculoskelet. Disord. **15**, 137 (2014)

10. Haveman, M.E., et al.: Telemedicine in patients with peripheral arterial disease: is it worth the effort? Expert Rev. Med. Devices **16**(9), 777–786 (2019)

11. Ata, R., et al.: VascTrac: a study of peripheral artery disease via smartphones to improve remote disease monitoring and postoperative surveillance. J. Vasc. Surg. **65**, 115S-116S (2017)

12. Constant, N., et al.: A smartwatch-based service towards home exercise therapy for patients with peripheral arterial disease. In: 2019 IEEE International Conference on Smart Computing (SMARTCOMP), pp. 162–166 (2019)

13. Shalan, A., Abdulrahman, A., Habli, I., Tew, G., Thompson, A.: YORwalK: desiging a smartphone exercise application for people with intermittent claudication. Stud. Health Technol. Inform. **247**, 311–315 (2018)

14. Costa, A., Julián, V., Novais, P.: Advances and trends for the development of ambient-assisted living platforms. Expert Syst. **34**(2), e12163 (2017)

15. Costa, A., Rincon, J.A., Carrascosa, C., Julian, V., Novais, P.: Emotions detection on an ambient intelligent system using wearable devices. Future Gener. Comput. Syst. **92**, 479–489 (2019)

16. Martinez-Martin, E., Costa, A., Cazorla, M.: PHAROS 2.0—A PHysical Assistant RObot System improved. Sensors **19**(20), 4531 (2019)

17. Rincon, J.A., Costa, A., Novais, P., Julian, V., Carrascosa, C.: ME3CA: a cognitive assistant for physical exercises that monitors emotions and the environment. Sensors **20**(3), 852 (2020)

18. McDermott, M.M., et al.: Unsupervised exercise and mobility loss in peripheral artery disease: a randomized controlled trial. J. Am. Heart Assoc. **4**(5), e001659 (2015). (in Eng)

19. Vileikyte, L.: Diabetic foot ulcers: a quality of life issue. Diabetes Metab. Res. Rev. **17**(4), 246–249 (2001)

20. Bali, M.: Drools JBoss Rules 5.X Developer's Guide. Packt Publishing, Birmingham (2013)

21. Alharbi, R.F., Berri, J., El-Masri, S.: Ontology based clinical decision support system for diabetes diagnostic. In: 2015 Science and Information Conference (SAI), pp. 597–602 (2015)

Intelligence as a Service: A Tool for Energy Forecasting and Security Awareness

Sinan Wannous[✉] [iD], Isabel Praça[iD], and Rui Andrade[iD]

School of Engineering, (ISEP/IPP), Research Group on Intelligent Engineering and Computing for Advanced Innovation and Development (GECAD), Polytechnic of Porto, Porto, Portugal
{sinai,icp,rfaar}@isep.ipp.pt

Abstract. Forecasting is of an immense importance in energy markets, it aims to build accurate forecasting models to inspect future scenarios. It can also be used to monitor energy profiles to detect faults and other security concerns. Many tools and services have been introduced to automate the forecasting process. However, the 'ideal' tool highly depends on how much it perfectly fulfills the desired behavior in the targeted application. In this paper, we introduce a configurable energy forecasting tool, which extends a set of machine learning models to provide dynamic energy forecasting services. The developed tool aims mainly to predict energy generation/consumption, build forecasting models, compare predictions, and fine-tune prediction models. Then, we utilize this tool to conduct two case studies. The first aims to compare the performance of different prediction models in residential and office buildings, using multiple experiments with variations of input fields. The second one investigates the role of the energy forecasting tool to raise awareness regarding security incidents in a shop floor. Results from both case studies emphasized the prospective role of the developed tool in energy forecasting and security awareness.

Keywords: Energy forecasting · Security awareness · Machine learning · Forecasting models · Energy forecasting tools

1 Introduction

Energy forecasting is crucial in the context of energy markets. Inspecting energy patterns leads to wiser decisions for better balance between consumption and generation values. In this context, there is always a need to have reliable models to forecast energy demands. Such models have immense implications in energy monitoring, planning, operation and optimization of buildings and utilities. Normally, forecasting models are primarily used for analyzing the energy consumption and providing future scenarios. However, they can also be utilized to monitor building systems to detect faults over time, and to facilitate the integration of clean energy sources. On the other hand, literature incorporates a wide range of research and studies covering energy forecasting in various contexts. Most of which seeks to compare various forecasting models in different application fields, circumstances, and data sets, with the aim to reach the most accurate model for the

© Springer Nature Switzerland AG 2021
F. De La Prieta et al. (Eds.): PAAMS Workshops 2021, CCIS 1472, pp. 176–186, 2021.
https://doi.org/10.1007/978-3-030-85710-3_15

given case. Likewise, energy-related forecasting tools and services have been developed to automate the forecasting process, some of them are free and open-source, while the majority is paid and used in private conditions. In this context, there is always a necessity to perform energy forecasting services for multiple purposes. While there is no ideal tool for energy forecasting, the case highly depends on how much the tool fulfills the desired behavior in the targeted application.

In this paper, we introduce a customized tool to support dynamic energy forecasting services. In the following Sect. 2 we present a state of the art of related research works. In Sect. 3, we describe our developed tool and its specifications. To check the prospective roles of the developed tool, we describe two undertaken case-studies in Sects. 4 and 5. Then, we finalize with a conclusion in Sect. 6.

2 State of the Art

Energy forecasting can be categorized according to time horizons into short-term, medium-term, and long-term predictions. It usually utilizes the most common input fields of weather data, time contextual data, and preceding power values [1]. On the other hand, artificial intelligence (AI) and machine learning (ML) techniques have been adapted to forecast energy for over three decades [2], primarily supervised machine learning and artificial neural networks (ANN) [3, 4].

Authors of Deb et al. [5] analyzed nine ML techniques for energy forecasting. They observed that each technique possesses a set of advantages and disadvantages. Another study by Ahmad et al. [6] proposed four supervised ML models for utilities and buildings energy forecasting. They considered short and long-term horizons and estimated the forecasting accuracy. Furthermore, the application of ANNs for forecasting energy use/demand has been analyzed [7]. Results indicated that most applications were applied to commercial buildings using hourly data. A case study by Vinagre et al. [8] revealed better accuracy of Support Vector Machines for energy consumption forecasting over ANN. Regression tools were also evaluated in the context of urban area load forecasting [9]. As a result, Random Forest provided better short-term predictions while k-Nearest Neighbor was better for long-term predictions.

Furthermore, ensemble learning [10] is a common approach that combines independent base "weak" models. Authors of Pirbazari et al. [11] propose an ensemble energy prediction approach for household communities. The approach performs multi-hour ahead load/generation forecasting using three input factors: time, meteorological, and consumption records. Furthermore, authors in Pinto et al. [12] utilize three ensemble methods (Gradient Boosted Regression, Random Forests and Adaboost) for an hour-ahead forecast of the electricity consumption of an office building. They also compared their results to fuzzy rule-based models and SVM [13]. The outputs exposed relatively close results with superiority of the ensemble models.

Apart from forecasting models, energy monitoring has been used to increase security. Silva et al. [14] discover the usage of power consumption and energy monitoring to identify security risks for buildings. The authors propose a system that generate alarms whenever abnormal energy consumption values are detected within a given context. On the other hand, different tools for energy planning and forecasting have been introduced.

According to a study of energy-related forecasting tools and services [15], most services are private and not freely available. Another study reviewed 68 computer tools for renewable energy systems [16]. Authors found that the 'ideal' energy tool is dependent on the targeted objectives. Further studies presented tools for energy prediction presenting key attributes for each model [17, 18]. However, although most forecasting tools are not freely accessible, widely used free solutions are also available. LEAP, the Low Emissions Analysis Platform (originally, Long-range Energy Alternatives Planning) [19], is an integrated software to track energy consumption developed at the Stockholm Environment Institute [20]. It has been widely used for energy planning and forecasting [21–23]. OSeMOSYS (Open Source Energy Modeling System) [24] and Temoa (Tools for Energy Model Optimization and Analysis) [25] are also other free and open source systems for energy planning and forecasting.

To conclude, it is explicit, to a large extent, that there is no optimal model or tool for energy forecasting. The best tool largely depends on how much it perfectly fulfills the desired behavior and fits the case of the targeted application.

3 Energy Forecasting Tool

3.1 Overview

We developed an energy forecasting tool that extends a set of ML models to provide dynamic services. It aims mainly to predict energy generation/consumption, build forecasting models, compare predictions, and fine-tune prediction models. This tool deals with hourly consumption, contextual data, such as day of week and season, and weather data (see Table 1). It is worth mentioning that the contextual fields are not subject to a specific timestamp. They are being handled as independent numbers indicating the current time parts when the consumption/generation value is registered.

Table 1. Fields of historical input data sets for the energy forecasting tool.

Field	Type	Description
hour	Contextual	The hour of the day (values: 0–23)
day_w	Contextual	The day of the week (values: 1–7)
day_m	Contextual	The day of the month (values: 1–31)
month	Contextual	The month of the year (values: 1–12)
year	Contextual	The year
temp	Weather	The temperature value
prev_val_n	Previous value	The nth preceding registered value
consumption/generation	Targeted attribute	The actual registered value

Figure 1 presents a sample of a historical energy consumption data set. However, the tool is totally configurable to let the user decide the types of fields to be considered.

hour	day_w	day_m	month	year	temp	prev_val_1	prev_val_2	prev_val_3	consumption
5	2	17	4	2018	5	66232.43333	62255.46667	71972.53333	65668.26667
6	2	17	4	2018	5	65668.26667	66232.43333	62255.46667	66869.5
7	2	17	4	2018	8	66869.5	65668.26667	66232.43333	66678.56667
8	2	17	4	2018	10	66678.56667	66869.5	65668.26667	83451.43333
9	2	17	4	2018	13	83451.43333	66678.56667	66869.5	88926.76667

Fig. 1. A sample of a historical energy consumption dataset.

In general, the developed tool aims to forecast energy consumption or generation for short and medium-term horizons. Nevertheless, future prediction is not the only objective of this tool, further advanced tasks such as model training and tuning might introduce additional outputs and give the user an additional flexibility in optimizing models results.

3.2 Specifications and Implementation

The tool uses the combinations of five forecasting models, two model validation techniques, and a variety of provided services. Furthermore, the tool brings into use sophisticated interfaces to control and adjust prediction configurations as needed.

Prediction Models. The energy forecasting tool utilizes five supervised machine learning models/estimators. Such estimators investigate the underlying link between the independent fields (contextual, weather, and previous values), and the dependent target field (consumption or generation). Used models include three ensemble learning methods: Adaboost.R2 (Ada.) [26], Random Forest Regressor (RF) [27], and Gradient Boosting Regressor (GBR) [28]. In addition to Support Vector Regression (SVR) [29] and Linear Regression (LR) [30]. However, the tool provides rich forms to adjust the multiple parameters of each estimator. Figure 2 displays the control over configurations of 3 prediction models.

Fig. 2. An example of configurating 3 prediction models used in model training.

Model Validation. An essential part of the prediction mechanism, the tool maintains validation mechanisms to (a) evaluate the estimator performance, (b) estimate the accuracy of the resulted predictions, and (c) compare predictions of different models and input data sets. The main validation approach is to randomly split the input data set into two sub-sets, one used to train the model, and the other one used to test the trained model. In this context, our tool comes with the two common validation mechanisms: Train Test Split and Cross Validation. The former performs only one train-test cycle, while the later executes multiple train-test cycles and averages the results. Yet, configurations of both methods can be controlled as needed (see Fig. 3). Nevertheless, the tool measures two accuracy metrics: R^2 score (Coefficient of Determination) [31], and Mean Absolute Error (MAE) [32].

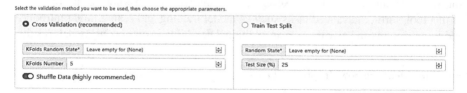

Fig. 3. Specifying the model validation mechanisms.

Tool Features. Services provided by this tool include, but are not limited to:

- Training: aims to build downloadable forecasting models to be used later for forecasting energy consumption/generation.
- Prediction: aims to use trained models to make predictions for the future.
- Tuning: aims to tune forecasting models using combinations of hyperparameters.

Implementation. Technically speaking, the energy forecasting tool is a standalone web-based application, provides its services using interactive graphical user interfaces. It is built in Python/Django web framework [33] and scikit-learn library [34]. Furthermore, some features are also provided remotely using Restful API services.

4   Case Study #1: Tuning Energy Forecasting

In this case study, we aim to investigate the prospective role of the proposed tool in comparing the performance of different prediction models. Besides, we seek to understand how the variations of input data sets or input fields might positively/negatively influence the accuracy of predictions.

Material and Methods. In this case study, we consider two different data sets, the first one is gathered from the real monitoring of an *office* building in the campus of ISEP/GECAD. The building is occupied in daily basis by approximately 30 people every working day. The data sources provide the energy consumption of the mentioned campus from different devices, electrical sockets, lighting, and HVAC, as well as other measurements such as the temperature, luminosity, and humidity. Samples of these data sets are available online at [35]. However, a data sample of about 3 months has been internally collected; and converted from 10-s time interval to an hourly base energy consumption log. On the other hand, the second data set is much bigger and covers approximately 6 years of energy consumption in a *residential* building in Porto. The building is occupied by one family and provides only energy consumption in a 15-min time interval. Likewise, values have been averaged to an hourly base, and then, merged with temperature data of the exact location of the building retrieved from a weather API by [36]. However, the obvious difference in data size and sources is deliberate in terms of assessing transparently the forecasting models, as well as evaluating the effect of data diversity on predictions. Finally, once pre-processed, both data sets were re-formatted into MS Excel documents as per the template mentioned in Table 1.

We used the tuning module of our tool to perform multiple predictions as the following: for each data set, we conducted 17 experiments, each of which covers a different combination of input fields (see Table 2). Furthermore, for each experiment, we tuned the five prediction models using multiple combinations of hyperparameters. Finally, we cross validated the accuracy of each tuning process and registered the best averaged prediction accuracy. We ended up with 85 energy forecasting instances for each data set with a total of 170 different experiments.

Table 2. Tuning experiments, including the input fields considered for each experiment.

Experiment	Pre-values number	Contextual data	Weather data
Exp[1]	0	day_m, month, hour, year, day_w	temp
Exp[2]	1	day_m, month, hour, year, day_w	temp
Exp[3]	3	day_m, month, hour, year, day_w	temp
Exp[4]	10	day_m, month, hour, year, day_w	temp
Exp[5]	3	day_m, month, hour, year, day_w	n/a
Exp[6]	3	n/a	temp
Exp[7]	3	n/a	n/a
Exp[8]	0	day_m, month, hour, year, day_w	n/a
Exp[9]	0	n/a	temp
Exp[10]	0	day_m	n/a
Exp[11]	0	Month	n/a
Exp[12]	0	Hour	n/a
Exp[13]	0	Year	n/a
Exp[14]	0	day_w	n/a
Exp[15]	0	hour, day_w	n/a
Exp[16]	0	day_m, hour, day_w	n/a
Exp[17]	0	day_m, month, hour, day_w	n/a

Results and Discussion. We present in Figs. 4 and 5 the detailed accuracy results (R^2 score) for predictions of the *office* and *residential* data sets, respectively.

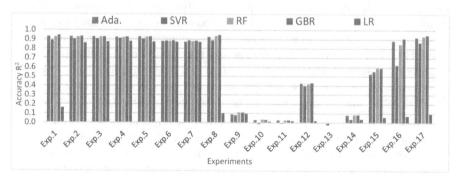

Fig. 4. Prediction accuracy (R^2) for each experiment (Exp) for the *office* building dataset.

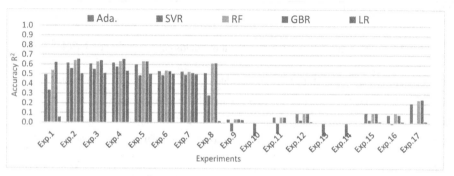

Fig. 5. Prediction accuracy (R^2) for each experiment (Exp) for the *residential* building dataset.

Comparing the outcomes of the tuning process, results clearly show that the accuracy of the *office* building predictions was, in general, much better than the accuracy of the *residential* building. This might be due to the slightly consistent usage of energy appliances in a heavily occupied office environment. Especially when compared to a limited members' family-based environment, where the absence of a family member could significantly affect the energy usage. It is also obvious that predictions of both data sets are usually higher when including all contextual data fields and/or the preceding values (Exp$^{1-8}$). While there is no significant impact of only weather data on our predictions (Exp^9). We can also conclude that the "hour" field has the most tangible effect among contextual fields (Exp^{12}), and the accuracy increases when appending more contextual attributes (Exp$^{14-17}$). As for the prediction models, results show slightly close accuracy in the first 8 experiments, with some deficiency of Linear Regression model. However, both data sets indicate that Adaboost, Random Forest and Gradient Boosting Regression were able to provide the best results in almost all experiments. Eventually, GBR was able to provide the most accurate predictions of both the *office* building ($R^2 \approx 0.95$ for Exp^8 & Exp^{17}) and *residential* building ($R^2 \approx 0.66$ for Exp^4).

5   Case Study #2: Security Awareness

This case study investigates the role of energy forecasting to raise awareness regarding security incidents. Here, our tool might act as an early warning mechanism to monitor and protect physical and informational assets.

Material and Methods. The data set used is a livestream of the actual energy consumption of 10 sensors/analyzers, installed and operate in different sections of a textile industry shop floor in Porto. Analyzers are: *Compressor, Jacquard Loom, Drawing, Printing, Ratiér Loom, Cutting Division, Dyeing, Warehouse, Weaving and Commercial Area* analyzers. To secure a real time monitoring, analyzers' data was provided via an internal secure API and fed to the tool in a 5-min time interval. For each analyzer, consumption records, when requested by the tool, are being instantly processed and averaged to an hourly base and fit into the default input structure (Table 1). In this case study, we consider all contextual fields with no weather or preceding values.

As we have a continues data streaming, we specify the historical time window of the consumption data to be collected. We also provide the future contextual data samples for the next period to be used for consumption prediction. Using a predefined prediction model, collected data is being used to train the model and predict the future consumption. Nevertheless, obtained results demonstrate (a) the analyzer's daily consumption profile, as well as (b) the consumption predictions for this analyzer for the future period. For the sake of this case study, we investigated two analyzers, the *Drawing* analyzer, and the *Cutting Division* analyzer. For each analyzer, as we are dealing with day-ahead forecast, we obtained the consumption values of the previous 3 months to calculate the analyzer's consumption profile and predict its consumption for the next 24 h.

Results and Discussion. The following Figs. 6 and 7 present the results for the *Drawing* and *Cutting Division* analyzers, respectively. Left charts represent the average consumption daily profile, while right charts represent the consumption prediction for the next 24 h. As we could notice in each figure, the predictions of the next 24 h for both analyzers are close to the analyzers' profiles, in spite of the difference in prediction performance. We could also notice the variation in consumption values between *Drawing* analyzer's profile and prediction, which explains the relatively low prediction accuracy of this analyzer ($R^2 \approx 0.67$). Such diversity might refer to unstable energy consumption of this analyzer in comparison to the other one with consistent consumption and prediction accuracy of $R^2 \approx 0.88$.

On the other hand, another key benefit of such results is to monitor the behavior of each analyzer. To make sure it is consistent and matches both the consumption profile and the prediction. With that said, an abnormal actual consumption behavior that does not match the prediction results/profile should give an alert. Which aims to check the deficiency cause and effects in the area where the analyzer is installed. An abnormal consumption in this scenario could be for example a high level of consumption in the night period. As we can see in both studied sections, the consumption profile between mid-night and 6 AM is very low. Thus, a spike in consumption in this period could be a reason to trigger an alert. While, a sudden and unexpected drop of the consumption during the daily hours could mean a problem in the looms or other machines of the shop-floor. The detection of the abnormal behaviors is now under investigation as machine

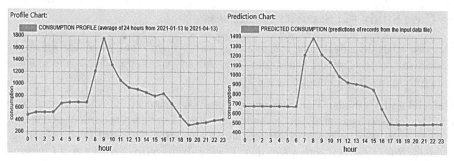

Fig. 6. Daily consumption profile (left chart) and next 24 h prediction results (right chart) for the *Drawing* analyzer, prediction accuracy $R^2 \approx 0.67$.

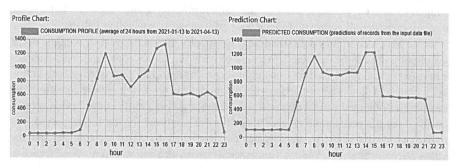

Fig. 7. Daily consumption profile (left chart) and next 24 h prediction results (right chart) for the *Cutting Division* analyzer, prediction accuracy $R^2 \approx 0.88$.

learning models will be included for that. However, despite the installation of our tool in this shop floor environment is still being investigated, we were able to obtain promising results. Especially while integrating the tool with monitoring and security systems to produce automatic alerts.

6 Conclusion

In this paper, we introduced a configurable energy forecasting tool that extends common ML models to provide dynamic energy forecasting services. Features provided by this tool varies from energy model training, tuning, and predictions, to other security monitoring services such as energy profile predictions. Furthermore, we evaluated the role of the developed tool in two distinct case studies, one aims to compare and find accurate forecasting models, and another one acts as an early warning mechanism to protect organization assets. The developed tool was able to serve our requirements in different circumstances and can be reused and extended for other similar scenarios.

However, despite there is no ideal tool for energy forecasting, the development should continue to automate the forecasting process. Since there is a definite set of forecasting models with known input parameters and evaluation mechanisms, future works might focus on providing tools that combine as many of the prediction models.

Furthermore, the performance of such tools might be a challenging task, especially for complex models and huge historical data sets. Consequently, further research could be carried on investigating the implementation of big data and distributed environments based tools for dynamic energy forecasting.

Acknowledgement. This work has been supported by Project CyberFactory#1 (ITEA-17032/ANI|P2020 40124) co-funded by Portugal 2020, and from FEDER Funds through COMPETE program and from National Funds through FCT under project SPET–PTDC/EEI-EEE/029165/2017 and 507 UIDB/00760/2020.

References

1. Raza, M.Q., Khosravi, A.: A review on artificial intelligence based load demand forecasting techniques for smart grid and buildings. Renew. Sustain. Energy Rev. **50**, 1352–1372 (2015)
2. Hong, T., Pinson, P., Wang, Y., Weron, R., Yang, D., Zareipour, H.: Energy forecasting: a review and outlook. IEEE Open Access J. Power Energy **7**, 376–388 (2020)
3. Antonopoulos, I., et al.: Artificial intelligence and machine learning approaches to energy demand-side response: a systematic review. Renew. Sustain. Energy Rev. **130**, 109899 (2020)
4. Ahmad, T., Chen, H.: A review on machine learning forecasting growth trends and their real-time applications in different energy systems. Sustain. Cities Soc. **54**, 102010 (2020)
5. Deb, C., Zhang, F., Yang, J., Lee, S.E., Shah, K.W.: A review on time series forecasting techniques for building energy consumption. Renew. Sustain. Energy Rev. **74**, 902–924 (2017)
6. Ahmad, T., Huanxin, C., Zhang, D., Zhang, H.: Smart energy forecasting strategy with four machine learning models for climate-sensitive and non-climate sensitive conditions. Energy **198**, 117283 (2020)
7. Runge, J., Zmeureanu, R.: Forecasting energy use in buildings using artificial neural networks: a review. Energies **12**, 3254 (2019)
8. Vinagre, E., Pinto, T., Ramos, S., Vale, Z., Corchado, J.M.: Electrical energy consumption forecast using support vector machines. In: 2016 27th International Workshop on Database and Expert Systems Applications (DEXA), pp. 171–175 (2016)
9. Johannesen, N.J., Kolhe, M., Goodwin, M.: Relative evaluation of regression tools for urban area electrical energy demand forecasting. J. Clean. Prod. **218**, 555–564 (2019)
10. Dietterich, T.G., et al.: Ensemble learning. Handb. Brain Theory Neural Netw. **2**, 110–125 (2002)
11. Pirbazari, A.M., Sharma, E., Chakravorty, A., Elmenreich, W., Rong, C.: An ensemble approach for multi-step ahead energy forecasting of household communities. IEEE Access **9**, 36218–36240 (2021)
12. Pinto, T., Praça, I., Vale, Z., Silva, J.: Ensemble learning for electricity consumption forecasting in office buildings. Neurocomputing **423**, 747–755 (2021)
13. Jozi, A., Pinto, T., Praça, I., Vale, Z.: Day-ahead forecasting approach for energy consumption of an office building using support vector machines. In: 2018 IEEE Symposium Series on Computational Intelligence (SSCI), pp. 1620–1625 (2018)
14. Silva, F., Santos, G., Praça, I., Vale, Z.: A context-based building security alarm through power and sensors analysis. Energy Inform. **1**, 349–353 (2018)
15. González Ordiano, J.Á., Waczowicz, S., Hagenmeyer, V., Mikut, R.: Energy forecasting tools and services. Wiley Interdiscip. Rev. Data Min. Knowl. Discov. **8**, e1235 (2018)
16. Connolly, D., Lund, H., Mathiesen, B.V., Leahy, M.: A review of computer tools for analysing the integration of renewable energy into various energy systems. Appl. Energy **87**, 1059–1082 (2010)

17. Giebel, G., Landberg, L., Kariniotakis, G., Brownsword, R.: State-of-the-art Methods and software tools for short-term prediction of wind energy production. In: EWEC 2003 (European Wind Energy Conference and Exhibition) (2003)
18. Gargiulo, M., Gallachóir, B.Ó.: Long-term energy models: principles, characteristics, focus, and limitations. Wiley Interdiscip. Rev. Energy Environ. **2**, 158–177 (2013)
19. LEAP. https://leap.sei.org/default.asp?action=home. Accessed 21 Apr 2021
20. Stockholm Environment Institute: bridging science and policy. https://www.sei.org/. Accessed 21 Apr 2021
21. Khan, S.I., Islam, A., Khan, A.H.: Energy forecasting of Bangladesh in gas sector using LEAP software. Glob. J. Res. Eng. **11**(1), 15–20 (2011)
22. Shabbir, R., Ahmad, S.S.: Monitoring urban transport air pollution and energy demand in Rawalpindi and Islamabad using leap model. Energy **35**, 2323–2332 (2010)
23. Huang, Y., Bor, Y.J., Peng, C.-Y.: The long-term forecast of Taiwan's energy supply and demand: LEAP model application. Energy Policy **39**, 6790–6803 (2011)
24. Howells, M., et al.: OSeMOSYS: the open source energy modeling system: an introduction to its ethos, structure and development. Energy Policy **39**, 5850–5870 (2011)
25. Hunter, K., Sreepathi, S., DeCarolis, J.F.: Modeling for insight using tools for energy model optimization and analysis (Temoa). Energy Econ. **40**, 339–349 (2013)
26. Drucker, H.: Improving regressors using boosting techniques. In: ICML, pp. 107–115 (1997)
27. Breiman, L.: Random forests. Mach. Learn. **45**, 5–32 (2001)
28. Friedman, J.H.: Greedy function approximation: a gradient boosting machine. Ann. Stat. **29**, 1189–1232 (2001)
29. Chang, C.-C., Lin, C.-J.: LIBSVM: a library for support vector machines. ACM Trans. Intell. Syst. Technol. **2**, 1–27 (2011)
30. Hutcheson, G.D.: Ordinary least-squares regression. L. Moutinho GD Hutcheson, SAGE Dict. Quant. Manag. Res. 224–228 (2011). https://us.sagepub.com/en-us/nam/the-sage-dictionary-of-quantitative-management-research/book230815
31. Coefficient of determination. In: The Concise Encyclopedia of Statistics, pp. 88–91. Springer, New York, (2008). https://doi.org/10.1007/978-0-387-32833-1_62
32. Fürnkranz, J., et al.: Mean absolute error. In: Sammut, C., Webb, G.I. (eds.) Encyclopedia of Machine Learning, pp. 652–652. Springer, Boston (2010). https://doi.org/10.1007/978-0-387-30164-8_525
33. Django: The Web framework for perfectionists with deadlines. https://www.djangoproject.com/. Accessed 13 Apr 2021
34. Pedregosa, F., et al.: Scikit-learn: machine learning in {P}ython. J. Mach. Learn. Res. **12**, 2825–2830 (2011)
35. Open Data Sets: IEEE PES Intelligent Systems Subcommittee. https://site.ieee.org/pes-iss/data-sets/. Accessed 10 May 2021
36. World Weather Online. https://www.worldweatheronline.com/. Accessed 11 May 2021

Workshop on Multi-Agent-Based Applications for Modern Energy Markets, Smart Grids, and Future Power Systems (MASGES)

Workshop on Multi-Agent-Based Applications for Modern Energy Markets, Smart Grids, and Future Power Systems (MASGES)

Future power systems will probably be characterized by very large penetrations of renewables (towards 100%) and support the operation of wholesale markets (e.g., day-ahead and balancing markets) together with local markets. Electricity markets are a complex and evolving reality, meaning that researchers are lacking insight into numerous open problems that are being raised (e.g., the need of new market designs to manage the variability and uncertainty of the increasing levels of renewable generation). Also, future power systems will integrate a large number of distributed energy resources and new players. Smart grids are intrinsically linked to the challenges raised by new power systems and are expected to improve their efficiency and effectiveness, while ensuring reliability and a secure delivery of electricity to end-users. They should be capable of autonomously and intelligently configuring themselves to make the most efficient use of the available resources, to be robust to different kinds of failures and energy production deviations, and to be extendable and adaptable in face of the rapidly changing technologies and requirements.

The focus of this workshop is on the modeling and simulation of modern power systems, supporting electricity markets capable of integrating large levels of variable renewable energy, and also the existence of emerging technologies, such as distributed generation, demand response, energy storage, smart homes, and electric vehicles.

Organization

Organizing Committee

Fernando Lopes — National Laboratory of Energy and Geology, Portugal
Zita Vale — Polytechnic Institute of Porto, Portugal

Program Committee

Alberto Fernández	Universidad Rey Juan Carlos, Spain
Alexander Pokahr	University of Hamburg, Germany
Dongmo Zhang	University of Western Sydney, Australia
Fernando Lopes	LNEG, Portugal
Frank Dignum	Utrecht University, The Netherlands
Helder Coelho	Universidade de Lisboa, Portugal
Ivana Kockar	University of Strathclyde, Scotland
Jörg Müller	Clausthal Unversity of Technology, Germany
Juan A. Rodríguez-Aguilar	IIIA-CSIC, Spain
Koen Hindriks	Delft University of Technology, The Netherlands
Laurent Vercouter	INSA de Rouen, France
Matthias Klusch	DFKI, Germany
Massimiliano Giacomin	University of Brescia, Italy
Murat Sensoy	University of Aberdeen, UK
Morten Lind	DTU, Denmark
Nikos Hatziargyriou	National Technical University of Athens, Greece
Olivier Boissier	ENS Mines Saint-Etienne, France
Paolo Torroni	University of Bologna, Italy
Paul Valckenaers	Katholic University Leuven, Belgium
Pavlos Moraitis	Paris Descartes University, France
Sascha Ossowski	Universidad Rey Juan Carlos, Spain
Souhila Kaci	Artois University, France
Tiago Pinto	ISEP/IPP, Portugal
Wojtek Jamroga	Clausthal University of Technology, Germany
Zita do Vale	ISEP/IPP, Portugal

Agent-Based Phase Space Sampling of Ensembles Using Ripley's K for Homogeneity

Jörg Bremer[1]([✉]), Johannes Gerster[1], Birk Brückner[1], Marcel Sarstedt[2], Sebastian Lehnhoff[1], and Lutz Hofmann[2]

[1] Department of Computing Science, University of Oldenburg,
26129 Oldenburg, Germany
{joerg.bremer,johannes.gerster}@uol.de
[2] Institute of Electric Power Systems, Leibniz University Hannover,
Appelstraße 9A, 30167 Hannover, Germany

Abstract. In future energy systems, decentralized control will require delegation of liabilities to small energy resources. Distributed energy scheduling constitutes a complex multi-level optimization task regarding the underlying high-dimensional, multi-modal and nonlinear problem structure. The multi-level issue as well as the requirement for model independent algorithm design are substantially supported by appropriate machine learning flexibility models. Generating training sets by digital twins works well for single energy units. Combining training sets from individually modeled energy units, on the other hand, results in folded distributions with unfavorable properties for training. Nevertheless, this happens to be a quite frequent use case, e.g. when an ensemble of distributed energy resources wants to harness the joint flexibility for some control task. A fully decentralized agent-based algorithm is proposed that samples from distributed twins maximizing coverage of flexibility and simultaneously minimizing the discrepancy of the sample by using Ripley's K measure. Applicability and effectiveness are demonstrated by several simulations using established models for energy unit simulation.

Keywords: Phase space sampling · Discrepancy · MAS · Scheduling

1 Introduction

For climate protection reasons, electrical energy supply in many countries is currently undergoing fundamental changes. Large, fossil generation is gradually replaced by (DERs). DERs are often based on renewables like wind and solar energy or characterized by efficient usage of resources, e.g. in the co-generation case. The paradigm shift from few centralized plants to a numerous DERs is challenging due to integration into existing electricity markets, because DERs are usually owned and operated by independent stakeholders. The often rather low flexibility potential of a single DER does not justify the transaction costs

© Springer Nature Switzerland AG 2021
F. De La Prieta et al. (Eds.): PAAMS Workshops 2021, CCIS 1472, pp. 191–202, 2021.
https://doi.org/10.1007/978-3-030-85710-3_16

for direct integration into energy markets. A well-known approach to tackle this problem is the concept of (VPPs) [26]. The basic idea is to aggregate a multitude of small DERs to a jointly controlled entity, which is large enough to participate in energy markets. Besides distributed electricity generation, e.g. (CHP), photovoltaic or wind power, VPPs can include controllable consumption such as shiftable loads, heat pumps or air conditioning. Tapping the demand side flexibility potential can compensate for the poorer planning ability of generation suffering from uncertainty. In case of additional flexibility demand, VPPs can be complemented by battery storages. A common use case in VPP control is scheduling the operation of participating DERs for a day-ahead planning horizon. This task is a variant of the unit commitment problem [11]. The goal is to select an active power schedule for each energy unit – from an individual search space of feasible schedules – such that some global objectives are met.

Agent-based approaches have developed into a relevant branch of research for VPP control and are widely discussed [23]. Usually, with agent-based approaches a software agent has to decide on a schedule for its corresponding energy resource at some point. In doing so, it must take into account the individual technical operational constraints because only feasible schedules may be considered in the optimization. The individual constraints are based on the capabilities of the unit, operation conditions (weather etc.) and cost restrictions, among others. To allow for unit independent algorithm design and generic software agents that are able to represent different types of DERs, a flexibility model is required which abstracts from DER specific constraints. Independently of the type of DER, the operational flexibility can be characterized by a set of feasible schedules, whereby feasible means operable by the energy unit without violating any operational constraints. In [3] a support vector based model has been introduced that builds upon such a representation of flexibility as a set of feasible schedules. From a methodological perspective, the concept presented in [3] realizes the abstraction from the technical system in several steps: First, in a simulation based sampling process, a set of example schedules is generated by a digital twin. These schedules are interpreted as vectors in an high dimensional space. This allows for a geometric interpretation of the units phase space and opens up the possibility to learn the surface boundary which separates valid from invalid schedules by means of Support Vector Data Description (SVDD). In [8] the support vector based approach was extended by a decoder which allows for a mapping of infeasible schedules to neighboring feasible schedules and thus systematic generation of feasible instances of the unit's phase space without domain knowledge on the (possible situational) operations of the controlled DER. Doing so, the decoder takes over the constraint handling which enables the use of standard optimization heuristics in the succeeding load planning phase.

In decentralized self-organized algorithms, typically each agent is responsible for one single resource and locally decides on the best schedule for the own unit. Newer use cases additionally demand the representation an ensemble of DERs e.g. when a hotel, a small business, a school or a neighborhood with an ensemble of co-generation, heat pump, solar power and controllable consumers wants to jointly participate. The same applies when thinking beyond the use case considered in this paper. E.g., for the provision of ancillary services for higher network levels, it would be conceivable to represent the flexibility of an entire low-voltage network by a single grid agent, as the aggregated grid flexibility is mostly made up from the individual flexibilities of the grid connectees [28,29]. All cases have in common that individual flexibilities have to be aggregated. Thereby a problem arises. Generating a single decoder for handling all constraints and feasible operations is challenging due to statistical problems when combining training sets from individually sampled flexibility models. Due to the convoluted densities only a very small portion of the feasible region (the dense region) is captured by the machine learning process [5]. But, a combined training set is needed if one wants to train a single decoder for an ensemble. In [5] the problem is bypassed by treating the ensembles as individual sub-VPPs. In contrast, [6] and [7] propose an approach that attacks the problem already during the sampling phase by taking the sampling as optimization problem with the aim of minimizing the convolution. The latter approaches differ in the optimization method used. While [7] uses Simulated Annealing, in [6] (CMA-ES) is applied.

So far, all solutions propose a centralized approach. This contribution proposes a distributed algorithm for seamless integration into the likewise distributed control algorithm. We formulate the sampling as a distributed optimization problem and use Ripley's K function [10] for evaluating the quality of the distribution of the combined sample schedules.

2   Distributed Sampling of Ensemble Flexibility

2.1   Flexibility Modeling

Flexibility modeling is the task of modeling constraints for DERs. Flexibility denotes the sub vector space of schedules that a DER might operate without violating any (technical or economic) constraint. A schedule of a DER is a vector $x = (x_0, \ldots, x_d) \in \mathcal{F} \subset \mathbb{R}^d$ with each element x_i denoting mean power generated (or consumed) during the ith time interval. Popular methods treat constraints as separate objectives or penalties, leading to a

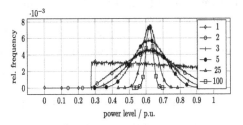

Fig. 1. Density of different folded distributions of operable CHP power levels.

transformation into an unconstrained many-objective problem [17,30]. For optimization in smart grid scenarios, black-box models capable of abstracting from the intrinsic model are more useful [7]. As the number of constraints quickly grows for ensembles, penalty approaches often fail. Penalties towing into different directions mutually hamper each other in finding feasible solutions. A powerful, yet flexible way of constraint-handling is the use of a decoder that systematically constructs feasible solutions [9]. A decoder imposes a relationship between a decoder solution and a feasible solution and gives instructions on how to construct a feasible solution [9]. Modern decoder approaches are based on machine learning and capture the feasible region from exemplary schedules generated by digital twins [8]. For generating a training set of as input for machine learning decoders, [4] developed a method that samples the phase space of a single DERs. Sometimes, a decoder is needed to cover the aggregated flexibility of an ensemble consisting of individually operated energy units. A digital twin that covers the joint operation of an ensemble is usually not available for sampling.

Randomly combining training sets of individual DER by adding up instances from each training set to gain a training set for the joint behavior is not targeted. An aggregated training set exhibits a density (of operable power levels) that results from folding of the source distributions. Figure 1 shows an example from [2]. Uniformly distributed values for levels of power fold up in case of ensembles. The situation gets worse with growing number of resources. The more individual training sets (and thus energy units in the ensemble) are folded, the more leptokurtic the pdf gets. This leads to an aggregated training set that is dense in the middle and sparse at the outskirts. Thus, instances from the outer parts are neglected as outliers when trying to learn a model. Large portions of the flexibility are not incorporated. For this reason, we designed an agent-based approach that circumvents this folding problem.

2.2   Sampling as Distributed Optimization Problem

The goal is to find a sample $\mathcal{X} \in \mathbb{R}^n \times \mathbb{R}^d$ of n joint schedules. Each row in matrix $\mathcal{X}$ denotes a joint schedule with dimension d. The distributed sampling problem can be reduced to a series of independent simpler problems: the repeated search for the next instance of a joint schedule. We assume that a sample of $0 < m < n$ instances already exist to which we want to add a new instance. For the goodness of fit of the new instance into the already existing sample, we need a measure of the discrepancy of the sample. The discrepancy of a set $X = \{x_1, \ldots, x_n\}$ measures how equidistributed X is. A general definition is given by [20]:

$$D_n(X) = \sup_{B \in \prod_{i=1}^{s}]a_1, b_i] = x \in \mathbb{R}^s | a_i \leq x_i < b_i} \left| \frac{A(B; P)}{n} - \lambda_s(B) \right|, 0 \leq a_i < B_i \leq 1 \quad (1)$$

with s-dimensional Lebesgue measure λ_s and $A(B; P)$ counting the number of points in P that fall into B. There exist several extension (e.g. the easier to calculate L_2 discrepancies [19]) to this general concept. A good overview can be found in [1].

We chose to use Ripley's K as statistical measure [10, 27]. In general, Ripley's K is defined as $K(r) = \lambda^{-1} E$, with E denoting the number of events (occurrence of other schedule) within distance r and λ denoting the density (count per unit area). Regarding points in Euclidean space the following estimator is often used:

$$\hat{K}(r) = \lambda^{-1} \sum_{i} \sum_{i \neq j} \frac{I(\delta_{ij} < r)}{n} \quad (2)$$

for n data samples, $I(\delta_{ij} < r)$ counting the number of data point within a distance less than r within a circle around data point i; λ measures the average density in n/A for the total area A. In our case $A = 1$, because all schedules are scaled to be within the unit hypercube.

Within a homogeneous set in the plane, points are distributed such that approximately the same number of points occurs in any circular region of a given area. If the set lacks homogeneity, it may be spatially clustered at a certain scale. Thus, $\hat{K}(r)$ is compared with the expected number of points $\lambda\pi r^2$. If the number of measured points is larger than the expected one, clusters are present, because the mean number of closer points is higher than expected. We want to minimize such mismatch and avoid clustering of samples and minimize the difference between expected and measured count of schedules. The latter is our degree of freedom, because we may move schedules within the feasible phase space in order to optimize the sample. For full homogeneity the integral over all possible r would have to be taken into account. We approximate this integral by

$$\tilde{K} = \sum_{r \in R} \left| \hat{K}(r) - nA_S(r) \right|. \tag{3}$$

The set R defines different distances $\{r_1, \ldots, r_k\}$ with $0 < r_i < 1$. A distance larger than 1 does not make any sense as all joint schedules are scaled to the unit hypercube. $A_S(r)$ denotes the volume of the hypersphere with radius r to cope with arbitrary dimensions [24]: $A_S(r) = \frac{\pi^{d/2}}{\Gamma(\pi/2+1)} r^n$ with $\Gamma(x) = (x-1)!$ [21]. With $\tilde{K}$ we have the objective function for our sampling optimization problem that is now solved in a distributed way using a multi agent system.

2.3   Solving with COHDA

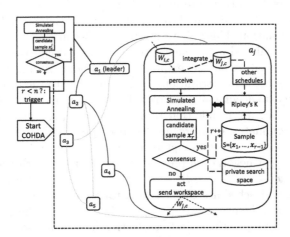

Fig. 2. General concept of distributed ensemble sampling with COHDA.

For distributed solving we used the Combinatorial Optimization Heuristic for Distributed Agents (COHDA), which was introduced in [14] and has been successfully applied to a variety of smart grid applications [13,22,23]. The general idea behind COHDA is an asynchronous iterative approximate best-response behavior [18], where each agent reacts to updated information from other agents by adapting its own selection with respect to local and global objectives.

Originally, COHDA had been designed as a fully distributed solution to the predictive scheduling problem in smart grid management. In this scenario, each agent in the multi-agent system is in charge of controlling exactly one distributed energy resource (generator or controllable consumer) with procuration for negotiating the energy. For the original predictive scheduling problem, it was the goal to find exactly one schedule for each energy unit such that (1) each assigned schedule can be operated by the respective energy unit without violating any hard technical constraint, and (2) the difference between the sum of all targets and a desired given target schedule is minimized.

An agent in COHDA does not represent a complete solution as for instance in population-based approaches [15,25]. Each agent represents a class within a multiple choice knapsack problem. Each class is represented by a decoder as model for the flexibility. Each agent chooses schedules as solution candidate only from the set of feasible schedules given by the decoder. Each agent communicates with a limited neighborhood. The neighborhood (communication network) is defined by a small world graph [14]. Agent collect information from the direct neighborhood, but each received message also contains (not necessarily up-to-date) information from the transitive neighborhood. Each agent may accumulate information about the choices of other agents and thus gains his own local belief of the aggregated schedule that the other agents are going to operate. With this belief each agent may choose a schedule for the own controlled energy unit in a way that the coalition is put forward best.

All choices for schedules are rooted in incomplete knowledge and beliefs in what other agents do; gathered from messages. The taken choice (together with the decision-base) is communicated to all neighbors and thus spreads successively throughout the coalition. This process is repeated. Because all information about schedule choices is labeled with an age, each agent may decide easily whether the own knowledge repository has to be updated. Any update results in recalculating of the own best schedule contribution and spreading it to the direct neighbors. By and by all agents accumulate complete information and as soon as no agent is capable of offering a schedule that results in a better solution, the algorithm converges and terminates. Convergence has been proved in [12].

This concept can be easily adapted to our sampling problem: we start the above sketched agent negotiation procedure several times. Each time the agents are given a list $x = \{x_1, \ldots, x_{ell}\}$ of ℓ already existing (from previous negotiations) aggregated schedules instead of a target schedule. The agents then negotiate on a new schedule $x = \sum_{1 \leq i \leq n} s_i$. Figure 2 shows the general concept and pipeline. Using Eq. 3, the objective function for this negotiation is

$$\arg\min_{s_j \in S_j} \quad \tilde{K}\left(\left(s_j + \sum_{i \neq j} s_i\right) \cup X\right); \tag{4}$$

i.e. agent a_j may alter s_j (as long as contained in the individual search space S_j) to find the one that minimizes $\tilde{K}$. In order to ensure the feasibility of s_j, we applied a support decoder as described in [8]. Such decoder is given as a mapping function $\gamma : \mathbb{R}^d \to \mathbb{R}^d \subseteq S$. Thus, after mapping a genotype solution with γ to the feasible sub-region, the result is a schedule that is operable by the energy device. Such support vector decoder can be trained with a set of feasible schedules derived from a simulation model of the energy resource.

Each time an agent decides on a schedule for the own energy device, optimization problem Eq. (4) has to be solved. This happens several times during negotiation. Thus, the overall sampling problem is a bi-level problem. In general, any optimization algorithm that integrates with a decode as constraint-handling technique could be used to solve Eq. (4). So far, we tested and compared random search as baseline, simulated annealing [16] as instance of evolution strategies, and particle swarm [25] as example of swarm based algorithms.

3   Results

As energy resource model for our simulations, we used a modulating cogeneration plant and the simulated thermal demand of a detached house. The used models have already served in several projects for evaluation [7,13,23].

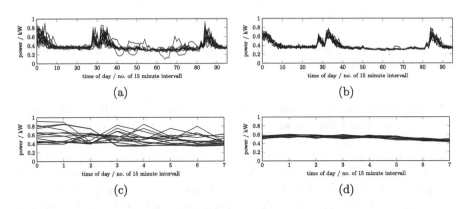

Fig. 3. Comparison of optimized ((a) and (c)) and naive combined samples ((b) and (d)) for 96 dimensions and 10 energy units (top) and 8 dimension and 100 energy units (bottom).

Figure 3 gives two examples of the optimization improvement potential by two examples. We optimized these examples with all three optimization approaches. For parameterization we used recommendations from [25] for the PSO and [16] for simulated annealing.

An example for the resulting curve of $\hat{K}$ for different radii r for all algorithms is compared in Fig. 4. The right figure enlarges the low radius portion by a logarithmic axis for better visibility. Low values of K mark a better result. For small radii, even the naive sampling achieves a good result. This is immediately clear, because even within the too small region that is covered by the naive sampling, homogeneity is preserved. The main problem is the lack of coverage of the outer flexibility. With growing radius, naive sampling quickly degrades to almost no homogeneity within the whole feasible region. All schedules are completely clustered within a single cluster. The best result is achieved by simulated annealing; closely followed by random search; PSO was not that good. The good performance of random search is a bit surprising but might be explained by the fact that the purpose of the procedure is random sampling, which is closely related to random search except for the number of tries. Nevertheless, for the remaining experiments we went with simulated annealing.

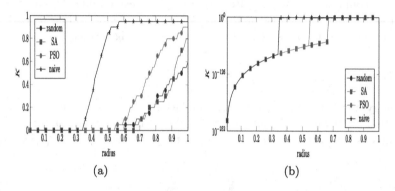

(a)   (b)

Fig. 4. Example result of random search, simulated annealing, PSO and naive sampling comparing Ripley's K for different radii.

In order to demonstrate the achieved improvement over the naive combination of individual samples, we calculated the (point cloud) diameter of the samples. Table 1 shows the mean results for different scenarios (with schedule dimension d and number of agents n). For each scenario randomly initialized simulation models for the co-generation plants have been instantiated to train a support vector decoder for the agent negotiation. Naive sampled sets were directly aggregated from these individual samples. The agents used simulated annealing with a budget limitation of 1000 objective evaluations for each decision routine run per agent. This budget was introduced to keep negotiation fast enough as simulated annealing is executed each time an agent tries to improve the coalition's result. Table 2 shows a significant improvement in all scenarios regarding the size of the covered flexibility (in terms of sample diameter). Table 1 shows also the number of sent messages as indicator for the number of conducted individual agent decisions; although this is not a complete 1:1 relation. Of course, for the naive approach no messages are sent.

Table 1. Mean improvement in covered flexibility (measured as sample diameter) for different numbers of agents n and schedule dimension.

Scenario	Diameter		Messages
	SA	Naive	SA
$d = 8, n = 20$	0.8433 ± 0.0118	0.1699 ± 0.0118	29856 ± 2391
$d = 96, n = 10$	0.9837 ± 0.2570	0.5900 ± 0.0355	15683 ± 6812
$d = 8, n = 100$	0.7737 ± 0.0543	0.1230 ± 0.0138	1075570 ± 212800

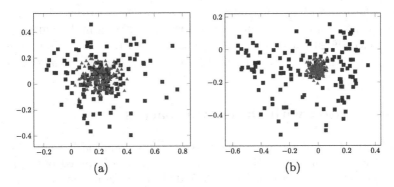

(a)   (b)

Fig. 5. Gain in occupied vector space through optimization with a 20 agent example on the left and a 50 agent example on the right. (Color figure online)

As indicator for the homogeneity of the aggregated samples, we additionally calculated the anchored L_2-discrepancy after [19]. All samples are from the unit hypercube. The unanchored version is reflection invariant and better copes with instances at the boundary. Thus, this measure may evaluate the effectiveness of the objective function on outer instances. Table 2 shows the mean results for the same scenarios as Table 1. Again, smaller values are better. For all experiments 20 runs have been conducted generating aggregated samples of 20 instances each. To get an impression of the gain in occupied sub-space for high-dimensional examples, we used dimension reduction to lineup naive and optimized samples. Figure 5 shows two examples based on principal component analysis. Figure 5a shows a 96-dimensional example with 20 agents comparing the restricted flexibility encoded by the original, naive sampled set (red) and the gain achieved after optimization (blue). Figure 5b gives an example with 50 agents.

Table 2. Mean improvement in L_2-discrepancy for different scenarios.

Scenario	SA	Naive
$d = 8, n = 20$	$2.9823 \times 10^{-3} \pm 1.1852^{-5}$	$9.2176^{-2} \pm 7.0655 \times 10^{-4}$
$d = 96, n = 10$	$3.3077 \times 10^{-32} \pm 9.3493^{-34}$	$7.4541^{-3} \pm 9.2321 \times 10^{-5}$
$d = 8, n = 100$	$3.2052 \times 10^{-3} \pm 3.9740^{-5}$	$9.5238^{-2} \pm 5.8712 \times 10^{-4}$

Table 3. Comparison of achieved flexibility coverage measured by sample diameter.

Scenario	Distributed SA	Central SA	Non-budgeted SA
s1	0.9919 ± 0.0237	0.7395 ± 0.0224	0.8488 ± 0.0172
s2	0.8468 ± 0.0043	0.9943 ± 0.0036	1.0693 ± 0.0683
s3	0.8072 ± 0.0309	0.7752 ± 0.0249	0.8156 ± 0.0355

Table 4. Comparison of achieved homogeneity measured by L_2-discrepancy.

Scenario	Distributed SA	Central SA	Non-budgeted SA
s1	$8.244^{-4} \pm 6.419^{-5}$	$1.159 \times 10^{-3} \pm 2.485 \times^{-5}$	$7.097 \times 10^{-4} \pm 1.011 \times 10^{-5}$
s2	$1.361^{-16} \pm 7.126^{-18}$	$1.282 \times 10^{-16} \pm 3.511 \times^{-18}$	$1.148 \times 10^{-16} \pm 3.134 \times 10^{-18}$
s3	$1.002^{-3} \pm 6.596^{-5}$	$1.661 \times 10^{-3} \pm 1.419 \times^{-4}$	$1.002 \times 10^{-3} \pm 9.773 \times 10^{-5}$

4   Comparison with Other Approaches

To the best of our knowledge, there is so far no approach that addresses this specific problem in a distributed way. Thus, we compared our approach with a centralized algorithm. Tables 3 and 4 show results for three scenarios: s1 ($d = 8, n = 10, m = 20$), s2 ($d = 48, n = 30, m = 20$), and s3 ($d = 8, n = 50, m = 10$). Again, we compared achieved diameter to assess the gain in encoded flexibility and the L_2-discrepancy to assess homogeneity. As centralized algorithm we use simulated annealing. For unfolding in [7] also simulated annealing had been used as centralized approach. As can be seen from the results, the distributed approach is competitive with the centralized approach despite a lack of global information. For the centralized approach, we used two versions: with and without budget. For performance reasons, the distributed approach uses simulated annealing with a budget of 1000 evaluations per decision. In order to get full control over the overall budget, we introduced a second condition restricting each agent to a maximum of 5 times trying to improve. This restriction result in a overall budget of $n \cdot 1000 \cdot 5$ for n agents. The same budget is set for the budgeted simulated annealing.

When looking at the achieved diameters, the distributed approach outperforms even the unbudgeted SA for low-dimensional problems. Regarding the homogeneity of the sample, the SA without budget always succeeds because it has the budget to go the extra mile for precision work in shuffling the sample to the ideal place. The same effect could be achieved with the distributed approach by increasing the budget there. But, this would at the same time result in more (maybe tiny) improvements made by the agent. Each improvement made by an agent results in triggering several other agents trying to improve these new results even further. Thus, the whole process is disproportionately slowed down. Here, further research has to be conducted to find the best trade-off.

5   Conclusion

Machine learning for flexibility modeling enables efficient and domain knowledge independent implementation of distributed optimization methods. So far, these models were only applied to single energy units, because distributions of power levels in the training sets of single units fold up when aggregating them to ensemble training sets. Such training set renders useless for appropriately learning a model for the joint flexibility of a group of energy units. Agent-based solutions are widely seen as the most promising approach to cope with the growing problem instances in the future smart grid. We presented an agent-based approach for ensemble sampling that is able to circumvent the folding problem and demonstrated applicability and effectiveness. As an agent-based approach, it can seamlessly be integrated into different decentralized coordination algorithms. Scrutinizing these interplay issues and application of our approach for aggregating the flexibility potential of entire network levels in the context of grid control and ancillary service provision, will be the upcoming tasks of this work.

Acknowledgement. This work was funded by the Deutsche Forschungsgemeinschaft (DFG, German Research Foundation) – 359921210.

References

1. Beck, J., Sós, V.T.: Discrepancy Theory, pp. 1405–1446. MIT Press, Cambridge (1996)
2. Bremer, J., Lehnhoff, S.: Sensitivity in multi-ensemble scheduling. In: FedCSIS. Annals of Computer Science and Information Systems, vol. 15, pp. 215–223 (2018)
3. Bremer, J., Rapp, B., Sonnenschein, M.: Support vector based encoding of distributed energy resources' feasible load spaces, pp. 1–8. IEEE PES (2010)
4. Bremer, J., Sonnenschein, M.: Sampling the search space of energy resources for self-organized, agent-based planning of active power provision. In: Page, B., Fleischer, A.G., Göbel, J., Wohlgemuth, V. (eds.) EnviroInfo 2013. Shaker (2013)
5. Bremer, J., Lehnhoff, S.: Hybrid multi-ensemble scheduling. In: Squillero, G., Sim, K. (eds.) EvoApplications 2017. LNCS, vol. 10199, pp. 342–358. Springer, Cham (2017). https://doi.org/10.1007/978-3-319-55849-3_23
6. Bremer, J., Lehnhoff, S.: Phase-space sampling of energy ensembles with CMA-ES. In: Sim, K., Kaufmann, P. (eds.) EvoApplications 2018. LNCS, vol. 10784, pp. 222–230. Springer, Cham (2018). https://doi.org/10.1007/978-3-319-77538-8_16
7. Bremer, J., Lehnhoff, S.: Unfolding ensemble training sets for improved support vector decoders in energy management, vol. 2, pp. 322–329. Science and Technology Publications (2018)
8. Bremer, J., Sonnenschein, M.: Constraint-handling with support vector decoders. In: Filipe, J., Fred, A. (eds.) ICAART 2013. CCIS, vol. 449, pp. 228–244. Springer, Heidelberg (2014). https://doi.org/10.1007/978-3-662-44440-5_14
9. Coello, C.A.C.: Theoretical and numerical constraint-handling techniques used with evolutionary algorithms: a survey of the state of the art. Comput. Methods Appl. Mech. Eng. **191**(11–12), 1245–1287 (2002)
10. Dixon, P.M.: Ripley's K Function. American Cancer Society (2013)

11. Guan, X., Zhai, Q., Papalexopoulos, A.: Optimization based methods for unit commitment: Lagrangian relaxation versus general mixed integer programming. IEEE PES General Meet. **2**, 1095–1100 (2003)
12. Hinrichs, C.: Selbstorganisierte Einsatzplanung dezentraler Akteure im Smart Grid. Ph.D. thesis, Carl von Ossietzky Universität Oldenburg (2014)
13. Hinrichs, C., Bremer, J., Sonnenschein, M.: Distributed hybrid constraint handling in large scale virtual power plants. In: IEEE PES Conference on Innovative Smart Grid Technologies Europe. IEEE Power & Energy Society (2013)
14. Hinrichs, C., Lehnhoff, S., Sonnenschein, M.: A decentralized heuristic for multiple-choice combinatorial optimization problems. In: Helber, S., et al. (eds.) Operations Research Proceedings 2012. ORP, pp. 297–302. Springer, Cham (2014). https://doi.org/10.1007/978-3-319-00795-3_43
15. Karaboga, D., Basturk, B.: A powerful and efficient algorithm for numerical function optimization: artificial bee colony (ABC) algorithm. J. Global Optim. **39**(3), 459–471 (2007). https://doi.org/10.1007/s10898-007-9149-x
16. Kirkpatrick, S., Gelatt, C.D., Vecchi, M.P.: Optimization by simulated annealing. Science **220**(4598), 671–680 (1983). https://doi.org/10.1126/science.220.4598.671
17. Kramer, O.: A review of constraint-handling techniques for evolution strategies. Appl. Comput. Intell. Soft Comput. **2010**, 1–19 (2010)
18. Littman, M.L., Stone, P.: Leading best-response strategies in repeated games. In: Seventeenth Annual International Joint Conference on Artificial Intelligence Workshop on Economic Agents, Models and Mechanisms (2001)
19. Matouček, J.: On the L2-discrepancy for anchored boxes. J. Complex. **14**(4), 527–556 (1998)
20. Niederreiter, H.: Random Number Generation and Quasi-Monte Carlo Methods. Society for Industrial and Applied Mathematics, Philadelphia (1992)
21. Nielsen, N.: Handbuch der theorie der gammafunktion. Teubner (1906)
22. Nieße, A., Beer, S., Bremer, J., Hinrichs, C., Lünsdorf, O., Sonnenschein, M.: Conjoint dynamic aggregation and scheduling for dynamic VPP. In: Ganzha, M., Maciaszek, L.A., Paprzycki, M. (eds.) FedCSIS, Warsaw, Poland, September 2014
23. Nieße, A., et al.: Market-based self-organized provision of active power and ancillary services: an agent-based approach for Smart Distribution Grids, pp. 1–5. IEEE (2012)
24. Peters, M.H.: On the shrinking volume of the hypersphere. Coll. Math. J. **46**(3), 178–180 (2015). https://doi.org/10.4169/college.math.j.46.3.178
25. Poli, R., Kennedy, J., Blackwell, T.: Particle swarm optimization. Swarm Intell. **1**(1), 33–57 (2007). https://doi.org/10.1007/s11721-007-0002-0
26. Pudjianto, D., Ramsay, C., Strbac, G.: Virtual power plant and system integration of distributed energy resources. IET Renew. Gener. **1**(1), 10–16 (2007)
27. Ripley, B.D.: The second-order analysis of stationary point processes. J. Appl. Probab. **13**(2), 255–266 (1976). https://doi.org/10.2307/3212829
28. Sarstedt, M., et al.: Standardized evaluation of multi-level grid control strategies for future converter-dominated electric energy systems. at-Automatisierungstechnik **67**(11), 936–957 (2019)
29. Sarstedt, M., Kluß, L., Gerster, J., Meldau, T., Hofmann, L.: Survey and comparison of optimization-based aggregation methods for the determination of the flexibility potentials at vertical system interconnections. Energies **14**(3), 687 (2021)
30. Smith, A., Coit, D.: Penalty functions. In: Handbook of Evolutionary Computation, p. Section C5.2. Oxford University Press and IOP Publishing, Department of Industrial Engineering, University of Pittsburgh, USA (1997)

Analysis and Simulation of Local Flexibility Markets: Preliminary Report

Jorge Morais[1]($\boxtimes$), Fernando Lopes[2], and Anabela Pronto[3]

[1] NOVA School of Science and Technology|FCT NOVA, Caparica, Portugal
jmm.morais@campus.fct.unl.pt
[2] LNEG - National Laboratory of Energy and Geology, Lisbon, Portugal
fernando.lopes@lneg.pt
[3] Centre of Technology and Systems/UNINOVA, Quinta da Torre, 2829-516 Caparica, Portugal
amg1@fct.unl.pt

Abstract. Flexibility markets are novel markets that allow distributed energy resources to remunerate changes in their baseline electricity consumption/production profiles. Given the pioneer status of these markets, the number of trades performed is still relatively small, not allowing for a detailed analysis of the quantities traded and the price formation mechanisms. The use of agent-based simulation tools is a promising approach to accurately model and analyze the behavior of flexibility markets, allowing for a more detailed understanding of the behavior of the agents and the transaction prices. In this paper, we carry out a systematic survey of ongoing flexibility markets projects. We then proceed to describe our ongoing work to develop a local flexibility market, by extending the MATREM system. Finally, we describe a forthcoming study to be carried out with the help of MATREM and involving scenarios related to the Iberian market.

Keywords: Energy markets · Local flexibility markets · Transmission and distribution system operators · Distributed energy resources · MATREM system

1 Introduction

Energy markets and power systems in general are going through a period of unprecedented changes (see, e.g., [1]). Over the past decade, we have witnessed a rapid deployment of renewable energy sources (RES) in electrical networks. More recently, we have also seen the emergence of new distributed energy resources (DERs), such as battery storage (BESS) and electric vehicles (EVs), as well as changes in electricity consumption patterns by end-users.

Market-based tools that allow DERs to trade their flexibility are a promising way to adequately remunerate their flexibility services, thus creating new investment opportunities. The development of the so-called flexibility markets is taking the first steps (see, e.g., [2]). Different market configurations are being studied at the pilot project level, although some of them are already in a commercial exploration phase. However, and given the pioneer status of these projects, the number of transactions carried out is

© Springer Nature Switzerland AG 2021
F. De La Prieta et al. (Eds.): PAAMS Workshops 2021, CCIS 1472, pp. 203–214, 2021.
https://doi.org/10.1007/978-3-030-85710-3_17

still relatively small, not allowing for a detailed analysis of the behavior of the agents involved, nor the prices considered. We therefore believe that there is an opportunity to develop a simulation tool allowing for a more detailed analysis of the behavior of agents and market prices.

In this paper, we perform a systematic survey of the ongoing flexibility market projects and compare their main characteristics. We then proceed to describe our ongoing efforts to develop a flexibility market to be integrated into the MATREM system [3, 4]. Finally, we propose a case study to be performed with the help of MATREM and involving scenario related to the Iberian market.

2 Flexibility Markets

2.1 Overview

The increase in energy production from renewable energy sources, associated with the general trend towards the electrification of economic activities, are creating an opportunity for consumers/producers (prosumers) to be paid for deciding what part of their energy use is not critical or time dependent. If this flexibility is offered in the market, it will contribute to a better balance between supply and demand, and also to solve a wide range of problems experienced by system operators, notably preventing congestions and avoiding or postponing network reinforcement investments.

Traditionally, flexibility was provided by large operators. Currently, the small traders and prosumers are increasingly seeking to value their flexibility. This trend is strongly supported by the European Union [5, 6]. Flexibility markets are thus being increasingly recognized as an important tool for the management and optimization of electrical networks, and more generally for the overall reduction of system costs. We present next some examples of real projects already underway or under study and compare their main characteristics. For this purpose, we carried out a bibliographic review on the topic [7–10] and a consultation of public available data on ongoing projects.

2.2 Examples of Flexibility Markets

PICLO FLEX. The UK based software company Piclo started operation in the energy sector in 2013 [11]. The Piclo Flex market was developed with funding from the UK Government's Department of Business, Energy, and Industrial Strategy. In 2018, the test of the platform encompassed the six distribution system operators (DSOs) in UK. Subsequently, Piclo signed commercial contracts with those DSOs in order to support their developing flexibility procurement activities. The first tenders were launched in 2019, to meet the flexibility needs for both the 2019–20 and 2020–21 periods.

NODES. The NODES flexibility market [12], established in early 2018, is a joint project between the Norwegian DSO Agder Energi and the European energy exchange Nord Pool (PX). Nord Pool runs the leading power market in Europe, offering both day-ahead and intraday markets to customers. Agder Energi is one of the leading companies in the Norwegian renewable energy sector and has been an active aggregator and supplier of flexibility in several European countries.

ENERA. The ENERA project [13] is the result of the German Federal Ministry of Economic Affairs and Energy program Smart Energy Showcases – Digital Agenda for the Energy Transition (SINTEG), and aims at developing and demonstrating scalable standard solutions with a high share of renewable energies within selected regions in the country.

GOPACS. (Grid Operator Platform for Congestion Solutions) is a new software platform jointly developed by the Dutch TSO TenneT and the regional grid operators (DSOs). Its main objective is to mitigate the capacity shortages in the electricity grid (congestions), thus contributing to keep the Dutch grid reliable and affordable [14].

IREMEL. OMIE, the Spanish Iberian electricity spot Market Operator, in collaboration with IDAE, Institute for the Diversification and Energy Saving, launched the IREMEL project, aiming at facilitating and promoting the implementation and efficient utilization of distributed energy resources in distribution networks. To validate the capabilities and advantages of the proposed model, IREMEL includes 5 pilots on local flexibility markets in different Spanish areas, with different participants and under different conditions [15].

ENEDIS is the main DSO of the French electricity market (more than 90% of market share). Following the Nice Smart Valley pilot (INTERFLEX Project), the integration of local flexibility was validated as a potential solution for solving congestion and/or deferring network investments [16]. For this purpose, ENEDIS built a proprietary Web platform (E-FLEX).

TEPCO V2G. Initiative carried out in Japan, involving TEPCO (TSO/DSO), Mitsubishi Motors, Hitachi Systems and Shizuoca Gas [17]. It aims at demonstrating the feasibility of aggregating electric vehicles in virtual power plants (VPPs) in order to provide system balance services (replacement reserve) through vehicle-to-grid system. These services will be traded in the balancing market.

POWER POTENTIAL. This project aims at creating a new market for reactive energy for flexibility providers, in order to generate additional capacity in the network, and deal with voltage/thermal constraints in the grid of the Southeast of England. The project is led by NGESO (TSO), with the support of UKPN (DSO) [18].

CLEM. Cornwall Local Energy Market (CLEM) is a flexible service market project targeting both the local DSO (WPD) and the TSO (NGESO), in order to minimize the congestion problems resulting from the high production of energy from renewable energy resources [19]. It is the result of an initiative by Centrica (an aggregator) in conjunction with WPD and NGESO.

2.3   Comparison of Projects

Table 1 lists the main characteristics of the aforementioned projects. Despite the diversity of solutions adopted, we found that most projects aim at providing flexibility solutions to DSOs and/or TSOs for network congestion management. In this sense, they constitute local markets where the principal buyers are DSOs and TSOs, who for this purpose define the constraint areas (where flexibility procurement will be made).

Potential suppliers are typically subject to a prior qualification process, in which the validation of the technical characteristics of the assets to be used is considered. Also, a reference baseline is established for flexibility offers (usually based on the historical analysis of consumption/production). Based on it, there seems to be a multiplicity of differentiating characteristics between projects, which we will subsequently detail.

Market Agents. On the supply side (sell offers), the markets are open to DERs, whether or not they behave as balance responsible parties (BRPs), individually or through aggregation services. On the demand side (buy offers), the markets may be open to DSOs (e.g., Piclo Flex, ENEDIS, IREMEL), DSOs and TSOs (e.g., ENERA, TEPCO V2G), or DSOs, TSOs and BRPs (e.g., GOPACS, NODES).

Procurement Mechanism. There are two main types of procurement mechanisms: periodic tender and ID continuous matching. Procurement by tender has generally a relatively long service delivery horizon (1 year or more) and is mainly used when TSOs/DSOs are searching for solutions that allow investment deferral in network reinforcement. This is the case, for example, of UKPN (DSO), which regularly launches multi-annual tenders on the Piclo Flex platform [11].

Procurement by ID continuous matching has a more immediate delivery horizon (it can go from a day to 15 min after clearing) and essentially aims at timely resolving network congestion problems and minimizing the need to reduce production (curtailment). This is particularly the case for the GOPACS and NODES markets.

Trading Period. It can range from months-ahead (for example, in Piclo Flex) to 15 min before delivery (for example, in NODES, GOPACS and ENERA).

Remuneration. Includes usually a capacity term and a utilization term. In the case of continuous ID markets, remuneration is mostly for utilization.

Price Rule. The general rule for most markets is pay-as-bid. Buyers use different evaluation formulas (for example, the comparable rate from UKPN) that combine these two terms to rank the proposals to be selected. Note that in this case there is no price offer from buyers. They may eventually indicate a maximum acceptable price range (for example, Piclo Flex and ENEDIS).

In the case of continuous ID markets (for example, ENERA and NODES), the price-setting mechanism results from the matching of buy and sell offers in accordance with existing rules for the wholesale markets. In the case of GOPACS, both buyers and sellers receive the offered price, the difference (spread) being supported by DSOs/TSOs [20].

Minimum Offer. There is a great variability in the minimum size of acceptable offers, which range between 0.1 MW and 1 MW. Naturally, the greater the minimum acceptable offer, the lower the overall liquidity of the market, and consequently the need for smaller capacity DERs to resort to aggregators.

Table 1. Comparison of pioneer projects

PROJECT NAME	Project partners	Use of independent platform	Problem to be solved	Market agents (sellers)	Market agents (buyers)	Type of procurement
PICLO FLEX	Piclo + 6 DSO	Yes (Piclo Flex)	Congestion; investment deferral	Flex. providers, aggregators	DSO	Tender
POWER POTENTIAL	NGESO TSO), UKPN (DSO), U. Cambridge; U. Oxford	No (proprietary DERMS interface run by UKPN)	Voltage and congestion constraints	Flex. providers, aggregators	TSO	Tender
CLEM	Centrica (aggregator) NGESO (TSO) WPD (DSO)	Yes (N-SIDE)	Congestion	Flex. providers through CENTRICA	phase 2: DSO + TSO	Phase 1: tender phase 2: auction
NODES	Nord Pool (PX); Agder Energi (DSO)	Yes (NODES)	Congestion; balancing	Flex. providers, aggregators	DSO + TSO + BRP	ID continuous market
ENERA	EPEX SPOT (PX); TenneT (TSO); 2 DSO	Yes (ENERA Flexmarkt)	Congestion	Flex. providers, aggregators	DSO + TSO	ID continuous market
GOPACS	TenneT (TSO) + 4 DSO	No (GOPACS not a Marketplace);	Congestion; TSO/DSO coordination	Flex. providers, aggregators	DSO + TSO + BRP	ID continuous market
ENEDIS	ENEDIS (DSO)	No (E-FLEX proprietary platform)	Congestion; investment deferral	Flex. providers, aggregators	DSO	Tender
IREMEL	OMIE (PX), IDEA	Yes	Congestion; investment deferral	Flex. providers, aggregators	TBD	TBD
V2G	TEPCO (TSO/DSO); Mitsubishi; Hitachi	No	Congestion; balancing; voltage constraints	Aggregators	DSO/TSO	Auction

Flexibility Products. Table 2 presents the main characteristics of some of the flexibility products available on the markets (e.g., Piclo Flex, NODES, ENERA and GOPACS). It shows the similarity of product specifications, concretely with some products traded in wholesale continuous markets (e.g., NODES, ENERA and GOPACS).

From what was discussed above, it can be concluded that flexibility markets are just taking their first steps, with transaction volumes still insignificant, when compared to

Table 2. Comparison of flexibility products

PROJECT NAME	Product name	Type	Remuneration	Contract duration	Minimum increment	Minimum price
PICLO FLEX	UKPN Secure	Regulation Up	Availability + utilization	1 to 7 years	N.A	N.A
NODES	WPD Intraflex	Regulation Up/Down	Availability + utilization	30 min	0,01 £/MW	
ENERA	RES/Non RES; Hour/quarter_Hour	Regulation Up/Down	Utilization	1 h; 15 min	0,1 €/MWh	−9999,9/−50/MWh
GOPACS	IDCONS (Buy and Sell Orders)	Regulation Down/Up	Utilization	15 min multiples		

the volumes of wholesale markets. The main motivation for the development of these markets is to provide DSOs/TSOs with additional tools, in the form of flexibility products to deal with network constraints.

The commercialization of flexibility does not seem to require a particular market design (with specific characteristics). In this sense, the existing designs of wholesale electricity markets seem to be a good starting point for the design of flexibility markets. In particular, the cases studied can roughly be divided into two groups: procurement by periodic tender and procurement by ID continuous market.

There is still a great diversity in the specifications of the flexibility products. However, the products traded in continuous flexibility markets are roughly similar to the products traded in wholesale continuous markets. Also, the issues related to DSO/TSO and BRP/DER coordination are not yet completely addressed. The direct connection of flexibility markets with existing wholesale and balancing markets needs to be completely operationalized.

3   Overview of the MATREM System

Intelligent agents and multi-agent systems (MAS) technologies represent an innovative approach to design and implement complex systems. They have been used to solve problems in a variety of commercial and industrial applications. These applications range from personal software assistants to distributed systems, where agents are constituted as processing elements in computational systems. Electricity markets (EMs) are open systems that promote competition between suppliers and offer consumers a varied choice of services. EMs are by nature distributed and complex and can encompass a wide range of transaction techniques. Agent-based simulation (ABS) presents itself as a promising approach to accurately model and analyze in detail the behavior of EMs over time [3, 4].

MATREM (for Multi-Agent Trading in Electricity Markets) allows the user to perform simulations of energy markets under a variety of conditions. In each simulation, different agents are used to emulate the heterogeneity of the markets, namely producers, traders, aggregators, small and large consumers, market operators and system operators. Agents are developed using the JADE [21] and JADEX [22] platforms.

The Java Agent Development Framework (JADE) platform was developed using the JAVA programming language. This platform has properties that facilitate the development of computational agents, such as agent communication and mobility, making possible to run systems on different machines and operating systems. The JADEX platform consists of a reasoning engine that runs on JADE, allowing the development of belief-desire-intention (BDI) agents.

MATREM supports a spot market and a derivatives market. The spot market comprises a day-ahead market and an intraday market (see, e.g. [23, 24]). The derivatives market comprises a futures market. The tool also supports the negotiation of tailored (or customized) bilateral contracts (see, e.g. [25–27]). In addition, MATREM supports six different types of market entities: generation companies, traders, aggregators, consumers, market operators and system operators.

4 New Local Flexibility Market

A major goal of this work is to extend the MATREM system with a new local flexibility market. To this end, we intend to take into account a key aspect of the previous market comparison, namely the fact that the commercialization of flexibility does not seem to require a particular market design with specific characteristics. As such, the existing design of wholesale electricity markets seems to be a good starting point. In particular, our ongoing work considers a continuous market (similar to some intraday continuous markets), with pay-as-bid as the pricing mechanism.

Literature review seems to support this choice. For example, in [28], the authors suggest that continuous trading promotes price efficiency and better suits the trading mechanism preferences of the investors. An in [7], the authors suggest that continuous trading might be more suitable for markets with low liquidity.

The market design that we are envisioning is therefore a transmission/distribution-level market that clears continuously, with a pay-as-bid pricing rule. Market agents include TSOs/DSOs as buyers of flexibility products, and DERs and aggregators as flexibility providers. The matching algorithm will be based on some of the Iberian market rules [29].

Table 3. Flexibility assets

Flexibility provider	Nominal flex. capacity (MW)	Asset type
DER 1 => DER 4	0,05	vehicle_charging
DER 5 => DER 20	0,05	battery
DER 21	0,10	vehicle_charging
DER 22	0,28	vehicle_charging/battery
DER 23	0,49	vehicle_charging/battery
DER 24 => DER 37	0,50	mixed
DER 38	0,70	vehicle_charging/battery
DER 39 => DER 48	1,00	mixed
DER 49	1,05	vehicle_charging/battery
DER 50	1,40	vehicle_charging/battery
DER 51	1,75	vehicle_charging/battery
DER 52	2,10	mixed
DER 53 => DER 54	2,45	vehicle_charging/battery
DER 55 => DER 58	2,60	mixed
Total	*41,17*	

5 Case Study

In as much as the present reality of the Portuguese market is, local flexibility markets are yet nonexistent, either at an operating or design level.

Accordingly, a forthcoming study will be based on the secondary and tertiary reserve markets operated by the Portuguese TSO and inspired by the TEPCO V2G project (discussed above). Our believe is that it would be compelling for the Portuguese TSO to have access to additional balancing solutions in the form of flexibility products traded in a local flexibility market (as is already the case of other European TSOs). This would also have the additional benefit of opening the possibility for local DERs and aggregators (presently without access to existing energy markets) to create value from their untapped flexibility potential.

Previous work by the Portuguese regulating authority ERSE on this matter has led to the creation of a pilot project designed to allow DERs to participate in the National balancing market, which ran until the end of 2020 [30]. However, strictly speaking, this was not a local market, as DERs were allowed to participate at a nation-wide level.

On the supply side, we intend to consider a representative set of 58 local DER assets (Table 3), including electric vehicles and batteries, as presented in Fig. 1. On the demand side, the study will involve a single agent. For simplicity, a single flexibility product (Up Regulation) will be considered.

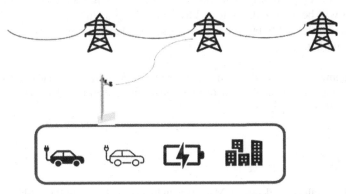

Fig. 1. Schematic representation of local flexibility providers.

Some details about the procedure to be adopted in order to define the bids to submit to the market are shown in Table 4. Basically, it will involve the following: for each hourly period, each nth DER will bid a price corresponding to nth sub-interval of that hourly price range. In Table 4, m represents the minimal hourly price, M the maximum hourly price, Yn a randomized percentage, and Cn the flexibility capacity of DER n.

Table 4. Bids/offers of DERs for a particular hour of the market horizon.

Agent	Flex. quantity offered (MWh)	Flex. price (€/MWh)
DER 1	$Y_1 \cdot C_1$	$p_1 = m$
DER 2	$Y_2 \cdot C_2$	$p_2 = m + ((M - m)/N) \cdot 2$
...	...	...
DER n	$Y_n \cdot C_n$	$p_n = m + ((M - m)/N) \cdot n$
...	...	...
DER N	$X_N \cdot C_N$	$p_N = M$

6 Conclusions

Local Flexibility markets are just taking their first steps, with transaction volumes still insignificant, when compared with the volumes of wholesale markets. Accordingly, there seems to be a good opportunity to extend the MATREM system with a new local flexibility market, allowing for a more detailed analysis of market behavior and transactions.

Efforts to develop a new local flexibility market are being undertaken by the authors. The market will be analyzed and tested by considering a study involving a number of DERs and some flexibility buyers, and will take into account scenarios associated with the Iberian market.

Acknowledgements. This work was developed and supported by FCT Fundação para a Ciência e a Tecnologia (CTS multiannual funding) under the framework of project (2020–2023) UIDB/00066/2020.

References

1. Lopes, F., Coelho, H.: Electricity Markets with Increasing Levels of Renewable Generation: Structure, Operation Agent-based Simulation and Emerging Designs. Springer, Cham (2018). https://doi.org/10.1007/978-3-319-74263-2
2. Lopes, F.: From wholesale energy markets to local flexibility markets: structure, models and operation, Chap. 3. In: Local Electricity Markets. Academic Press, London (2021)
3. Lopes, F.: MATREM: an agent-based simulation tool for electricity markets. In: Lopes, F., Coelho, H. (eds.) Electricity Markets with Increasing Levels of Renewable Generation: Structure, Operation, Agent-based Simulation, and Emerging Designs. SSDC, vol. 144, pp. 189–225. Springer, Cham (2018). https://doi.org/10.1007/978-3-319-74263-2_8
4. Lopes, F., Coelho, H.: Electricity markets and intelligent agents Part II: agent architectures and capabilities. In: Lopes, F., Coelho, H. (eds.) Electricity Markets with Increasing Levels of Renewable Generation: Structure, Operation, Agent-based Simulation, and Emerging Designs. SSDC, vol. 144, pp. 49–77. Springer, Cham (2018). https://doi.org/10.1007/978-3-319-74263-2_3

5. European Comission, Memo: New Electricity Market Design: a Fair Deal for Consumers, November (2016)
6. EU: Directive (EU) 2019/944 of the European Parliament and of the Council of 5 June 2019 on Common Rules for the Internal Market for Electricity and Amending Directive 2012/27/EU, Electricity and Amending Directive, vol. 944 (2019)
7. Schittekatte, T., Mêeus, L.: Flexibility markets: Q&A with project pioneers. Util. Policy **63**, 101017 (2020)
8. Anaya, K., Pollitt, M.: A review of international experience in the use of smart electricity platforms for the procuremente of flexibility services, Milestone 1. University of Cambridge (2020)
9. SmartEn: Design Principles for (Local) Markets for Electricity System Services, Smart Energy Position Paper (2019)
10. Dronne, T., Roques, F., Saguan, M.: Local flexibility markets for distribution network congestion-management: which design for which needs? (2020)
11. Johnston, J.: Piclo flexibility marketplace, October (2018)
12. Deuchert, B.: NODES – a new market design to trade decentralized flexibility (2019)
13. Sommer, H.: Local flexibility markets: beyond the Status Quo. A truly European Power Exchange, EPEX Spot (2020)
14. Hirth, L., Glismann, S.: Congestion management: from physics to regulatory instruments, pp. 1–23. ZBW – Leibniz Information Centre for Economics, Kiel (2018)
15. IDAE: OMIE, and Ministerio para la Transición Ecológica, Proyecto IREMEL: Integración de Recursos Energéticos através de Mercados Locales de Electricidad (2019)
16. ENEDIS: Feuille de Route pour la Transformation des Méthodes de Dimensionnement des Réseaux et l'intégration des Flexibités (2020)
17. Hitachi Systems Power Service, Ltd. and Hitachi Solutions, Ltd.: V2G demonstrator project using EVs as virtual power plant resource (2018)
18. Power Potential: Power potential market procedures (2018)
19. Bray, R., Woodman, B., Judson, E.: Future prospects for local energy markets: lessons from the cornwall LEM (2020)
20. STEDIN, Liander, Tennet, and Enexis: IDCONS Product Specification GOPACS (2019)
21. Bellifemine, F., Caire, G., Greenwood, D.: Developing Multi-Agent Systems with JADE. Wiley, Chichester (2007)
22. Braubach, L., Pokahr, A., Lamersdorf, W.: JADEX: a BDI-agent system combining middleware and reasoning. In: Unland, R., Klusch, M., Calisti, M. (eds.) Software Agent-Based Applications, Platforms and Development Kits. WSSAT, pp. 143–168. Springer, Basel (2005). https://doi.org/10.1007/3-7643-7348-2_7
23. Algarvio, H., Couto, A., Lopes, F., Estanqueiro, A., Santana, J.: Multi-agent energy markets with high levels of renewable generation: a case-study on forecast uncertainty and market closing time. In: Omatu, S., et al. (eds.) Distributed Computing and Artificial Intelligence. AISC, pp. 339–347. Springer, Cham (2016). https://doi.org/10.1007/978-3-319-40162-1_37
24. Algarvio, H., Lopes, F., Couto, A., Estanqueiro, A.: Participation of wind power producers in day-ahead and balancing markets: an overview and a simulation-based study. WIREs Energy Environ. **8**(5), e343 (2019)
25. Lopes, F., Mamede, N., Novais, A.Q., Coelho, H.: Negotiation tactics for autonomous agents. In: 12th International Workshop on Database and Expert Systems Applications (DEXA), pp. 1–5. IEEE (2001)
26. Lopes, F., Mamede, N., Novais, A.Q., Coelho, H.: Negotiation in a multi-agent supply chain system. In: Third International Workshop of the IFIP WG 5.7 Special Interest Group on Advanced Techniques in Production Planning & Control, pp. 153–168. Firenze University Press (2002)

27. Lopes, F., Coelho, H.: Concession behaviour in automated negotiation. In: Buccafurri, F., Semeraro, G. (eds.) E-Commerce and Web Technologies: 11th International Conference, EC-Web 2010, Bilbao, Spain, September 1–3, 2010. Proceedings, pp. 184–194. Springer, Heidelberg (2010). https://doi.org/10.1007/978-3-642-15208-5_17
28. Lauterbach, B., Ungar, M.: Switching to continuous trading and its impact on return behavior and volume of trade. J. Financ. Serv. Res. **12**(1), 39–50 (1997). https://doi.org/10.1023/A:1007965627691
29. OMIE: Day-ahead and intraday electricity market operating rules, vol. 8, no. 5, p. 55 (2019)
30. ERSE: Projeto-Piloto De Participação Do Consumo No Mercado De Reserva De Regulação - Relatório Previsto No Artigo 16º da Diretiva Nª 4, 2019" (2020)

Semantic Interoperability for Multiagent Simulation and Decision Support in Power Systems

Gabriel Santos[1,2] , Tiago Pinto[1,2(✉)] , Zita Vale[2] , and Juan M. Corchado[3]

[1] GECAD Research Group, Porto, Portugal
[2] Institute of Engineering, Polytechnic of Porto, Porto, Portugal
{gajls,tcp,zav}@isep.ipp.pt
[3] BISITE Research Group, University of Salamanca, Salamanca, Spain
corchado@usal.es

Abstract. Electricity markets are complex and dynamic environments with very particular characteristics. Ambitious goals, including those set by the European Union, foster the increased use of distributed generation, essentially based on renewable energy sources. This requires major changes in electricity markets and energy systems, namely through the adoption of the smart grid paradigm. The use of simulation tools and the study of different market mechanisms and the relationships between their stakeholders are essential. One of the main challenges in this area is developing decision support tools to address the problem as a whole. This work contributes to increasing interoperability between heterogeneous systems, namely agent-based, directed to the study of electricity markets, the operation of smart grid, and energy management. To this end, this work proposes the use of ontologies to ease the interaction between entities of different natures and the use of semantic web technologies to develop more intelligent and flexible tools. A multiagent systems society, composed of several heterogeneous multiagent systems, which interact using the proposed ontologies, is presented as a proof-of-concept.

Keywords: Electricity markets · Multi-agent systems · Ontologies · Semantic interoperability · Smart Grids

1 Introduction

The electricity sector, traditionally run by monopolies and powerful utilities, has undergone major changes in the last couple of decades [1, 2]. The goals of the European Union (EU) have played a significant role in these changes with the "20-20-20" targets [3] and, more recently, with the regulation (EU) 2019/943 on the internal electricity market [4]. The most significant changes are the increase of renewable and distributed generation penetration, which led to the adoption of the Smart Grids (SG) paradigm [5]; the introduction of a competitive approach in the electricity wholesale market; and, more recently, in some aspects of retail and local markets [4]. SG quickly evolved from a

© Springer Nature Switzerland AG 2021
F. De La Prieta et al. (Eds.): PAAMS Workshops 2021, CCIS 1472, pp. 215–226, 2021.
https://doi.org/10.1007/978-3-030-85710-3_18

concept widely accepted by the involved parties to an industrial reality [6]. The restructuring of wholesale electricity markets (EM) has been another major concern of the EU, particularly with the formation of a Pan-European EM. An important step in this direction was taken in early 2015 when several European EM were coupled on a common daily market platform [7].

In this context, the use of simulation tools to study the different market mechanisms and relationships among their stakeholders becomes essential. Multi-agent simulators are particularly well suited for analyzing complex interactions in dynamic systems such as EM [8]. These must be able to cope with the rapid evolution of EM, translated into new models and constraints, providing its participants with adequate tools to adapt themselves to the markets. Some of the key advantages of agent-based approaches are the facilitated inclusion of new models, market mechanisms, types of participants, and different types of interactions [9]. Several modeling tools have emerged over the years, such as the Agent-based Modeling of Electricity Systems (AMES) [10], the Electricity Market Complex Adaptive System (EMCAS) [11], and the Multi-Agent Simulator of Competitive Electricity Markets (MASCEM) [9]. One of the key challenges in this area is developing decision support tools to address the problem as a whole. For this, it is fundamental to provide interoperability between different systems to allow us to study specific parts of the global problem [8]. Ontologies facilitate interoperability between heterogeneous systems giving semantic meaning to information exchanged between the various parties [12]. The advantage lies in the fact that all the members in a particular domain know them, understand, and agree with the concepts defined therein. There are, in the literature, several proposals for the use of ontologies within the SG framework [12, 13]. All are based on the Common Information Model [14], which defines a common vocabulary describing the components used in the transport and distribution of electricity. However, these ontologies are focused on the utilities' needs, leaving aside relevant information to the consumer. The development of ontologies to represent diverse knowledge sources is essential, aiming to ease the interaction between entities of different natures and interoperability between heterogeneous systems, namely agent-based, aimed at the study of EM, SG operation, and consumer energy management.

This work proposes a semantically interoperable multi-agent systems (MAS) society for the simulation and study of EM, SG, and consumer energy management, taking advantage of existing simulation and decision support tools [9, 15, 16]. These tools are complemented by newly developed ones, ensuring interoperability between them. It is considered the use of real data for simulations as realistic as possible. Data are acquired from databases or in real-time through the infrastructure already installed in the research lab. Ontologies are primarily used for the knowledge representation in a common vocabulary, facilitating interoperability between the various systems. Besides interoperability, ontologies and semantic web technologies enable developing more intelligent and flexible tools through the appliance of semantic reasoners and rules. The following section (Sect. 2) overviews relevant work regarding existing MAS and ontologies directed to different power and energy systems (PES) areas. Section 3 presents the proposed approach to address the identified issues. Section 4 presents a simulation scenario to demonstrate the use of ontologies and semantic web technologies. Section 5 ends the document with the conclusions and the next steps to take.

2 Related Work

This section introduces relevant background on existing MAS and ontologies for PES simulation. Subsect. 2.1 overviews the existing MAS developed at the authors' research group that motivated this work. In turn, Subsect. 2.2 presents existing ontologies publicly available and developed for various PES domains.

2.1 Power Systems Agent-Based Simulation

The Multi-Agent Simulator of Competitive Electricity Markets (MASCEM) [9, 17] is a simulation and modeling tool developed to study the operation of the restructured, complex, and competitive EM. It provides a diversity of market models (e.g., auction-based pools, bilateral contracting, and forward markets), including agents representing the EM's main stakeholders: market operator, system operator, and participating players. MASCEM enables the simulation of three European EM: MIBEL, EPEX SPOT, and Nord Pool. By selecting a combination of the available market models, hybrid markets' simulation is also available. The Multi-Agent Smart Grid simulation Platform (MAS-GriP) [16, 18] models and simulates the most relevant entities at the microgrid and SG levels as software agents, including different types of operators, aggregators, and energy resources, such as consumers (e.g., residential, commercial, industrial), producers (e.g., wind farms, solar plants, co-generation units), electric vehicles, among others. It considers both fully simulated agents and agents connected to physical infrastructures for the automatic management and control of the respective resources, allowing to test complex alternative approaches in realistic settings. The Adaptive Decision Support for Electricity Markets Negotiations (AiD-EM) [15, 19, 20] is a decision-support tool for EM participating players. It is composed of multiple MAS supporting different negotiation types (e.g., auction-based markets, bilateral negotiations). Each system uses artificial intelligence (AI) methodologies to provide players with the best possible decision according to the current context. AiD-EM also performs portfolio optimization for EM participation, context-awareness to adapt the players' strategies to the appropriate context, and an Efficiency/Effectiveness (2E) balance management mechanism to determine the balance between the quality of results and the execution time of the simulation.

2.2 Ontologies for Multi-agent Interoperability Within Power Systems

The Foundation for Intelligent Physical Agents (FIPA) [21] *"is an IEEE Computer Society standards organization that promotes agent-based technology and the interoperability of its standards with other technologies"*. Thus, the use of FIPA standards promotes heterogeneous MAS interoperability. However, even if agents use the same communication and content languages, they can't effectively communicate unless they share a common vocabulary. Ontologies ease heterogeneous systems' interoperability by providing a common shared vocabulary for the correct interpretations of the messages exchanged, enabling effective communication without misunderstandings. Thus, this work gathers and extends existing ontologies for the EM and SG domains to develop a shared semantic model for PES simulation.

The Electricity Markets Ontology (EMO) [22] describes abstract concepts and axioms from the EM domain to extend and reuse in developing market-specific ontologies. It is a modular ontology developed to provide semantic interoperability between MASCEM and external agent-based systems. Additionally, the AiD-EM (ADM) ontology module extends EMO for the interoperability between EM players and the AiD-EM decision-support tool. The Smart Energy Aware Systems (SEAS) [23] ontology describes the SEAS project[1] knowledge model as the basis for the semantic interoperability between the tools within the project's ecosystem. It reuses and aligns existing standards covering the project's vocabulary while being extensible to other cases. The SEAS knowledge model is composed of several modules for different domains, allowing to expose, exchange, reason, and query knowledge in a semantically interoperable way. Recently, the SEAS and the Smart Appliances REFerence ontologies were aligned [24]. The Smart Appliances REFerence (SAREF) [25] ontology aims to ease the matching of existing assets in the smart appliances domain. It supplies building blocks that can be separated or combined according to the users' needs. SAREF gathers semantics from buildings and household smart appliances. Additionally, it merges data from different organizations while fitting into the machine-to-machine (M2M) architecture of the European Telecommunications Standard Institute (ETSI). Finally, SAREF has been extended to meet industry standards [26].

3 Proposed Solution

There are several agent-based tools developed in the scope of various domains within the PES. These tools by themselves are still limited as they are directed only to specific areas of the PES, unable to surpass the lack of decision-support solutions able to simulate, test, study, and validate the PES as a whole. To this end, systems interoperability is mandatory. This work proposes a solution to address the lack of interoperability between PES agent-based tools, providing the means to achieve more complex and inclusive simulations, taking advantage of existing simulation and decision-support tools [9, 15, 16], while complementing them with new ones. The solution produces a MAS society, composed of multiple simulation and decision support tools, for PES simulation, test, study, and validation. Interoperability is achieved using ontologies and semantic communications. Besides promoting semantic interoperability, ontologies also provide knowledge representation in a common vocabulary. Additionally, using ontologies and semantic web technologies provide the means for developing more intelligent and flexible systems. On the one hand, by keeping the systems agnostic to the (semantic) data models used, and on the other, by using semantic reasoners and rules instead of coded business rules. Finally, it uses real data to run simulation scenarios as realistically as possible. The systems collect data from databases or devices through the infrastructure already installed at the authors' research lab. Figure 1 illustrates the proposed solution.

On the left side of Fig. 1 are represented, in grey, the existing MAS introduced in Subsect. 2.1, namely: MASCEM, AiD-EM, and MASGriP, while in green are illustrated the newly developed tools, i.e., the Semantic Services Catalog (SSC) [28, 29], the Intelligent Decision Support Services (IDeS), the Data Access Service (DAS), the Device

---

[1] https://itea3.org/project/seas.html.

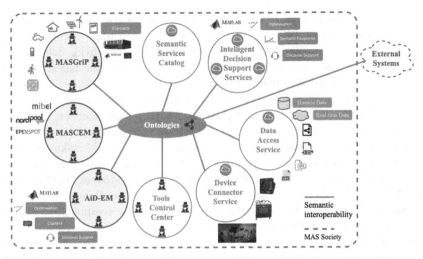

Fig. 1. Society of MAS in the scope of PES [27]. (Color figure online)

Connector Service (Dev-C), and Tools Control Center (TOOCC) [30, 31]. External systems are also able to participate in the MAS society co-simulations using the proposed ontologies. SSC [28, 29] is a flexible and configurable tool providing a common ground for registering and searching both web and agent-based services. It overcomes the complex and error-prone manual configurations of distributed MAS to communicate with each other and web services. Typically, this configuration is made beforehand, sometimes hardcoded, others with configuration or properties files. However, this may lead to errors when dealing with multiple distributed MAS and web services configurations, besides the burden of reconfiguring each system for each simulation. SSC provides the means for searching a specific service or MAS returning all the required data for an automatic connection configuration, eliminating the burden and error-prone of configuring the systems at each simulation.

IDeS is a configurable and distributed containerized platform providing intelligent and decision-support algorithms (e.g., forecast, scheduling, optimization, etc.) to the MAS society. Each container holds an algorithm, keeping them distributed across the MAS community intranet. This option brings several benefits, from which we highlight improved performance, stability, and automation. A new IDeS container is started and configured for the first time to add an algorithm to the MAS society. Its configuration includes the algorithm file(s) to publish, a human-readable description, the respective documentation for the service's webpage, a semantic description to register the service on SSC, and, optionally, an input example for a test page. DAS is the service responsible for providing historical and real-time data to the MAS society. It gathers several sources to provide historical and near real-time data in a common vocabulary, independently of the data source. Data sources are databases, real-time readings, stylesheets, text files (e.g., CSV, XML, JSON), or web repositories. It is also possible to upload data files in the most common formats, such as XML, JSON, CSV, and RDF[2]. Additionally, data must

---

[2] https://www.w3.org/wiki/RdfSyntax.

be meaningful, i.e., make implicit semantics explicit, turning raw data into knowledge. Thus, DAS provides data following the linked data best practices[3] according to the ontologies of the MAS society. Alternatively, it is also able to provide data in JSON format for non-semantic tools. DAS facilitates historical and real-time data access to the agent community through simple REST requests.

Dev-C provides agents with connection to physical devices enabling data readings from real hardware (e.g., sockets, lights, sensors, air-conditioning, etc.) at a given timestep and the control of devices when applicable. This way, it is possible to test scenarios in real-world environments and apply results to devices, making them act accordingly. Devices may be dummy, connected to a Programmable Logic Controller (PLC), or smart appliances. To this end, Dev-C considers both Modbus[4] and HTTP protocols. TOOCC [30, 31], in turn, provides users with a centralized interface to control the simulations within the MAS society. It allows to: run the co-simulation of all or some of the systems/algorithms, or the simulation of each independently; determine the sequence of execution and mappings between the output of a tool to the following input; and, if required, to automatically analyze and compare simulation results. TOOCC also takes advantage of SSC to know, at each moment, what services and MAS are available for simulation.

Ontologies and semantic communications provide interoperability between the various MAS. Being the ontologies publicly available enables external systems to participate in the MAS society simulations. Following ontology development best practices, the MAS society ontologies include EMO, SEAS, and SAREF for reuse and extension, since these ontologies already gather relevant concepts. OWL-S[5] is reused and extended for the semantic description of services in SSC. In addition to semantic interoperability, ontologies are also valuable to describe data models and business rules of agent's roles. Using ontologies and semantic web technologies enables to keep the systems agnostic to the data models and business rules, as demonstrated in [32, 33]. The following section presents a simple scenario, using the MAS society, showing how to take advantage of the ontologies and semantic web technologies for multi-agent semantic interoperability.

4   Case Study

The present case study demonstrates how using ontologies and semantic web technologies benefit the development of flexible, configurable, and semantically interoperable agent-based systems. It presents an energy balance (EB) with four agents: a Balance Responsible Party (BRP), a Consumer, a Producer, and a Prosumer. The BRP agent is responsible for keeping the grid's EB, whereas the remaining agents provide their hourly consumption (C) and generation (G) when requested. The BRP determines the amount of energy needed from the Utility Grid, or to be sent, at each hour, given by Eq. (1). Figure 2 illustrates this scenario.

$$EB = C - G + UG \tag{1}$$

---

[3] https://www.w3.org/TR/ld-bp/.

[4] https://www.modbus.org/.

[5] https://www.w3.org/Submission/OWL-S/.

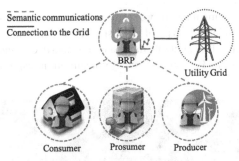

Fig. 2. Energy balance scenario.

The agents communicate using the publicly available ontologies Register BRP[6] (RBRP) and Energy Balance[7] (EBO). RBRP provides a vocabulary for registering in the BRP for EB, while the EBO describes the necessary concept for the execution of the EB. Each agent receives his knowledge base (KB) at the start-up, setting up his role accordingly. The BRP waits for the players' registration, which is the first step of the remaining agents. To prepare the register requests, the players use a SPARQL template file with tags to replace with the respective values from the KB, namely the agent's name, the service type, and the languages and ontologies he understands. Figure 3 shows the Prosumers' register request. After receiving a registration request, the BRP validates it against a SPARQL query. If valid, he gets the player's data to make the registrations and responds with a registration acceptance message. Otherwise, the BRP responds with a registration decline message. Figure 4 illustrates the registration acceptance sent by BRP to the Prosumer agent. The registration acceptance informs the player about the language and ontology to use in the EB communications.

The EB simulation starts at the user's request. The BRP also uses SPARQL templates to generate hourly consumption and generation requests for the next hour. Figure 5 displays the hourly consumption request sent to the Consumer and Prosumer agents for

```
1   @base        <http://www.gecad.isep.ipp.pt/AAMAS2021-Tutorial-CPMAS/mascd/1.0/>
2   @prefix owl:   <http://www.w3.org/2002/07/owl#>
3   @prefix rdf:   <http://www.w3.org/1999/02/22-rdf-syntax-ns#>
4   @prefix indiv: <http://www.gecad.isep.ipp.pt/AAMAS2021-Tutorial-CPMAS/mascd/1.0/indiv/#>
5   @prefix xsd:   <http://www.w3.org/2001/XMLSchema#>
6   @prefix rdfs:  <http://www.w3.org/2000/01/rdf-schema#>
7   @prefix rbrp:  <http://www.gecad.isep.ipp.pt/AAMAS2021-Tutorial-CPMAS/mascd/1.0/register-brp.ttl#>
8
9   indiv:ProsumerRegisterRequest
10      rdf:type        rbrp:RegisterRequest
11      rbrp:agentName  "Prosumer" ;
12      rbrp:language   "JSON-LD" , "Turtle" ;
13      rbrp:ontology   "http://www.gecad.isep.ipp.pt/AAMAS2021-Tutorial-CPMAS/mascd/1.0/energy-balance.ttl"
14                      "http://www.gecad.isep.ipp.pt/AAMAS2021-Tutorial-CPMAS/mascd/1.0/register-brp.ttl" ;
15      rbrp:serviceType "PROSUMER" .
16
17   indiv:  rdf:type    owl:Ontology ;
18           owl:imports rbrp:
19
```

Fig. 3. Prosumer's register request

---

[6] http://www.gecad.isep.ipp.pt/AAMAS2021-Tutorial-CPMAS/mascd/1.0/register-brp.ttl.

[7] http://www.gecad.isep.ipp.pt/AAMAS2021-Tutorial-CPMAS/mascd/1.0/energy-balance.ttl.

the first hour. Upon receiving the hourly consumption or generation requests, players use SPARQL queries to validate the type of request and for which hourly period. With this data, players query their KB to generate the respective hourly consumption or generation response. Figure 6 presents Prosumer's hourly consumption response for the first hour.

```
1   @base      <http://www.gecad.isep.ipp.pt/AAMAS2021-Tutorial-CPMAS/mascd/1.0/> .
2   @prefix owl:    <http://www.w3.org/2002/07/owl#> .
3   @prefix rdf:    <http://www.w3.org/1999/02/22-rdf-syntax-ns#> .
4   @prefix indiv:  <http://www.gecad.isep.ipp.pt/AAMAS2021-Tutorial-CPMAS/mascd/1.0/indiv/#> .
5   @prefix xsd:    <http://www.w3.org/2001/XMLSchema#> .
6   @prefix rdfs:   <http://www.w3.org/2000/01/rdf-schema#> .
7   @prefix rbrp:   <http://www.gecad.isep.ipp.pt/AAMAS2021-Tutorial-CPMAS/mascd/1.0/register-brp.ttl#> .
8
9   indiv:ProsumerRegistrationAcceptance
10      rdf:type        rbrp:RegistrationAcceptance ;
11      rbrp:language   "Turtle" ;
12      rbrp:ontology   "http://www.gecad.isep.ipp.pt/AAMAS2021-Tutorial-CPMAS/mascd/1.0/energy-balance.ttl" .
13
14  indiv:  rdf:type        owl:Ontology ;
15          owl:imports  rbrp: .
16
```

Fig. 4. Prosumer's registration acceptance.

```
1   @base      <http://www.gecad.isep.ipp.pt/AAMAS2021-Tutorial-CPMAS/mascd/1.0/> .
2   @prefix ebo:    <http://www.gecad.isep.ipp.pt/AAMAS2021-Tutorial-CPMAS/mascd/1.0/energy-balance.ttl#> .
3   @prefix owl:    <http://www.w3.org/2002/07/owl#> .
4   @prefix rdf:    <http://www.w3.org/1999/02/22-rdf-syntax-ns#> .
5   @prefix indiv:  <http://www.gecad.isep.ipp.pt/AAMAS2021-Tutorial-CPMAS/mascd/1.0/indiv/#> .
6   @prefix xsd:    <http://www.w3.org/2001/XMLSchema#> .
7   @prefix rdfs:   <http://www.w3.org/2000/01/rdf-schema#> .
8
9   indiv:HourlyConsumptionRequestHour1
10          rdf:type        ebo:HourlyConsumptionRequest ;
11          ebo:requests  indiv:HourlyConsumptionHour1 .
12
13  indiv:  rdf:type        owl:Ontology ;
14          owl:imports  ebo: .
15
16  indiv:HourlyConsumptionHour1
17          rdf:type   ebo:HourlyConsumption ;
18          ebo:hour   "1"^^xsd:unsignedShort .
19
```

Fig. 5. Hourly consumption request for the first hour.

After receiving all responses, the BRP agent runs the EB optimization for the next hour to inform the Utility Grid accordingly. The process repeats for the rest of the day. During the simulation, each agent displays one or more charts with the amount of energy of each period. The BRP agent shows the daily consumption, daily generation, daily EB, and the daily grid. Figure 7 illustrates the daily EB results from the BRP's perspective. From Fig. 7, one can see that from hour 11 to hour 16, the agent community supplies energy to the grid. In the remaining periods, the grid is satisfying the agents' needs.

```
1   @base           <http://www.gecad.isep.ipp.pt/AAMAS2021-Tutorial-CPMAS/mascd/1.0/> .
2   @prefix ebo:    <http://www.gecad.isep.ipp.pt/AAMAS2021-Tutorial-CPMAS/mascd/1.0/energy-balance.ttl#> .
3   @prefix owl:    <http://www.w3.org/2002/07/owl#> .
4   @prefix rdf:    <http://www.w3.org/1999/02/22-rdf-syntax-ns#> .
5   @prefix indiv:  <http://www.gecad.isep.ipp.pt/AAMAS2021-Tutorial-CPMAS/mascd/1.0/indiv/#> .
6   @prefix xsd:    <http://www.w3.org/2001/XMLSchema#> .
7   @prefix rdfs:   <http://www.w3.org/2000/01/rdf-schema#> .
8
9   indiv:ProsumerHourlyConsumptionResponse
10      rdf:type        ebo:HourlyConsumptionResponse ;
11      ebo:responds    indiv:ProsumerHourlyConsumption .
12
13  indiv:  rdf:type        owl:Ontology ;
14      owl:imports     ebo: .
15
16  indiv:ProsumerHourlyConsumption
17      rdf:type            ebo:HourlyConsumption ;
18      ebo:hour            "1"^^xsd:unsignedShort ;
19      ebo:hourlyPowerUnit "Wh" ;
20      ebo:val             "747.393723" .
21
```

Fig. 6. Prosumer's hourly consumption response for the first hour.

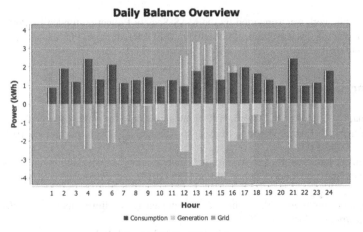

Fig. 7. Daily EB results.

5   Conclusions

A key challenge in PES is the lack of suitable decision-support tools to address problems as a whole. Several tools emerged to assist different stakeholders in their planning and operation. However, these tools only address specific problems and do not provide means to add interoperability with other systems.

This work proposes and presents an innovative and advanced approach to provide interoperability between MAS in the scope of PES. To this end, it is considered the use of ontologies and semantic web technologies. Ontologies ease semantic interoperability by providing a common vocabulary agreed and shared between the agents' community for meaningful communications. External systems can also participate in the simulations and be part of the agent-based community using the proposed ontologies. The use of semantic web technologies also enables the development of tools agnostic to the ontologies and business rules. This approach makes the systems more flexible to updates since it reduces the need to re-code them, which is a relevant feature since ontologies and rules must evolve accordingly with the PES domain. The integration of multiple MAS and services complementing each other results in the so-called MAS Society. The case study demonstrates how the use of ontologies and semantic web technologies provides flexible and interoperable MAS. It is a simple example to ease the reader's understanding and follow-up.

As future work, there's a new version of the ontologies in development to be published and publicly available soon. IDeS and Dev-C, which only respond in JSON format, will soon be responding using the linked data principles. This way, agents from the MAS society will use semantic data directly without translating it from JSON to RDF.

Acknowledgments. The authors would like to acknowledge the support of the Fundação para a Ciência e a Tecnologia (FCT) through the Ph.D. studentship SFRH/BD/118487/2016 and the project CEECIND/01811/2017.

Funding. This work was supported by the MAS-Society Project co-funded by Portugal 2020 Fundo Europeu de Desenvolvimento Regional (FEDER) through PO CI and under grant UIDB/00760/2020.

References

1. Sharma, K.C., Bhakar, R., Tiwari, H.P.: Strategic bidding for wind power producers in electricity markets. Energy Convers. Manag. **86**, 259–267 (2014). https://doi.org/10.1016/j.enconman.2014.05.002
2. Gencer, B., Larsen, E.R., van Ackere, A.: Understanding the coevolution of electricity markets and regulation. Energy Policy **143**, 111585 (2020). https://doi.org/10.1016/j.enpol.2020.111585
3. European Commission: 2020 climate & energy package—Climate action. https://ec.europa.eu/clima/policies/strategies/2020_en
4. European Parliament: REGULATION (EU) 2019/943 OF THE EUROPEAN PARLIAMENT AND OF THE COUNCIL - of 5 June 2019 - on the internal market for electricity (2019)
5. Lund, H.: Renewable Energy Systems - A Smart Energy Systems Approach to the Choice and Modeling of 100% Renewable Solutions. Academic Press, Cambridge (2014)
6. Gangale, F., Vasiljevska, J., Covrig, C.F., Mengolini, A., Fulli, G.: Smart grid projects outlook 2017: facts, figures and trends in Europe (2017). https://doi.org/10.2760/15583
7. APX: Italian Borders Successfully Coupled (2015)
8. Santos, G., et al.: Multi-agent simulation of competitive electricity markets: autonomous systems cooperation for European market modeling. Energy Convers. Manag. **99**, 387–399 (2015). https://doi.org/10.1016/j.enconman.2015.04.042
9. Santos, G., Pinto, T., Praça, I., Vale, Z.: MASCEM: optimizing the performance of a multi-agent system. Energy **111**, 513–524 (2016). https://doi.org/10.1016/j.energy.2016.05.127
10. Li, H., Tesfatsion, L.: Development of open source software for power market research: the AMES test bed. Iowa State University, Department of Economics. Staff General Research Papers 2 (2009). https://doi.org/10.21314/JEM.2009.020
11. Thimmapuram, P., Veselka, T.D., Koritarov, V., Vilela, S., Pereira, R., Silva, R.F.: Modeling hydro power plants in deregulated electricity markets: integration and application of EMCAS and VALORAGUA. In: 2008 5th International Conference on the European Electricity Market, EEM (2008). https://doi.org/10.1109/EEM.2008.4579096

12. den Hartog, F., Daniele, L., Roes, J., IEEE: Toward semantic interoperability of energy using and producing appliances in residential environments. In: 2015 12th Annual IEEE Consumer Communications and Networking Conference, pp. 170–175 (2015)

13. Doğdu, E., et al.: Ontology-centric data modelling and decision support in smart grid applications a distribution service operator perspective. In: 2014 IEEE International Conference on Intelligent Energy and Power Systems, IEPS 2014 - Conference Proceedings, pp. 198–203 (2014). https://doi.org/10.1109/IEPS.2014.6874179

14. Ravikumar, G., Khaparde, S.A.: A common information model oriented graph database framework for power systems. IEEE Trans. Power Syst. **32**, 2560–2569 (2017). https://doi.org/10.1109/TPWRS.2016.2631242

15. Pinto, T., Vale, Z.: AID-EM: adaptive decision support for electricity markets negotiations. In: IJCAI International Joint Conference on Artificial Intelligence, pp. 6563–6565. International Joint Conferences on Artificial Intelligence (2019). https://doi.org/10.24963/ijcai.2019/957

16. Gomes, L., Faria, P., Morais, H., Vale, Z., Ramos, C.: Distributed, agent-based intelligent system for demand response program simulation in smart grids. IEEE Intell. Syst. **29**, 56–65 (2014). https://doi.org/10.1109/MIS.2013.2

17. Praça, I., Ramos, C., Vale, Z., Cordeiro, M.: MASCEM: a multiagent system that simulates competitive electricity markets (2003). https://doi.org/10.1109/MIS.2003.1249170

18. Oliveira, P., Pinto, T., Morais, H., Vale, Z.: MASGriP—A multi-agent smart grid simulation platform. In: 2012 IEEE Power and Energy Society General Meeting, pp. 1–8 (2012). https://doi.org/10.1109/PESGM.2012.6345649

19. Pinto, T., Sousa, T.M., Praça, I., Vale, Z., Morais, H.: Support Vector Machines for decision support in electricity markets' strategic bidding. Neurocomputing **172**, 438–445 (2016). https://doi.org/10.1016/j.neucom.2015.03.102

20. Pinto, T., Praça, I., Vale, Z., Morais, H., Sousa, T.M.: Strategic bidding in electricity markets: an agent-based simulator with game theory for scenario analysis. Integr. Comput. Aided. Eng. **20**, 335–346 (2013). https://doi.org/10.3233/ICA-130438

21. Foundation for Intelligent Physical Agents: Welcome to the Foundation for Intelligent Physical Agents. http://www.fipa.org/

22. Santos, G., Pinto, T., Vale, Z., Praça, I., Morais, H.: Electricity markets ontology to support MASCEM's simulations. In: Bajo, J., et al. (eds.) PAAMS 2016. CCIS, vol. 616, pp. 393–404. Springer, Cham (2016). https://doi.org/10.1007/978-3-319-39387-2_33

23. Lefrançois, M., Kalaoja, J., Ghariani, T., Zimmermann, A.: SEAS knowledge model (2016)

24. Lefrançois, M.: Planned ETSI SAREF extensions based on the W3C&OGC SOSA/SSN-compatible SEAS ontology patterns. In: CEUR Workshop Proceedings, Amsterdam, Netherlands, p. 11p (2017)

25. Daniele, L., den Hartog, F., Roes, J.: Created in close interaction with the industry: the Smart Appliances REFerence (SAREF) ontology. In: Cuel, R., Young, R. (eds.) FOMI 2015. LNBIP, vol. 225, pp. 100–112. Springer, Cham (2015). https://doi.org/10.1007/978-3-319-21545-7_9

26. Daniele, L., Solanki, M., den Hartog, F., Roes, J.: Interoperability for smart appliances in the IoT world. In: Groth, P., et al. (eds.) ISWC 2016. LNCS, vol. 9982, pp. 21–29. Springer, Cham (2016). https://doi.org/10.1007/978-3-319-46547-0_3

27. Pinto, T., Santos, G., Vale, Z.: Practical application of a multi-agent systems society for energy management and control: demonstration. In: Proceedings of the International Joint Conference on Autonomous Agents and Multiagent Systems, AAMAS, Montreal QC, Canada, pp. 2378–2380 (2019)

28. Canito, A., Santos, G., Corchado, J.M., Marreiros, G., Vale, Z.: Semantic web services for multi-agent systems interoperability. In: Moura Oliveira, P., Novais, P., Reis, L.P. (eds.) EPIA 2019. LNCS (LNAI), vol. 11805, pp. 606–616. Springer, Cham (2019). https://doi.org/10.1007/978-3-030-30244-3_50

29. Santos, G., et al.: Semantic services catalog: demonstration of multiagent systems society co-simulation (2021). https://doi.org/10.5281/ZENODO.4717828
30. Teixeira, B., Pinto, T., Silva, F., Santos, G., Praça, I., Vale, Z.: Multi-agent decision support tool to enable interoperability among heterogeneous energy systems. Appl. Sci. **8**, 328 (2018). https://doi.org/10.3390/app8030328
31. Teixeira, B., Santos, G., Pinto, T., Vale, Z., Corchado, J.M.: Application ontology for multi-agent and web-services' co-simulation in power and energy systems. IEEE Access **8**, 81129–81141 (2020). https://doi.org/10.1109/ACCESS.2020.2991010
32. Santos, G., Vale, Z., Faria, P., Gomes, L.: BRICKS: building's reasoning for intelligent control knowledge-based system. Sustain. Cities Soc. **52**, 101832 (2020). https://doi.org/10.1016/j.scs.2019.101832
33. Santos, G., Faria, P., Vale, Z., Pinto, T., Corchado, J.M.: Constrained generation bids in local electricity markets: a semantic approach. Energies **13**, 3990 (2020). https://doi.org/10.3390/en13153990

Energy Management Strategy of Solar Hydrogen Based Micro-grid and Flexible Market

Sriparna Roy Ghatak[1]($\boxtimes$), Fernando Lopes[2], and Parimal Acharjee[3]

[1] Kalinga Institute of Industrial Technology, Bhubaneswar, India
[2] LNEG- National Laboratory of Energy and Geology, Lisbon, Portugal
fernando.lopes@lneg.pt
[3] National Institute of Technology, Durgapur, India

Abstract. An optimal energy management strategy of micro-grid consisting of solar energy sources and hydrogen system consisting of fuel cell and electrolyzer is presented in this paper. The uncertainty aspects of solar energy source and load is also considered in this work. Hydrogen and battery storage devices are used as long term and short-term devices respectively. A 24-h power dispatch strategy is proposed, considering both the minimization of operating costs and the environment costs due to carbon emission. Various operational constraints such as power equality, maximum and minimum power of generating sources etc. are considered in an operational strategy of the microgrid. An IEEE 13 bus system is considered as the test micro-grid. Further, this paper introduces a forthcoming study to be conducted by the authors to investigate the unique challenges of energy markets with large-scale penetrations of renewables, focusing on flexibility markets, with the main aim of placing the work on micro-grids described in the paper into a broader context, related to energy markets and power systems generally.

Keywords: Micro-grids · Uncertain solar energy source · Hydrogen · Energy management · Energy markets · Local flexibility markets · MATREM system

1 Introduction

In recent years, due to high climatic and environmental concerns, countries across the globe are vastly shifting towards renewable and sustainable source to meet their increasing energy demands. In this context, the concept of micro-grid is gaining a huge importance worldwide, which consists of distributed energy sources, storage devices and controllable loads [1]. In the present conditions, solar energy source has emerged as an appropriate choice for sustainable energy supply in micro-grids. The output of solar energy source is highly uncertain in nature which varies with time, weather conditions, solar irradiance and temperature of the place. This uncertainty or intermittent characteristics of solar energy source creates challenges for system operators in balancing generation with load demand and maintaining system constraints. Therefore, in order to design a safe and reliable micro-grid it is essential to model the solar energy source taking into account its randomness. Considering the intermittent characteristic of PV,

© Springer Nature Switzerland AG 2021
F. De La Prieta et al. (Eds.): PAAMS Workshops 2021, CCIS 1472, pp. 227–236, 2021.
https://doi.org/10.1007/978-3-030-85710-3_19

the assimilation of storage devices in a micro-grid environment is essential for achieving resilience and increasing the penetration level of renewables [2]. Hydrogen is a possible solution for long term storage of energy which unlike battery storage has lower rate of self-discharge. Green Hydrogen refers to generating hydrogen onsite utilizing the surplus energy of renewable system enabling environmental sustainability. Moreover, using hydrogen will also reduce the overdependence of the countries on minerals and rare earth materials-based battery storage [3].

For effective, operation of this scheme it is essential to ensure a robust energy management strategy which can determine the amount of power generated by each resource at a precise time with an aim to reduce the working cost, enhance the energy efficiency and system reliability [4]. Now-a-days, many researchers are working in this area to obtain maximum benefit from it. Some of them are highlighted here. In [5], researchers studied the techno-economic feasibility of hydrogen-based energy storage in remote areas. Researchers developed a model of self-sustaining integrated renewable electricity network self and tested it in Jeju island of Republic of Korea [6]. In [7], authors found out the optimal energy management scheme of PV wind hydrogen battery hybrid with the aim of reducing operating costs and increase the life·span of the device. In [2], authors determined the optimal resource management strategy of PV fuel cell and battery with load characterization.

However, in most of the previous work a rule-based strategy is used for energy management, which may not give the optimal result for operation. In some of the previous work, uncertainty, or intermittent characteristic of solar is not considered. Moreover, very few pieces of work have focused on both economic and environment benefits while designing the schemes of energy management.

In this paper an optimized energy management strategy for operation of a solar hydrogen based microgrid system is proposed, considering minimization of operating costs and maximization of environment benefits. Various security constraints pertaining to power equality, battery state of charge (SOC), and maximum and minimum power of generating sources are considered. Extended nondominant sorted genetic algorithm (E_NSGAII) [8] is utilized to resolve the multi-objective problem. Solar power is used as primary source of energy. Considering the practical aspects, uncertainty of solar power source and load is also considered in this work.

Fuel cells (FC) are used as the secondary power source. The excess energy of the solar PV panels is used to provide electric energy to electrolyzer and to charge the batteries. Hydrogen produced in the electrolyzer acts as a long-term storage device and batteries will be used as short-term storage. In this microgrid, the provisions are made to connect the microgrid with the main grid for enhancing the system reliability.

The last part of the paper introduces a forthcoming study to be conducted by the authors to investigate the unique challenges of energy markets with large-scale penetrations of renewables, focusing on flexibility markets, with the main aim of placing the work on micro-grids into a broader context, related to energy markets and power systems generally.

2 Modeling of System Components

Designing of operating strategy of PV hydrogen -based system is a complicated task as it needs development of accurate mathematical models intended for each system components. In the following section mathematical modeling of system components are given.

2.1 Uncertainty Model of Solar Irradiance

To express the random solar output beta probability density function $f(s^t)$ [8] is used in this paper.

$$f(s^t) = \begin{cases} \frac{\Gamma(a+b)}{\Gamma(a)\Gamma(b)} (s^t)^{a-1} (1 - s^t)^{b-1} & \text{if } 0 \le s^t \le 1 a, b > 0 \\ 0 & \text{otherwise} \end{cases} \tag{1}$$

The shape parameters are represented as a and b and can be expressed in the following equation

$$a = \frac{\mu \times b}{1 - \mu} \quad b = (1 - \mu) \times ((\mu(1 + \mu))\big/\sigma^2 - 1) \tag{2}$$

In Eq. 2., μ and σ represents mean and standard deviation which is calculated from the historical data. The maximum power $P(s)$ of a PV system is formulated as.

$$P(s) = N \times FF \times V \times I \tag{3}$$

N in Eq. (3) is the module number of PV panels. FF is the fill factor, V and I are the voltage and current of solar array as given in Eq. (4) and (5).

$$V = V_{Oc} - K_{Voltage} \times T_{Cell} \tag{4}$$

$$I = s^t[I_S + K_I \times (T_{Cell} - 25)] \tag{5}$$

I and V_{Oc} in Eq. (4) and (5) are the short circuit current and voltage on open circuit respectively. T_{Cell}, K_I and $K_{Voltage}$ are the cell temperature of solar panels, temperature coefficient of current and voltage respectively. To enhance the accurateness of the outcome every hour is subdivided into number of states (NS). The probability of every state is evaluated as given Eq. (1). Expected hourly output of solar is calculated as follows:

$$P(s)_{hour} = \int_{i=1}^{NS} f(s^t) \times P_o(s^t) \tag{6}$$

2.2 Uncertainty Model of Load

Power demand in micro-grid exhibits distinctive uncertainty as it varies with time, season etc. To model the random nature of real and reactive load Probabilistic method of Gaussian normal distribution $(f(l_t))$ [8] can be used which is given as follows

$$f(l_t) = \frac{1}{\sigma\sqrt{2\pi}}e^{\frac{-(l_t-\mu)^2}{2\sigma^2}} \tag{7}$$

σ and μ in (7) represents standard deviation and mean of historic load data.

$P(t)$ and $Q(t)$ are the expected real and reactive power at time t. $P_{o(t)}$ and $Q_{o(t)}$ are the real and reactive power measured with smart meter at the time instant t.

2.3 Hydrogen System

The hydrogen system consists of Fuel cells, electrolyzer and metal hydride storage to store hydrogen.

FC are pledging technology for generating electric power as it possess high efficiency and low carbon emissions. Hydrogen generated in electrolyzer comes in the FC and a chemical reaction occurs which generates electrons and protons. The power produced by the FC is mathematically expressed as follows

$$P_F = n_{fc} * V_{fc}\, I_f \tag{8}$$

V_{fc} is the voltage of fuel cells. n_{fc} is the number of fuel cell stack. I_f is the current in the fuel cell. Electrolyzer consists of cells which are series connected and water electrolysis method is adopted to generate hydrogen. Amount of hydrogen generated is given by the following expression.

$$H_{2gen} = \eta_f \frac{\text{Ncell } i_{EI}}{zF} \tag{9}$$

Where η_f and F stands for Faraday s efficiency and Faraday constant, respectively. i_{EI} is the current in the electrolyzer. A metal hydride storage tank is used in this paper because it is safe and compact.

3 Modeling of Fitness Function

In the present work the energy management strategies are framed in a way such that the operating costs and the emission costs will be minimum as given in Eq. (1) and (2). The reference power settings of the energy sources at a particular time instant (t) is selected accordingly. $OC_{battery}$, $OC_{fuelcell}$ and $OC_{electrolyzer}$ is the operating cost per KW of battery, fuel cell and electrolyzer respectively.

$$\text{Operating cost (t)} = OC_{battery}P_{battery}(t) + OC_{fuel\ cell}P_{fuel\ cell} + OCgrid(t)grid(t) \tag{10}$$

The cost due to carbon emission is given by the following equation

$$Emission\ cost(t) = CE_{battery}P_{battery}(t) + CE_{fuel\ cell}P_{fuel\ cell}(t) + CEgrid\ Pgrid \quad (11)$$

Abiding by the security constraints is the most important aspect for safe, secure operation of microgrid. Therefore, security constraints must be considered while designing the microgrid.

Some of the security constraints that are considered are as follows

$$P_{grid,t} + P_{renewable,t} - P_{load,t} = 0 \quad (12)$$

$$SOC_{minimum} \leq SOC_t \leq SOC_{maximum} \quad (13)$$

$$P_{fuelcell}^{minimum} \leq P_{fuelcell}^t \leq P_{fuelcell}^{maximum} \quad (14)$$

$$P_{electrolyzer}^{minimum} \leq P_{electrolyzer}^t \leq P_{electrolyzer}^{maximum} \quad (15)$$

4 Multi-objective Algorithm

In microgrid designing there may be two or more than two objectives to be fulfilled which may be contradictory in nature. Therefore, it becomes essential to utilize robust multi-objective algorithm to solve it. Deb et al. developed Non-Dominant Sorting Genetic Algorithm [9], which is one of the most popularly used procedures as it can handle efficiently many objectives and are applied successfully in many power and energy problems [10, 11]. However, evolution of NSGA II algorithm is also vital to overcome some limitations such as early convergence, larger distance among the attained Pareto front and global Pareto front along with absence of diversity amongst the attained Pareto optimal solutions. Extended non-dominant sorted genetic algorithm (E_NSGAII) is utilized in the current process to solve the proposed design problem. A concept of parental inheritance is introduced in the conventional NSGA II algorithm in which the preliminary selection process of parent population a superior pool is created. This will generate finer pool of child chromosome and hence assists in improving the speed of convergence to the true optimal global Pareto front. The process of non-dominant sort, Parent inheritance, dynamic crowding distance, simulated binary crossover, tournament selection, and polynomial mutation are used in E_NSGA II to obtain the Pareto front. Fuzzy logic is applied to get the single compromised solution among all the obtained Pareto solutions.

5 Case Study

In the present problem an IEEE 13 bus test system [12] is considered as a microgrid. This system consists of two capacitors; one is connected at bus number 675 and at bus 611. The one-line diagram of the test microgrid is shown in Fig. 1. Hourly values of solar and load obtained by applying probability density functions is given in Fig. 2. The PV panels and the hydrogen system along with battery storage is placed in bus number 675. 10 PV panels are considered for this work. The input to the problem is the expected value of solar and load calculated using probability density functions, operating costs, and the environment parameters. The output is the 24 h optimum power dispatch to the load such that the operating cost is minimized, and the environment benefit is maximized while satisfying the operational constraints. At a certain time, t, each generating source that participates on the bus is according to the decision provided by the multi-objective operating strategy. The Extended nondominant sorting genetic algorithm (E_NSGA II) [8] is applied as the multi-objective algorithm in this paper. In Table 1, the parameters used in solving the problem using E_NSGAII is given. Table 2 shows all the data pertaining to the generating source. Battery SOC and level of hydrogen is the most important control parameter and accordingly the switching decisions are taken in the proposed operating strategy. Battery SOC is maintained between 40–90 and whenever the battery SOC reaches less than 40, battery is charged. At the time when the PV output is more than load the extra power is used to charge the battery and once battery SOC reached 80% the power is used to run the electrolyzers. Moreover, the fuel cell is switched off when the level of hydrogen in the tank is low. At every point of time safe and reliable power supply to the load will be ensured.

Table 1. Parameters

Parameter	Values
Number of iterations	450
Population size	100
Probability of crossover	0.9
Probability of mutation	0.3

Table 2. Renewable generation in microgrid system

Parameter	Values
CE_{CO2}	10 \$/ton CO_2
PV panel	
Rated power	10 KW
O&M cost	5 \$/year
Fuel cells	
O&M cost	0.01 \$/hr/KW
Rated power	5 KW
Battery	
O&M cost	1 \$/year
Battery capacity	96000 Ah

Figure 3 shows the power management strategy of each generating source at each hour, considering minimization of operation cost and maximization of environment benefit. As observed from the figure fuel cells work only during nighttime as secondary power source. Battery SOC is maintained between 40% and 90%.

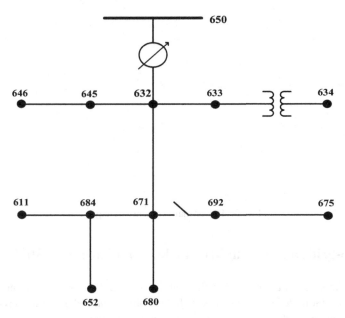

Fig. 1. Single line diagram of IEEE 13 bus system

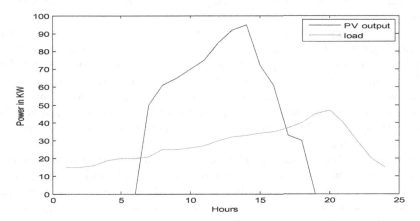

Fig. 2. Hourly variation of solar output and load.

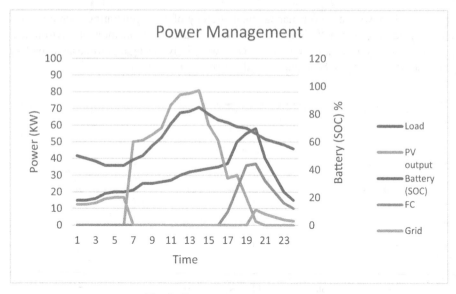

Fig. 3. Power management strategy

6   Micro-grids and Flexibility Markets: Forthcoming Study

Energy markets (EMs) are built on well-established rules of transparency and competition. The 'common' design framework includes both day-ahead and intra-day-markets, operating together with forward markets, and complemented with balancing markets. This framework was developed, however, when the majority of power plants were fuel-based, meaning that their production could be controllable with limited economic impact.

The clean energy transition creates unique challenges in the design and operation of energy markets. Chief among these is the need to incentivize increasing levels of flexibility in a cost-effective way to manage the rising variability and uncertainty of the net load [13]. Also, the increasing deployment of decentralized resources able to offer demand-side flexibility is starting to be thought provoking due to need to incorporate them in a cost-effective manner. This is particularly true for microgrids and their key components, typically offering excellent opportunities to provide flexibility to the grid and the power system in general.

Flexibility markets are starting to be recognized as a promising tool to incentivize decentralized resources to trade flexibility products [14]. These markets are essentially markets to be used by system operators to redispatch their grids, allowing the participation of micro-grids, balancing responsible parties (BRPs) and distributed energy resources, either individually or through aggregation services.

A forthcoming study to be conducted by the authors will look at using an agent-based tool, called MATREM (for Multi-Agent TRading in Electricity Markets), to investigate emerging and new markets designs involving flexibility markets [15]. At present, MATREM supports a day-ahead market, an intra-day market, and a balancing market (see, e.g., [16]). Also, the tool supports a futures market for trading standardized bilateral contracts and a marketplace for negotiating tailored (or customized) bilateral contracts (see, e.g., [17]).

The major goal of the study is to help managing the flexibility challenges of EMs with large-scale penetrations of renewables. This involves the extension of MATREM with a new local flexibility market. The agents allowed to participate in this market are either flexibility buyers or flexibility providers. The former include transmission system operators, distribution systems operators and BRPs. The latter involve aggregators, BRPs, and mainly micro-grids, particularly the micro-grid described in the paper.

7 Conclusion

An optimized energy management strategy of a solar hydrogen based microgrid is proposed in this paper. PV energy sources are considered as primary and Fuel cells are considered as the secondary power source of the microgrid. The uncertainty aspects of solar and load are considered in the proposed work. To mitigate the uncertainty or intermittent characteristics of solar energy source hydrogen is used as the long-term storage and battery as the short-term storage. To enhance the reliability of the microgrid provisions of grid connection is there in the system. An IEEE 13 bus system is considered as the test microgrid. A multi-objective E_NSGAII procedure is applied to solve the problem of optimum energy management. In this paper, a 24-h optimum power dispatch to the load is obtained as the result considering the minimization of the operating costs and the costs due to environmental emissions. Operating constraints pertaining to power equality, battery SOC, maximum and minimum power of generating sources is considered in the proposed work. At, a certain time, t, each generating source that participates on the bus is according to the decision provided by the multi-objective operating strategy.

At the last the paper introduces a forthcoming study to be conducted by the authors to investigate the unique challenges of energy markets with large-scale penetrations of renewables. The study will look at using an agent-based tool, called MATREM to investigate emerging and new markets designs involving flexibility markets. In this way, the work presented in this paper constitutes part of a larger project plan and represents an important step towards a major goal, related to renewable generation, energy trading and distributed energy resources, including microgrids.

References

1. Alam, M., Kumar, K., Dutta, V.: Design and analysis of fuel cell and photovoltaic based 110 V DC microgrid using hydrogen energy storage. Energy Storage 1(3), e60 (2019)
2. Cingoz, F., Elrayyah, A., Sozer, Y.: Optimized resource management for PV–fuel-cell-based microgrids using load characterizations. IEEE Trans. Ind. Appl. 52(2), 1723–1735 (2015)
3. Duman, A.C., Güler, Ö.: Techno-economic analysis of off-grid PV/wind/fuel cell hybrid system combinations with a comparison of regularly and seasonally occupied households. Sustain. Cities Soc. 42, 107–126 (2018)
4. Petrollese, M., Valverde, L., Cocco, D., Cau, G., Guerra, J.: Real-time integration of optimal generation scheduling with MPC for the energy management of a renewable hydrogen-based microgrid. Appl. Energy 166, 96–106 (2016)

5. Marocco, P., Ferrero, D., Gandiglio, M., Ortiz, M.M., Sundseth, K., Lanzini, A., Santarelli, M.: A study of the techno-economic feasibility of H_2-based energy storage systems in remote areas. Energy Convers. Manage. **211**, 112768 (2020)

6. Hwangbo, S., Nam, K., Heo, S., Yoo, C.: Hydrogen-based self-sustaining integrated renewable electricity network (HySIREN) using a supply-demand forecasting model and deep-learning algorithms. Energy Convers. Manage. **185**, 353–367 (2019)

7. García, P., Torreglosa, J.P., Fernandez, L.M., Jurado, F.: Optimal energy management system for stand-alone wind turbine/photovoltaic/hydrogen/battery hybrid system with supervisory control based on fuzzy logic. Int. J. Hydrogen Energy **38**(33), 14146–14158 (2013)

8. Ghatak, S.R., Sannigrahi, S., Acharjee, P.: Multiobjective framework for optimal integration of solar energy source in three-phase unbalanced distribution network. IEEE Trans. Ind. Appl. **56**(3), 3068–3078 (2020)

9. Deb, K.: Multi-objective Optimization Using Evolutionary Algorithm, 1st edn, pp. 203–207, Wiley (2001)

10. Kumar, M., Guria, C.: The elitist non-dominated sorting genetic algorithm with inheritance and its jumping gene adaptations for multi-objective optimization. Inf. Sci. **382–383**, 15–37 (2017)

11. Jeyadevi, S., Baskar, S., Babulal, C.K., Iruthayarajan, M.W.: Solving multiobjective optimal reactive power dispatch using modified NSGA-II. Int. J. Electr. Power Energy Syst. **33**(2), 219–228 (2011)

12. Hayat N., Roy Ghatak S., Rani Pani, S., Mishra, S.: Performance improvement of three phase unbalance distribution system using DG and DSTATCOM. In: IEEE Calcutta Conference (CALCON), pp. 200–205 (2020)

13. Lopes, F., Coelho, H.: Electricity markets with increasing levels of renewable generation: structure, operation, agent-based simulation and emerging designs, Springer, Cham (2018). https://doi.org/10.1007/978-3-319-74263-2

14. Lopes, F.: From wholesale energy markets to local flexibility markets: structure, models and operation. In: Local Electricity Markets. Academic Press, London (2021)

15. Lopes, F.: MATREM: an Agent-based simulation tool for electricity markets. In: Electricity Markets with Increasing Levels of Renewable Generation: Structure, Operation, Agent-Based Simulation and Emerging Designs, pp. 189–225, Springer, Cham (2018). https://doi.org/10.1007/978-3-319-74263-2_8

16. Algarvio, H., Couto, A., Lopes, F., Estanqueiro, A., Santana, J.: Multi-agent energy markets with high levels of renewable generation: a case-study on forecast uncertainty and market closing time. In: Omatu, S., et al. (ed.) 13th International Conference on Distributed Computing and Artificial Intelligence, pp. 339–347. Springer, Cham (2016)https://doi.org/10.1007/978-3-319-40162-1_37

17. Lopes, F., Mamede, N., Novais, A.Q., Coelho, H.: Negotiation tactics for autonomous agents. In: 12th International Workshop on Database and Expert Systems Applications (DEXA), IEEE, pp. 1–5 (2001)

Workshop on Smart Cities
and Intelligent Agents (SCIA)

Workshop on Smart Cities and Intelligent Agents (SCIA)

Smart cities represent a new way of thinking about urban space by shaping a model that integrates aspects like energy efficiency, sustainable mobility, protection of the environment, and economic sustainability. These aspects represent the goals for future software developments. Current cities provide potentially unlimited settings for intelligent agents to display their ability to react, act proactively, interact between themselves, or otherwise plan, learn, etc. in an intelligent, or rather human, manner.

Therefore, the objective of this workshop is to discuss the use of agent technology in the area of smart cities with the goal of providing intelligence to the cities. We welcome any paper about experiences on the use of agents in smart cities tackling issues related to smart architectures, urban simulations, intelligent infrastructure, smart transport, open data, ... We also aim to address specific methodological and technological issues raised by the real deployment of agents in rich environments such as smart cities.

Organization

Organizing Committee

Vicente Julián	Universitat Politècnica de València, Spain
Adriana Giret	Universitat Politècnica de València, Spain
Juan Manuel Corchado	Universidad de Salamanca, Spain
Alberto Fernández	Universidad Rey Juan Carlos, Spain
Holger Billhardt	Universidad Rey Juan Carlos, Spain
Sara Rodríguez-González	Universidad de Salamanca, Spain

Program Committee

Adriana Giret	Universitat Politècnica de València, Spain
Alberto Fernandez	University Rey Juan Carlos, Spain
Angelo Costa	University of Minho, Portugal
Carlos A. Iglesias	Universidad Politécnica de Madrid, Spain
Carlos Carrascosa	Universidad Politecnica de Valencia, Spain
Holger Billhardt	University Rey Juan Carlos, Spain
Alfonso González-Briones	Universidad Complutense de Madrid, Spain
Javier Palanca	Universitat Politècnica de València, Spain
José Antonio Castellanos	University of Salamanca, Spain
Javier Prieto	University of Salamanca, Spain
Alberto Rivas	University of Salamanca, Spain
Guillermo Hernández	AIR Institute, Spain
Fernando de la Prieta	University of Salamanca, Spain
Juan Manuel Corchado	University of Salamanca, Spain
Marin Lujak	IMT Lille Douai, France
Pablo Chamoso	University of Salamanca, Spain
Ramon Hermoso	University of Zaragoza, Spain
Roberto Centeno	Universidad Nacional de Educacion a Distancia, Spain
Sara Rodríguez	University of Salamanca, Spain
Sascha Ossowski	University Rey Juan Carlos, Spain
Vicente Julian	Universitat Politècnica de València, Spain
Pasqual Martí	Universitat Politècnica de València, Spain
Jaume Jorda	Universitat Politècnica de València, Spain
Juan M. Alberola	Universitat Politècnica de València, Spain
Radu-Casian Mihailescu	Malmö University, Sweden
Victor Sánchez-Anguix	Universitat Politècnica de València, Spain

Services Extraction for Integration in Software Projects via an Agent-Based Negotiation System

David Berrocal-Macías[1]([✉]) [iD], Zakieh Alizadeh-Sani[1]([✉]) [iD],
Francisco Pinto-Santos[1]([✉]) [iD], Alfonso González-Briones[1,2,3]([✉]) [iD],
Pablo Chamoso[1,3]([✉]) [iD], and Juan M. Corchado[1,3,4,5]([✉]) [iD]

[1] BISITE Research Group, University of Salamanca. Edificio Multiusos I+D+i,
37007 Salamanca, Spain
dabm@air-institute.org, {zakieh,franpintosantos,
alfonsogb,chamoso}@usal.es, jm@corchado.net
[2] Research Group on Agent-Based, Social and Interdisciplinary Applications
(GRASIA), Complutense University of Madrid, Madrid, Spain
[3] Air Institute, IoT Digital Innovation Hub, Carbajosa de la Sagrada,
37188 Salamanca, Spain
[4] Department of Electronics, Information and Communication, Faculty
of Engineering, Osaka Institute of Technology, Osaka 535-8585, Japan
[5] Pusat Komputeran dan Informatik, Universiti Malaysia Kelantan,
Karung Berkunci 36, Pengkaan Chepa, 16100 Kota Bharu, Kelantan, Malaysia

Abstract. The great development of the internet and all its associated
systems has led to the growth of multiple and diverse capabilities in the
field of software development. One such development was the emergence
of code repositories that allow developers to share their projects, as well
as allowing other developers to contribute to the growth and improvement of those projects. However, there has been such a growth in the
use of these systems that there are multiple works with very similar
names and themes that it is not easy to find a repository that completely adapts to the developer's needs quickly. This process of searching
and researching for repositories that fit the initial needs has become a
complex task. Due to the complexity of this process, developers need
tools that allow them to process a large amount of information that can
be downloaded and analysed programmatically. This complexity can be
solved by approaches such as big data and scraping. This paper presents
the design of a data ingestion system for libraries, components and repositories in a multi-agent programming environment.

Keywords: Data ingest · Service intake · Multi-agent · Big data

1 Introduction

Software development has greatly benefited from the order, classification and
availability of code provided by software repositories. Repositories provide a

© Springer Nature Switzerland AG 2021
F. De La Prieta et al. (Eds.): PAAMS Workshops 2021, CCIS 1472, pp. 241–252, 2021.
https://doi.org/10.1007/978-3-030-85710-3_20

meeting point for developers to evolve the work they host. The use of repositories quickly became widely adopted by companies in the development environment, so that development is stored and a record is kept of when changes have been made. These logs provide information on which developers contribute the most or go back to previous versions to identify and fix problems that have arisen in new versions.

The vast majority of software development companies use private repositories that do not make their development code available to other developers, but many developers upload their projects to public repositories such as Github, Gitlab, Bitbucket and others. The use of public repositories encourages collaborative work that integrates developers who are interested in the project. In this way, public repository projects improve and evolve (improving their functionality, security, quality, etc.) by detecting and solving problems that the original developer has not detected. Repositories are a tool to be taken into account in any software development.

Repositories have contributed greatly to software development, creating a breakthrough in the free software development community. However, there are currently a large number of projects with similar names, technologies, themes and almost identical objectives, which complicates the task of searching for a project or service that meets the needs of the developer who is searching. In addition, the existence of multiple repositories means that some projects are often replicated in them, being different versions due to the contributions of users in different ways in one or the other.

However, the vast majority of repositories include data and metadata that can be used by tools to try to carry out a search process automatically. In this way, this tedious task can be performed in a much simpler way in its elaboration, more accurate in its search and much faster in its development. To this end, tools or systems must be developed that, given a token or a series of tokens, are capable of performing a search for the services that implement this functionality, using the data and metadata presented by each of the repositories. For this reason, this work has created a tool for searching and extracting repositories that correspond to a specific token or set of tokens, and subsequently, this tool carries out a selection process of those services that best adapt to the user's needs so that this service or set of services can be included in the software project in which the user wishes to integrate the service sought.

The rest of the paper is structured as follows. Section 2 reviews state-of-the-art proposals in the service extraction from repositories. Section 3 presents the Service extraction approach in multi-agent paradigm. Section 4 describes the evaluation of proposed extraction methodology and the key results. Finally, Sect. 5 draws some conclusions and future work.

2   Related Works

Web-based public repositories have a standard structure in their API responses (e.g., JSON, XML). These structured responses provide automatic crawling using web-based repositories, which due to collect an extensive dataset collection. Therefore, over the past decades, most research in collecting data has emphasized web crawling [1]. However, this form of collection creates noisy data. To this end, Much of the current literature on collecting data pays particular attention to the use of Natural Language Processing (NLP) and feature extraction techniques [2–4].

Collected data from web feed AI algorithms in several research areas. The objective of this study is to provide data collection for intelligent software or service selection. In general, modern software development includes 1) Identifying system requirements, 2) Finding and collecting available services or libraries from open source repositories, 3) Classifying the discovered services or libraries with the same functionality, 4) Ranking selected services or libraries with the same functionality.

This study aims to provide data for the second step, which investigates available software collection from web pages, code repositories, and public web service registries.

According literature gathering data can fall into two categories: 1) Gathering software data which include source code and metadata [5–8] 2) Gathering service data which usually include service meta data [9,10]. The service can be considered as resemble software that performs a single or a few limited tasks. The significant difference between software and service data is that the source code of service data can not be available.

In general, databases that include source codes have been utilized for smart software development tools, such as code completion [11,12], code search [13], etc.

More recent attention [5,6] has focused on the Github APIs [14], which can help to define software features. The following features can be extracted from GitHub APIs: 1) User rate 2) ReadMe file 3) Software License 4) vulnerability alerts 5) Last commit date 6) Requirement of software 7) Number of issues 8) Data or parameter Media type 9) Number of pull request comments. Prana et al. [15] have provided a manual annotation of 4,226 README file sections from 393 randomly sampled GitHub repositories. They have used extracted data for multi-label classification. However, In real-world problem manual annotating can cost more and suffer from human mistakes, as well. The majority of source code collections apply code mining approaches [16,17] which assume code as structured text.

Collecting approaches that only collect service or software meta-data information can be used for automatic service discovery and service composition. Nabli et al. [18] have discussed the Cloud-based services and their discovery challenges. They have proposed a model called CSOnt which allowing the crawler to automatically collect and categorize Cloud services using Latent Dirichlet Allocation (LDA). However, their services include well-annotated cloud services such as amazon services [19] or Azure [20], which provide certain services. They have not provided details on the services witch have can provide several functionality with less documentation.

According to the literature, most proposed datasets either include software data (source code and metadata) or are performed for a service discovery

process that only includes service metadata. This study proposes an approach that provides a large labeled dataset that include software and service
information.

3   Service Extraction, Integration and Negotiation Techniques in Multi-agent Paradigm

This part of the article will be taken up with discussing and investigating services
data collection from web pages, code repositories, and classic registries.

The creation of the data frames will be detailed below based on the information that can be obtained from each method. The main workflow is detailed in
Fig. 1.

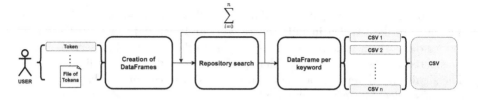

Fig. 1. Pipeline of the service extraction process

3.1   Gathering Services from Websites

In general, a website offering services includes names, descriptions and service
links. The service binding contains the WSDL of the service or a list of service
methods, input, output.

The main source used to gather information has been programableweb, which
has a long list of application programming interfaces (API) services, software
development kits (SDKs), source code, mashups and API-libraries which they
keep up to date and classified, it also includes a glossary and a classification of
services by key words.

Using crawling techniques has scoured the web and it has been able to create
a series of scripts that obtain the data provided by the website to finally create
a series of data sets which will be detailed as follows, however, only well-known
services have full annotations.

Based on what the web page provides, the final entries sought to build the
data set have been:

– **In terms of obtaining APIs:**

- Name
- Description
- Categories

- Number of followers
- Endpoint
- Portal URL

- Provider
- Type of authentication
- Version
- Version status
- Type

- Architecture
- Requests formats
- Response formats
- Is official?

- **Concerning the software development kit data:**

  - Name
  - Description
  - Category
  - Related APIs
  - Date submitted

  - Provider URL
  - Asset URL
  - Repository URL
  - Languages

- **Concerning the source code data:**

  - Name
  - Description
  - Category

  - Source Code URL
  - Repository URL
  - Languages

- **Concerning the mashups data:**

  - Name
  - Description
  - Category
  - Date submitted
  - Related APIs

  - Categories
  - URL
  - Company
  - App Type

- **Concerning the API library data:**

  - Related APIs
  - Category
  - Date Published
  - Languages
  - Related Frameworks
  - Architectural Style
  - Provider

  - Asset URL
  - Repository URL
  - Terms Of Service URL
  - Type
  - Docs Home URL
  - Request Formats
  - Response Formats

- **Concerning the framework data:**

  - Name
  - Description
  - Date published
  - Languages

  - Provider
  - Asset URL
  - Repository URL
  - Terms Of Service URL

3.2 Gathering Services from Service Code Repositories

In the following section is presented the workflow followed to obtain a series of data sets through the most popular code repositories, as well as to obtain metadata for each of them through key words searches using crawling techniques.

In order to search for services, a list of 505 keywords related to API services was obtained from the previous website. To focus the search on service repositories, 30 additional service-specific keywords were subsequently added to the website, such as WSDL, SOAP, PASS, IASS, microservice etc.

It has been decided to use the three most popular code repositories - GitHub, GitLab and Bitbucket - to perform this type of search, witch are known for hosting a large number of publicly licensed code repositories. Using its API, both file and keyword searches can be performed.

For all cases the following a script has been built that using the set of key words mentioned above fetches a number of code repositories related to the key, additionally the script accesses each repository found and downloads extra useful data.

The scripts have been prepared to support both bulk and targeted keyword searches, in both cases it uses threading to increase its efficiency, but due to API limitations, fetching the data can be delayed to hours or even days.

After the raw data collection, a filtering of noisy data was carried out, reducing the final number of valid repositories considerably.

The data collected from each service code repositories have been:

- **Data set from GitHub:**

  - Repository URL (the user name and repository are implied)
  - Description
  - Topics
  - Number of Stars
  - Number of Forks

- **Data set from GitLab:**

  - Name
  - Description
  - Repository URL
  - Date Created
  - Tags
  - Number of stars
  - Number of forks

- **Data set from Bitbucket API:**

  - Name
  - Description
  - Repository URL
  - Related Website URL
  - Date created
  - Updated on
  - Owner name
  - Owner organization

Web crawling techniques have been also used to collect information from the repositories, has been used Bitcuket's public search engine with authentication.

However this technique is limited in terms of the amount of information that can be collected from the results compared to using the API:

– **Data set from Bitbucket Web:**

- Name
- Description
- Repository URL

- Date updated
- Number of watchers
- Related key word

3.3 Gathering Services from Service Registries

As a service registry it has been decided to collect data from Docker Hub containers. For the search it has been agreed to use the docker binary filtering by number of stars, a small parameterised script has been built that makes calls to the docker binary file and collects the response to be formatted and stored, resulting in a data set with the following entries:

– **Data set from Docker Hub:**

- Name
- Description
- Number of stars

- Is official?
- GitHub Repository URL
- Related key word

4 Evaluation of Proposed Extraction Methodology

The results obtained from the previous approach as well as the difficulties and possible improvements will be presented and discussed in the following sections.

4.1 Data Sets Obtained from Websites

Six data sets have been obtained from this web resource with the following entries:

Programableweb	
Resource	Valid entries
API	22.295
SDK	19.394
Source code	15.389
Mashups	6.448
API-library	1.670
Framework	555
Total	65.749

4.2   Data Sets Obtained Service Code Repositories

Overall 535 key words have been used to construct the data sets.

Data Set from GitHub using two API access tokens, took 50 h at a rate of about 10 key words per hour.

In total, 838.588 entries of keyword-related code repositories have been fetched.

Data Set from GitLab using one API access token, took 8 h at a rate of about 67 key words per hour.

In total, 874.623 entries of keyword-related code repositories have been fetched.

Data Set from BitBucket because of API limitations, 1.000 per hour, the repository retrieval process was delayed for 6 days, using 10 API tokens.

In total the script was able to retrieve 141.840 entries of keyword-related code repositories before the data collection process was turned off by timeout.

To increase the number of web requests from 60 to 60,000 per hour, as mentioned previously, web screening techniques were used. This new implementation took 38 h, at a rate of about 14 key words per hour.

In total, 961.908 entries of keyword-related code repositories have been fetched.

Service code repositories	
Service C.R	Valid entries
BitBucket Web	961.908
GitLab	874.623
GitHub	812.024
BitBucket API	141.840
Total	2.790.395

4.3   Data Sets Obtained from Service Registries

Similar to service code repositories, the list of 535 key words mentioned in the previous paragraphs has been used.

The direct use of the docker binary is limited to 100 elements per keyword, but is able to filter based on popularity.

Data Set from Docker Hub took 2 h at a rate of about 260 key words per hour.

In total, 357.917 entries of keyword-related code repositories have been fetched.

Service registries	
Registry	Valid entries
Docker Hub	357.917

4.4 Missing Values

In order to get an overview of the collected entries and the amount of information from the fields described in the previous section, the distribution of missing values for each resource will be shown below (Fig. 2).

As mentioned previously, only the most popular entries have complete data available, but almost all of them have a description field which can be a starting point for using machine learning methods to classify the entries, in expectation of API-library which do not contain a description field (Figs. 3 and 4).

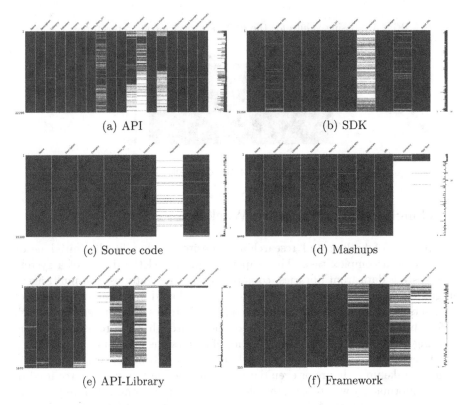

(a) API

(b) SDK

(c) Source code

(d) Mashups

(e) API-Library

(f) Framework

Fig. 2. Missing values for the data set: programmableweb

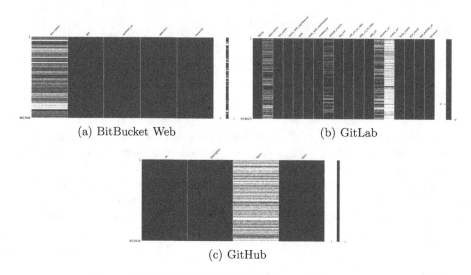

(a) BitBucket Web   (b) GitLab

(c) GitHub

Fig. 3. Missing values for the data set: service code repositories

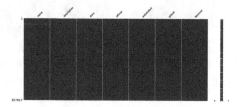

Fig. 4. Missing values for the data set: DockerHub

5   Conclusions and Future Work

The process of finding and researching repositories that fit the initial needs has become a complex task. This paper has presented the design of a system for ingesting data from libraries, components and repositories in a multi-agent programming environment [21]. The workflow followed for obtaining a series of data sets through the most popular code repositories was presented, as well as for obtaining the metadata of each of them through keyword searches using crawling techniques. For all cases, a series of scripts has been built that, using a set of keywords, retrieves useful data, but due to API limitations, fetching the data can take up to hours or even days. For this reason the main source used to gather information was programmableWeb which has a long list of application programming interface (API) services, software development kits (SDKs), source code, mashups and API libraries that are kept up to date and classified thanks to its great community.

Combining both approaches a total of 3.214.061 code service entries have been retrieved using a total of 535 keywords, forming a data set with extra descriptions and annotations that will allow future research work on keyword-driven service recommendation using fields such as description or desired inputs or outputs from a series of petitions to an API. For the future work in terms of data gathering, it has been agreed to expand these data sets to include more keywords and gather more web resources for the creation of new ones.

Acknowledgments. This research has been supported by the European Union's Horizon 2020 research and innovation programme under grant agreement No 871177.

References

1. Kumar, M., Bhatia, R., Rattan, D.: A survey of web crawlers for information retrieval. Wiley Interdisc. Rev. Data Mining Knowl. Discovery **7**(6), e1218 (2017)
2. Dang, S., Ahmad, P.H.: Text mining: techniques and its application. Int. J. Eng. Technol. Innovations **1**(4), 866–2348 (2014)
3. Rivas, A., González-Briones, A., Cea-Morán, J.J., Prat-Pérez, A., Corchado, J.M.: My-Trac: system for recommendation of points of interest on the basis of Twitter profiles. Electronics **10**(11), 1263 (2021)
4. Rivas, A., Gonzalez-Briones, A., Hernandez, G., Prieto, J., Chamoso, P.: Artificial neural network analysis of the academic performance of students in virtual learning environments. Neurocomputing **423**, 713–720 (2021)
5. Markovtsev, V., Long, W.: Public git archive: a big code dataset for all. In: Proceedings of the 15th International Conference on Mining Software Repositories, pp. 34–37 (2018)
6. Karampatsis, R.-M., Babii, H., Robbes, R., Sutton, C., Janes, A.: Big code!= big vocabulary: open-vocabulary models for source code. In: 2020 IEEE/ACM 42nd International Conference on Software Engineering (ICSE), pp. 1073–1085. IEEE (2020)
7. Krutz, D.E., et al.: A dataset of open-source android applications. In: 2015 IEEE/ACM 12th Working Conference on Mining Software Repositories, pp. 522–525. IEEE (2015)
8. Luan, S., Yang, D., Barnaby, C., Sen, K., Chandra, S.: Aroma: code recommendation via structural code search. Proc. ACM Program. Lang. **3**(OOPSLA), 1–28 (2019)
9. Programmableweb, Dataset [16] (2014). https://www.programmableweb.com/api/. Accessed 2020
10. QWSdata, Dataset (2007). https://qwsdata.github.io/citations.html. Accessed 2018
11. TabNine, Autocompletion with deep learning (2019). https://www.kite.com/. Accessed 2020
12. Priya, R., Wang, X., Hu, Y., Sun, Y.: A deep dive into automatic code generation using character based recurrent neural networks. In: 2017 International Conference on Computational Science and Computational Intelligence (CSCI), pp. 369–374. IEEE (2017)
13. Balog, M., Gaunt, A.L., Brockschmidt, M., Nowozin, S., Tarlow, D.: DeepCoder: learning to write programs. arXiv preprint arXiv:1611.01989 (2016)
14. Github API (2019). https://developer.github.com/v3/. Accessed 2020
15. Prana, G.A.A., Treude, C., Thung, F., Atapattu, T., Lo, D.: Categorizing the content of GitHub readme files. Empirical Softw. Eng. **24**(3), 1296–1327 (2019)

16. Pham, H.S., et al.: Mining patterns in source code using tree mining algorithms. In: Kralj Novak, P., Šmuc, T., Džeroski, S. (eds.) DS 2019. LNCS (LNAI), vol. 11828, pp. 471–480. Springer, Cham (2019). https://doi.org/10.1007/978-3-030-33778-0_35

17. Allamanis, M., Sutton, C.: Mining idioms from source code. In: Proceedings of the 22nd ACM SIGSOFT International Symposium on Foundations of Software Engineering, pp. 472–483 (2014)

18. Nabli, H., Djemaa, R.B., Amor, I.A.B.: Efficient cloud service discovery approach based on LDA topic modeling. J. Syst. Softw. **146**, 233–248 (2018)

19. AWS Services (2006). https://aws.amazon.com/ec2/. Accessed 2021

20. Azure, Microsoft (2006). https://azure.microsoft.com/en-us/services/virtual-machines/. Accessed 2021

21. González-Briones, A., Prieto, J., De La Prieta, F., Demazeau, Y., Corchado, J.M.: Virtual agent organizations for user behaviour pattern extraction in energy optimization processes: a new perspective. Neurocomputing (2020)

Transfer Learning for Arthropodous Identification and its Use in the Transmitted Disease Diagnostic

David Garcia-Retuerta$^{(\boxtimes)}$ ⓘ, Roberto Casado-Vara ⓘ, and Sara Rodríguez ⓘ

University of Salamanca, Patio de Escuelas Menores, 37008 Salamanca, Spain
dvid@usal.es

Abstract. Outdoors's activities and sporadic nature getaways are becoming more and more common in recent years. Warm and humid climates without extreme temperatures favor insects or small organisms to live (and proliferate), which can cause potentially serious health problems if we do not have a minimum knowledge of what to do if we are bitten or stung. One of such concerning animals are the arthropodous. The objective of this work is to provide doctors and patients a machine learning-based tool to obtain a fast initial diagnostic based on a picture of the specimen which bit them. The developed model achieved over a 93% accuracy score based on a dataset of 493 color images. Three species have been categorized and analyzed, and the possible diseases they may transmit identified. The proposed system is effective and useful for a future real-life integration into a platform.

Keywords: Computer vision · Arthropodous · Fast diagnostic

1 Introduction

Tick-borne infections have been well known for more than 100 years. They occur with varying incidence in relation to time and geographical location, depending on different circumstances, such as animal reservoirs, climate, ecological conditions and lifestyles. Preventive measures, such as the use of repellents and clothing covering most parts of the body, offer only limited protection. Vaccine prevention is only available for some tick-borne infections and even then, it is not always sufficiently used [2].

One of the most common tick-borne diseases is the Lyme disease. It was first described in the mid-1970s. The name of the disease comes from the geographical location of the original outbreak in the vicinity of Old Lyme, Connecticut, USA. The causative agent is transmitted through the bite of vectors of the Ixodes kind. The incidence of canine Lyme disease is seasonal and corresponds to the feeding periods of Ixodes vectors. Since it was first diagnosed in Old Lyme, the disease has been detected in several countries (mainly in the east and south-west of the USA, Austria and Slovenia) [3]. Approximately 365,000 cases are detected per year.

The best practise to prevent the spread of tick-related diseases is to avoid the initial bite by expanding prevention measurements such as protective clothing, repellents, etc.

© Springer Nature Switzerland AG 2021
F. De La Prieta et al. (Eds.): PAAMS Workshops 2021, CCIS 1472, pp. 253–260, 2021.
https://doi.org/10.1007/978-3-030-85710-3_21

Nevertheless, when the patient is already infected, an early and accurate diagnostic may significantly reduce the morbidity and the mortality rate [4].

In order to achieve successful results, it is mandatory to involve all parties: governments, international and private organizations, the agrochemical industry, rural professionals, etc. Once the policy makers are convinced of the importance of adopting new innovative strategies and solutions, then the veterinarians and farmers will be responsible of their implementation [5].

One of the most promising new technologies in the state-of-the art is deep learning, and transfer learning in particular. Machine learning and data mining techniques have achieved successful results in numerus real-world applications recently [6]. Moreover, its ability to learn on its own solely based on new data makes it more flexible and less labor demanding, promoting higher productivity record in its adoption institutions.

The state of the art for anthropod identification focuses on training CNNs from scratch using custom datasets [8], after a powerful image preparation. Convolutional Neural Networks are a common tool in computer vision which provides good results, although it requires extensive training and large datasets. A proposed solution in this regard was to create a unit through which the insects must pass at some point. The unit is then equipped with a camera and the video flow can be used as the main dataset [9]. The species of each specimen is assessed with the computer vision algorithm, and then it is straight forward to list the possible diseases it could have transmitted.

When there is a need to create powerful machine learning models with limited computer power and a medium-sized dataset, transfer learning is the best alternative. It has been developed due to the difficulties and cost of obtaining additional data in some cases, and to the common proverb in computer science: *theres no need to reinvent the wheel*. The transfer learning methodology consists on most of the structure and weights of a successful neural network, and re-training only its very last layers so that it adapts to the considered problem [7].

Healthcare provides could take advantage of such a state-of-the-art method for democratising diagnosis and improving healthcare coverage, as well as improve customer satisfaction and the platform's value.

This article covers such a question and it is structured as follows: Sect. 2 describes the used data and the method developed to take the images with the correct format, as well as examples of the input data. In Sect. 3, the developed model is described in detail, the data preparation shown graphically and the obtained results presented. Lastly, Sect. 4 draws some conclusions of the current study and proposes future research lines.

2 Data and Method

This research is focused on a particular subset of arthropodous: the ticks of Castile and León region, in Spain. They are ubiquitous in the countryside. People living in rural areas, working in slaughterhouses and dog owners are very familiar with them.

A database containing images all the ticks analyzed by the hospital of Salamanca (Spain) has been used to perform the experiments. The database has color images of ticks extracted from patients and manually examined by an expert to resolve which species it belongs to. Two images are generally taken of each specimen, and the labels correspond with the previous species assessment. The number of images is limited as it only includes specimens retrieved in 2021, because the method for taking the images was developed in 2021 as well. Nevertheless, the dataset is constantly expanding with new received ticks.

There are five species of ticks which can be found in Castile and León region every year:

- **Ixodes**. It is characterized by its dorsal shield without grooves, without eyes and elongated face.
  The diseases it can transmit are: Lyme disease, anaplasmosis and the central European encephalitis.
- **Hyalomma**. It is characterized by its elongated face, eyes, dotted back, ringed legs or marbled and long legs.
  The only disease it can transmit is the Crimean–Congo hemorrhagic fever.
- **Rhipicephalus**. It is characterized by its hexagonal base of capitulum, with eyes, with scallops, with triangular palps.
  The only disease it can transmit is the Boutonneuse fever, also called Mediterranean spotted fever.
- **Dermacentor**. It is characterized by its ornamented shield.
  The diseases it can transmit are: rickettsiosis, tick-borne lymphadenopathy (TIBOLA) – also called Dermacentor-Borne Necrosis Erythema Lymphadenopathy (DEBONEL).
- **Haemaphysalis**. It is characterized by its scalloped, no eyes, rectangular capitulum base, no grooves.
  The only disease it can transmit is the rickettsiosis.

In this work we do not use the gathered data of Haemaphysalis ticks as their number is not statistically significant. Only around five specimens are analyzed every year because they bit a person, and the current database only contains two images of this category (belonging to the same specimen). Moreover, the Rhipicephalus dataset was problematic and it is not considered either. It will be included in future research.

The dataset contains images taken with a HD camera and with a smartphone (similar to the devices which rural doctors currently have). Figure 1 shows examples of the four main categories considered for developing the model which clearly show the most characteristic features of each species. However, the final model only takes three of them into consideration as previously mentioned.

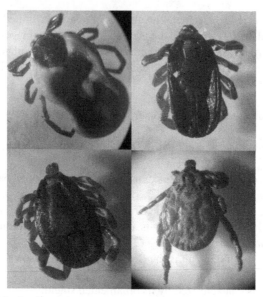

Fig. 1. Ticks found in Castile and León every year. Ixodes (top left), Rhipicephalus (top right), Hyalomma (bottom left) and Dermacentor (bottom right).

A method has been developed so that any individual can take a useful picture and perform the analysis:

1. The tick is extracted from the patient's skin.
2. The tick specimen is placed on top of a flat surface, on a piece of paper. Most ticks are dead when extracted from the skin, so is very unlikely that it will run away.
3. The phone is positioned 20 cm above the chosen surface, and the picture taken with the back camera (which often has a higher resolution).
4. The photo is opened by an app or webpage which make use of the developed method.

3   Machine Learning Approach

Recent advantages in computer vision allow us to automate complex tasks which have always been carried out by specialized professionals. Face recognition is a well-known example, but state-of-the-art neural networks allow researchers to bring the benefits of deep learning to particular problems of their field. Moreover, transfer learning contributed to a democratization of deep learning, allowing researcher without vast computer resources to make use of pre-trained deep convolutional neural networks.

This research works makes extensive usage of transfer learning by combining the pre-trained ResNet50 network with a SVM. The original images are prepared for obtaining a better suitability to the networks, and it resulted in a high performance. This process is described in the current section.

3.1 Data Preparation

The original dataset contains around 2200 images, of which 460 are labeled and show no apparent flaw. Only the images taken using a HD camera were used for these tests, as the images taken with a normal smartphone presented several problems due to the lower quality. The final subset includes 141 training images and 33 validation images. The train-test split was approximately 80%–20% respectively, and carried out manually so that different images of the same tick always belong to the same subset.

For each image, a preparation process is carried out. It works as follows:

1. The image is converted to grayscale.
2. A low-pass filter is applied to remove the image noise. In this case, a Gaussian filter was selected.
3. A threshold is defined to transform the image into black and white. As the background of the picture is a piece of paper, the black is expected to correspond with the mite.
4. A bounding rectangle which includes all the black segments is then defined. Using its coordinates, the corresponding area of the original image is selected.
5. The cropped image is returned. The resulting image is expected to contain a well-centered arachnid and no extra pixels around it.

This process is similar to the most common state-of-the-art preprocessing methods for face recognition [1]. A real example of the result of this data preparation in the used dataset can be found in Fig. 2.

Fig. 2. Tick image preprocessing. The area of the image containing the animal is selected and a new image obtained with only the centered arachnid.

One problem found with the proposed preparation method is that some images contain mites with broken legs, resulting in an abnormally large bounding rectangle.

3.2 Transfer Learning – The Network

Transfer leaning is a method for obtaining knowledge from a network trained for an initial purpose, and the adapting it for solving a new problem. It is a great leap forward in computer vision projects, as it allows to use powerful networks which would otherwise require a supercomputer for training.

In this case, the ResNet50 network was select as it was the best-performing option. Xception, Mobile NASNet and Inception v3 networks were also tested but their performance was between a 21 and 26.3% lower. Resnet50 is based on the ResNet network which won the ImageNet challenge on 2015. It became a milestone as it was the first time an algorithm obtained a better classification error than humans.

ResNet50 is used in combination with a Support Vector Machine (SVM) which is trained the gathered mite images, preprocessed by the network. The SVM fits into the network as a new last layer, therefore taking advantage of all the pre-trained weights and adapting itself to the new problem.

3.3 Results

The developed model has been tested with images never seen by the network. A random train-test split was initially considered and dismiss, as two pictures of same mite are often found. In the case of dead specimen, both pictures are almost identical so good results could be obtained if the model learnt the images by heart (instead of learning to recognize the kind of mite shown). Therefore, the train-test split was carried out manually.

The validation dataset consisted of 33 images of 3 different categories, belonging to the mite species "Dermacentor", "Hyalomma" and "Ixodes". The accuracy score was 0.93939394 and the mean squared error was 0.06060606. The confusion matrix of the model can be found in Fig. 3.

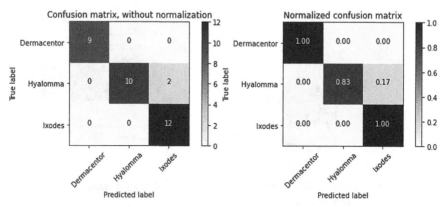

Fig. 3. Confusion matrix without normalization (left) and normalized confusion matrix (right) of the best developed model.

As it can be seen, the model had a great performance and provided strong results within the limited dataset. A real-world deployment of the model could even be considered as the benefits of using this algorithm clearly overcome the risks. Many lives could be saved by speeding up diagnosis in developed territories, and by easing the access to health analysis in underdeveloped areas.

Nevertheless, the limitations of this initial study must be taken into account when analyzing the previous numbers: the datasets used were relatively small for a computer vision problem. Although this obstacle was partially avoided by using transfer learning, the authors are cautious and will perform additional analyses when more data is available.

4 Conclusion

A novel method for tick identification has been successfully developed and, after future tests and verifications, it has the potential to speed up the diagnostic of thousands of patients and to bring advanced deep learning techniques to rural areas.

The performance of the initial tests based on high quality images were successful (94% accuracy), so the following step in this research line is to fine-tune the current model so that it can be used with smartphone-quality images. Camera focus and pixel quality are the main challenges, but based on the obtained results it is expected that they will be overcome.

Moreover, the usage of transfer learning allows institutions with a low budget to re-train the model using a normal computer (as opposed to a powerful server's cluster) and to execute the trained network on devices with limited processing power (such as smartphones or even IoT devices).

In conclusion, the proposed model is currently capable of assisting experts in their laboratories to speed up the tick identification and subsequent disease diagnosis. It provided strong results so a real-world application is also possible to democratizes this analysis tool and allow any smartphone user to have access to a fast, accurate diagnosis; therefore improving their life quality. Technology at the service of the citizens, human-centered advantages.

Acknowledgments. This research has been supported by the project "Intelligent and sustainable mobility supported by multi-agent systems and edge computing (InEDGE-Mobility): Towards Sustainable Intelligent Mobility: Blockchain-based framework for IoT Security", Reference: RTI2018–095390-B-C32, financed by the Spanish Ministry of Science, Innovation and Universities (MCIU), the State Research Agency (AEI) and the European Regional Development Fund (FEDER).

The research was partially supported by the project "Computación cuántica, virtualización de red, edge computing y registro distribuido para la inteligencia artificial del futuro", Reference: CCTT3/20/SA/0001, financed by Institute for Business Competitiveness of Castilla y León, and the European Regional Development Fund (FEDER).

References

1. Masi, I., Wu, Y., Hassner, T., Natarajan, P.: Deep face recognition: a survey. In: 2018 31st SIBGRAPI Conference on Graphics, Patterns and Images (SIBGRAPI), pp. 471–478. IEEE October 2018
2. Mutz, I.: Las infecciones emergentes transmitidas por garrapatas. Annales Nestlé (Ed. española) **67**(3), 123–134 (2009). https://doi.org/10.1159/000287275
3. Steere, A.C., Coburn, J., Glickstein, L.: The emergence of Lyme disease. J. Clin. Investig. **113**(8), 1093–1101 (2004)

4. Bratton, R.L., Corey, G.R.: Tick-borne disease. Am. Fam. Phys. **71**(12), 2323–2330 (2005)
5. de Castro, J.J.: Sustainable tick and tickborne disease control in livestock improvement in developing countries. Vet. Parasitol. **71**(2–3), 77–97 (1997)
6. Weiss, K., Khoshgoftaar, T.M., Wang, D.: A survey of transfer learning. J. Big Data **3**(1), 1–40 (2016). https://doi.org/10.1186/s40537-016-0043-6
7. Pan, S.J.: Transfer learning. Learning **21**, 1–2 (2020)
8. Gutiérrez, S., Hernández, I., Ceballos, S., Barrio, I., Díez-Navajas, A.M., Tardaguila, J.: Deep learning for the differentiation of downy mildew and spider mite in grapevine under field conditions. Comput. Electron. Agric. **182**, 105991 (2021)
9. Bjerge, K., Frigaard, C.E., Mikkelsen, P.H., Nielsen, T.H., Misbih, M., Kryger, P.: A computer vision system to monitor the infestation level of Varroa destructor in a honeybee colony. Comput. Electron. Agric. **164**, 104898 (2019)

Autonomous Distributed Intersection Management for Emergency Vehicles at Intersections

Cesar L. González[1,3], Juan J. Pulido[2], Juan M. Alberola[1(✉)], Vicente Julian[1], and Luis F. Niño[2]

[1] Institut Valencià d'Investigació en Intel.ligència Artificial (VRAIN), Universitat Politècnica de València, Valencia, Spain
{cegonpin,jalberola,vinglada}@dsic.upv.es
[2] Universidad Nacional de Colombia, Bogotá, Colombia
{jjpulidos,lfnino}@unal.edu.co
[3] Universidad ECCI, Bogotá, Colombia

Abstract. In recent years, numerous approaches have attempted to develop traffic control strategies at intersections. The complexity of a dynamic environment with different vehicles crossing in different directions and in some cases, with multiple conflict points, is a major challenge for the traffic optimisation, especially in urban areas. Work has focused on developing systems that range from intelligent traffic lights to complex centralised protocols that evaluate the policies to be met by vehicles at the intersections. In general, a traffic control system at intersections gives the green light to one lane, while keeping all other lanes on red light. But, what happens when there are several levels of vehicle priority or when there are emergency vehicles in the lanes? This feature needs a special protocol because of the high risk of collisions with other vehicles and the possible improvement in waiting times for emergency vehicles. Therefore, this paper proposes an emergency vehicle attention protocol with an algorithm that implements rules based on the protocol called Distributed Intersection Management (DIM) that is used by autonomous vehicles while negotiating their cross through the intersection. This proposal also seeks to avoid affecting the traffic flow of normal vehicles while the algorithm gives priority to emergency vehicles.

Keywords: Autonomous distributed intersection management · Emergency vehicle · Vehicle coordination

1 Introduction

Nowadays, the challenges of research in transportation systems have been complemented with the use of technologies capable of assuming the complexity associated with the possibility of communication and interaction between vehicles and with the infrastructure. These technologies must take into account that vehicles always meet the conditions necessary to maintain safety on the road. When

© Springer Nature Switzerland AG 2021
F. De La Prieta et al. (Eds.): PAAMS Workshops 2021, CCIS 1472, pp. 261–269, 2021.
https://doi.org/10.1007/978-3-030-85710-3_22

a vehicle does not meet these safety conditions, the control of the implemented technology has to intervene to avoid a possible collision of the vehicle, especially, at an intersection. Although there are still numerous problems to be solved in this type of system, the use of intelligent algorithms explores new and better ways to solve these problems.

Apart from safety, other important objectives of transportation systems research are the optimisation of flow, reduction of pollution or travel time used by vehicles in their movements. All this must be taken into account in order to validate in which type of road infrastructures it is necessary to make greater contributions.

Communication between vehicles facilitates their coordination in order to achieve the aforementioned objectives. In recent years, many studies have focused on providing a certain degree of coordination between autonomous vehicles, mainly at the moment of crossing, since this is one of the most critical situations that require the collaboration of vehicles circulating on different roads. Some examples can be found at [1–6].

Most of the proposals focus on offering centralised solutions by means of some type of infrastructure, although there are also decentralised solutions where vehicles arriving at an intersection form a network that collaboratively decide on the actions to be taken to speed up the flow through the intersection. An example of this type of proposal is presented in [7], where a series of crossing rules are proposed for the coordination management of autonomous vehicles. Thus, a collaborative behaviour emerges if the vehicles follow the rules.

A key element in this type of conflict situations at vehicle intersections is the management of vehicles with possible priorities such as emergency vehicles. In this particular case, we can also find previous works that try to speed up the flow of emergency vehicles in intersections versus non-priority vehicles.

In [8], the authors showed how it is possible to integrate the specific features of attention of emergency vehicles in a vehicular flow simulator. Moreover, in [9] authors implement a strategy about attention emergency vehicles where the policy gives more priority at the lanes where there is emergency vehicles, consequently, the delays on emergency vehicles will be less than normal vehicles. The approach that can be found in [10] tries to avoid delays in the emergency vehicles giving the priority of crossing in the lane where there is emergency vehicle without affecting with long delays other lanes with other vehicles. In a similar way, in [11] they present a centralised proposal taking into account the distance of the emergency vehicle to the intersection and the arrival probability to the intersection. The centralised control changes the traffic lights, including the traffic light for pedestrians.

In a different way, semi-centralised approaches can be found, for instance, the work in [12] includes some low cost infrastructure in the lanes improving the traffic light system. There exists communication between the different control systems of the proposed infrastructure adjusting the traffic light when there are emergency vehicles. Self-organised approaches are also proposed, for instance, in [13] authors use a protocol called VTL-PIC, where they change the normal traffic lights in the intersections into a virtual traffic light. The protocol establishes that when several vehicles arrive at the intersection and if they detect a possible conflict, then a leader is elected who will manage the traffic in the intersection. Finally, [14] presents an IoT-based approach for emergency vehicle priority and self-organised traffic control at intersections. An intersection controller gets emergency vehicle positions (through GPS devices installed in the emergency vehicles) and vehicle density data at each lane approaching an intersection. The controller can adjust the traffic lights according to detected traffic.

As can be seen, numerous works have been carried out to optimise the flow of emergency vehicles at intersections. Most of these works focus on proposing centralised solutions. In an alternative way, this paper presents an extension of the work presented in [7] where a distributed coordination management system for intersections of autonomous vehicles was proposed. This extension focuses on prioritising the crossing of emergency vehicles, while minimising the impact on the flow of normal vehicles. Some experimentation was carried out on the SUMO[1] simulator to demonstrate the feasibility of the proposal.

The rest of this paper is structured as follows. In Sect. 2, we describe the Distributed Intersection Management model for Emergency vehicles. In Sect. 3, we show several experiments in order to validate the proposal. Finally, in Sect. 4, we draw some concluding remarks and suggest some future research lines.

2   Emergency Vehicles Model

In this section, we present the coordination model for emergency vehicles. This model is based on the Distributed Intersection Management (DIM) model [15], which provides autonomous vehicles with the capacity to negotiate and manage crossings at intersections. The DIM model is composed by three parts: the traffic flow model, the autonomous vehicle model, and behavioral roles. The traffic flow model is based on the LAI [16] model for large traffic networks simulation. Basically, this model represents the mechanism to maintain safe distances among the vehicles, guaranteeing safe driving, by defining the following rules:

- A vehicle a_i can accelerate as long as exists a distance D_{acc} between this vehicle and the vehicle that comes before a_{i+1}.
- A vehicle a_i keeps its velocity as long as exists a distance $D_{keep} < D_{acc}$ between this vehicle and the vehicle that comes before a_{i+1}.
- A vehicle a_i has to decrease its velocity if exists a distance $D_{brake} < D_{keep}$ between this vehicle and the vehicle that comes before a_{i+1}.

Autonomous vehicles can be represented as a group of agents $A = a_0, ..., a_n$. Each vehicle a_i includes sensors to detect other vehicles that are inside an area. Each vehicle is also provided with a wireless communication system to send messages and request information to other vehicles. Taking into account this

---

[1] https://www.eclipse.org/sumo/.

model, autonomous vehicles are be able to negotiate their own crossing without help of devices like traffic lights, sensors or traffic infrastructure.

Finally, an autonomous vehicle can play two different roles: follower (F) and negotiator (N). These roles depend on the information and the specific actions that a vehicle can carry out. The follower role is played by autonomous vehicles that are moving just behind another vehicle. In contrast, the negotiator role is played by autonomous vehicles that do not detect other vehicles inside their communication areas and before the next intersection. In Algorithm 1 we can observe the coordination algorithm for intersection crossing. This algorithm determines which autonomous vehicle should cross an intersection when a conflict with other vehicles occurs.

Algorithm 1. Coordination intersection crossing

Require: An autonomous vehicle a_i with role N.
Ensure: Cross the intersection; otherwise stop.
1: **while** a_i arrives at intersection k **do**
2:     Broadcast its distance and velocity over k
3:     **if** There is not a response by any vehicle **then**
4:        a_i can cross with priority the intersection k
5:     **else**
6:        a_i should evaluate crossing for avoiding collisions and block the intersection k
7:        **if** There is a fleet of autonomous vehicles crossing the intersection k in a conflicting way **then**
8:           a_i must remain stopped until the intersection k becomes clear
9:        **else if** There is a vehicle a_j that answers the broadcast message with 0 velocity and e position regarding the intersection k **then**
10:          a_i must remain stopped until the position e becomes clear to avoid blocking the intersection
11:        **else if** There is a vehicle a_j that answers the broadcast message with exactly the same conditions as a_i regarding the intersection k **then**
12:          a_i and a_j apply a negotiation protocol to decide which one gets the priority to cross the intersection.
13:        **end if**
14:     **end if**
15: **end while**

2.1   Emergency Vehicles

An emergency vehicle a_e is a vehicle that plays an emergency role (E). This vehicle has the priority of intersection crossing over the rest of vehicles. We should note that we assume only two lines in conflict way at each intersection.

In order to define the behavior of emergency vehicles is required to introduce the two radius that determine the behavior of autonomos vehicles in the DIM model: the perception radius and the communication radius. The perception radius P_i of a vehicle a_i defines a detection area inside which, other autonomous vehicles are detected by the sensors of a_i. The communication radius C_i defines a communication area inside which, other autonomous vehicles receive messages sent by a_i. Messages can be delivered to specific receivers or can be broadcasted to any receiver inside this area.

When an emergency vehicle a_e arrives at an intersection k, this vehicle has the priority for crossing the intersection unless other vehicles are already crossing the intersection in a conflict way. To represent this behavior, a_e sends a broadcast message to those vehicles that are situated inside its communication radius C_e. In this message, a_e is identified as an emergency vehicle. According to this, the following situations may occur:

- If a_e does not receive any response to its broadcast message, then crosses the intersection with priority.
- If other vehicles are already crossing the intersection in a conflict way, the vehicle a_i that is playing the negotiator role (N) in this crossing, determines whether it can stop before arriving at the intersection. Thus, a_i reduces the velocity until stopping at the intersection, remaining stopped until a_e finishes the intersection crossing.
- If other vehicles are already waiting to cross the intersection, the vehicle a_i that is playing the negotiator role (N) broadcasts a message in order to stop the traffic in the conflict way.
- If two emergency vehicles arrive at the same time at the intersection k, each one in a different conflict way, therefore:
  1. If there are not any other vehicle already waiting at the intersection, then, both emergency vehicles take the same behavior of a negotiator role (i.e. they apply a negotiation protocol in order to take the decision about who has the crossing priority).
  2. If there are other vehicles waiting in the intersection, they follow the default behavior of a negotiator role until one of the emergency vehicles crosses the intersection.

It must be noted that emergency vehicles are only considered when they are inside the specific radius. Therefore, the flow of the global traffic system is not influenced by emergency vehicles.

3   Results

In this section we show several experiments focused on testing the performance of the emergency vehicles model. We used the SUMO simulator for urban mobility. SUMO provides functionalities to simulate traffic in cities composed by streets and intersections (Fig. 1). For the purpose of these experiments, we considered four intersections for different traffic densities, ranging from 0 to 1. Emergency vehicles may appear with a prior probability of 1 vehicle per each 3600 vehicles.

In order to test the performance of the model proposed, we compare our DIM model for emergency vehicles with a Green Wave model, which is the traditional approach that provides a traffic intersection management based on traffic lights.

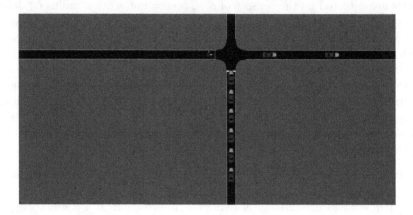

Fig. 1. SUMO simulator showing an intersection with regular vehicles (yellow) and emergency vehicles (red). (Color figure online)

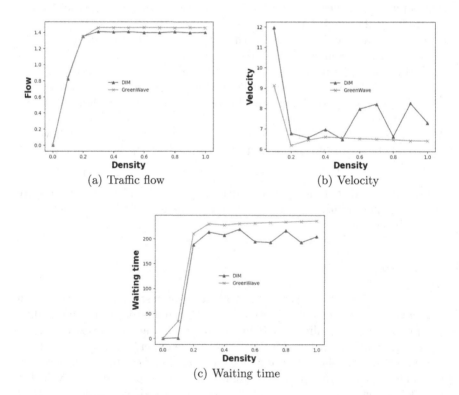

(a) Traffic flow

(b) Velocity

(c) Waiting time

Fig. 2. Models comparison without emergency vehicles

In Fig. 2, we show the performance of both models in cities without emergency vehicles. Figure 2(a) represents the traffic flow depending on the density of the city. As it can be observed, the flow increases in both models until a density of 0.3. From this density on, the traffic flow stabilizes. This can be explained since the intersections may be blocked for large values of traffic flow.

As it can be appreciated, the performance of the Green Wave model is slightly worse than DIM. This behavior is repeated in Fig. 2(b), which shows the average velocity of vehicles and in Fig. 2(c), which shows the average waiting time. Both variables, velocity and waiting time are slightly worse for the Green Wave model. This can be explained since the DIM model provides a coordination mechanism based on the traffic, which is adapted depending on the traffic scenario. In contrast, the Green Wave considers a fixed amount of time to give crossing priorities. This strategy may penalize blocked lines.

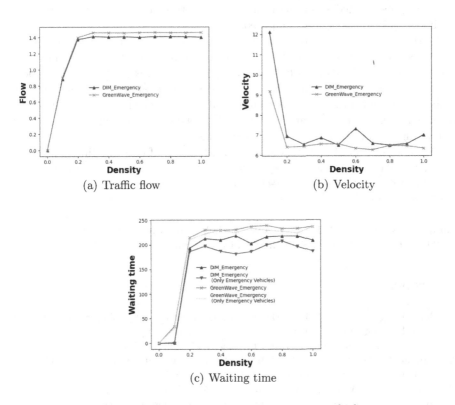

(a) Traffic flow

(b) Velocity

(c) Waiting time

Fig. 3. Models comparison with emergency vehicles

In Fig. 3, it can be observed the performance of both models when emergency vehicles are introduced. Similar to the previous experiment, both the traffic flow and the velocity are quite stable from densities values higher than 0.2. In

Fig. 3(c) we can observe the average waiting time of emergency vehicles and the average waiting time of regular vehicles (i.e. non-emergency vehicles). As it can be observed, the Green Wave model does not give significant priority to emergency vehicles. In contrast, the DIM model provides a mechanism that allows the emergency vehicles to considerably reduce the average waiting time compared with the rest of vehicles. Moreover, these differences become significant when the traffic density is higher than 0.2.

4   Conclusions

Intersections represent point of conflict since autonomous vehicles from different lines need to cross. Centralised solutions provide coordination mechanisms in order to determine priorities for crossing. In addition, emergency vehicles are required to get the highest priority as possible when crossing the intersection. Therefore, distributed solutions that can adapt to changes in the environment (such as, traffic densities) are required.

In this paper, we propose a distributed coordination management system that considers emergency vehicles. This system provides crossing mechanisms at intersections in a distributed fashion. According to the experiments, this model provides a better performance than other centralised approaches managed by traffic lights regarding variables such as traffic flow, velocity and waiting time. What is more, this performance is eventually better for emergency vehicles that require highest priorities than the rest of vehicles.

One assumption of our work is the consideration of one-way lines. In future works, we plan to extend this approach in order to consider several lines for each direction. This would be specially interesting when emergency vehicles are considered.

Acknowledgements. This work was partially supported by MINECO/FEDER RTI2018-095390-B-C31 project of the Spanish government.

References

1. Derlis Gregor, S., Toral, T.A., Barrero, F., Gregor, R., Rodas, J., Arzamendia, M.: A methodology for structured ontology construction applied to intelligent transportation systems. Comput. Stan. Interfaces **47**, 108–119 (2016)
2. Kaplan, J.: Digital trends-cars (2018). https://www.digitaltrends.com/cars/every-company-developing-self-driving-car-tech-ces-2018/
3. Morgan, P.L., Williams, C., Flower, J., Alford, C., Parkin, J.: Trust in an autonomously driven simulator and vehicle performing maneuvers at a T-junction with and without other vehicles. In: Stanton, N. (ed.) AHFE 2018. AISC, vol. 786, pp. 363–375. Springer, Cham (2019). https://doi.org/10.1007/978-3-319-93885-1_33
4. Fagnant, D.J., Kockelman, K.: Preparing a nation for autonomous vehicles: opportunities, barriers and policy recommendations. Transp. Res. Part A Policy and Practice **77**, 167–181 (2015)

5. Bertozzi, M., Broggi, A., Cellario, M., Fascioli, A., Lombardi, P., Porta, M.: Artificial vision in road vehicles. Proc. IEEE **90**(7), 1258–1271 (2002)
6. Schwarting, W., Alonso-Mora, J., Rus, D.: Planning and decision-making for autonomous vehicles. Ann. Rev. Control Robot. Auton. Syst. **1**, 187–210 (2018)
7. González, C.L., Zapotecatl, J.L., Gershenson, C., Alberola, J.M., Julian, V.: A robustness approach to the distributed management of traffic intersections. J. Ambient. Intell. Humaniz. Comput. **11**(11), 4501–4512 (2020)
8. Bieker-Walz, L., Behrisch, M., Junghans, M.: Analysis of the traffic behavior of emergency vehicles in a microscopic traffic simulation. EPiC Ser. Eng. **2**, 1–13 (2018)
9. Dresner, K., Stone, P.: Human-usable and emergency vehicle-aware control policies for autonomous intersection management. In: Fourth International Workshop on Agents in Traffic and Transportation (ATT), Hakodate, Japan (2006)
10. Hajiebrahimi, S., Iranmanesh, S.: An adaptive control method of traffic signal-timing under emergency situations for smart cities. In: 2018 3rd IEEE International Conference on Intelligent Transportation Engineering (ICITE), pp. 225–230. IEEE (2018)
11. Kapileswar, N., Santhi, P.V., Chenchela, V.K.R., Venkata Siva Prasad, C.H.: A fast information dissemination system for emergency services over vehicular ad hoc networks. In: 2017 International Conference on Energy, Communication, Data Analytics and Soft Computing (ICECDS), pp. 236–241. IEEE (2017)
12. Athul Krishna, A., Kartha, B.A., Nair, V.S.: Dynamic traffic light system for unhindered passing of high priority vehicles: wireless implementation of dynamic traffic light systems using modular hardware. In: 2017 IEEE Global Humanitarian Technology Conference (GHTC), pp. 1–5. IEEE (2017)
13. Viriyasitavat, W., Tonguz, O.K.: Priority management of emergency vehicles at intersections using self-organized traffic control. In: 2012 IEEE Vehicular Technology Conference (VTC Fall), pp. 1–4. IEEE (2012)
14. Khan, A., Ullah, F., Kaleem, Z., Rahman, S.U., Anwar, H., Cho, Y.-Z.: EVP-STC: emergency vehicle priority and self-organising traffic control at intersections using internet-of-things platform. IEEE Access, **6**, 68242–68254 (2018)
15. Gonzalez, C.L., Zapotecatl, J.L., Alberola, J.M., Julian, V., Gershenson, C.: Distributed Management of Traffic Intersections. In: Novais, P., et al. (eds.) ISAmI2018 2018. AISC, vol. 806, pp. 56–64. Springer, Cham (2019). https://doi.org/10.1007/978-3-030-01746-0_7
16. Lárraga, M.E., Alvarez-Icaza, L.: Cellular automaton model for traffic flow based on safe driving policies and human reactions. Phys. A **389**(23), 5425–5438 (2010)

Carsharing in Valencia: Analysing an Alternative to Taxi Fleets

Pasqual Martí(✉), Jaume Jordán, and Vicente Julian

Valencian Research Institute for Artificial Intelligence (VRAIN),
Universitat Politècnica de València, Camino de Vera s/n, 46022 Valencia, Spain
pasmargi@vrain.upv.es, {jjordan,vinglada}@dsic.upv.es
http://vrain.upv.es/

Abstract. The awareness of pollution in urban areas is currently rising. Among the various possible solutions, the reduction of carbon dioxide emissions from the use of fossil-fuel-powered vehicles stands out. To this end, private vehicles and other services such as taxis could be replaced by more sustainable alternatives, including carsharing fleets. This type of vehicle, generally electric, is being introduced in more and more cities, offering a green mobility alternative. In this paper, we analyse the efficiency of the current taxi fleet in Valencia through multi-agent simulations. We then assess possible carsharing fleets with different configurations. Our results show the potential that a combination of the two types of fleets would have to meet the current demand and, at the same time, improve the sustainability of the city.

Keywords: Urban mobility · Sustainability · Carsharing · Simulation · Intelligent agents

1 Introduction

In the last few years, both city managers and the general public have become aware of the importance of pollution in urban areas. Thus, there are more and more initiatives to enhance sustainability and reduce the carbon footprint of cities. The European Union's 2030 climate and energy framework has as the key target to reduce at least 40% the greenhouse gas emissions (for 1990 levels)[1]. In this context, laws are being promoted by various city councils that apply significant restrictions on polluting vehicles, especially in city centres. This is intended to improve the air quality of cities, thereby improving sustainability and quality of life for citizens. There are cities where there is a total ban on all private combustion vehicles, both petrol and diesel, while other cities are less restrictive and only the most polluting vehicles are banned (usually defined by their age or emissions according to their technical datasheet).

---

[1] 2030 climate & energy framework: https://ec.europa.eu/clima/policies/strategies/2030_en.

© Springer Nature Switzerland AG 2021
F. De La Prieta et al. (Eds.): PAAMS Workshops 2021, CCIS 1472, pp. 270–282, 2021.
https://doi.org/10.1007/978-3-030-85710-3_23

In parallel to all this, new models of mobility services have appeared that are better adapted to the demands of users. The most well-known among them is the "ridesourcing" service, which allows its users to book a ride on-demand, usually through a multi-platform app. Interested in how this new services impact urban transit, authors in [8] compared many of them (like Uber or Lyft) to taxi services in the city of San Francisco, in the United States. Their findings indicate that despite the similar aspects of taxi and ridesourcing fleets, they differed in waiting time and number of served trips. Also, at least half of the ridesourcing trips were a substitute for public transport and private vehicle rides, and not only taxi services, as one might have thought.

The introduction of new modes of transportation does not simply substitute the previously existent but creates new transportation trends among their users. Because of that, one measure that could alleviate both excess pollution and the amount of traffic in cities would be the inclusion of electric carsharing fleets [3]. This type of service consists of users who need to travel to specific places without using the available public transport lines (metro, bus, etc.) being able to reserve a carsharing vehicle within their reach, walk to the vehicle and make their journey in that vehicle. At the end of the journey, the vehicle can be used by another user. This implies a reduction in the number of private vehicles circulating in the city, as users could have their needs covered with the carsharing service and public transport. The work in [6] shows a reduction in the average household vehicle ownership in Vancouver, Canada, after two different carsharing systems were introduced. In addition, in the future, it may mean that many users will not need to own a vehicle, which has a significant impact on sustainability at various levels, both for the vehicles present in cities and for polluting manufacturing processes, among others. On the other hand, many taxi users would be willing to use carsharing services as it may suit them from an economic point of view if such a service is competitively priced. However, not all taxi demand can be covered by carsharing vehicles, e.g. people who are unable to drive vehicles, or with other types of needs that mean that taxis cannot be substituted.

Carsharing fleets have the potential to be a low-carbon and sustainable alternative to traditional urban fleets, such as taxi or dial-a-ride services. Carsharing fleets emit less carbon dioxide as empty trips (trips without passenger) are nonexistent [2]. In addition, this type of fleet can be easily implemented using hybrid or fully electric vehicles, as they perform great in urban areas. Because of this, even if the carsharing is only serving a percentage of the city's taxi demand, it would be achieving a less polluted area. In this line, authors analyse in [1] when does a carsharing service, located in the city of Beijing, outperforms in terms of travel-cost a taxi service. Other Beijing-centred works, as [9], explore carsharing fleet configurations to study their performance through simulation.

As it is shown above, most of the works that analyse the performance of vehicle fleets refer to a concrete city or urban area. This makes sense as one of the crucial factors for a good urban fleet performance is how well it adapts to the citizen's movement trends and travelling preferences. Our work follows this trend by localising our analysis on the city of Valencia, Spain. The authorities of

Valencia have been very interested in developing the United Nation's Sustainable Development Goals (SDG) during the past few years. The most relevant to our work would be SDG 11: *Sustainable Cities and Communities*, which the city council is implementing by banning the use of private vehicles in certain central areas of the city, pedestrianising squares, creating new green areas, and promoting the use of electric vehicles. Valencia did not have any carsharing services before and only recently a small enterprise called *Cargreen*[2] just started offering this service through a fleet of 100 electric cars on 9 May 2021. Because of that, we do not have access to carsharing GPS data. Nevertheless, we have information about population, traffic, as well as social media activity that we use to reproduce the movement trends of Valencia's citizens.

Many of the aforementioned studies base their findings on surveys and the analysis of fleet data. Instead, in our work, we apply the multi-agent modelling paradigm to reproduce the users of the different transportation services and their behaviours. In addition, we make use of SimFleet, a multi-agent-based simulator, to execute our simulations and collect the relevant data for its subsequent analysis. Our main objective is to examine the performance of Valencia's public taxi fleet in terms of user satisfaction and carbon dioxide emissions and research the features a free-floating carsharing fleet should have to offer a competitive, more sustainable alternative to a part of the mobility demand.

The rest of the paper is structured as follows. Section 2 introduces the software used for the simulations and the system modelling of this work. Then, Sect. 3 details how our experiments were carried out and the metrics that evaluate different fleet configurations. Section 4 shows the obtained results and their analysis. Finally, in Sect. 5 we present our conclusions and future work.

2   Simulation Environment

In this section, we describe the software we used to create and execute our simulations as well as how the system is modelled.

2.1   SimFleet

The simulations are carried out by a modified version of SimFleet [7]. SimFleet is a multi-agent-based urban fleet simulator, which is focused on the implementation and comparison of agent strategies.

For the setup of our taxi fleet simulations, we use SimFleet's FleetManager Agent as a centralized entity that chooses to which taxi each customer request is forwarded. The strategy followed for this is to send the request to the closest available taxi. Taxis are modelled by Transport Agents, who are in charge of picking up customers at their origin and dropping them off at their destination. Finally, customers of the taxi fleet are represented by Customer Agents. These agents create a travel request (from their origin to their destination) and pass

---

[2] http://cargreen.es/.

it to the FleetManager. Then, once they get confirmation that their request has been assigned to a taxi, they simply wait for the pick-up.

In contrast, to simulate carsharing fleets, we make use of a modified version of SimFleet, presented in [4]. This version includes new behaviours for the three aforementioned agents so that they act as a *free-floating carsharing fleet*. The FleetManager has the role to inform the customers of any available (non-booked) vehicle together with its location. Transport agents have a more passive role, they simply remain parked at their origin positions and wait for a booking request. As for the Customer Agents, they now can choose which vehicle they are booking according to their own needs. In addition, they have to walk to their booked vehicle to make use of it. The distance they can walk is limited by user-defined parameter. Once they are inside their vehicle, they drive to their destination and leave the vehicle parked and available to any other customer. For a more detailed description of the agent's strategy, please refer to [4]. Bear in mind that all simulations have the same goal, which is for every customer to reach their destination.

2.2   Generators

A simulation is only as good as the data it uses to build the scenario. Because of that, we aimed to base our simulations on real data of the city of Valencia, Spain; which we chose to set our experiments in. Thanks to open data portals, provided by the regional[3] and national governments[4], we have access to geolocated data indicating the amount of population per area, average traffic intensity on each city road, and the location of every taxi stop.

The aforementioned data are used by our *Load Generators*, presented in [5]. Their purpose is to create realistic simulation scenarios by distributing the elements of the simulation (agents, resources, etc.) according to real city data.

The generators work by first dividing the area where the simulation takes place in many subareas. The amount of subareas is defined by the *granularity* of the generator. Then, it creates a probability distribution over the whole area, assigning to each subarea a selection probability. Such a probability is computed following the amounts of population, traffic, and social activity that occur within the subarea. The different factors are joined by Eq. 1, where O_i indicates a subarea, p_i, t_i, and a_i the amounts of population, traffic, and social activity within O_i, respectively; and w_p, w_t and w_a are weights that control the influence of each type of data over the probability. The amount of data in a subarea is divided by the amount of the same type of data occurring in the whole area.

$$prob(O_i) = w_p \cdot \frac{p_i}{\sum_{j=1}^{N} p_j} + w_t \cdot \frac{t_i}{\sum_{j=1}^{N} t_j} + w_a \cdot \frac{a_i}{\sum_{j=1}^{N} a_j}; \text{ with } w_p + w_t + w_a = 1 \quad (1)$$

Agents are assigned origin and destination subareas semi-randomly, according to the probabilities. Varying the values of the weights (w_p, w_t, w_a), we can

---

[3] *Govern Obert.* www.valencia.es/val/ajuntament/govern-obert.

[4] *Instituto Nacional de Estadística* (INE). www.ine.es/index.htm.

increase the importance of the different factors depending on the type of agent we are creating. For instance, for customers, more weight is given to population and social activity with respect to traffic. With this, our simulations can reproduce the movement trends of real city users.

2.3 System Modelling

The simulations are set over the city of Valencia, Spain, as we have data regarding its population, traffic per road, and geolocalized Twitter activity. The data is used by the *Load Generators* (Sect. 2.2) to populate the scenario with customer and transport agents, and assign realistic movement to them.

The scenario is loaded by SimFleet (Sect. 2.1) and the simulation is executed. During the development of the simulation, the system keeps track of many parameters corresponding to elapsed times and travelled distances. At the end of the simulation, these metrics are collected and grouped in an output file.

For taxi fleet simulations, the taxis spawn available in different points of the city. Customers spawn and send a travel request to the fleet manager who, in turn, forwards it to the available taxi which is closer to the customer. If there were no available taxis in the area, the customer would wait and ask the fleet manager again. Once a taxi is assigned a travel request, it will drive to the customer's location, pick her up and drop her off at her destination. Then, the customer agent will finish its execution and the taxi agent will inform the fleet manager that it is available again. Customer agents have a parameter that indicates the time they are willing to wait to book a vehicle (maximum waiting time). If a customer is not picked up by a taxi after its maximum waiting time elapsed, it will be marked as "unsatisfied" and stop its execution.

Regarding carsharing fleet simulations, the vehicles (electric cars or e-cars) also spawn available in various points of the city. Customers spawn and send an information request to the fleet manager, which replies with the location of every available vehicle. In addition to their maximum waiting time, carsharing system customers have a specific parameter that determines the distance they are willing to walk to a vehicle (maximum walking distance). A customer usually books the closest vehicle among the available vehicles within reach (according to its maximum walking distance). Once the vehicle is booked, the customer walks to it, drives to its destination and finishes its execution upon arrival. The vehicle is left available for new bookings on the previous customer's destination. If a customer can not book any vehicle after its maximum waiting time elapsed, it will be marked as "unsatisfied" and finish its execution.

Both taxi and carsharing fleet simulations finish once every customer is either at their destination or unsatisfied.

3 Experimental Setup

Following, we introduce our system's metrics and the configurations used to analyse Valencia's taxi fleet. Experimentation is performed over 6-hour simulations of the city's transit with a fixed demand generation and different types of fleets.

3.1 Metrics

The performance of a fleet is measured by analysing many metrics regarding customer's time and fleet vehicle distances. Most of the metrics are general, although some of them are only meant for carsharing or taxi fleet's transports and customers. All metrics are presented in Table 1.

Table 1. Metrics for the evaluation of fleet performance. Customer and Transport metrics apply to individual agents, whereas Simulation metrics show global indicators of customers' satisfaction and vehicle fleets' performance.

Customer metrics	
Walked distance	Distance walked by the customer to its booked transport's location
Waiting time for a booking	Time elapsed from customer's spawn until receiving confirmation of a booking
Waiting time for a pick up	Time elapsed from customer's spawn until being picked up by a taxi
Satisfaction	Boolean that indicates whether a customer has reached its destination
Transport metrics	
Assignments	Number of customers that the vehicle served
Empty distance	Distance travelled by a taxi without a customer
Customer distance	Distance travelled by a vehicle with a customer inside
Simulation metrics	
Avg. customer booking time	Average of every satisfied customer's waiting for booking time
Avg. customer waiting time	Average of every satisfied customer's waiting for pick up time
Avg. customer walked dist.	Average of every satisfied customer's walked distance
Satisfaction %	Percentage of satisfied customers
Total assignments	Sum of every transport's assignments
Avg. assignments	Average number of assignments per transport
Avg. empty distance	Average of every transport's empty distance
Avg. distance	Average distance travelled by fleet transports
Unused vehicles	Number of transports never used by a customer

With these metrics, we can evaluate the performance of a fleet from two different perspectives. Firstly, from the point of view of a customer, lower times and shorter walked distances indicate higher satisfaction. Secondly, regarding the economic and environmental sustainability of the fleet, shorter empty distances and a higher number of assignments and occupied distances are preferable. The global simulation metrics are useful to see the effects of a different number of vehicles and/or customers in different scenarios.

3.2 Configurations

Valencia has a total of 2,841 registered taxis. However, not all of them are in service at the same time. The maximum number of taxis in service is 1,044, but this highly varies depending on the weekday and time of the day, going down to 200 or fewer taxis in periods of low demand. Unfortunately, as there is no recorded data about the number of active taxis per hour, we chose to represent it as a percentage of the total number of taxis. We created a baseline simulation

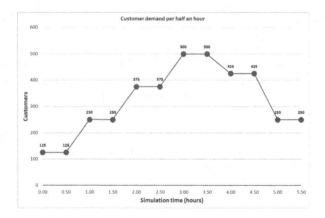

Fig. 1. Mobility demand in terms of the number of customers per simulation hour. The X-axis indicates simulation hours in increments of 30 min (0.5 h). Y-axis indicates the number of customers that spawn simultaneously at the indicated time.

scenario with 840 taxis, which is 80% of the maximum number of active taxis. With this, we aim to compensate for periods with higher and lower taxi amounts.

As for the demand, we modelled customers as individual persons with a spawning time, a location and a destination that was at least 2 km away from their origin. Our simulations reproduce 6 h of city activity. The real amount of demand per hour is also changing, reaching a maximum of up to 1000 requests per hour and minimums of around 50. Aiming to reproduce this, we divided a total of 3850 customers into 30-min intervals as shown in Fig. 1. As it can be seen, we have a minimum of 250 customers per hour at the beginning of the simulation and a maximum of 1000 customers during the third hour.

The simulation of the taxi fleet served as a baseline to compare its performance with different carsharing fleet configurations. For this purpose, five other simulation scenarios were defined. Each of them preserved the demand, but customers were served by a carsharing fleet. The different scenarios varied in number of vehicles of the fleet: *Cs-1000*, *Cs-840*, *Cs-560*, *Cs-280*, and *Cs-140*, which had 1000, 840, 560, 280 and 140 vehicles, respectively. Measuring the percentage of satisfied customers allows us to approximate how much of the mobility demand can be covered by the different carsharing fleet configurations. In addition, we can also compare each fleet's carbon dioxide emissions as a function of their number of vehicles and the total distance travelled by the whole fleet.

The simulations were executed fixing a speed of 40 km/h for the vehicles and 4 km/h for pedestrians (carsharing customers). This was done to use an average speed among the maximum of 50 km/h in urban roads and 30 km/h in residential areas, as well as waiting time at traffic lights. As for pedestrians, we reduced the average walking speed of 5 km/h by 1 to take into account the time spent waiting at traffic lights. Every customer had a maximum waiting time of 12 min (720 s) and carsharing users had their maximum walking distance set to 1000 m. Therefore, 12 min after their spawning time, if a customer has not had the chance to book a vehicle or has not been picked up by a taxi, it will be marked as unsatisfied and finish its execution.

4   Results and Discussion

This section presents three different experiments. First, the differences among carsharing simulation outputs are examined to define the parameters of a competitive carsharing fleet that can deal with part of the mobility demand. Then, a reduction in the number of vehicles of Valencia's current taxi fleet is assessed. Finally, we present a hybrid configuration that presents a joint mobility model where the demand is served by two different fleets.

4.1   Carsharing Fleets Performance

The first experiment shows a comparison of the different carsharing fleets performance against the baseline configuration (Taxi-840) presented in Table 2. Time values must be understood as an optimistic reference and not exact time, as phenomena like traffic congestion or traffic lights are not considered. For the baseline simulations, the customer booking time (Table 2, first row) indicates the time taken to call the taxi company and ask for a cab. Consequently, the customer waiting time shows how much the taxi took to pick up the client, on average. This is different for carsharing fleets, where booking time reflects the time the user has been checking the app waiting for an available vehicle to book, whereas waiting time displays the time spent walking towards the booked vehicles. The rest of the metrics describe the same factors for both types of fleets (see Table 1 for a detailed explanation of each metric).

Table 2. Comparison of global simulation metrics of the different carsharing fleets (labelled as "Cs-" followed by the number of vehicles they contain) against the baseline taxi fleet of 840 vehicles.

	Taxi-840	Cs-1000	Cs-840	Cs-560	Cs-280	Cs-140
Avg. cust. booking time (min)	1	1	1	1	1.1	1.8
Avg. cust. waiting time (min)	1.5	4.4	5.5	6.1	7.4	9.1
Avg. cust. walked dist (m)	0	487	497	529	572	610
Satisfaction %	100	97	93.4	86.4	60	37.1
Total assignments	3850	3738	3597	3325	2310	1429
Avg. assignments	5.12	3.85	4.76	6.11	8.31	10.28
Avg. dist. per assignment (Km)	5.8	5.4	5.4	5.4	5.4	5.4
Unused vehicles	87	30	85	16	2	1
Total empty distance (Km)	1727	0	0	0	0	0
Total distance (Km)	22230	19890	19121	17671	12308	7624

We have plotted in the graph of Fig. 2 the evolution of demand (in terms of customers waiting to be served) and the number of unsatisfied customers throughout the simulations. The number of waiting customers is indicated by the left vertical axis and represented with areas of a different colour. It can be seen how the demand peaks at the times where batches of customers are introduced in the simulation. Then, it can be observed how the demand decays faster as the number of vehicles in a fleet increases. For fleets with a greater number of vehicles (*Cs-1000, Cs-840*) most of the waiting customers are served. However, in the rest of the fleets, a sharp drop is observed, coinciding with the end of the maximum waiting time for customers. The right vertical axis indicates the number of unsatisfied customers, represented by lines with different patterns. These lines grow by steps each time a batch of waiting customers reach their maximum waiting time and, therefore, become unsatisfied. As it can be seen, the lower the number of vehicles in a fleet, the faster the lines increase.

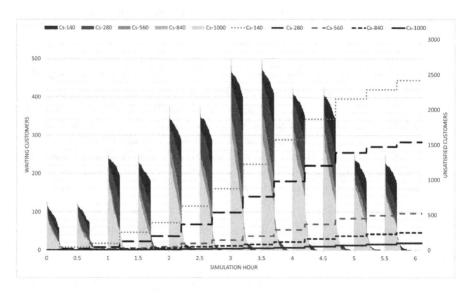

Fig. 2. Visualisation of the evolution of the amounts of waiting clients (left vertical axis) and unsatisfied clients (right vertical axis) in the different carsharing simulations according to the simulation time (in hours). Simulations are labelled with "Cs-" followed by the number of vehicles in their fleet.

Analysing the results from the customer satisfaction perspective, the baseline taxi service consistently offers lower waiting times and higher satisfaction ratios. The different carsharing fleets can not serve every customer with the restrictions we have introduced for their vehicle use. We are aware, however, that a direct comparison of taxi and carsharing fleets is not fair, as they are very different. Taxi services are generally used for short, one-off journeys. Some carsharing vehicles are used for the same purpose, although some users use them as a substitute for private vehicles. On the other hand, carsharing users must be willing to drive a vehicle themselves and park to it. Nevertheless, the results show that part of the taxi customers could be served by a carsharing fleet (up to 37.1% with a carsharing fleet of only 140 vehicles, 60% with a fleet of 280 vehicles, or even 86.4% with 560 vehicles), thus reducing emissions due to the smaller number of vehicles and the fact that they are not driven empty at any time.

From the point of view of fleet sustainability, it is interesting to see how the average number of assignments per vehicle increases as the number of unused vehicles is reduced. Fewer vehicles mean less impact on the environment, both in terms of vehicle manufacture and its subsequent maintenance. In addition, it implies less risk of traffic congestion, which also reduces pollution and generally improves the quality of life for all users of the urban transport system.

The usage of carsharing vehicles has an obvious yet forceful advantage: the avoidance of empty vehicle movement. Our results show that around 1727 km could be saved each 6 h by avoiding empty journeys. Assuming an average city consumption of 5 L/100 km[5], this represents a saving of 0.20 tonnes of CO_2. If the carsharing fleet was implemented by fully electric vehicles, the savings would be much higher. For instance, the fleet in *Cs-140* amounts to 7624 km every 6 h. Such an amount of distance, being travelled with cars with the above-average consumption, would have an impact of 0.83 tonnes of CO_2. If every vehicle was electric all of the emissions could be avoided.

4.2 Taxi Fleet Reduction

With the previous results in mind, we run new taxi fleet simulations reducing the number of vehicles, aiming to find out how much of a reduction could be applied without worsening customer satisfaction ratios. The results can be seen in Table 3. Simulations *Taxi-560* and *Taxi-280* are able to comply with the generated demand, meanwhile for *Taxi-140* the system gets overloaded and only a 56.7% of customers can be served. As the number of vehicles is reduced, higher empty and total distances appear. Nevertheless, that is to be expected, as vehicles will generally be further away from their customers. In addition, as we commented above, the economic and environmental benefits of lower vehicle manufacturing and maintenance must be considered.

4.3 Hybrid Configuration

Lastly, we developed a hybrid simulation that contained a fleet of 280 carsharing vehicles and another one with 140 taxis. With the results of this experiment (Table 4) we show how a reduced taxi fleet could aid the carsharing service in serving the customers that otherwise would remain unsatisfied. In addition, even though carsharing may be a more sustainable approach, a taxi service will always be necessary for certain types of users (people who are unable to drive vehicles, or with other types of needs).

---

[5] Value obtained as an average of the gas consumption of vehicle models generally used for taxis in Valencia.

Table 3. Comparison of global simulation metrics of the different taxi fleets (labelled as "Taxi-" followed by the number of vehicles they contain) against the baseline taxi fleet of 840 vehicles.

	Taxi-840	Taxi-560	Taxi-280	Taxi-140
Avg. cust. booking time (min)	1	1	1	4.7
Avg. cust. waiting time (min)	1.5	1.5	2.2	9.1
Avg. cust. walked dist (m)	0	0	0	0
Satisfaction %	100	100	99.9	56.7
Total assignments	3850	3850	3850	3850
Avg. assignments	5.12	7.06	13.75	27.5
Avg. dist. per assignment (Km)	5.8	6.0	6.4	8.2
Unused vehicles	87	15	0	0
Total empty distance (Km)	1727	2418	4163	11049
Total distance (Km)	22230	22921	24666	31552

The combination of the two fleets with a total of 420 vehicles can cover all customer demand. This is a very positive result as customers are well served with both alternatives, and the total number of potentially polluting vehicles (taxis) needed is lower than in previous experiments. Additionally, this last approach is closer to how real cities work. Having many options, authorities would ideally promote those with a lower carbon footprint. This could be achieved by making them more attractive from an economic perspective. Any measure that starts to change how society perceives transportation is useful to work towards the sustainability of future cities.

Table 4. Global simulation metrics for a carsharing (*Cs-280*) and a taxi (*Taxi-140*) fleet executed in the same configuration.

Hybrid configuration		
	Cs-280	Taxi-140
Avg. cust. booking time (min)	1.1	1
Avg. cust. waiting time (min)	7.4	4
Avg. cust. walked dist (m)	572	0
Satisfaction %	100	100
Total assignments	2310	1540
Avg. assignments	8.3	11
Avg. dist. per assignment (Km)	5.4	7.5
Unused vehicles	2	0
Total empty distance (Km)	0	3183
Total distance (Km)	12308	11429

5   Conclusions

In this paper we have studied the introduction of a carsharing system in the city of Valencia, Spain, aiming to provide a more sustainable alternative to its current taxi fleet. We have developed simulations grounding agent movement and distribution on real city data. Our results indicate that meanwhile, some type of taxi service will always be necessary, carsharing has a high potential to reduce carbon dioxide emissions in the city and reduce traffic congestion, at the expense, of course, of some of the customers' satisfaction.

In addition, a hybrid approach, in which the use of taxi fleets is combined with green carsharing services, shows potential to cover all the customers' demand while also lowers the carbon footprint. This would be ideal for a transition towards fully electric urban mobility, thus achieving a more sustainable city.

The current work opens several research paths for the future. On the one hand, we would like to explore more realistic demand generation approaches. For this, we would need a reliable source of data and a subsequent selection of the appropriate features. On the other hand, we want to introduce another means of transportation to our simulations, aiming to analyse more thoroughly the amounts of the total mobility demand that each system covers. Vehicles of the public transportation system of Valencia, like busses, bikes or metro lines would make a great addition for better simulations of the city transportation.

Acknowledgements. This work was partially supported by MINECO/FEDER RTI2018-095390-B-C31 project of the Spanish government. Pasqual Martí is funded by grant PAID-01-20-4 of Universitat Politècnica de València.

References

1. Dong, X., Cai, Y., Cheng, J., Hu, B., Sun, H.: Understanding the competitive advantages of car sharing from the travel-cost perspective. Int. J. Environ. Res. Public Health **17**(13), 4666 (2020)
2. Firnkorn, J., Müller, M.: What will be the environmental effects of new free-floating car-sharing systems? The case of car2go in Ulm. Ecol. Econ. **70**(8), 1519–1528 (2011)
3. Katzev, R.: Car sharing: a new approach to urban transportation problems. Anal. Soc. Issues Public Policy **3**(1), 65–86 (2003)
4. Martí, P., Jordán, J., Palanca, J., Julian, V.: Free-floating carsharing in simfleet. In: Intelligent Data Engineering and Automated Learning - IDEAL 2020, pp. 221–232. Springer, Cham (2020)
5. Martí, P., Jordán, J., Palanca, J., Julian, V.: Load generators for automatic simulation of urban fleets. In: De La Prieta, F., et al. (eds.) PAAMS 2020. CCIS, vol. 1233, pp. 394–405. Springer, Cham (2020). https://doi.org/10.1007/978-3-030-51999-5_33
6. Namazu, M., Dowlatabadi, H.: Vehicle ownership reduction: a comparison of one-way and two-way carsharing systems. Transp. Policy **64**, 38–50 (2018)
7. Palanca, J., Terrasa, A., Carrascosa, C., Julián, V.: Simfleet: A new transport fleet simulator based on mas. In: International Conference on Practical Applications of Agents and Multi-Agent Systems. pp. 257–264. Springer (2019)

8. Rayle, L., Dai, D., Chan, N., Cervero, R., Shaheen, S.: Just a better taxi? a survey-based comparison of taxis, transit, and ridesourcing services in San Francisco. Transp. Policy **45**, 168–178 (2016)
9. Yoon, T., Cherry, C.R., Ryerson, M.S., Bell, J.E.: Carsharing demand estimation and fleet simulation with EV adoption. J. Clean. Prod. **206**, 1051–1058 (2019). https://doi.org/10.1016/j.jclepro.2018.09.124

Simulation Analysis of the Break Assignment Problem Considering Area Coverage in Emergency Fleets

Dora Novak[1] and Marin Lujak[2]([⊠])[ID]

[1] Faculty of Mechanical Engineering and Naval Architecture, University of Zagreb, Zagreb, Croatia

[2] CETINIA, Universidad Rey Juan Carlos, Madrid, Spain
marin.lujak@urjc.es

Abstract. Real time allocation of vehicles to incidents in emergency fleets is a challenging optimization problem due to time and location uncertainty in incident appearance. In addition, to ensure high responsiveness and efficiency of emergency vehicle crews, their work shifts need to be well balanced with enough break times. These two aspects are simultaneously taken into consideration in Break Assignment Problem Considering Area Coverage (BAPCAC) proposed by Lujak et al. in [1]. Because of its multiple dimensionality and complex mixed linear integer programming structure, this problem is computationally expensive. In this paper, we test in simulations the performance of the BAPCAC problem and propose a simplification of the model so that it can be solved in close-to real time.

Keywords: Break assignment problem · Emergency fleet coordination · Area coverage

1 Introduction

Efficiency of an emergency service fleet can be greatly impacted by fatigue, decreasing the responsiveness of emergency vehicle crews if they do not get sufficient rest. The crews must deal with stressful situations during the whole work shift and be ready to assist urgent accidents at any time. It is, therefore, crucial to ensure crews' high alertness by assigning enough breaks in terms of length and frequency.

Incidents are often urgent and require assistance within certain target time, e.g. for an ambulance assistance of an out-of-hospital emergency patient, it is 20 min from the call. Chances of saving lives are higher if response is faster. A minimum number of emergency vehicles that dynamically evolves through time should always be available for incident assistance to minimize both morbidity and mortality. The work load of emergency vehicles cannot be predicted with certainty due to the stochastic appearance of incidents both in terms of location

© Springer Nature Switzerland AG 2021
F. De La Prieta et al. (Eds.): PAAMS Workshops 2021, CCIS 1472, pp. 283–295, 2021.
https://doi.org/10.1007/978-3-030-85710-3_24

and time. Neither is the minimum number of vehicles needed to assist the incidents known with certainty and it can only be predicted by applying forecasting methods on historical data.

This problem is mathematically formulated as Break Assignment Problem Considering Area Coverage (BAPCAC) [2,3], which combines two previously investigated problems: break scheduling and maximization of area coverage. BAPCAC aims to minimize both the area uncovered by vehicles and the fatigue of vehicle crews. The aim of the model is to position crews' vehicles so that they are able to assist given incidents but also to ensure enough rest time so that their fatigue is controlled.

BAPCAC is a mixed-integer linear programming (MILP) problem combining the computationally expensive break scheduling problem (BSP) and the maximal coverage location problem (MCLP) and, as such, highly computationally complex as described in Sect. 2. Since it is a multidimensional spatio-temporal problem that finds for each vehicle work breaks and best locations throughout a work shift, we explore in simulated experiments in Sect. 3 its complexity in 3 dimensions: time, space, and the fleet's size. The dimension that contributes the most to the computational cost is revised and simplified in Sect. 4. The paper concludes in Sect. 5.

2   Preliminaries and Related Work

The BSP problem aims to find the optimal break schedule for a work shift, which can be of great importance for, e.g., police patrols and out-of-hospital emergency medical assistance, working long stressful hours and requiring enough rest time. In the BSP problem, shifts and various types of breaks are planned by satisfying different constraints, legal and other, while avoiding or minimizing fatigue (e.g., [4–10]). Conversely, the MCLP problem focuses on minimizing the area that is not covered by available units. The goal is to distribute these units according to the spatial distribution of demand with a temporal dimension. Developed solution approaches should be able to dynamically distribute the units, while closing the gap between demand and supply, i.e., relocate the units in real time, depending on how the demand distribution changes (e.g., [11–17]).

However, when solving these two problems separately and sequentially, parts of the issue crucial for optimal functioning of the fleet are omitted. This is why it is important to solve them simultaneously in a mathematical program that unites them both. Lujak et al. [1–3] proposed the break assignment problem considering area coverage (BAPCAC) as a combination of BSP and MCLP, both NP hard. BAPCAC takes in consideration both spatial and temporal dimension of the dynamically evolving demand as the main input while assigning breaks and relocating fleet's vehicles over the region of interest according to this demand. For the self-sufficiency of this work, we present next the BAPCAC mathematical program. More details can be found in [1].

(BAPCAC):

$$\min \; w \cdot \sum_{i \in \mathcal{I}, \tau \in \mathcal{T}} \left((1-\gamma)\delta_{i\tau} + \gamma dev_{i\tau} \right) + (1-w) \cdot \sum_{a \in A, \tau \in \mathcal{T}} \left(1 - y_{a\tau} \right), \tag{1}$$

such that:

$$dev_{i\tau} \geq \bar{\delta} - \delta_{i\tau}, \forall i \in \mathcal{I}, \tau \in \mathcal{T} \tag{2}$$

$$dev_{i\tau} \geq \delta_{i\tau} - \bar{\delta}, \forall i \in \mathcal{I}, \tau \in \mathcal{T} \tag{3}$$

$$\sum_{a \in A} \left(z_{a\tau i} + \bar{z}_{a\tau i} \right) = D_{i\tau} - \delta_{i\tau}, \forall i \in \mathcal{I}, \tau \in \mathcal{T} \tag{4}$$

$$z_{a\tau i} \leq \sum_{j \in \mathcal{J} | N_{ij}=1} D_{i\tau} x_{a\tau j}, \forall a \in A, \tau \in \mathcal{T}, i \in \mathcal{I} \quad \cdot \tag{5}$$

$$\bar{z}_{a\tau i} \leq \sum_{j \in \mathcal{J} | \bar{N}_{ij}=1} D_{i\tau} x_{a\tau j}, \forall a \in A, \tau \in \mathcal{T}, i \in \mathcal{I} \tag{6}$$

$$z_{a\tau i} \leq D_{i\tau}(1 - y_{a,\tau}), \forall a \in A, \tau \in \mathcal{T}, i \in \mathcal{I} \tag{7}$$

$$\bar{z}_{a\tau i} \leq D_{i\tau} y_{a,\tau}, \forall a \in A, \tau \in \mathcal{T}, i \in \mathcal{I} \tag{8}$$

$$\sum_{i \in \mathcal{I}} z_{a\tau i} \leq 1, \forall \tau \in \mathcal{T}, a \in A \tag{9}$$

$$\sum_{i \in \mathcal{I}} \bar{z}_{a\tau i} \leq 1, \forall \tau \in \mathcal{T}, a \in A \tag{10}$$

$$\sum_{j \in \mathcal{J}} x_{a\tau j} = 1, \forall \tau \in \mathcal{T}, a \in A \tag{11}$$

$$x_{a\tau j} + x_{a(\tau+1)j'} \leq 1 + IM_{jj'}, \forall a \in A, \tau \in [1, |\mathcal{T}| - 1], j, j' \in \mathcal{J} \tag{12}$$

$$y_{a\tau} \geq \sum_{b \in B} \sum_{k=0}^{\Delta_b^{MIN}-1} \alpha_{ab(\tau-k)}, \ \forall a \in A, \ \tau \in [\max_{b \in B}(\Delta_b^{MIN}), |\mathcal{T}|] \tag{13}$$

$$y_{a\tau} \leq \sum_{b \in B} \sum_{k=0}^{\Delta_b^{MAX}-1} \alpha_{ab(\tau-k)}, \ \forall a \in A, \ \tau \in [\max_{b \in B}(\Delta_b^{MAX}), |\mathcal{T}|] \tag{14}$$

$$\sum_{b \in B} \sum_{k=0}^{\Delta_b^{MAX}-1} \alpha_{ab(\tau-k)} \leq 1, \ \forall a \in A, \ \tau \in [\max_{b \in B}(\Delta_b^{MAX}), |\mathcal{T}|] \tag{15}$$

$$\sum_{\tau'=\tau}^{\tau+MAX_b^w-1} \alpha_{ab\tau'} \geq 1, \ \forall a \in A, b \in B, \tau \in [1, |\mathcal{T}| - MAX_b^w + 1] \tag{16}$$

$$\sum_{b \in B} \alpha_{ab\tau} \leq y_{a\tau}, \ \forall a \in A, b \in B, \tau \in [1, |\mathcal{T}|] \tag{17}$$

$$z_{a\tau i}, \bar{z}_{a\tau i}, \delta_{i\tau} \geq 0, x_{a\tau j}, y_{a\tau}, \alpha_{ab\tau} \in \{0,1\}, \forall i \in \mathcal{I}, j \in \mathcal{J}, \tau \in \mathcal{T}, a \in A \tag{18}$$

BAPCAC contains three dimensions: time, space, and fleet size. Objective function (1) consists of two parts: minimizing uncovered area and maximizing the number of breaks assigned to the vehicle agents. These two functions are opposed to each other, and therefore, weight w, where $0 \leq w \leq 1$, is introduced.

Constraints (2) and (3) introduce deviation parameter $dev_{i\tau}$ since (1) considers only the summation of the values over time periods and geographical areas (cells) in a region of interest, but it does not consider their temporal and spatial distribution. Constraints (4) link the covered area part with *idle* and *on-break* vehicles. The sum of all density parts assigned to the *idle* and *on-break* vehicles in each area and time slot should amount to a maximum of the density of covered area. The coverage variable $\bar{z}_{a\tau i}$ in the constraint assumes that the breaks are preemptive and can be ended if an incident needs to be assisted by the *on-break* vehicle. (5) and (6) limit the coverage of each idle (vehicle) agent and an agent on-break to at most incident density $D_{i\tau}$ of unit area $i \in \mathcal{I}$ at time slot $\tau \in \mathcal{T}$ if it is positioned within the travel time defined by adjacency matrix N_{ij} and $\bar{N}_{ij}$, respectively. These constraints ensure that part $z_{a\tau i}$ of the coverage of the area i by an idle agent and an agent on-break, respectively, is at most the sum of the densities of the areas $j \in \mathcal{J}$ within its reach at time $\tau \in \mathcal{T}$. Furthermore, (7) and (8) limit idle coverage and the coverage on-break vehicle agents only to idle ones and those at break, respectively. Moreover, (9) guarantee that the incident density covered by each idle agent sums up to at most 1 at time $\tau \in \mathcal{T}$ due to the unitary vehicle capacity, i.e. each agent can assist only one incident at once. Similarly, (10) limits the capacity for the coverage of each agent on-break.

(11) assigns to each agent a at each time slot τ a unique location $j \in \mathcal{J}$, by means of location variable $x_{a\tau j}$, while (12) constraints agents' positions $x_{a\tau j}$ in two consecutive time slots t, $t + 1$ to be within the maximum allowed distance travelled established by parameter $IM_{jj'}$ with binary values.

Minimal and maximal break durations are imposed by (13) and (14). (15) prohibit the assignment of more than one break type during a maximal duration of each break. For a time window starting at each time slot with the duration of a maximum uninterrupted work time MAX_b^w, each break type should start at least once according to (16). Moreover, (17) prohibits the start of more than one break type at a time, while (18) represents non-negativity and range constraints on decision variables. The solution of the BAPCAC problem is supposed to be found in the rolling time horizon, thus for the next $|\mathcal{T}|$ periods. Since this is a strongly NP-hard problem, to be able to perform the optimization fast enough, mathematical complexity of the model is experimentally analyzed, critical dimension found, and its size reduced.

3   Simulation Experiments

The simulations are performed in IBM ILOG CPLEX Optimization Studio 12.10, a decision optimization software using mathematical programming. The simulation experiments are created in random scenarios and are run on Dell laptop with Intel Core i7-7560U CPU running at 2.40 Ghz and with 16 Gb of RAM. Simulation time limit is 1 h. Moreover, two break types are defined, long and short breaks. Parameters for each type are as follows. For short breaks, both the minimum Δ_b^{MIN} and maximum length of break Δ_b^{MAX} equal 20 min, while maximum allowed work time before assigning a short break MAX_b^w equals 1 h 40 min. For long breaks, $\Delta_b^{MIN} = 40$ min, $\Delta_b^{MAX} = 1$ h 20 min and $MAX_b^w = 3$ h 20 min. The simulations are performed in a square environment, where the used parameters are randomized following the continuous uniform distribution.

Because of the high-complexity of the BAPCAC problem, two simplifications are considered. First, deviation parameter $dev_{i\tau}$ from (1) is removed, which implies elimination of constraints (2) and (3), which create exponential increase in number of parameters by linearizing an initially non-linear variable $dev_{i\tau}$. By removing deviation from the model, $|\mathcal{I}| \times |\mathcal{T}|$ number of constraints would be eliminated twice, one time for each constraint removed. Second simplification will consider elimination of the variable $\bar{z}_{a\tau i}$, concerning assignment of incidents to on-break vehicles. Thus, constraint (6), (10) will be excluded, while constraint (4) will be simplified when only considering assigning incidents to the idle vehicles, i.e. only variable $z_{a\tau i}$. Without (6) and (10), $|\mathcal{I}| \times |\mathcal{T}| \times |\mathcal{A}|$ and $|\mathcal{T}| \times |\mathcal{A}|$ number of constraints will be removed respectively. These two simplifications will be implemented for all simulation experiments and analysis of the BAPCAC model.

For each simulation instance there are three dimensions that can be changed: number of vehicles, number of time periods and area size. Weight w will vary from 0 to 1, with a change of 0.1.

Figure 1 represents graphically the change in uncoverage and fatigue with the change in w. Even though the trend is as expected, smoother transition would be desirable. Ideally, uncoverage values would be gradually decreasing together with weight w, while fatigue would monotonically increase. At lower values of w model assigns all the importance to fatigue. When $w < 0.5$, model assigns breaks to all the idle vehicles for all the 12 time periods. Obtained results are different if additional constraints on the upper bound on time spent on break are added.

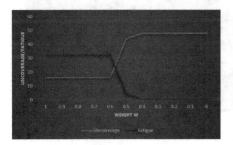 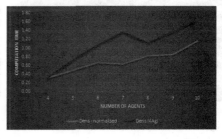

Fig. 1. Uncoverage & fatigue vs. weight w

Fig. 2. Average computational time

Next, we vary the number of available vehicles and consider the densities normalised according to the number of vehicles and a constant density normalised for the same number of vehicles. Figure 2 shows the average computational time between normalised incident density and constant incident density for $|\mathcal{A}| = 4$. Computational time increases in each case proportionally with the increasing number of vehicles. However, in the experiments, this time is higher for the constant than for the normalised incident density. In the case of constant incident density, it is assumed that supply is higher than the demand, which directly leads to greater number of coverage possibilities. Experiments show that CPLEX consumes more computational time when the possibilities are diversified.

System Balance. We next investigate how the model performance indicators change with respect to the incident density.

In continuation, we use the term of "saturation point", which represents the case when supply and demand are balanced, meaning there are enough available vehicles to cover all the estimated demand at the given time, $D_{i\tau} = \sum_{a \in A} z_{a\tau i} \forall i \in \mathcal{I}, \tau \in \mathcal{T}$. A "saturated system" will have uncoverage value $\delta_{i\tau} = 0$.

First, incident densities set for 6, 8 and 10 agents have been compared. For this comparison, weight w is held constant with its value being 1. Therefore, only area coverage problem needs to be taken into account. Figure 3 represents the change in uncoverage per agent versus the number of vehicles. With increase in vehicle number, uncoverage per vehicle drops as expected. Also, when different incident densities are applied, this variable increases in value and reaches the saturation later. Uncoverage for all densities decreases when more vehicles are added to the system, and finally converges to 0 with similar trends. Gradient of all three curves is steeper with lower numbers of vehicles and is decreasing simultaneously with the uncoverage value.

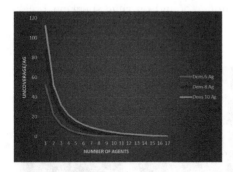   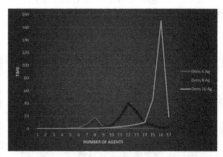

Fig. 3. Uncoverage per agent vs. incident density

Fig. 4. Computational time vs. incident density

BAPCAC complexity is represented by the computational time needed for the solver to find the optimal solution in Fig. 4. There is a clear peak for all instances, and that is when number of agents starts to outgrow the given demand. In Fig. 3, the most complex instances are the ones with the minimum value of uncoverage, but when uncoverage is still not 0, meaning not yet saturated. Figure 4 shows

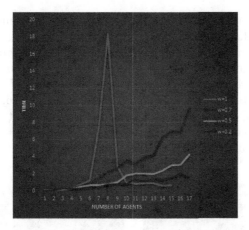

Fig. 5. Changes in computational time for different weight values

tendency that the most complex instances are near saturation point, while their complexity drops drastically after the saturation point is passed. The graph shows direct relation between the coverage area part of the problem and its complexity.

System Balance for Different Values of Weight w. Complexity of the model is analyzed through computational time. Figure 5 represents the change in computational time needed for CPLEX to solve an optimization problem with different instances as shown above. When value of weight w is less than 1, that means that model is considering both the problem of uncoverage and fatigue, Fig. 5 shows rather exponential growth in complexity as the number of vehicles grows. As the fatigue part of the objective function is in fact a sum over all the agents, it is expected that the computational time will grow with increasing number of agents. This graph shows the exponential trends, which are stronger at higher values of w, meaning that the break scheduling part of the problem is consuming less computational time, thus it is less complex to be solved. When applying weight $w = 1$, or when the only focus is on minimizing uncoverage, there is a clear peak on Fig. 5 when the number of agents employed is 7. Knowing a priori predicted demand, if fleet's size is slightly greater than given demand, computational time can be greatly reduced and the model can run in close to real time. However, this approach implies that saturation point is known.

3.1   Critical Dimension

Scalability of the BAPCAC model is manifested through either the computational time or optimality gap. Scalability analysis is conducted for weight $w = 0.7$ because it represents good balance between uncoverage and fatigue part of the model. Figures 6, 7 and 8 show linear change in number of variables when one of the dimensions (area size, number of time periods $|\mathcal{T}|$, number of vehicles) is increasing while other dimensions remain constant.

Figure 6 shows increase in number of variables for three different values of $|\mathcal{T}|$, where each point represents the difference in variable number for area 6 × 6 compared to 4 × 4. For example, the lowest point, when $|\mathcal{T}| = 12$ and $|\mathcal{A}| = 4$ shows that there are 3120 variables more when area is 6 × 6, compared to the smaller area 4 × 4 if all the other dimensions are kept constant. If we consider the highest linear change in this Figure, when $|\mathcal{T}| = 20$ and $|\mathcal{A}| = 10$, this difference is 12400 between same instance with 4 × 4 and 6 × 6.

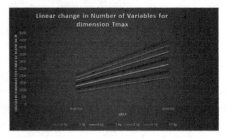

Fig. 6. Number of variables vs. area size

Fig. 7. Number of variables vs. $|\mathcal{T}|$

Figure 7 represents linear change in number of variables with the increase of $|\mathcal{T}|$ by 4, from $|\mathcal{T}| = 12$ to $|\mathcal{T}| = 16$ and the same values for increase from $|\mathcal{T}| = 16$ to $|\mathcal{T}| = 20$. Each line represents an instance for the constant number of available vehicles. This figure shows that increase in number of variables for increasing number of time periods $|\mathcal{T}|$ ranges from 880 to 4584, which is significantly lower than the increase in dimension area.

Contribution of the third dimension, number of vehicles available for assistance, to the model complexity is shown in Fig. 8, where each of the two green lines represent instances when area size is 4 × 4 and 6 × 6. Each point on the graph represents change in number of variables if number of available vehicles increases by 1. The figure shows that this linear change between different number of vehicles can range from 612 for least complex instances to 2220 added variables when the instance is at the highest complexity level (area 6 × 6 and $|\mathcal{T}| = 20$). It is clear that dimension with number of vehicles, i.e. agents, contributes to the model complexity less than two other dimensions.

Critical dimension analysis was carried out on a relative basis, comparing experiment instances that have been simulated. Least complex instance was compared to the most complex instance to understand how each of the dimensions contribute to the BAPCAC model complexity as a result of the increase in number of variables.

Regarding scalability, dimensions $|\mathcal{T}|$ and $|\mathcal{A}|$ are proven to contribute less to the computational complexity than the area size dimension. Therefore, small

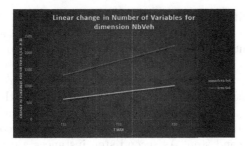

Fig. 8. Number of variables vs. fleet size

increase of these two dimensions would not make the model overly complexed for CPLEX, whereas with a minimum increase in area size CPLEX would not be able to find optimal solution within 1 h.

It is important to emphasize that increase in area size from 4 × 4 (16 area units) to 6 × 6 (36 area units) results in adding an extra 20 area units because of its quadratic form. This consequently leads to a larger increase in number of variables. However, this should be resolved with a simplification idea.

4   Simplification of the BAPCAC Model

To ensure BAPCAC model scalability it is needed to simplify it in terms of the most complex dimension. As analyzed earlier, dimension that contributes the most to computational complexity is area size, precisely instances with area 6 × 6. Therefore, a simplification that will allow CPLEX to solve instances with bigger areas within reasonable computational time will be proposed. As an example, this simplification will be implemented to instance with region of interest with 36 cells (area 6 × 6).

In order to simplify BAPCAC model for area dimension, it is necessary to decrease number of variables concerning each area. This can be done by simplifying some of the constraints that include area dimension. Thus, the number of area units needs to be sized down.

Two-step simplification is suggested as a solution for instance when region of interest has 36 cells (area 6 × 6). As earlier described, uncoverage part of the objective function 1 is more computationally complex than fatigue part, especially when area dimension is bigger. This is why proposed solution would solve the problem in two steps. First step will focus only on area coverage in simplified area, while second step will simultaneously solve both area coverage and break assignment problems.

As the first step, 36 cells (area 6 × 6) will be divided into 4 parts, each part consisting of 9 (area 3 × 3) cells, and will form new area 2 × 2 with 4 cells. Within this first step, only area coverage part of the problem will be considered and therefore, available agents would be distributed in 4 area units considering only associated demand. When distributed once, agents will not be able to move across area units but will stay in assigned unit for duration of all time periods and will be able to assist only the incidents in area units assigned to them. Regarding constraints, (5) and (12) need to be adjusted accordingly.

The second step includes solving BAPCAC problem for each of the 4 area parts. Each area part includes 9 area units within a 3 × 3 area. Having smaller area size consequently means lower model complexity and thus, less computational time needed. After distributing available agents throughout 4 area parts in the first step, only the smaller number of agents will be considered for each area part in the second step. As second step instances are greatly simplified, BAPCAC model will assign incident to both *idle* and *on-break* vehicles, meaning parameter $\bar{z}_{a\tau i}$ will be included together with $z_{a\tau i}$. This will contribute to minimization of area uncoverage by utilizing small number of agents, possibly employing them even when they are on break.

To test performance of the simplified model, its simulation results will be compared to the initial model results with the focus on model complexity as well as model output, meaning decision variables of uncoverage and fatigue.

Instance with 5 agents available, 16 time period and region of interest with 36 cells (area 6 × 6) is considered. When more importance is given to the uncoverage part of the problem, CPLEX does not find an optimal solution within limited time of 1 h. Focus is therefore put on resolving this particular problem.

As the second step involves 4 separate simulations of area 3 × 3 needed, sum of their solutions will be taken into account while analyzing the effectiveness of proposed model simplification. Comparison of decision variable results is provided in Figs. 9 and 10. Uncoverage is lower for all weights but for $w = 0.7$, which has negligibly higher uncoverage for simplified model. Regarding fatigue, it is considerably lower for higher values of weight w if simplification is implemented. This is a result of assigning incidents to *on-break* vehicles as well, i.e. including parameter $\bar{z}_{a\tau i}$.

   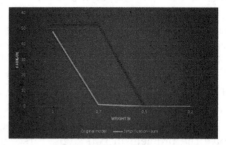

Fig. 9. Uncoverage vs. simplification

Fig. 10. Fatigue vs. model simplification

Figures 11 and 12 compare optimality gap and computational time respectively. The gap is significantly higher at $w = 1$ and $w = 0.7$ for model without simplification. Even though the gap values are lower for $w = 0.5$ and $w = 0.2$

Fig. 11. Gap vs. simplification

Fig. 12. Comp. time vs. simplification

for initial model, simplified model results are given as summation of acceptably low gap values. With simplification, the computational time does not exceed 2 s, while still maintaining good quality of solution, which was the main goal of this work.

5 Conclusion

The presented work is a summary of a Master's thesis that investigated computational limits of the BAPCAC problem considering area coverage, which addresses both the BSP and the MCLP problem.

BAPCAC is intended for emergency vehicle fleets with a receding horizon urgent dynamic and stochastic demand. This imposes requirement for finding the solution in close to real time. To ensure the balance between the solution quality and computational time, BAPCAC was tested in simulated scenarios using IBM ILOG CPLEX Optimization Studio. Three dimensions were evaluated: area size, fleet size and time horizon size. Among these, it is found that area size contributes the most to the computational time.

Two-step BAPCAC model simplification, focused on reducing computational time by reducing of the number of areas in the region of interest was proposed and evaluated. This simplification resulted in a significant reduction of the computational time, offering the possibility of solving the problem in close to real time and showing satisfactory values for area uncoverage and agents fatigue.

Future analysis of the BAPCAC model should consider various system settings. This can involve different spatial arrangements of the area, improved break parameters considering minimal engagement of each agent, etc. We expect that by approximations, depending on particular needs of the operational setting that is being modeled, BAPCAC model will be sufficiently flexible and able to respond to all the additionally imposed requirements, while not contributing significantly to the computational cost.

Acknowledgment. This work has been partially supported by the "AGRIFLEETS" project ANR-20-CE10-0001 funded by the French National Research Agency (ANR) and by the Spanish MINECO projects RTI2018-095390-BC33 (MCIU/AEI/FEDER, UE) and TIN2017-88476-C2-1-R.

References

1. Lujak, M., Sánchez, A.G., Mier, M.O., Billhardt, H.: An overview of a break assignment problem considering area coverage (2021). https://hal.archives-ouvertes.fr/hal-03104345
2. Lujak, M., Billhardt, B.: Case study from short term scientific mission "emergency fleet break assignment problem considering area coverage". In: Handbook What is Industrial Mathematics? Case Studies from MI-NET. Mathematics for Industry Network (MI-NET) COST ACTION TD1409, p. 30 (2019)
3. Lujak, M.: STSM "Break assignment in emergency fleets". In: Program & Abstracts Book. ICIAM 2019 Valencia, 9th International Congress on Industrial and Applied Mathematics, Valencia, Spain, July 15–19, p. 40 (2019)
4. Widl, M., Musliu, N.: The break scheduling problem: complexity results and practical algorithms. Memetic Comput. **6**(2), 97–112 (2014). https://doi.org/10.1007/s12293-014-0131-0
5. Di Gaspero, L., et al.: Automated shift design and break scheduling. In: Uyar, A., Ozcan, E., Urquhart, N. (eds.) Automated Scheduling and Planning, pp. 109–127. Springer, Heidelberg (2013). https://doi.org/10.1007/978-3-642-39304-4_5
6. Reikk, M., Cordeau, J.-F., Soumis, F.: Implicit shift scheduling with multiple breaks and work stretch duration restrictions. J. Sched. **13**(1), 49–75 (2010)
7. Quimper, C.G., Rousseau, L.M.: A large neighbourhood search approach to the multi-activity shift scheduling problem. J. Heuristics **16**, 373–392 (2010). https://doi.org/10.1007/s10732-009-9106-6
8. Robbins, T.R., Harrison, T.P.: A stochastic programming model for scheduling call centers with global Service Level Agreements. Eur. J. Oper. Res. **207**, 1608–1619 (2010)
9. Fei, H., Meskens, N., Chu, C.: A planning and scheduling problem for an operating theatre using an open scheduling strategy. CAIE **58**, 221–230 (2010)
10. Aickelina, U., Dowslandb, K.A.: An indirect genetic algorithm for a nurse-scheduling problem. Comput. Oper. Res. **31**, 761–778 (2004)
11. Church, R., ReVelle, C.: The maximal covering location problem. In: Addison-Wesley Papers of the Regional Science Association (1974)
12. Gallais, A., Carle, J.: An adaptive localized algorithm for multiple sensor area coverage. In: 21st International Conference on Advanced Information Networking and Applications (AINA 2007), Niagara Falls, ON, pp. 525–532 (2007)
13. Brotcorne, L., Laporte, G., Semet, F.: Ambulance location and relocation models. Eur. J. Oper. Res. **147**(3), 451–463 (2003)
14. Gendreau, M., Laporte, G., Semet, F.: A dynamic model and parallel tabu search heuristic for real-time ambulance relocation. Par. Comp. **27**, 1641–1653 (2001)
15. Gendreau, M., Laporte, G., Semet, F.: The maximal expected coverage relocation problem for emergency vehicles. J. Oper. Res. Soc. **57**, 22–28 (2006)
16. Maxwell, M.S., Restrepo, M., Henderson, S.G., Topaloglu, H.: Approximate dynamic programming for ambulance redeployment. INFORMS J. Comput. **22**, 266–281 (2010)
17. Naoum-Sawaya, J., Elhedhli, S.: A stochastic optimization model for realtime ambulance redeployment. Comput. Oper. Res. **40**, 1972–1978 (2013)

18. Alrifaee, B., Mamaghani, M.G., Abel, D.: Centralized non-convex model predictive control for cooperative collision avoidance of networked vehicles. In: 2014 IEEE ISIC (2014)
19. Ullman, J.D.: NP-complete scheduling problems. J. Comput. Syst. Sci. **10**, 384–393 (1975)
20. Burer, S., Letchford, A.N.: Non-convex mixed-integer nonlinear programming: a survey. Surv. Oper. Res. Manage. Sci. **17**(2), 97–106 (2012)

A Template-Based Approach to Code Generation Within an Agent Paradigm

Francisco Pinto-Santos[1]([✉]) [iD], Zakieh Alizadeh-Sani[1], David Alonso-Moro[1,3],
Alfonso González-Briones[1,2,3] [iD], Pablo Chamoso[1,3] [iD],
and Juan M. Corchado[1,3,4,5] [iD]

[1] BISITE Research Group, University of Salamanca, Edificio Multiusos I+D+i,
37007 Salamanca, Spain
{franpintosantos,zakieh,chamosog}@usal.es
[2] Research Group on Agent-Based, Social and Interdisciplinary Applications
(GRASIA), Complutense University of Madrid, Madrid, Spain
alfonsogb@usal.es
[3] Air Institute, IoT Digital Innovation Hub, Carbajosa de la Sagrada,
37188 Salamanca, Spain
davidalonso@air-institute.org
[4] Department of Electronics, Information and Communication, Faculty
of Engineering, Osaka Institute of Technology, Osaka 535-8585, Japan
jm@corchado.net
[5] Pusat Komputeran dan Informatik, Universiti Malaysia Kelantan, Karung
Berkunci 36, Pengkaan Chepa, 16100 Kota Bharu, Kelantan, Malaysia

Abstract. Today, the paradigm of multi-agent systems has earned a place in the field of software engineering thanks to its versatility to adapt to various domains. However, the construction of these systems is complex, which leads to additional costs in the implementation process. In recent years, however, several frameworks have emerged to simplify this task by providing functionalities that these systems need as a basis, or even tools to generate code related to this paradigm. These tools are based on a single framework, protocol and language, which sets many limits to the code generation capacity of these tools. Therefore, this paper proposes a tool for code generation of complete multi-agent systems, focused on the elimination of the restrictions of programming language, framework, communication protocol, etc. through the use of model-driven and template-driven development.

Keywords: Multi-agent · Model driven development · Software engineering · Code generation · Template code generation

1 Introduction

In order to improve productivity and software quality, a series of software development paradigms emerged to avoid programmer errors. One of the most popular paradigms was Model Driven Development (MDD) which, through a process guided by models, and in collaboration with other tools, allows the generation

© Springer Nature Switzerland AG 2021
F. De La Prieta et al. (Eds.): PAAMS Workshops 2021, CCIS 1472, pp. 296–307, 2021.
https://doi.org/10.1007/978-3-030-85710-3_25

of code from these models. MDD reached maturity at the end of the 20th century using UML as one of its most advanced standards, although there are other modelling languages that can be used to the same level of satisfaction. Although the development and advancement that this software development paradigm has experienced, the software development industry still cannot respond with the necessary speed to organisations that need to include these methodologies to rapidly change their business models.

Model-driven development is also known as Model Driven Engineering (MDE), from which different proposals are derived. The Model Driven Architecture (MDA) proposed by the Object Management Group (OMG) is possibly the best known. However, there are other proposals such as Adaptive Object Models and Metamodels, which attempt to facilitate the construction of dynamic and adaptable systems. The latter strategy is highly related to business rules research, specifically when means are needed to describe business rules and automatically generate implementations.

The MDD paradigm covers a wide spectrum of research areas that should be taken into account such as modelling languages for model description, the definition of transformation languages between models, the construction of tools to support the tasks involved in modelling, the application of the concepts in development methods and in specific domains, among others. While the MDD proposes the use of a set of standards such as MOF, UML and QVT, which are very well documented and applied with great success, others have a long way to go in terms of definition and design.

Due to the needs in the software industry to enable the integration of various software technologies in a fast and transparent way, as well as to adapt quickly to the changing needs of the business logic, the Model Driven Development (MDD) model has been adopted. In this development paradigm, a semi-automatic generation of software from models is carried out. Under this approach, a business expert can express his or her knowledge in a formal modelling language and the IT team defines how it will be implemented. And if desired, the same model can be implemented towards different platforms (Java, .Net, CORBA). This allows to generate several platform-dependent artefacts with less development effort, through the same platform-independent model, which represents the business knowledge [1].

Although this paradigm presents numerous benefits, it also presents certain aspects that must be taken into account in order to allow its integration into the internal systems of any architecture that contemplates a long-term vision. In this work, a review of code generation under the MDD paradigm is carried out to produce complete multi-agent systems from code templates. For this purpose, a five-phase code generation model has been proposed, which uses a BPMN notation file for the specification of agents.

The rest of the paper is structured as follows. Section 2 reviews state-of-the-art proposals in this area. Section 3 presents the Template based code generation approach, with special emphasis on aspects of inclusion different phases that make up the process. Section 4 describes the evaluation process of the generated systems and the key results. Finally, Section 5 draws some conclusions and future work.

2 Code Generation Background

Monolithic applications have been used in traditional software architecture for decades. The problem is that managing reliability and scalability is difficult when they become larger. To this end, Some software architecture like services-oriented architecture has emerged. Regarding modern SOA complexity, several approaches based on model-driven, automatic code generation, and agent-based models have been introduced.

Model-driven approaches rely on high-level abstraction which is more understandable for humans. One of the promising Model-driven techniques is template-based code generation which uses model-to-text transformations. According to the literature, template-based code generation can fall into two categories:1)Full-automatic software generation [2,3] 2) Semi-automatic code generation [4,5].

In the first category, code generation does not solve the particular problem. The emphasis on this automation is generation all software files and codes using pre-defined templates. These techniques have been used in web applications. In most web application frameworks, code generator automatically generate the skeleton of the website and code some common portal site features. Although, web framework had most advantage of template base code generation, template code generation can find in most area which needs automatic code generation. As instance, Benato et al. have suggested template-based code generation in self-adaptive software that can autonomously react to modifications in its execution setting [3].

Their generator module of source code, has 3 major levels: 1) metamodel 2) template Engine 3) source Code. The template engines work as the heart of their it which contains all logic of generator module of source code and uses new metamodel as its input.

In the second category, users need to defines what they expect from the program. BPMN editors are well-known visual programming tools. Moreover, low-code and no-code development can use template-based code generation utilizing visual modeling software. [6]. The idea behind these techniques is that complex code can demonstrate as graphical blocks. These blocks can include UML diagrams [7], modules, services [8], etc. This black box items can represent the system behavior in a simple and transparent manner.

Moreover, Distributed application has different modules on several resources; therefore, automatic code generation can bring Complexity reduction, Error reduction, and Consistency enhancement. Regarding these features, service composition research has utilized them in order to automatic code generation. [9] has explored the MDA transformation technique to model the whole service for providing adaptive service composition. MDA transformation entails transforming models from one level to another in the same system. The transformation between these levels are automatic, which are divided into two main categories: 1) Model to Model 2) Model to Text. Automatic code generators are a type of model-to-text transformations. Regarding these ability.

Modern software development platforms are smart environments with more interactive behavior. To this end, multi-agent has mixed with MDA.

A significant study by Ferber et al. combined multi Agent with MDA techniques. They introduced a model called AALAADIN which has The proposed model enables humans to meta-modeling concepts of groups, agents, and roles [10].

With emerging Agent-Oriented Software Engineering, several studies have investigated such as Challenges, and trends [11], Evaluation of agent-oriented methodologies [12], increasing integration by power-type-based language [13], etc. However, there is no agreement on which standard has to be used in this area of research. However, most of the works [10,14], have related to UML and its extensions.

By using multi-agent concept, researchers have been able to provide more efficient solution in distributed systems. Ivanova et al. have introduced a solution based on MDA and composition models for Advanced Metering Infrastructure (AMI). AMI are complex systems that can provide communication between the control center and distributed agents. Therefore, techniques such as high abstraction modeling, reusability, adaptability are essential. To this end, their proposed model considers all of AMI system requirements such as self-describing, rich knowledge representation, service discovery [15].

Keogh et al. have proposed MAS Organisations considering runtime execution. The proposed model tries to provide acceptable flexibility by recognizing behavioural characteristics [16].

Ferber et al. have applied agent-based models in MDA in order to accelerate software development in multi-agent systems [10]. Also, Gomez-Sanz et al. have introduced a related tools for the INGENIAS [17]. The introduced tool provides a graphical editor which presents abstraction levels of items. However, it provides code editors which allow users to customize their codes, as well. Moreover, It provides some recommendations during implementation for guiding users.

According to the literature, most proposed frameworks or tools for multi agent systems are either very general or presented for a specific purpose. This study proposes a tool for code generation of complete multi-agent systems. Using SOA architecture brings multi-purpose ability and helps to support a wide range of third-party technologies and programming languages.

3   Template Based Code Generation Approach

In order to produce complete multi-agent systems from code templates, a five-phase code generation model is proposed, which starts from an agent specification file. This file will contain a definition of agents, and is structured in an agent definition language such as BPMN; However, any structured text format (such as XML or JSON) that allows to define the agents individually and their connections, is appropriate for this purpose. The essence of this language is to structure the elements used in this notation in a canvas using graphic tools. These elements can be divided into the following groups:

- Flow objects are the main elements, in them we have events, activities and gateways.

- Events describe events and are represented by circles. Depending on the type the outer circle can be simple (start), double (intermediate) or thick (end).
- Activities are the aggregation of tasks required for a program fraction that is subsequently added to the main program. They are represented by rectangles with rounded corners. If they are specific, they are indicated by an icon in the upper left corner.
- Gateways are control structures represented by diamonds.
- Connection objects relate each of the flow objects and can be sequences, messages or associations.

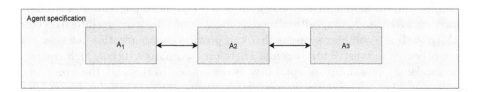

Fig. 1. Agent specification in file

The agent specification file, is parsed in order to extract the structure with the information of the different events, objects and connections, to later generate a structured system from them. Therefore, to generate the multi-agent system's code, it is necesary to have a repository of metamodels, which will consist of code templates, whose parameters are provided in the agent specification file.

The starting point for code generation is the agent specification file, and an example of the graphical representation of the content of this file can be found in the Fig. 1. For the generation of this code, several phases have been defined and are described as follows:

- Phase I: The file is processed to obtain the list of objects modeled in it, such as agents, events, etc., as well as the information associated with them, such as parameter mappings between components, type of service, associated template and other metadata of each component and event. This results in an object representation within a software application, formed by a flow of information between the agent specification, as shown in Fig. 2.
- Phase II: For each agent to be generated, the templates associated to each one are retrieved, then, the individual code of each one is generated. This results in an information flow as shown in Fig. 3, in which the functionality of each agent is already generated, but they are not communicated.

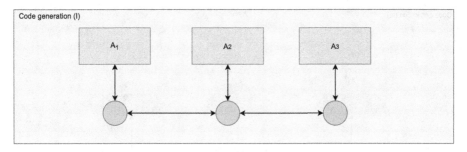

Fig. 2. Phase I of code generation process

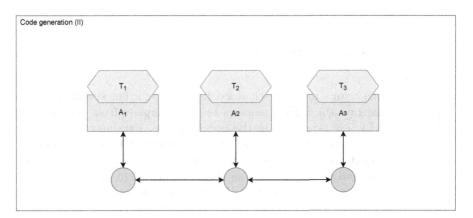

Fig. 3. Phase II of code generation process

– Phase III: Each component is taken and also by means of templates, a protocol communication adapter is generated as interface within the internal behavior of the agent and the rest of the organization. It is worth to highlight, that in this case, due to the fact that the database of metamodels used for the tags is mostly made up of REST services whose functionality is to be incorporated into a multi-agent organization, HTTPS middleware has been used as protocol adapter. For the generation of this protocol adaptor, a template is also used, after which the parameter mapping is generated, resulting in a structure similar to the one shown in Fig. 4.

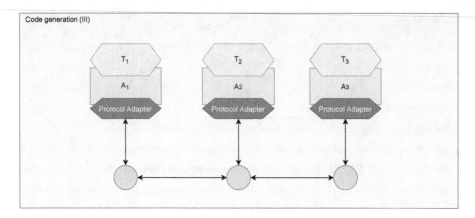

Fig. 4. Phase III of code generation process

– Phase IV: The communication schema defined in the agent specification file is used to generate the HTTP requests to each template from the interface offered by API rest generated in the previous step. Parameter mapping is also performed between each agent so that the output of one can be matched to the input of the next, resulting in a set of communicating agent as shown in Fig. 5. It should be noted that the programming language in which each template is written may vary, due to the protocol adapter.

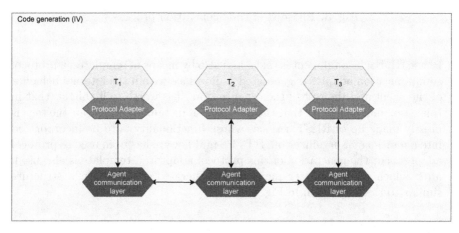

Fig. 5. Phase IV of code generation process

The advantages of this code generation model is that it allows the integration of components from different programming languages into a multi-agent system, in order to communicate with a standard and efficient protocol, as long as the parameter mapping between each of the components (defined in templates) is specified.

4   Evaluation of Generated Systems

This section describes a code generation use case with the proposed system, focusing especially on the part of code generation and integration in the multi-agent organization.

For this purpose, a use case is proposed in which it is desired to create a multi-agent organization, composed of three agents. Each of them will perform a sentiment analysis of the same text with different technics. Subsequently, by means of negotiation techniques, the result of the three agents will be composed in order to select the most appropriate one for the organization.

For this purpose, three templates implementing sentiment analysis have been used, one for each agent, which have been described in Listing 1.1. The reference to the template and how to perform the mapping of input and output parameters has been established.

In this file, other aspects have also been defined, such as the selected negotiation for the agents, which consists of agreement technologies [18]. However, other simpler ones have been implemented in the system, such as the composition by mean or median.

Listing 1.1: Agent organization specification file

```xml
<?xml version="1.0" encoding="UTF-8" ?>
<organization>
  <meta>
    <name>O1</name>
  </meta>
  <negotiator>argumentation-based-negotiator</negotiator>
  <agents>
    <name>A1</name>
    <template>a6dfed16-761d-47f0-adbe-6652508ad6d0-sentiment-analysis-1</template>
    <meta-template>
      <input-params>
        <name>text</name>
        <type>string</type>
        <requited>true</requited>
      </input-params>
      <output-params>
        <name>sentiment-compound</name>
        <type>dict</type>
      </output-params>
    </meta-template>
  </agents>
  <agents>
    <name>A2</name>
    <template>a6dfed16-761d-47f0-adbe-6652508ad6d0-sentiment-analysis-2</template>
    <meta-template>
      <input-params>
        <name>input_text</name>
        <type>string</type>
        <requited>true</requited>
      </input-params>
      <output-params>
```

```
        <name>sentiment-result</name>
        <type>array</type>
      </output-params>
    </meta-template>
  </agents>
  <agents>
    <name>A3</name>
    <template>a6dfed16-761d-47f0-adbe-6652508ad6d0-sentiment-analysis-3</template>
    <meta-template>
      <input-params>
        <name>t</name>
        <type>string</type>
        <requited>true</requited>
      </input-params>
      <output-params>
        <name>sentiment</name>
        <type>float</type>
      </output-params>
    </meta-template>
  </agents>
</organization>
```

After applying the code generation with this input file, the code files corresponding to the three agents have been generated. In this article in the snipets Code Listing 1.2 and Code Listing 1.3 are attached respectively an example of the result of the integration using the python API that wraps the sentiment analysis component of agent 1 and the java class that implements the integration with the analysis functionality of agent 1, since the agents are developed in JADE and communicate through ACL.

No examples of the code generated for the negotiation are attached, since it consists of another template derived from [19], which implements the selected negotiation.

Listing 1.2: Generated HTTP rest adapter

```
import flask
from flask import request, jsonify
from a6dfed16_761d_47f0_adbe_6652508ad6d0_sentiment_analysis_1 import analyze

app = flask.Flask(__name__)

@app.route('/', methods=['POST'])
def behaviour():
    result = {}
    result['sentiment-compound'] = analyze(request.json.text)
    return jsonify(result)

app.run()
```

Listing 1.3: Java generated code from agent side

```java
public class AgentAdapter{

    public void adapt(String url, Map<String,String>params){
        OkHttpClient client = new OkHttpClient().newBuilder().build();
        MediaType mediaType = MediaType.parse("application/json");
        RequestBody body = RequestBody.create(mediaType, Utils.serialize(params));
        Request request = new Request.Builder().url(url).method("POST", body)
            .addHeader("Content-Type", "application/json").build();
        Response response = client.newCall(request).execute();
        JSONObject json = new JSONObject(response.body().string());
        String result = json.getString("sentiment-compound");
        return result;
    }
}
```

As a result of the deployment, a multi-agent organization is obtained, which is able to negotiate by obtaining the sentiment analysis of the provided text, reaching the result described in the Table 1. The weights assigned in the table described above have been negotiated with agreement technologies [18] by calculating the distance of the result to the average of all the results.

Table 1. Table with results of the negotiation

Agent	Sentiment result	Weight
A1	0.91	0.21
A2	0.83	0.67
A3	0.64	0.12
Total		0.824

5   Conclusions

The proposed system is capable of generating code for multi-agent systems focused on the integration of specific technology into one. This system generates the code using existing templates, customizing them by using a protocol adapter, after which it generates the corresponding calls to integrate the generated components in JADE templates that communicate via ACL with a negotiation specified previously to the code generation. The result of this process is a multi-agent organization generated from templates that allows the use of a programming paradigm in multiple programming languages, facilitating the integration of these in the system.

Among the future lines of work that will be exploited from this work, are the study through more use cases, incorporating a system of template ingestion to increase the existing database of templates and incorporating more algorithms for negotiation between agents.

Acknowledgment. This research has been supported by the European Union's Horizon 2020 research and innovation programme under grant agreement No 871177.

References

1. Pavón, J., Gómez-Sanz, J.J., Fuentes, R.: The ingenias methodology and tools. In: Agent-Oriented Methodologies, pp. 236–276. IGI Global (2005)
2. Uyanik, B., ŞAHİN, V.H.: A template-based code generator for web applications. Turk. J. Electr. Eng. Comput. Sci. **28**(3), 1747–1762 (2020)
3. Benato, G.S., Affonso, F.J., Nakagawa, E.Y.: Infrastructure based on template engines for automatic generation of source code for self-adaptive software domain. In: SEKE, pp. 30–35 (2017)
4. Rademacher, F., Sorgalla, J., Wizenty, P., Sachweh, S., Zündorf, A.: Graphical and textual model-driven microservice development. In: Bucchiarone, A., et al. (eds.) Microservices, pp. 147–179. Springer, Cham (2020). https://doi.org/10.1007/978-3-030-31646-4_7
5. Blas, M.J., Gonnet, S.: Computer-aided design for building multipurpose routing processes in discrete event simulation models. Eng. Sci. Technol. Int. J. **24**(1), 22–34 (2021)
6. Waszkowski, R.: Low-code platform for automating business processes in manufacturing. IFAC-PapersOnLine **52**(10), 376–381 (2019)
7. Sunitha, E.V., Samuel, P.: Automatic code generation from UML state chart diagrams. IEEE Access **7**, 8591–8608 (2019)
8. Jörges, S.: Construction and Evolution of Code Generators: A Model-Driven and Service-Oriented Approach. LNCS, vol. 7747. Springer, Heidelberg (2013). https://doi.org/10.1007/978-3-642-36127-2
9. Zatout, S., Boufaida, M., Benabdelhafid, M.S., Berkane, M.L.: A model-driven approach for the verification of an adaptive service composition. Int. J. Web Eng. Technol. **15**(1), 4–31 (2020)
10. Ferber, J., Gutknecht, O.: A meta-model for the analysis and design of organizations in multi-agent systems. In: Proceedings International Conference on Multi Agent Systems (Cat. No. 98EX160), pp. 128–135. IEEE (1998)
11. Zambonelli, F., Omicini, A.: Challenges and research directions in agent-oriented software engineering. Auton. Agent. Multi-Agent Syst. **9**(3), 253–283 (2004)
12. Jazayeri, A., Bass, E.J.: Agent-oriented methodologies evaluation frameworks: a review. Int. J. Softw. Eng. Knowl. Eng. **30**(09), 1337–1370 (2020)
13. Garcia-Magarino, I.: Towards the integration of the agent-oriented modeling diversity with a powertype-based language. Comput. Stand. Interfaces **36**(6), 941–952 (2014)
14. Bauer, B., Müller, J.P., Odell, J.: Agent UML: a formalism for specifying multiagent software systems. In: Ciancarini, P., Wooldridge, M.J. (eds.) AOSE 2000. LNCS, vol. 1957, pp. 91–103. Springer, Heidelberg (2001). https://doi.org/10.1007/3-540-44564-1_6
15. Ivanova, T., Batchkova, I.: Approach for model driven development of multi-agent systems for ambient intelligence. In: Artificial Intelligence in Industry 4.0: A Collection of Innovative Research Case-studies that are Reworking the Way We Look at Industry 4.0 Thanks to Artificial Intelligence, pp. 183–198 (2021)
16. Keogh, K., Sonenberg, L.: Designing multi-agent system organisations for flexible runtime behaviour. Appl. Sci. **10**(15), 5335 (2020)
17. Gomez-Sanz, J.J., Fuentes, R., Pavón, J., García-Magariño, I.: Ingenias development kit: a visual multi-agent development environment. In: Proceedings of the 7th International Joint Conference on Autonomous Agents and Multiagent Systems: Demo Papers, pp. 1675–1676 (2008)

18. González-Briones, A., Prieto, J., De La Prieta, F., Herrera-Viedma, E., Corchado, J.M.: Energy optimization using a case-based reasoning strategy. Sensors **18**(3), 865 (2018)
19. Briones, A.G., Rodrıguez, J.M.C., Omatu, S.: A multi-agent architecture for optimizing energy consumption using comfort agreements. Ph.D. thesis, Universidad de Salamanca (2018)

A Low-Cost Human-Robot Negotiation System

Jaime Andres Rincon[1]($\boxtimes$), Angelo Costa[2]($\boxtimes$), Vicente Julian[1]($\boxtimes$),
Carlos Carrascosa[1]($\boxtimes$), and Paulo Novais[3]($\boxtimes$)

[1] Universitat Politècnica de València, Institut Valenciá d'Investigació en
Intel.ligència Artificial (VRAIN), Valencia, Spain
{jrincon,carrasco}@dsic.upv.es, vjulian@upv.es
[2] MVRLab, University of Alicante, Alicante, Spain
angelogoncalo.costa@ua.es
[3] ALGORITMI Centre, Universidade do Minho, Braga, Portugal
pjon@di.uminho.pt

Abstract. In this paper we present a platform composed of a low-cost
robot and a multi-agent system that uses deep learning algorithms, whose
objective is to establish a negotiation process and persuasively sell items,
maximising their price, thus gain. To this, we have focused on developing an interactive process that is able to interact with humans using
a camera, microphone and speaker, to establish all negotiation process
without physical contact. This is relevant due to the current COVID-19
situation and arisen issues of human contact. Validation processes with
university students have revealed high interest and success in products'
negotiation.

Keywords: EDGE AI · Assistant robot · Emotion detection ·
Automated negotiation

1 Introduction

In various types of human-computer interactions there is a sense of uneasiness
affecting humans when having to trust the decision or advice of a computer,
not because they think that the computer will deceive them but because they
uncertain about the computer expertise [1]. This means that there is an inherent
distrust towards these systems, and often they are disregarded. Several studies
have shown that providing an embodiment of a person, either video-based or
robot-based, may improve the human's acceptance values [2]. Non-verbal cues
play an important role in trust and acceptance, as they can provide information
about intrinsic states, such as sincerity and confidence [3]. Therefore, it is clear
that text-based interaction with computers may be ineffective due to the lack
of "human" verbal and non-verbal traits. Several studies show that, when producing verbal and non-verbal cues, robots and avatars are met with high trust
and acceptance values, with preference towards robots [2,4,5]. Nonetheless, the

F. De La Prieta et al. (Eds.): PAAMS Workshops 2021, CCIS 1472, pp. 308–317, 2021.
https://doi.org/10.1007/978-3-030-85710-3_26

same studies find that interaction protocols have to be followed to demonstrate that these virtual actors are experts, as low-levels of distrust are common upon interacting with them. From this, it is clear that the virtual actor that has more success rate is the robot, as having a physical presence appears to positively influence trust and increase the social interaction [2].

For this project we have designed and built a low-cost robot that is an expert in trading and selling tasks. The objective is to provide a full human-like buying experience, visually identifying the object the user (in this case acting as a buyer) wants to buy, to orally interact with the user while negotiating the price. To infer the negotiation process we use a multi-agent system that levels the current prices, availability and demand and calculates the lowest price possible, being the utility function the gain maximisation. Thus, the negotiation follows a bazaar-like style, where user and robot try to maximise their utility functions in each interaction. While, at the current stage, the visual aspect of the robot is bare-bones, the features are enriched and designed to maintain a fluid conversation without the user having to touch any kind of screen or control to interact with it. Validation of the robot was performed with university students', revealing high interaction and interest, and classification success rate of 83.690%, proving the usability of such platforms.

This paper is structured as follows: Sect. 2 presents different previous works and similar approaches in the area; Sect. 3 details the different components of the proposed low-cost robot trading assistant; and, finally, Sect. 4 presents some conclusions.

2 State of the Art

In recent years, much work has been done to provide more appropriate forms of interaction between humans and agents. Human-agent interaction has been evolving in an attempt to adapt more and more to human-human interactions. In this sense, as indicated in [6] people try to interact as they are used to interacting, with face-to-face interactions and building social relationships. Thus, it seems unlikely that rules for human-agent interaction can be established that are very different from what humans normally know and use in their everyday interactions. Therefore, human-agent or human-robot interaction needs to be similar to human-to-human interaction to ensure truly meaningful interactions and relationships.

If we apply this idea to the interaction in human-robot negotiation processes, it is necessary to integrate the well-known strategies typically employed in automatic negotiation with the basic skills that are presupposed for humans as prerequisites for interaction and communication. Examples of such basic skills are the correct interpretation of gestures and emotions during the interaction process.

Regarding works related to human-agent negotiation, we can find several works and studies such as the work presented in [7] where a negotiator agent, called NegoChat is presented. NegoChat tries to achieve agreements with people using natural language in a chat environment. Another example is presented in [8,9] where also presents an agent called IAGO that attempts to gain the most value for itself in the negotiation by employing several human-negotiation techniques. IAGO can conduct a simple multi-issue bargaining task featuring four issues at five different levels.

Other works try to integrate the expression of emotions during the negotiation process, as in the experiments carried out at [10] where authors explore whether expression of anger or happiness by negotiator agents can produce effects similar to effects seen in human-human negotiation. The paper presents an experiment where participants play with agents that express emotions in a multi- issue negotiation task. In a similar way, in [11] present an agent capable of operating in environments where several humans converse with each other and interact with the agent in an interleaved manner. Moreover, in [12] authors develop an agent based on a cognitive architecture called ACT-R. The agent incorporates a model based on theory of mind, and uses this model to attempt to infer the adversary's strategy and respond according to the model. According to the experimentation carried out, the agent replicates some aspects similar to how humans act in negotiation processes. Finally, in [13] it is presented a comparison of mind perception in strategic exchanges between agents and humans. Concretely analyses how perceived minds of agents shape people's behavior in the dictator game, ultimatum game, and negotiation against artificial agents.

As can be seen there exist several proposals that try to achieve real negotiating robots in the near future. More recent works focus on taking into account the emotional aspects in a negotiation process, while others try to integrate the typical human interfaces. All these works focus on being able to mimic human behaviors in negotiation processes. Accordingly, this paper presents a proposal for a low-cost robot trading assistant that incorporates all the necessary components to establish complex negotiation processes with humans. The following section presents the proposal in detail.

3   Robot Trading Assistant

This section describes the operation of the robot trading assistant, detailing the different software and hardware tools used for the creation of the system. The proposed system is shown in the Fig. 1.

The proposed system runs on Robot Operating System (ROS),[1] which provides a set of software libraries and tools to help you create robotic applications allowing the integration of motor controllers, state-of-the-art algorithm, among other tools. ROS was designed to be a loosely coupled system in which a process is called a node and each node must be responsible for a task. Communication between nodes is done by message passing, this message passing is done through logical channels called topics. Each node can send or get data from another node using the publish/subscribe model. In our system, each of the modules (speech, vision and negotiation module) runs on independent nodes, the system subscribes to the topics offered by each node. This subscription allows the flow of information between nodes, achieving a decentralised execution of the system.

---

[1] https://www.ros.org/.

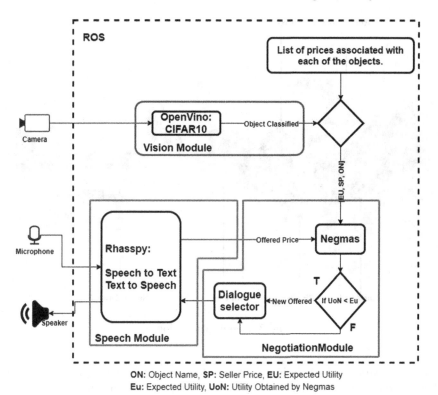

ON: Object Name, **SP:** Seller Price, **EU:** Expected Utility
Eu: Expected Utility, **UoN:** Utility Obtained by Negmas

Fig. 1. Proposed system architecture.

3.1 Hardware Description

This section describes the different hardware devices used to build the robot (Fig. 2). The system is based on a Rapsberry Pi 3B, which is connected to a series of accessories that allow it to recognise speech, classify objects and interact with other subsystems (such as the spray control). In order to be able to perform speech recognition, the system needs to be equipped with hardware that allows it to capture these sounds. For this purpose, the robot is equipped with the Matrix-Voice system, which is a series of MEMS (Micro-ElectroMechanical System) components. Matrix-Voice[2] has eight of which seven are distributed around a circumference, with a microphone spacing of 51°. The eighth microphone is located in the centre of the circumference, giving the system the ability to pick up omnidirectional sound.

To incorporate a Raspberry Pi 3B+, which is a small board or low-cost computer. By having this configuration and not being able to improve its features, such as increasing the RAM memory, processor speed, etc. This poses a problem when trying to develop applications involving deep learning models. However,

---

[2] https://www.matrix.one/products/voice.

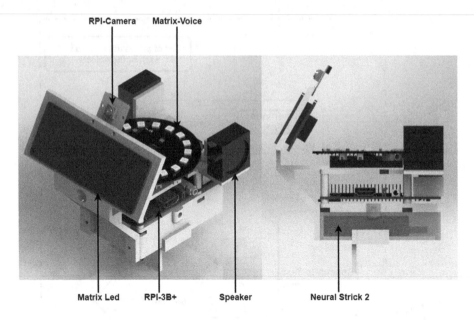

Fig. 2. Robot negotiation.

in recent years, devices designed to use deep learning models have appeared, allowing the trained model to be optimised and at the same time being able to be used in this type of mini-computers. There are devices on the market such as the Goolge Coral[3] and the Intel Neural Stick 2,[4] our robot uses the Intel device as an external system to optimise object classification using the Raspberry Pi 3B+. In this way, the robot was able to classify the objects in the CIFAR-10 database in a relatively short time. As the main purpose of the robot is to interact with a person, it was necessary to incorporate LED arrays. These arrays allow the robot's eyes to be displayed, thus helping to improve interaction with the human. The robot can represent up to five expressions (Fig. 3).

3.2   Software Description

As mentioned above, our system uses ROS to support the execution of the system. The described system incorporates a different software tools, which allow it to recognise objects using the CIFAR-10 database,[5] Rhasspy[6] to perform voice interaction (speech recognition and text-to-speech conversion) and Negmas which is responsible for performing negotiation. Object recognition is an important part used by the system, as it allows to identify the object that the

---

[3] https://coral.ai.
[4] https://software.intel.com/content/www/us/en/develop/hardware/neural-comput e-stick.html.
[5] https://www.cs.toronto.edu/~kriz/cifar.html.
[6] https://rhasspy.readthedocs.io/en/latest/.

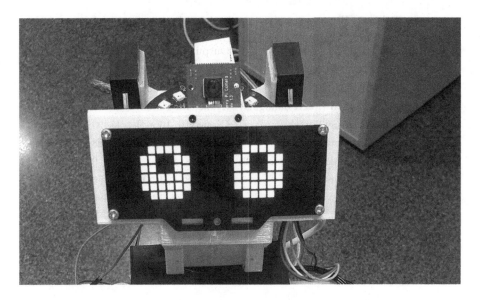

Fig. 3. Robot negotiation.

user wants to buy. To carry out this identification, a ROS[7] node has been created
to perform this task, OpenVino[8] and the CIFAR-10 database were used to carry
out this classification. Since the main objective of the system is to negotiate
the sale of any of the objects present in the CIFAR-10 database, to do this it is
necessary that each of the objects present in the database be assigned a property
list.

The hyperparameters that compose the proposed network to perform the
classification of the images of the CIFAR-10 database are presented in Table 1
and 2. The hyperparameters in Table 1 were obtained after several experiments
and are related to the optimisation process of the model.

Table 1. Hyperparameters for thew optimization of the model.

Learning rate	Momentum	Min batch size	Number of epochs
0.001	0.9	64	100

Moreover, Table 2 shows the final hyperparameters of the specific model,
composed of different convolutional layers with small 3 × 3 filters. The input
layer has a structure of 32 × 32 × 3 inputs and the output layer has 10 nodes
one for each object to be classified.

---

[7] https://www.ros.org.
[8] https://software.intel.com/content/www/us/en/develop/tools/openvino-toolkit.
   html.

Table 2. Hyperparameters obtained for the specific model.

Layer (type)	Output shape	Param #
conv2d (Conv2D)	(None, 32, 32, 32)	896
conv2d_1 (Conv2D)	(None, 32, 32, 32)	9248
max_pooling2d (MaxPooling2D)	(None, 16, 16, 32)	0
conv2d_2 (Conv2D)	(None, 16, 16, 64)	18496
conv2d_3 (Conv2D)	(None, 16, 16, 64)	36928
max_pooling2d_1 (MaxPooling2)	(None, 8, 8, 64)	0
conv2d_4 (Conv2D)	(None, 8, 8, 128)	73856
conv2d_5 (Conv2D)	(None, 8, 8, 128)	147584
max_pooling2d_2 (MaxPooling2)	(None, 4, 4, 128)	0
flatten (Flatten)	(None, 2048)	0
dense (Dense)	(None, 128)	262272
dense_1 (Dense)	(None, 10)	1290

To evaluate the performance of the proposed classification system, a number of attributes were extracted to determine whether the model correctly classifies the objects displayed by the user. The obtained classification accuracy can be seen in the Fig. 4. The accuracy obtained was 83.690% which can be considered quite adequate. Other scores used to determine the efficiency in the classification of the objects are the F1 score and the Recall. The F1 score was 0.83, it should be noted that the closer this value is to 1.0, the better the classifier will be. Lastly, the Recall was 0.82, which indicates that the model found a high number of positives when classifying the images.

Moreover, Fig. 5 shows the normalised confusion matrix of the classification model. It can be seen that the model is able to classify the different objects in the database with acceptable accuracy.

This list can be modified by the user, adding new properties to each of the objects. These properties would be taken into account in the negotiation. In our system, we have decided to use only the price that the seller gives to the object (SP) and the profit that the seller expects to obtain from the sale (EU). The result of this process returns a triplet consisting of the name of the object (ON), the seller's price (SP) and the expected utility (EU).

Once the system recognises the object the user wants to negotiate the purchase of, the user makes an offer indicating the price he or she is willing to pay. The system uses Rhasspy, an open source tool, fully offline voice assistant services used to many languages. Rhasspy converts the human voice in a text, in this text the system extract the price that he or she will to pay for the object. The price offered by the user, is used for Negmas to obtain the profit of the transaction. If the profit from the transaction is less than expected, the system makes a new offer telling the user that the offer is too low. This system resembles the

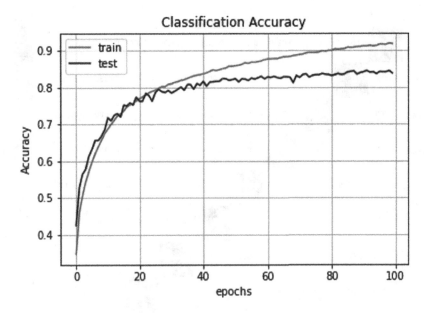

Fig. 4. Accuracy obtained during training and validation.

Table 3. Examples of the dialogues considered in the proposed system.

The price you are offering me is very cheap
Why don't you offer me a better price?
I can sell it for...
I can offer you...
The object price includes...
Someone made a better bid
Ok, I'll sell it to you for...
Ok, I'll sell it for...

process of negotiation by haggling, where two users try to reach an agreement by trying to equalise their profits.

To carry out this negotiation process, the system incorporates a series of dialogues, these dialogues are voiced through Rhasspy using text-to-speech conversion. Some of the dialogues present in the system are shown in the following Table 3.

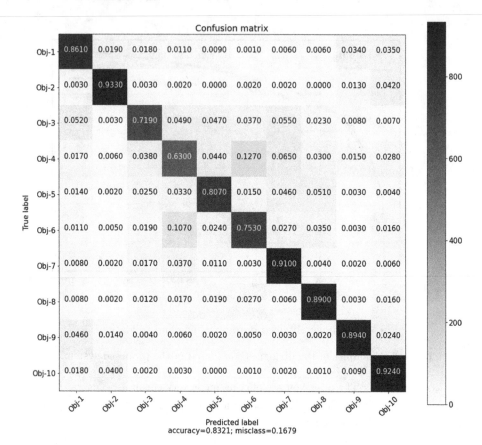

Fig. 5. Standardised confutation matrix.

4   Conclusions and Future Work

This paper presents the approach of using a physical presence in a system with human interaction. This physical presence of the system that facilitates the interaction is carried out by a low-cost robot described in the paper, and the interaction where this robot is used is a negotiation for trading objects. In the stage presented, the robot is engaged to sell the user the object he chooses and shows the robot. During the negotiation process, both negotiate the price to reach an agreement.

Using the robot and an speech-based dialogue system to interact with it, makes the user more comfortable and more interested in participate in the negotiation process than if this negotiation is made by a system with a more usual interface.

Acknowledgement. This work was partly supported by the Spanish Government (RTI2018-095390-B-C31) and Universitat Politecnica de Valencia Research Grant PAID-10-19.

References

1. Aseeri, S., Interrante, V.: The influence of avatar representation on interpersonal communication in virtual social environments. IEEE Trans. Vis. Comput. Graph. **27**(5), 2608–2617 (2021)
2. Pan, Y., Steed, A.: A comparison of avatar-, video-, and robot-mediated interaction on users' trust in expertise. Front. Robot. AI **3**, March (2016)
3. Williams, E.: Experimental comparisons of face-to-face and mediated communication: a review. Psychol. Bull. **84**(5), 963–976 (1977)
4. Kim, K., Boelling, L., Haesler, S., Bailenson, J., Bruder, G., Welch, G.F.: Does a digital assistant need a body? The influence of visual embodiment and social behavior on the perception of intelligent virtual agents in AR. In: 2018 IEEE International Symposium on Mixed and Augmented Reality (ISMAR). IEEE, October 2018
5. Suárez, G., Jung, S., Lindeman, R.W.: Evaluating virtual human role-players for the practice and development of leadership skills. Front. Virtual Reality **2**, April (2021)
6. Krämer, N.C., von der Pütten, A., Eimler, S.: Human-agent and human-robot interaction theory: similarities to and differences from human-human interaction. In: Zacarias, M., de Oliveira, J.V. (eds.) Human-Computer Interaction: The Agency Perspective. SCI, vol. 396, pp. 215–240. Springer, Heidelberg (2012). https://doi.org/10.1007/978-3-642-25691-2_9
7. Rosenfeld, A., Zuckerman, I., Segal-Halevi, E., Drein, O., Kraus, S.: NegoChat: a chat-based negotiation agent. In: Proceedings of the 2014 International Conference on Autonomous Agents and Multi-Agent Systems, pp. 525–532 (2014)
8. Mell, J., Gratch, J.: IAGO: interactive arbitration guide online. In: Proceedings of the 2016 International Conference on Autonomous Agents & Multiagent Systems, pp. 1510–1512 (2016)
9. Mell, J., Gratch, J.: Grumpy & Pinocchio: answering human-agent negotiation questions through realistic agent design. In: Proceedings of the 16th Conference on Autonomous Agents and Multiagent Systems, pp. 401–409 (2017)
10. de Melo, C.M., Carnevale, P., Gratch, J.: The effect of expression of anger and happiness in computer agents on negotiations with humans. In: The 10th International Conference on Autonomous Agents and Multiagent Systems, vol. 3, pp. 937–944 (2011)
11. Divekar, R.R., Kephart, J.O., Mou, X., Chen, L., Su, H.: You talkin' to me? A practical attention-aware embodied agent. In: Lamas, D., Loizides, F., Nacke, L., Petrie, H., Winckler, M., Zaphiris, P. (eds.) INTERACT 2019. LNCS, vol. 11748, pp. 760–780. Springer, Cham (2019). https://doi.org/10.1007/978-3-030-29387-1_44
12. Stevens, C.A., et al.: Using cognitive agents to train negotiation skills. Front. Psychol. **9**, 154 (2018)
13. Lee, M., Lucas, G., Gratch, J.: Comparing mind perception in strategic exchanges: human-agent negotiation, dictator and ultimatum games. J. Multimodal User Interfaces **15**(2), 201–214 (2021). https://doi.org/10.1007/s12193-020-00356-6

Author Index

Printed in the United States
by Baker & Taylor Publisher Services